Big Day Coming

Jesse Jarnow is a Brooklyn-based music journalist and hosts *The Frow Show* on WFMU, an independent free-form radio station in Jersey City. He writes for *The Village Voice* and elsewhere, and his work has appeared in *The Times* (UK), *Rolling Stone*, and other publications. He tweets @bourgwick.

Big Day Coming

YO LA TENGO and
the Rise of Indie Rock

JESSE JARNOW

GOTHAM BOOKS

GOTHAM BOOKS
Published by Penguin Group (USA) Inc.
375 Hudson Street, New York, New York 10014, U.S.A.
Penguin Group (Canada), 90 Eglinton Avenue East, Suite 700, Toronto, Ontario M4P
2Y3, Canada (a division of Pearson Penguin Canada Inc.); Penguin Books Ltd, 80
Strand, London WC2R 0RL, England; Penguin Ireland, 25 St Stephen's Green, Dublin
2, Ireland (a division of Penguin Books Ltd); Penguin Group (Australia), 250 Camber-
well Road, Camberwell, Victoria 3124, Australia (a division of Pearson Australia
Group Pty Ltd); Penguin Books India Pvt Ltd, 11 Community Centre, Panchsheel Park,
New Delhi – 110 017, India; Penguin Group (NZ), 67 Apollo Drive, Rosedale, Auckland
0632, New Zealand (a division of Pearson New Zealand Ltd); Penguin Books (South
Africa) (Pty) Ltd, 24 Sturdee Avenue, Rosebank, Johannesburg 2196, South Africa

Penguin Books Ltd, Registered Offices: 80 Strand, London WC2R 0RL, England

Published by Gotham Books, a member of Penguin Group (USA) Inc.

First printing, June 2012
10 9 8 7 6 5 4 3 2 1

LIBRARY OF CONGRESS CATALOGING-IN-PUBLICATION DATA
Jarnow, Jesse.
  Big day coming : Yo La Tengo and the rise of indie rock / Jesse Jarnow.
    p. cm.
  ISBN 978-1-59240-715-6
  1. Yo La Tengo (Musical group)   I. Title.
  ML421.Y6J37 2012
  782.42166092'2—dc23
  2011053088

Printed in the United States of America
Set in Egyptienne LT Std and Conduit ITC
Designed by Nora Rosansky

While the author has made every effort to provide accurate telephone numbers and
Internet addresses at the time of publication, neither the publisher nor the author
assumes any responsibility for errors, or for changes that occur after publication.
Further, the publisher does not have any control over and does not assume any responsibility for author or third-party websites or their content.

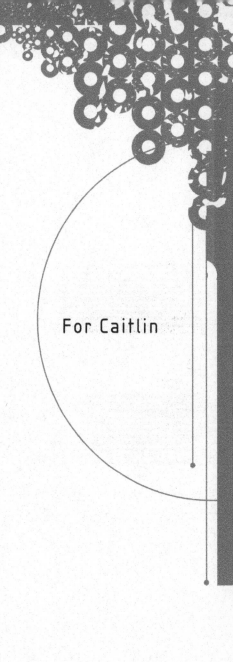

For Caitlin

Introduction

The Story of Yo La Tango

The first typo came with the second or third print appearance: "Wo La Tengo." It was in an ad by Maxwell's, even, the Hoboken club where the band's two primary members worked and veritably lived. The band had debuted there two months earlier, in December 1984, doing two sets at a party in the back room, and misspelled names were the least of their worries.

They opened with an instrumental—"Surfin' with the Shah" by UCLA band the Urinals—and that had gone well enough. The guitarist was a baby-faced twentysomething with an erupting halo of hair. When it came time for the night's first vocals, no words came from his mouth.

"Not exac. clear if anyone in the band had any sort of grip on their instruments," one contemporary writer noted of their early gigs. Despite the fact that they were a trio, the guitarist took no solos. That night and for many to follow, the drummer—a shy girl with round cheeks and a room-lighting smile—didn't sing at all.

The misspelled name would trail Ira Kaplan and Georgia Hubley in almost daily fashion through their career, an irony that was not lost on two people who regularly worked as free-lance copy editors. They kept a running tally.

There was a show as the classic "Yo La Tango" in 1995.

"Atlanta's Masquerade was always just like a home away from home to us, if the people in your family always spelled your name wrong and built the stage right above the pumping techno soundsystem," they later noted. The Florida Theater in Jacksonville offered a French twist, as "Yo Le Tengo." In Australia, a promoter managed to achieve the trifecta, getting vowels wrong in each word: Ya Lo Tango. Set to make their network television debut nine years after their first gig, Conan O'Brien squinted at a cue card and cheerily announced the next night's musical guest: "Yo Lo Tengo!"

They didn't always have such a troubling name. At first, they called themselves A Worrying Thing. Like the name they settled on—Yo La Tengo—they found it in a book about baseball.

"Doesn't matter what you did yesterday," Cleveland Indians pitcher Stanley Coveleski told writer Lawrence Ritter. "That's history. It's tomorrow that counts. So you worry all the time. It never ends. Lord, baseball is a worrying thing." When their own worries had them looking for a new name, Kaplan and Hubley passed on another similarly diminutive baseball term, the "Bad Hops," looking for a phrase that was meaningless enough for potential audiences to project onto. "Yo La Tengo" won.

Its source was a story about the New York Mets, a Kaplan obsession since his Hudson Valley youth. Born only five years before the Mets came into existence in the National League's 1962 expansion, the young Ira fell in love with the bumbling squad early in their arc upward from the worst season in modern baseball history, during which they lost 120 out of 160 games.

One reason for their losses was that center fielder Richie "Whitey" Ashburn often collided on fly balls with Venezuelan-born shortstop Elio Chacón, one of the first Latin American players in the Major Leagues. He didn't understand Ashburn's call of "I've got it." A Spanish-speaking teammate instructed Ashburn to try barking "yo la tengo!" the next time a fly ball came their way.

Ashburn did so. Chacón stopped, but crew-cut left fielder Frank Thomas barreled straight into Ashburn.

"What's a yellow tango?" he asked.

Kaplan and Hubley were tentative about playing music in front of people, and the image of a misplayed fly ball was one of innocent terror. Like the misspellings, it followed them, an ancient blooper reel stuck in loop. And when the name *was* spelled correctly, some were still left wondering if the band played Latin music. For years, famed New York radio host Vin Scelsa insisted on pronouncing it with a heavy Spanish accent.

The name remained eminently unspellable, even as they got better and bigger. In 1993 their label, Matador, sold 49 percent of itself to Atlantic Records, stepping up the distribution of their wares (including Yo La Tengo's latest) from a hard-built network of subcultural outposts to the full American marketplace. As part of its flirtation with the mainstream, the label released the soundtrack to *Amateur,* indie director Hal Hartley's own dalliance with Sony, featuring all-star Matador recording artist "Yo La Tango."

In 2006, more than twenty years into their career, the band appropriated the typo for a song title, "The Story of Yo La Tango," the twelve-minute final track on its new album, *I Am Not Afraid of You and I Will Beat Your Ass.* The disc's title, taken from another piece of pro-sports doggerel, was a sign of a confidence it was hard to imagine almost a quarter century earlier.

As a finale to the band's sets, "The Story of Yo La Tango" was seemingly nothing *but* guitar solo: a long, wild build to the moment Ira Kaplan removed the instrument from his neck and threw it around violently, as if to smash it, a sleight-of-wrist yanking it back into his arms at the last second. And then, to cue the last section, a dramatic rock guitar jump, feet flashing behind knees, executed as the only logical conclusion to whatever argument he'd been having.

But the song's lyrics, buried behind distortion, bravado moves, and a funny title, expressed no more certainty about the rock-and-roll process than the band had at its first show. In fact, the words expressed the uncertainty quite unmistakably. "We opened our hearts, it's true, but not to any of you," Kaplan sang inside the noise, in a manner as candid as the song's typo.

In their fifties by this time, Kaplan and Hubley more than resembled the couple they were two decades earlier. Though considerably more comfortable performing, Yo La Tengo was as unassuming as ever. Hubley and Kaplan still lived together a quick bike ride from Maxwell's, the neighborhood hangout where they continued to play often. Dressed in cool T-shirts, hoodies, and Converse All-Stars, they looked the same too—a nearly ageless rock-and-roll couple in loving bohemian matrimony.

But the band meant the lyric almost as literally as they could. It had taken some time for the world to come around to them. Even—or especially—in their own minds, there had long been a secondary quality to Yo La Tengo. Sonic Youth was noisier and had the more confidently sexy-cool downtown power couple of Thurston Moore and Kim Gordon. R.E.M. was janglier and, by the time Yo La Tengo started, already wildly successful. The Feelies and the dB's, the bands that nurtured them, were more established on the local scene. When it came to typos, they had good competition from Antietam, Mofungo, and the dB's, who once included a never-enforced typo fee in the tour rider they sent to venues.

So when Yo La Tengo did achieve success, they found it better to keep the world at arm's length sometimes. The lies they would occasionally feed journalists were little, sometimes hardly even lies at all. When a band member might nod along with a writer's misconception or not give a complete answer to a question, it was hardly at the level of Bob Dylan claiming to have traveled with a carnival as a teenager. They weren't malevolent gestures, or even provocative or particularly myth-making, but almost purely defensive, protecting something too rare and precious to share on command.

Ira and Georgia had started dating first, but the relationship was always fueled by music. It was how they met, seeing shows by other bands. "Some of those bands weren't all that popular, so there weren't that many people there," Georgia remembered later. "So it was kind of inevitable that you ended up knowing everyone in the room." The $3 Wednesdays that

Ira eventually helped book at Gerde's Folk City in Manhattan were titled, cheekily, Music for Dozens.

Much would be made later of lyrics that seemingly revealed the workings of Kaplan and Hubley's relationship. But it has been the intensity of their own fandom that has perhaps been the single unifying theme in their individual paths from before adolescence through (and including) the creation of their most mature work.

Since long before their first show, fueled by the same fandom, Kaplan and Hubley threaded themselves with the musical world around them, a pattern repeated by bassist James McNew, growing up ten years later in Virginia. At various points, the three operated professionally at nearly every level of the music scene—as journalists, managers, filmmakers, zine writers, sound engineers, sidemen, DJs, visual artists, designers, promoters, home recorders, producers, publicists, doormen, roadies, and label owners.

Kaplan and Hubley may have been shy about performing, but they were anything but socially inept. "Exceptionally well-connected" is how critic Robert Christgau began a very positive 1989 *Village Voice* review. In 1981, Ira was listed (along with Christgau) among ten rock critics in the country who dealt with American independent labels, a close-knit scene that would soon grow much larger.

The band's three members were hardly leaders, if there was even anything to lead, but they weren't passive, either. They didn't know everyone in the still-expanding music world around them, but they knew a lot. The sum total of their stories—Yo La Tengo's, their friends', and many others'—is an attempt to find a human-size passage through late twentieth-century capitalism (and eventually new-millennium craziness) in which to peacefully be musicians, a third path between do-it-yourself existential anarchy and fun-sucked squareness.

They were borne along on the currents sometimes. For a while, the vessel seemed to be called "college rock," like the *College Music Journal*, launched by Robert Haber the spring Ira moved to New York City in 1979. Or just "new," as in the

New Music Seminar, attended by two hundred musicians the following June. Robert Christgau coined "Amerindie," which didn't last all too long.

Kaplan and Hubley remained defiantly or accidentally outside underground trends that might draw them some attention. They liked the Kinks and folk music too much and were too old for hardcore, were too mild-mannered to be post-punks, and were too late-blooming to be part of the initial explosion of Hoboken bands in the early '80s. They were too unslick to be New Wave, too unassuming to be video stars. They worried over things. Patiently, always, they continued to make music.

The continuity begun in 1985 with the folk-rock of "The River of Water," their self-released first single, brought them squalling through reinventions, the addition of a full-time third member, distortion pedals, audible fascinations with exotica and free jazz and R&B, exquisitely quiet three-part harmonies, soundtracks to animation and French underwater documentaries, a unique connection to the comedy world, and decades-long collaborations with kindred spirits in bands from Nashville to New Zealand. It has also produced a canon of legitimate greatest hits, unidentified by any particular chart but hits that any Yo La Tengo fan (or audience applause-o-meter) would recognize: "Autumn Sweater," "Sugarcube," "Mr. Tough," "Tears Are in Your Eyes," "The Summer," "Stockholm Syndrome," and many others.

Ultimately, it was the tag "indie rock" that stuck. If the term would grow to make Yo La Tengo uncomfortable in its muddy imprecision, the word "independent" surely did not. Indeed, drummer Georgia Hubley's parents, Faith and John, were two of the most famously (and self-consciously) autonomous filmmakers of the postwar years.

"There's always been a strong moral sense in my family," Ira's younger brother Neil once remembered to *The New York Times*. "You believe in something, you act on your beliefs." Neil, then thirty-seven, had recently stopped a robbery in an east side subway tunnel and ended up in three hours of microsurgery to sew up a tendon-severing knife wound in his left wrist.

Yo La Tengo's independence was hardly the result of an arbitrary set of ideals. Grounded by Ira's steel-trap mind and nearly flawless memory, the same stubbornly freethinking personality traits manifested themselves again and again in each of the three band members as their music expanded, a sequence of daily decisions in their creative, personal, and business lives that created Yo La Tengo. For all their reasonable practices, though, sometimes they could be quite difficult.

"In some respects, they were the most demanding people," noted Bob Lawton, their longtime booking agent and Ira's occasional bandmate in Double Dynamite. "They just wanted to be right and could be quite upset when it wasn't right, whatever *right* was—a PA, a jerky monitor guy, an unheated club in February, the usual things that all bands gripe about. 'Why did we drive twelve hours to this complete shithole? We could have just taken the day off and arrived in Minneapolis a day early.'"

By the time the word "indie" came into vogue, its definition was anything but useful, although if you squinted at Yo La Tengo, you might see an exact resemblance of some version of the indie archetype: They wore Converse All-Stars, played noisy jams, sometimes sang quietly, released 7-inch records, got played on college radio, and recorded for an independent label. As the decades wore on, the term grew even blurrier.

At the heart of indie rock, though, was a well-worn network of clubs, publications, labels, college radio stations, record stores, and other institutions built—in the late 1970s and early 1980s—by a group of enterprising fans. And running between those clubs was a very specific kind of band, built atop the post–Velvet Underground continuum of underground rock, Yo La Tengo well among them, making instinctive human-scale music far from the MTV-dominated mainstream.

Like baseball, the game first played in its modern form on the same ground where Maxwell's stood, indie rock was not invented in any one place. But, also like baseball, if one had to pick somewhere to put a plaque, it might as well be Hoboken. Yo La Tengo's roots there ran deep. Desiccated in the mid-'70s to the point where $65 a month could get you a six-room apartment, Hoboken was as noble a canvas for a utopia as any, and a 30¢ PATH ride to the West Village. It was there that Yo La Tengo found themselves being sometimes-unwilling mirrors for indie rock as it passed into the mainstream of American culture and, eventually, they became something that hardly resembled Yo La Tengo at all.

"Be careful what you wish for," they have observed often about the modest but undeniable success they've achieved: big enough to be continuously sustaining, not large enough to retire. They have balanced a marriage, a business, and a serious artistic endeavor in the process.

Uninterested in living their lives completely publicly, Kaplan and Hubley's relationship remained a valuable source of creativity, and they fairly quickly became excellent musicians and songwriters in the process. "It was another way of writing about and to Georgia," Ira said of one of the band's most-loved songs, *Electr-o-Pura*'s "Tom Courtenay," which turned the stars of Hubley's favorite British films loose into a fantasia of their own.

It was an intimacy that the band both shared with its audience and kept intensely private. In that way, it drove one of rock and roll's most unique partnerships—a sweet and wholesome romantic iconography with a long, constantly renewing creative arc to sit in the pantheon next to reckless debauchers, concept-driven visionaries, mercurial songwriters, and countless other archetypes. It was a powerful myth and nearly totally true. Yo La Tengo were exactly who they seemed. They even sang about it.

The name they chose in 1984 would serve them with incredible effectiveness in the years to come. Spelled correctly or not, with or without meaning, "Yo La Tengo" was a durable shield.

Prologue

The Elysian Fields

Initially the tavern at 1039 Washington wasn't called anything at all, one more bar in a square mile of Hoboken that contained well over a hundred of them. There was a baseball field down the block where players came over from Manhattan, fleeing the city's blue laws. They'd been fleeing Manhattan for Hoboken for one reason or another since the mid-nineteenth century, beginning with the island's industrialization, and the baseball field that lingered in the train-track-crossed lot near the end of Eleventh Street by the Savannah shipping pier was the last remnant of the first place they'd played.

The ballplayers' favorite bar had itself been demolished only recently. Its location—paved over when Twelfth Street was extended to the water—was what determined the location of the first field. In fact, the field by William McCarty's tavern had been the first real baseball field anywhere.

They had arrived around 1843, carrying with them a new variation on rules to an ancient ball game, and disembarked from the Barclay Street ferry into a very different place from the Manhattan they'd just left. Stepping first onto a massive, manicured lawn surrounded by elm trees, they passed a merry-go-round, a ten-pin alley, and wax figures as they entered into

Col. John Stevens's Elysian Fields, a fantasy of Arcadian-American entrepreneurism and the first great public park in the New York City area, already some forty years old.

Housed behind a faux-Greek facade known as the Colonnade, McCarty's was down the River Walk, around the point, and set a little ways back from the Hudson. There was beer and chowder. If it wasn't heaven, it was close. Spread out before the ballplayers were the fields themselves, vast enough to hold 24,000 attendees at a P. T. Barnum–staged buffalo hunt in 1843. The buffalo escaped and caused mayhem.

At Elysian Fields, teams like the Knickerbockers found an environment suited for their kind of creativity. The Knicks wrote down their version of the rules. They regularized the distance between bases and established the concept of foul territory as a 270-degree angle made as an inverse from home plate. They thusly carved, however roughly, the first legitimate baseball diamond. Around McCarty's, a few more diamonds sprang up, and more ball clubs were chartered.

One Knickerbocker, Doc Adams—creator of the shortstop position—took responsibility for the manufacture of baseballs shared by the field's regular teams. "I found a Scotch saddler who was able to show me a good way to cover the balls with horsehide, such as was used for whip lashes," Adams remembered in 1896. "I used to make stuffing out of three or four ounces of rubber cuttings, wound with yarn and then covered with leather."

The teams preferred not to compete with one another, scheduling the diamonds on alternate days. "We used to have dinner in the middle of the day, and twice a week we would spend the whole afternoon in ball play," remembered one Knick. "We were all mature men and in business, but we didn't have too much of it as they do nowadays. There was none of that hurry and worry so characteristic of that present New York. We enjoyed life and didn't wear out so fast."

Games ended by sunset. Then, beer and cigars at McCarty's and an at least half-drunken ferry ride home amid sailboats and rowboats paddled by singing oarsmen.

The Knickerbockers' baseball diamonds, self-replicating art for the Industrial Age, jumped two rivers to Brooklyn, and soon the Civil War aided the dissemination of the New York baseball rules. As league play spread during the Reconstruction, including a touring craze in 1868, competitive baseball's structures hardened around the Knickerbockers' early relaxed joy. Some teams even charged admission. The Knicks remained an anomaly, content to play among themselves, eating well and getting drunk.

What the Knicks set into motion on the banks of the Hudson proved pleasing enough to repeat over and over again. The rules and organizational principles continued to twist as the games and statistics grew more marketable. Over the course of a century and a half, what began in Hoboken as a codification of a child's game would grow to become a $6-billion-per-year industry and a professional universe of tens of thousands of players and coaches on three continents. Like Hoboken's founding father, John Stevens, who'd built the first steamboat and an early railroad in Hoboken a few decades earlier, the Knicks were bona fide inventors, their diamonds ubiquitous across the globe.

In perfect visual synchronization with the Knickerbockers' hesitance to go professional, the ballplayers' Eden disappeared, swallowed by new streets and train tracks and the economic boom the Stevens family had long hoped for when they'd developed the fields. McCarty's became Roedenburg's, and—in the early 1870s—the Knickerbockers played their last game at Elysian Fields. They moved a few blocks inland and lasted another decade before folding.

Eventually, Twelfth Street extended to the water and the old bar and hotel at its end was torn down, replaced by a shipping warehouse. Baseball survived on the Hudson's banks for another twenty years. South of the former Colonnade, players shaped two last fields, called the Savannah Oval for the Ocean Steamship Company's Savannah line, which docked at the foot of Eleventh. The lot was big enough to accommodate two simultaneous games, outfields overlapping with players back-to-back in deepest center field.

Until Manhattan revoked its blue laws in 1918, crowds of six thousand still gathered on weekends to watch. Owner-manager John McGraw would lead his New York Giants from the Polo Grounds in upper Manhattan to Hoboken to play against local semi-pro teams. Other major leaguers, including Ty Cobb, roamed the Elysian Fields remnants there, too.

Near the new end of Eleventh Street, a strip of rowhouses had gone up around the time the Colonnade had come down. For at least the last seven years of big-time baseball in Hoboken, beginning around 1911, the four-story building at the corner of 1039 Washington owned by John W. Bremerman housed a new tavern, near where the last bit of park had been sewn into the grid.

By the time of the Depression, Hoboken was already well depressed. Dockside jobs disappeared even faster than they had before. The 1939 arrival of the Maxwell House coffee plant and its massive sign facing Manhattan—"the largest using neon tubing except at world's fairs," *The New York Times* breathlessly reported—was a godsend.

The company ran ads inviting interested coffee drinkers to order a booklet, modestly titled *Progress*, which would illuminate "the much talked about 'swing of industry' to New Jersey," and offered tours for summer vacationers. In the late '40s, the Hoboken workforce boomed to levels not seen since the turn of the century. The plant exploited the full scope of Hoboken's transportation system, importing beans by ship and exporting from the city's tangled dockside train hubs.

The bar at 1039 Washington formally appeared in the city's records as Maxwell's Tavern and Grill in 1952 next to the name of its newest owner, Ambrose Chius. He'd taken over from the Garibaldi family, owners since 1927, who'd merged the building with an adjoining storefront to create a back room.

Chius had called it Ambrose's at first, but soon changed to Maxwell's in deference to local usage. As Chius kept bar and served lunch, he sang songs in a high, keening Yugoslavian. "Beautiful. It sounded good," remembered one former patron and Maxwell House employee. "It sounded better after a few drinks." It was a daytime business, with booths in the front and back, and four or five beers lined up at the bar for lunchtime regulars. On paydays, factory workers cashed their checks at the bar and grabbed a sandwich and a drink while they were at it. Female patrons were infrequent.

In the back, Chius installed a jukebox stocked with Frank Sinatra, and a pair of pool tables that could be pushed aside for parties, communions, and the occasional wedding. While Manhattan thrived as a center of culture, Hoboken remained profoundly working-class. A Barbary Coast of desolate longshoremen's bars dotted the waterfront. The city's Italian and Puerto Rican communities existed mostly cut off from the Hudson, bound inland by factories and warehouses. Caffeinated air wafted over the city from the Maxwell House plant.

During the *Sgt. Pepper* year of 1967, Hoboken entered the federal Model Cities Program, part of the Great Society's War on Poverty, and ferry service was discontinued for the first time since the seventeenth century. Maxwell House faced a global coffee surplus that saw them a year and a half ahead of demand.

In 1971, Ambrose Chius returned to Yugoslavia. He sold the bar to Mary and Andrew McGovern. By the middle of the decade, even Maxwell House was laying people off, and nearly a quarter of the local population was on welfare. But a bar was a bar, even without a baseball field nearby.

Big Day Coming

CHAPTER 1

The Hudson Line

There came the magical afternoon Ira Kaplan was allowed to listen to the radio in the car. "I was out with my dad running errands, and I don't know that I *always* asked to listen to the radio, and I'm sure the answer was always no when I did," Ira remembered many years later. "Except one day he said yes."

A few years earlier, barely a month after Ira's seventh birthday, the Beatles had come through the living room on *The Ed Sullivan Show*. Abraham and Marilyn Kaplan would tell the story for years, of how Ira's eyes had positively lit up when the Liverpudlians hit the screen. Like countless others, Ira had been taken as the full British invasion cavalry mugged in black and white from the other side of the screen over the following months. It was like a spore inhaled. Ira grew insistent. Somewhat reluctantly, folk-loving Abraham brought home *Meet the Beatles*. Listening to rock music in the car took longer.

The first afternoon's magic was significantly abetted by the new Rolling Stones single "Ruby Tuesday," whose baroque piano, droning double bass, and mystic chorus entranced the ten-year-old. The next day, his mother brought him and his younger brother Neil to a local department store, and Ira left clutching the single, along with a copy of the second in the

Royal Guardsmen's trilogy of novelty 45s about Snoopy, "Return of the Red Baron." Many more records followed. He began to fill his head with music and found there was space for quite a lot of it.

Some thirty miles upriver from Manhattan in Croton-on-Hudson, the Kaplans weren't far from the big city. But they weren't close, either. Replete with Abraham and Marilyn planted on the far side of the generation gap, the family radiated a regional version of postwar suburban normal.

Abraham and Marilyn had arrived in green, leafy Croton by what amounted to traditional means, Abraham from Flatbush, where the Brooklyn Dodgers played, Marilyn from the Bronx. Both were the children of immigrants, one Austrian and three Russian parents between them. They married and lived in Queens, where Ira was born on January 7, 1957, one season before Abraham's beloved Dodgers abandoned Flatbush for sunny Los Angeles. Two years later, the Kaplans fled Brooklyn for Croton-on-Hudson.

For the young couple, Croton was a picturesque and natural decision. Abraham's sister lived there, and he thought it would be nice to learn how to sail. The town, fifteen stops north of Grand Central Station on the Croton Local, had become a logical destination for people like Abraham and Marilyn. That is, young, Jewish, and from New York's freeway-divided outer boroughs. Like many, the Kaplans made for the promised land at the new roads' far end.

A few decades earlier, a Chelsea real-estate agent named Harry Kelly had taken ads out in Manhattan newspapers to announce the sale of property on West Mount Airy Road. "A Community of Your Kind," Kelly headlined them. "Mt. Airy at Croton on the Hudson, 50 minutes from New York, 100 trains daily, is attracting artists, writers, intellectual workers—liberals and radicals, the very ones you would like for your neighbors," he wrote. Briefly home to John Reed, future founder of the American Communist Party, the nickname "Red Hill" soon followed.

When the music in the headphones slowed down and the lights blinked off, it meant it was time for dinner. Ira and his brother Neil had the downstairs in the new house to themselves. Neil was born just after the family arrived in Croton, followed by Adam, then Jeremy, most variations on a curly-headed theme.

"We could be sufficiently disconnected from them that we weren't driving them crazy with music," Ira said of the new setup. "I could listen to 45s all day without my mom wanting to kill herself. When the headphone era began, my dad would let us know that they needed us by flicking the power on and off from the circuit breaker."

Abraham, who worked in real-estate development in some capacity that Ira never fully understood, commuted to Manhattan every day. Just off Red Hill, the house he purchased for his growing family on Woodybrook Lane was three miles and a few steep rises from the village.

Down the road a little was Lee Hays, whose deep bass vocals anchored the Weavers, the genially radical folk quartet blacklisted in 1953. Former Weaver Pete Seeger—living twenty-five miles farther north in Beacon—was a regular presence around town.

"If there's a voice of growing up that's not family related, it's Pete Seeger," Adam Kaplan said. "I remember being by the Hudson River in Croton Point Park, and he was there. I found a dead fish and he showed me how to get rid of it. And then he pulled out a guitar, and there were like ten kids sitting around. It was great." The Weavers provided the soundtrack to the Kaplan boys' childhood, alongside children's LPs by the Baby Sitters, featuring Hays and actor Alan Arkin. Long before the Beatles, Marilyn and Abraham made sure that Ira and Neil had their own record player.

Small-town normalcy prevailed. Ira played Little League (first base for T&D Market) and marched in uniform with his team on Memorial Day. He babysat and begged his parents to take him to Palisades Park. Abraham, a rabid baseball and basketball fan, brought the boys out to Queens a few times a year to catch games by the New York Mets.

The bumbling, bombing team was perfect for Ira's child-like enthusiasm when he discovered baseball two years after the Mets' 1962 founding. "The golden era when both the Mets and the Yankees were bad," he fondly recalled of the mid-1960s. Soon the Mets captivated Ira solely. Neil, ever a freethinking Kaplan, remained a Yankees fan.

Despite Croton's progressive lineage, the '60s were slow to arrive, save for the records that Ira had started to accumulate at Woodybrook Lane. Not that his parents had exactly embraced his fandom. It had been a fight to get a transistor radio, even, but eventually he'd talked them into that, too.

Ira brought an analytical curiosity to bear on the records he listened to as he attempted to decipher the lyrics and intentions of the musicians who made them. "I remember vividly a babysitter bringing over a Paul Revere and the Raiders record and I thought that was great," Ira said. "The whole package, the guy with the ponytail on the cover, really helped me figure some things out." Another babysitter explained the drug references on *Sgt. Pepper* to the young listener. He wrote a letter to the Monkees, questions carefully included for all four members, and they sent back a form letter and invitation to join their fan club. One more thing figured out.

Though the world was alight with cultural revolution, the background to Ira's budding fandom was a downtown that, as late as 1970, was described as looking like "a set for a movie about small-town America." That same year, sleepy Woodybrook Lane was used to depict exactly that in a low-budget film penned by neighbor Eugene Price, later an Emmy-winning soap opera writer.

Directed by John G. Avildsen, six years from helming *Rocky, Guess What We Learned in School Today?* was an earnest romp about sex education and the hangups of modern society. It featured nudity, drugs, and communism to spare, but no rock and roll.

It also featured the neighbors. "All the kids were in the movie except the Lyons boys," Neil remembered, "because their parents were feuding with the Prices." Ira, Neil, and Adam appeared uncredited in a sex-ed scene, the older boys each with appropriately embarrassing dialogue. The Kaplan house was even used as a set.

"In one of the great Kaplan parent moments, the movie came out—three of the four Kaplan kids are in it, the house is in it, the road is in it—and my father's like, 'Well, let's wait till it comes around,'" Adam remembered. Other than a positive notice in *New York* magazine, the film was roundly panned. It closed almost instantly.

Ira's was a childhood of austere and logical fairness, communicated from Abraham and Marilyn's own Depression upbringings, which soon burned itself into their first son's mind. When Abraham had the last-minute opportunity to bring the boys to see the Mets play in the 1969 World Series, he calculated that they would miss several innings, and let somebody else take the tickets. Ira, in reply, calculated that they would have missed the first legendary catch made by outfielder Tommie Agee, but would have seen the second.

The Series was the Mets' great triumph. More often, Ira's favorite team only flirted with it. Earlier in the season, the Kaplans had been there to see Tom Seaver's near-perfect game against Ernie Banks and the Cubs, broken up with a single by rookie backup Jimmy Qualls in the ninth inning, a more bittersweet symbol of life as a young Mets fan.

Imperfect though it was, Ira's parents came up with a system by which he could hear new music, and so the well-behaved Ira waited patiently for the days when Marilyn and Abraham brought his lists to far-off department stores, Abraham to Korvette's on Forty-fifth Street in Manhattan, Marilyn to Alexander's in nearby White Plains. If his mom occasionally brought home albums like *Something Else* by Welsh pop crooner Shirley Bassey instead of the requested *Something Else by the Kinks*, well, that was a small price to pay to get some records to listen to until Abraham flicked the breaker and it was time for dinner.

There wasn't much to do in downtown Croton—no record store, no movie theater—but that was no reason not to hang out there sometimes. The return home for kids from Woodybrook Lane was uphill, and often involved a thumbed ride from a passing car. Hitching a lift from a famous folkie en route to Lee Hays's house wasn't uncommon, even though it still left a good deal of the climb.

Ira didn't say a word to Arlo Guthrie the day Woody's long-haired progeny picked up the shy fan, who most certainly owned a few (if not all) of the younger Guthrie's albums. Ira's tastes progressed with rapid logic through nearly anything he could absorb, folk-rock being an early favorite. Since the moment he'd clicked on with the Beatles, he had also displayed an uncommonly intense musical memory, each new experience slotted firmly into place.

One new one came the day Abraham announced that he would take Ira and his friends to Bill Graham's Fillmore East—a former Loews movie theater turned rock venue—in the East Village for Ira's twelfth birthday. "Not believing my good fortune, I panicked and picked a show that I wasn't that interested in, but it came up very quickly," Ira remembered. "I could have waited to see Jimi Hendrix or the Dead."

So panicked was the choice, in fact, that the show fell nearly a full month before his actual birthday. Headlining the mid-December show was Country Joe & the Fish. Just below them on the bill was an early version of the Peter Green–led Fleetwood Mac. "We went in all the time, for museums, dinner, puppet theater, kids' stuff," remembered Neil. But this city trip was different.

Abraham drove. En route, Ira, Neil, and friends speculated on whether Country Joe would lead the crowd in the "Fish" cheer from his "I-Feel-Like-I'm-Fixin'-to-Die Rag" or if the band would use the *other* word they'd supposedly used in concert and for which they'd been booted from *The Ed Sullivan Show* before even appearing.

But it was the first act that night that gave the Kaplans and friends their psychedelic money's worth. At the top of the stairs to the balcony, people placed polka-dot decals on audience members' foreheads. Abraham gamely received one. Ira didn't. As they took their seats, an usher warned Abraham that he was taking his kids to see a strip show.

It turned out to be a performance of the Japanese avant-garde artist Yayoi Kusama's *Self-Obliteration by Dots*. "Dots have taught me the proof of my existence," the artist recalled in 2006. "They scatter proliferating love in the universe and raise my mind to the height of the sky."

As the Kaplans and their guests took their seats, people onstage began to remove their clothes. Film collages flashed on screens. A policeman rushed on to shut the performance down. His clothes too were removed.

"I am told I was very vocal about not being happy with our seats," Neil said. "It was a very arty strip show."

And while indeed Country Joe & the Fish chanted "F-U-C-K" during their set, they were deemed boring. Fleetwood Mac was better.

Fillmore trips didn't become a regular practice, much to Ira's dismay. He was denied a trip to Woodstock but was soon the recipient of a Fender Stratocaster, just a few years old, and a Vibrolux amplifier. Ira scraped off the guitar's psychedelic paint job applied by the instrument's recently matriculated previous owner until it was an even red-brown and spent the summer playing it.

"It didn't have a casual quality," Adam remembered of his older brother's experiments, which soon included recording with two tape decks. Though he worked at it, Ira could not get comfortable. He put the Stratocaster in its case and came to favor the family piano, on which he was more proficient.

Though Ira was not bar mitzvahed, Marilyn and Abraham's intensely secular Judaism provided him passage into manhood when they brought a station wagon full of friends to see

Easy Rider. After the experience at the Fillmore, Abraham and Marilyn deemed the film too racy for Neil—he wasn't thirteen yet, after all—who sat in the adjoining theater with his dad, watching *Butch Cassidy and the Sundance Kid*. First-generation children of immigrants, the Kaplans found secularity was the American Dream incarnate, more freethinking independence than assimilation. After all, Croton was no place a Jewish family needed to assimilate.

Music accumulated. Ira brought records with him to school. "It seemed kinda natural at the time," he remembered later. "It showed what your identity was, what record you were holding." Marilyn, who worked at local hospitals, brought home an entire record collection filled with obscure garage and girl-group singles formerly belonging to an army veteran who had survived his tour of duty in Vietnam only to die tragically upon his return home. Ira and Neil tuned in to powerful rock stations like WNEW and WABC's FM affiliate, which had grown increasingly freeform.

One source of generational-gap tension between the elder and younger Kaplans was hair length. Older brothers of the boys' friends sometimes earned punch-ups because of their hippie appearance and, more specifically, their opposition to the Vietnam War. Abraham brought the boys to Washington, D.C., for a massive antiwar rally. Neil attended others with his friends and their parents.

As Ira entered high school, a skinny and bright-eyed obsessive, his fandom was marked by an increasing studiousness that any rabbinical scholar might appreciate. "I don't think that I ever felt that nothing mattered but music," Ira observed more recently. "Nothing mattered as much as music, but not to the exclusion of everything else."

Conscious or not, it was a pragmatic attitude. It mirrored what was becoming Ira Kaplan's dominant trait. Later in life, he would sometimes be identified as reserved or shy or even calculating, but he is probably most literally characterized as thoughtful. There was almost nothing not worth thinking through, a process often written across Ira's brow, most enthusiastically when it came to music. It didn't always go smoothly.

Around this time, Ira joined his first band. Called Heatwave, after the Martha and the Vandellas song, the seven-piece practiced in the living room on Woodybrook Lane. Ira pounded it out on their serviceable baby grand while a bandmate played Ira's Stratocaster. There were two guitarists, piano, drums, and bass. Occasionally, two guys played harmonica.

The band's setlist included "Heat Wave," Jefferson Airplane's "3/5 of a Mile in 10 Seconds," Jimmie Ainsworth and Earl Bud Lee's "Midnight Shift" (learned via Commander Cody's cover), Little Walter's "Boom Boom (Out Go the Lights)," and others. Marilyn and Abraham made themselves scarce during band practice. Neil and Adam hung around and watched.

"How could my parents not have not been into it?" Neil asked, clearly a Heatwave partisan. "This wasn't a bunch of guys messing around, these were serious musicians playing. They may have been high school kids, but they were working on arrangements. They weren't getting high and every now and then bashing out a chord, they were a band." And a band with occasional gigs, even, mostly at school dances.

So serious were the band's rehearsals that the experience proved utterly traumatic for Ira. "It was completely this group of really good friends, and we'd get together and make fun of each other [when we] sang. Whoever was singing was the butt of such abuse. I think back on how destructive that was," he remembered. He wouldn't try again until he was in his mid-twenties.

It was a late summer Wednesday when he was fifteen that Ira worked out two very important things. The first was how to get to the city.

Going to concerts had become a stressful albeit not unobtainable goal. "There was a Ten Years After show at Madison Square Garden that caused a bit of a scene, because the show ended much later than it was supposed to," Ira remembered. "My mom, waiting in the car, was not ecstatic." It was still more fun than hanging around Croton, anyway, maybe running into Neil and his group of friends, all carless at the back of the drive-in.

But then came the discovery of the Schaefer Music Festival concert series at Wollman Rink in Central Park, entering its fifth summer. Actively geared toward suburbanites, the shows started at six and were over by eight thirty. Ira could get himself there and back by train, and it was a train ride he came to know well—an escape from Croton, not only to Manhattan but to the ley lines where music existed in real life.

A $2.50 off-peak round-trip from the Croton North station, the train glided five hundred feet above the river, past the rail yards in Harmon-on-Hudson, and through a tunnel abutting the walls of Sing Sing prison. Then, under the Tappan Zee Bridge, through the Palisades, down the canal-like industrial zone of the Harlem River, and on into the elevated station at 125th Street before terminating at Grand Central.

Soon, the 125th Street station would evoke the Velvet Underground's "I'm Waiting for the Man," the lead song on *Live 1969*, which Ira borrowed from a friend (though he'd skipped immediately to the notorious "Heroin"). But before the Velvets, before any other band really, and the first reason for a solo city jaunt on the Croton Local to Grand Central Station, came the Kinks.

Marilyn had eventually brought home *Something Else . . .* and Ira had been intrigued by "Lola," a massive hit two summers earlier. He'd wanted to see them the year before at Carnegie Hall, but it hadn't worked out.

Under a nearly full moon, the Kinks drew seven thousand to Central Park. Members of the Kinks Preservation Society fan club had camped out since two a.m. to stake space in the front row and hang their banners from the stage scaffolding. About to embark on a series of theatrical concept albums, Ray Davies had recently entered his music hall phase. *Melody*

Maker magazine reported his entrance breathlessly: "And then, ladies and gentlemen, appeared the star of the show. White Telecaster wrapped around his groin, hands tapping his hair to get a bouncy edge to it, feet juggling in a little dance. The place just exploded."

Davies was far from the point of sobriety and spent time climbing the rafters. Fans would swarm his limo afterward, and spoke of the show reverently for years. "They did an encore that clearly wasn't planned," Ira remembered. "The house lights were on, and so was the music, so they just threw something together. It was a great show."

Ira's musical taste and curiosity were hardly limited. A few days later, he returned to Central Park to see country rockers Poco, and tried marijuana in the Wollman bleachers for the first time. But the second thing he'd worked out a few days earlier was that he *loved* the Kinks. The quartet from Muswell Hill captured his imagination.

He became a member of the Kinks Preservation Society, a local fan club, where he would encounter future members of the Smithereens, and acquired a bootleg cassette of the Central Park show, which stretched and developed gaps from repeated listens. And he saw the Kinks regularly as they passed through the New York area, some thirty shows over the next half decade.

"One of the things I really responded to was the way Ray as a performer seemed involved with the audience," Ira said. "There was a period [in May 1975] when I went to see them three nights in a row at the Beacon Theatre. I had tickets that were very close the first night. And at some break in the action, I yelled for 'Autumn Almanac,' and Ray responded with, 'Oh, that's a terrible song,' which was exciting and crushing simultaneously. The next night, I tried again with a different song, because I wasn't an idiot, and yelled for 'Dead End Street,' another song that was not in their repertoire. In that kind of way of his, I think he knew it was the same person, and he was almost apologizing. And he said, 'Oh, that's a good song, we'll do that one tomorrow,' which was like, 'That's *perfect*.' And they *did* it the next night, which was almost too good. I certainly ruined the show for people around me."

New freedoms abounded too, as high school progressed. Ira enthused over far more than the Kinks and the Velvets. With friends, he traveled as far as Springfield, Massachusetts, to see the Grateful Dead a half-dozen times during their mid-'70s peak. He brought Neil to the massive Roosevelt Stadium in Jersey City and taped the four-hour Dead show with mikes affixed to a pole held above the crowd. He did the same for the Beach Boys at Roosevelt Raceway later that summer.

In the fall of 1975, Ira enrolled at Sarah Lawrence College, slightly closer to Manhattan than Croton but still not close enough. There were interesting people to talk to at Sarah Lawrence, but Ira's interests lay beyond campus. Though he would graduate as scheduled in 1979, Ira had almost completely checked out of Sarah Lawrence two years earlier.

Neil breathed a sigh of relief when Ira came back from college with the debut by the Modern Lovers. "It was like, *Where have you been all my life?*" he remembered. It is a rock platitude to talk about everybody in the Velvet Underground's small audience going on to start their own bands, but it was certainly true of Jonathan Richman.

The Massachusetts-born singer had seen the Velvet Underground at the Tea Party in Boston, launching the Modern Lovers in 1970 to dish out ecstatic, Velvet-loving wryness. In Cleveland, high school students Peter Laughner and Jaime Klimek were regulars at the post–John Cale VU's appearances at La Cave, hanging out with Lou Reed between sets. Within a year, there was a small Ohio underground of bands like Klimek's Mirrors and Laughner's Rocket from the Tombs.

Much of what Richman, Laughner, Klimek, and others felt was Maureen Tucker's Bo Diddley-by-Babatunde Olatunji drums, thumped on a minimal kit, kick drum upturned, cymbal crashes almost entirely absent. Her simplicity created a language that supported skiffle twangs, gentle folk, classic R&B, Reed's tender pop, Nico's Nordic moans, and John Cale's fueled drone.

Tucker's beat became an anchor in a new rock-and-roll canon, also centered around the garage rock compilation *Nuggets*. Produced by Patti Smith Group guitarist (and first-generation VU fan) Lenny Kaye in 1972, Kaye—also a record clerk and critic—dubbed the no-star guitar bashing "punk-rock." Ira had held the set in his hands when it first came out, noting its price, but came around to it joyously soon enough. A decade and change earlier, Harry Smith's *Anthology of American Folk Music* had provided a standard collection of primordial recordings for emergent folk scenes; *Nuggets'* screaming guitars and Ace Tone organs did the same. Jonathan Richman became quickly part of the canon. Within a year of the Modern Lovers' debut album, John Cale himself was covering Richman's "Pablo Picasso."

Almost immediately after starting at Sarah Lawrence, Ira had headed for CBGB on Manhattan's Bowery, the bar whose fame had built to a steady boil over the past two years as the home to Patti Smith, Television, the Ramones, Suicide, and countless other bands. If they didn't all perform outright *Nuggets* or Velvets tributes, they at least knew them well. Cale and Reed were regulars. The scene around the bar had blossomed grandly, the city's livable rents producing a flowering of occasionally overlapping musical worlds between dwellers of TriBeCa jazz lofts, drone-loving minimalists, disco DJs, and scuzzy punks who had all inhaled spores of their own. Ira picked up a copy of Television's independently released single "Little Johnny Jewel" at a record show. It wasn't what he was expecting based on the "punk-rock" tag, but he was entranced by Tom Verlaine's and Richard Lloyd's celestially entwined guitars.

Ira's first trip to the Bowery was for Quacky Duck and His Barnyard Friends, an oddball country-glam act recently signed by Warner Bros. featuring two sons of Tony Bennett, teenage prodigy David Mansfield, and the cousin of the drummer in the now-disbanded Heatwave. It wasn't punk at all, but he'd found it. Ira went back frequently.

He repeatedly checked out the Ramones and brought an underage Neil to the Bowery to see the new trio Talking Heads, who soon added former Modern Lover Jerry Harrison to their lineup. Ira *loved* Television. He saw Patti Smith—and *Nuggets* compiler Lenny Kaye—for the first time at the Larry Richardson Gallery on Fourteenth Street. Smith dedicated "Time Is on My Side" to Ed Sullivan, whom she called "the father of rock and roll." With memories of the Beatles, the Dave Clark Five, and others still flickering in his mind, Ira could relate.

It began with a few record reviews for *The Phoenix*, Sarah Lawrence's newspaper, and soon Ira found the way in. One he wrote was about the new Alex Chilton 7-inch, "Singer Not the Song," released by the small independent label Ork, which was founded by scenester and Television benefactor Terry Ork. In the review, Ira was critical of producer Jon Tivens, and his comments came to the attention of Ork employees, some of whom shared (and were entertained by) the opinion of the insouciant college junior.

So charmed was the label that they mentioned the write-up to the New York rock monthly *Trouser Press*, as well as *SoHo Weekly News*, and from then on, Ira was part of the conversation. He began to file short record reviews with each. At the latter, especially, his clips landed at exactly the right moment. The publication's new music editor, Peter Occhiogrosso, was an avowed jazz listener, well plugged into the loft jazz scene, who had spawned its own network of microlabels and musician-operated clubs. But Occhiogrosso didn't know much about punk. When Ira's clips arrived on his desk, the new editor gave the twenty-year-old nearly instant carte blanche to cover whatever he wished. They were auspicious column inches to fill.

Launched in 1974 as a vehicle to fire salvos in an emerging

war on disco, Michael Goldstein had established *SoHo Weekly News*'s initial readership by distributing copies outside of Max's Kansas City, north of Union Square, where Andy Warhol's crowd hung out. One of the Max's regulars, the eternal rock insider Danny Fields, launched an eponymous gossip column to tend the New York art-rock flame in the wake of the Velvet Underground's breakup.

> **Lou Reed** is back from Europe, and wasted no time in checking out **Television** at CBGB, after he read somewhere that they had picked up where the **Velvets** left off. Lou, of course, was also anxious to hear his dear friend **Patti Smith**, and was seen grinning paternally as she performed his song "We're Gonna Have a Real Good Time Together" . . .

Fields moved on to *Sixteen* magazine, and—shortly thereafter—Ira had a gig.

After a few short reviews, his first real assignment was an inadvertent hazing into the rock critics' fraternity: to cover the band of a fellow writer—in this case the Geeks, featuring Ira's new *SoHo Weekly News* colleague Roy Trakin. The game was to flex one's writing chops enough to praise the band in a genuine, generous way without becoming too fulsome. Ira passed with flying colors.

"Although the Geeks don't have all-star instrumentalists to match [Lester] Bangs' Boys, they are a lot funnier and crazier than Lester. At Max's they were tuneful—or at least in tune." The following week, he reviewed Jonathan Richman's Modern Lovers at NYU, and appeared weekly after that. In some two hundred columns and reviews Ira wrote for *SoHo Weekly News* over the next five years, his persona rarely matched Fields's showbiz pizzazz, though he served much the same role: man on the scene.

"He was always very opinionated and feisty," Trakin said with a laugh of the twenty-year-old Ira. "Even as a young man, he was an old crotchety man." One with a new audience of around thirty thousand readers in the Manhattan area. After a few live reviews, Ira launched the "Swinging Singles" reviews column.

"Once people pass the age of 14 or so, they usually abandon the practice of buying 45's, save for fanatics," he declared. "It takes a rare dedication to rock and roll to be willing to sit by the turntable changing the record every two and a half minutes. But today's new groups—for reasons of economics and because many of the bands are record-loving fanatics themselves—have brought with them a renaissance of the 45. Dozens of singles are now available with the songs that will never be played while the speed selector is on 33 ⅓." It was a precise logic: no other way to hear the tunes.

Ira's coverage was vast. He kept up with British New Wave, megapop such as Electric Light Orchestra, local favorites such as Talking Heads, and noisy acts emerging out of the New York punk scene, such as Mars and Information. Though he did so readily enough, Ira found that dispensing judgment on bands and recordings didn't necessarily make him happy. But still, it was a reason to be close to the music scene unfolding on the Bowery. His interest in music never diminished in the slightest. When he actually *liked* a band, the job could be downright fun, his enthusiasm communicated in clean, smartly observed prose.

He was a ghost on the Sarah Lawrence campus, often seeing the same bands as many times as he could, typing up reviews in his dorm room between barely fulfilled course obligations.

"I love NRBQ and I am mystified by their commercial failure," he wrote. "To me, they embody everything I look for in a rock band. They play and sing well, have a sense of humor, and write simple, wonderful songs that I can sing in the shower. Cliché that it is, this is one band that plays for the fun of it. Their immense repertoire includes enough songs to construct a set that, repeated night after night, could conceivably result in fame and fortune. But it's a lot more fun for them to play what they want. That way even songs they've been doing for 10 years sound fresh. The Who can't make that claim."

Taking the train back and forth between school and the city, Ira remained somewhat of an outsider to the scene he covered. Even so, he began to absorb a sense of the way the business behind the music worked. "It's rock and roll reality," he noted in April 1978. "Sooner or later independent labels affiliate with one of the majors. We've seen it a lot of late. Stiff and Arista. ORK and Phonogram (just because it happens doesn't mean it's beneficial); Berserkly, then CBS." It was a new layer of the music world uncovered, deciphered through press releases, other columnists, talking with other fans, voraciously consumed rock texts, and (as always) the careful study of liner notes.

With most of his meticulously organized record collection back home in Croton, he would occasionally call to have Adam fact-check something from a sleeve. In that way, Ira turned his brother on to new music. "His questions led me places," Adam said. "He'd call to double-check who was on, like, the Sylvain Sylvain single. I'd never thought to look at what any of them did after the New York Dolls."

Ira covered big rock, including multiple nights of Elvis Costello, Bruce Springsteen at the Philadelphia Spectrum, and even a profile of Emmylou Harris, where the cub reporter went on the road with the Alabama-born country singer as she opened for Willie Nelson in New England. He had the most fun, he noticed, though, when the music was more casual. "Even if they never learn another song again, if they do nothing more than demonstrate how to go through life as inspired amateurs, we need the Heartbreakers," Ira would note of an ecstatic night getting drunk seeing Johnny Thunders and friends at Max's Kansas City.

He brought sixteen-year-old Adam to the unheated CBGB club to see the rockabilly-influenced punk band the Cramps.

"How many fans do you think they have?" Adam asked his brother.

"Oh, I'd say they're probably all here," Ira told him.

Ira had found himself in a very small world. In the early part of the year, he made contact with another local publication, and his first review appeared in September. *New York Rocker* was a natural fit, too, though its publication schedule was hardly as regular as *SoHo Weekly News*. Its founder, in fact, was a former *SoHo Weekly News* columnist named Alan Betrock. They were delighted to have an enthusiastic new writer who could make deadlines. Only eight months until graduation.

CHAPTER 2

New York Rockers

Ira's new address on the Upper West Side wasn't exactly hip, but the apartment was free. More important, it was in New York. He brought his Stratocaster with him when he moved too, but he rarely played it. "I plugged it into the stereo somehow," he remembered. "I would just solo on the high E string. I remember breaking it at one point and leaving it off for a year, to train myself to play on more than one string. But it didn't really work. To this day, I still primarily play on one string at a time."

During his senior year, as he'd penned the occasional *Rocker* piece, *SoHo Weekly News* gave him a new column, "Rocks Off." With its bold-faced markers of upcoming albums, gigs, and a little bit of semi-outsider gossip, Ira made an earnest attempt at capturing the whole of the worthwhile rock world in 1978: independent punk, mainstream standbys, and semi-forgotten heroes.

Ira's double life constrained him occasionally. His collection of more than one thousand LPs and 45s spilled between his Bronxville dorm room and the house on Woodybrook Lane, which necessitated constant calls to Adam. Most of all, Ira's new task required him to report what was going on in New York—both what he could get to and what he had to miss due to class and inconvenient train schedules.

"I managed to catch **Elvis Costello's** four numbers with **Richard Hell and the Voidoids** at CBGB's, as well as ex-Television **Richard Lloyd's** set with **the B-52's**," he noted once. "But when **Keith Richards** joined **Rockpile** at the Bottom Line for 'Down Down Down,' I was already on my way home."

He spent New Year's Eve seeing the New York Dolls. Though the Dolls were two years broken up, singer David Johansen (with former Dolls guitarist Sylvain Sylvain) headlined the Palladium while Johnny Thunders and the Delinquents featuring Jerry Nolan and Arthur Kane played at 19 Bleecker. Ira hit both.

While finishing at Sarah Lawrence in May, Ira furthered his music education, columning about trips to record conventions like Rock Ages and the Rock and Roll Flea Market, and their bounties of 45s to explore and absorb. He dug deep for sides by James Brown, the Searchers, P. F. Sloan, the Peppermint Trolley Company, the Hombres, Sandy Posey, and others.

The new apartment, at least, was near Hurrah on West Sixty-second Street, booked by Jim Fouratt beginning in 1978. Ira met dB's drummer Will Rigby there for the first time, and Rigby asked Ira how he was getting home. "I only live a few blocks from here," Ira told him. "Why, I might even *jog*."

Free rent or no, Ira still had to figure out how to make a living. Increasingly, he confirmed that big-time rock journalism—not to mention big rock—wasn't for him. Over the summer, he'd hit his nadir, traveling to Washington, D.C., to interview KISS for *SoHo Weekly News*. "I had a friend from college who lived there," Ira remembered. "I went to visit my friend, stayed up all night, and went to interview KISS. I wasn't a fan, either, and I was not a good interviewer. Any combination [might have worked]: if I was a fan, awake, or a good interviewer, or two out of three. It was pretty bad. Really bad.

"I think it was early in the morning. They weren't wearing makeup. It was in this big room in the hotel and they were just increasingly bored and perplexed as to why they were wasting their time with this comatose person who couldn't ask questions. They just started amusing themselves by talking about their days as junkies and shooting up heroin in their eyeballs and making up—or, for all I know, telling the truth—stories. Horrible, hilarious, pretty raunchy stories with their manager asking me, only half in jest, 'How much do you want for the tape?'"

Seeing the quartet in concert was about equally spectacular. "The stage show's major drawback is that all the special effects are telegraphed in advance," Ira noted. "Gene Simmons's [trip above the crowd in harness] was preceded by a longer than usual gap between songs, during which the darkened stage could not mask the roadies diddling with Gene Simmons's backside. The coolness quotient of Peter Criss's drum set spinning around was reduced considerably by the undisguised chaps doing the pushing."

Upon moving to New York in 1979, Ira's contributions to the *New York Rocker* increased in frequency. And, more pleasantly, he had good reason to visit the *Rocker* office.

There was an elevator operator at 166 Fifth Avenue, cattycorner from the Flatiron Building, but the *New York Rocker* office was on the second floor and it was just as easy to take the stairs. And, in an old New York way, the place was bustling.

Printed on tabloid-size newsprint with a color cover, the *Rocker* reached about ten thousand readers. Issues shipped COD to record stores in other cities and sold around town at independent book shops, record stores, and newsstands like Gem Spa, where CBGB regulars like Johnny Thunders and Dee Dee Ramone would go for egg creams following a heroin fix.

For founder Alan Betrock, *New York Rocker* was the culmination of a long climb out of rock's early, deep underground. Growing up in Queens, Betrock was a serious fan who launched his first homespun zines, *JAMZ* and *Rock Marketplace*, in the early '70s to research minutiae. Articles established catalog numbers and release dates for obscure garage rock singles and "American Punk Rock Groups," as Betrock told *The New York Times* in a 1972 interview, the year after he graduated from Queens College.

Betrock's forebears—including Paul Williams's *Craw-daddy!* and Greg Shaw's *Who Put the Bomp?*—had come to their fandom from science fiction, where homemade publications had been common for decades. Though Betrock didn't share the sci-fi background, he fit right in. He was a new kind of rock fan, with fierce obsessions of little interest to *Rolling Stone* and (from its perspective) its half million subscribers. With its wild and enthusiastic roster of contributors list, including Lester Bangs and Patti Smith, *Creem* offered some coverage, as did Robert Christgau at *Village Voice* but the indie underground was mostly gloriously new territory.

It was a world of bands and labels so independent that they often appeared like islands in a vast and poorly charted sea. Betrock found his way to gigs at CBGB not long after its December 1973 opening, when crowds didn't yet break twenty. Like Greg Shaw in Los Angeles, who waxed poetic about the importance of independence and began to release 7-inches on his own Bomp! Records, Betrock immersed himself completely. The following year, as he prepared for the launch of his next publication, he produced demos for Blondie.

The first issue of *New York Rocker*, dated February 1976, came on newsprint but was a fanzine in the truest sense of the word, perhaps slightly more civilized than John Holstrom, Ged Dunn, and Legs McNeil's *Punk*, which had launched a month earlier, but no less giddy. The first *Rocker* cover featured Television's Tom Verlaine and multiple articles about Patti Smith. Debbie Harry wrote about the Miamis, the Miamis wrote about Blondie, and Richard Hell wrote about himself. In the back was a crude map of lower Manhattan by painter Duncan Hannah, lines pointing to the abodes of Talking Heads, Blondie, the Ramones, and others. The second issue featured a popularity poll, song lyrics, and pictures of musicians' pets, including Television guitarist Richard Lloyd's cat, Puma; Talking Heads bassist Tina Weymouth's dog, Natasha; and Johnny Thunders's collie, Wolf. Future issues weren't so regular. The third came in May, the fourth in September.

There was early coverage of British punk, including pictures of a Sex Pistols gig credited to an eighteen-year-old Steven Morrissey, five years from cofounding the Smiths with Johnny Marr. But Betrock mostly focused on hometown heroes. Eventually, he took a windowless eight-by-twelve office across from the Flatiron Building. Posters spread wall to wall and, in places, back issues rose floor to ceiling.

Then, after two years, impulsively, he decided to fold the publication. "Alan was one of those people who plunged himself into something with tremendous enthusiasm and dedication, and when he was done with it, he was done," remembered Andy Schwartz, a native New Yorker who'd contributed to *Rocker* while attending college in Minneapolis.

While in Minnesota, Schwartz had worked behind the counter of Oar Folkjokeopus, the record store-cum-hangout spot that would soon nurture the Twin Cities' underground. He possessed a receding hairline, a puckish smile, and a level of committed fandom for music as a whole that could be mistaken for gruffness. Like Ira, Alan Betrock, and nearly everyone who would come to work in the *New York Rocker* office, Andy Schwartz had inhaled the spore too.

After moving back to New York in late 1977, he purchased *New York Rocker* lock, stock, and naming rights for $10,000, financed by his family. "I think Alan saw in me someone he could trust not to fuck the whole thing up," Schwartz said. "Even though I had never been involved in owning a business, running a business, or publishing or editing a publication."

The first order was to adhere to a regular production schedule. He hired a Minneapolis friend named Chris Nelson as art director. Andy manned a review column called "Panda's Platters" and held his passion for music inside an orderly personality and tight, lively copy. Under his leadership, *New York Rocker* could never again be referred to as a fanzine.

Andy's first issue was *Rocker*'s twelfth, published in February 1978. The cover featured the Clash, the first non-NYC band in that slot. "I took over this paper, not to transform it, but because I loved it too much for what it was to let it die," Andy wrote in an editorial. "I only hope that we can continue to provide exciting and informed coverage of ... what? ... When [the Patti Smith Group's] 'Because the Night' shatters the plastic placidity of AM airwaves; when my first spin of [Sham 69's] 'Borstal Breakout' nearly blows out the bedroom windows; when an unknown quantity of a band like The Rousers or the B-52s can blow me away on a chance visit to CBGBs— then I know that 1978 is a great time to be alive and in love with rock 'n' roll."

On the radio and the charts, disco reigned supreme, a style far from the boundary-bending mixes that powered the underground dance parties that emerged in lower Manhattan lofts a half decade earlier and that had given the genre its name. Disco's pop mutation oversaturated the record business. One could almost smell the crash coming, and the next year, it came, an industry-wide sales drop of 11 percent, the first industry decline since 1948.

Layoffs began the summer after Ira's May 1979 exit from Sarah Lawrence, with more than one thousand employees let go from the six major labels that controlled nearly 90 percent of the *Billboard* chart. These numbers, though duly reported in *New York Rocker*, meant little to its staff and readers, except perhaps as an affirmation that the world they occupied was the correct one—far from ex-Marines like Dick Asher, then the head of CBS Records, and his fellow music industrialists like Walter Yetnikoff, once described as a "rock warlord."

For *Rocker*, rock and roll existed someplace else. Though the punk bands signed to major labels—Patti Smith to Arista in 1975, Television to Elektra, the Ramones and Talking Heads to Seymour Stein's Sire—a world had opened up beyond them. In addition to the New York bands, Britain continued to supply hot copy from the recently imploded Sex Pistols to noted brainiac Elvis Costello to the waves of import singles washing ashore. But around the United States, other extraordinarily homegrown punk scenes flickered to life, each unique to its environs.

In Cleveland, the clique of Velvet Underground fans birthed

a series of bands. In Los Angeles, Greg Shaw turned *Who Put the Bomp?* into a label, and out in the south of L.A. suburbs, a teenage Greg Ginn sold refurbished radio gear through a company he'd dubbed Solid State Tuners. Launching his own band, Black Flag, he repurposed his electronics business into a record label, SST.

The South burned with the new music too. In Athens, Georgia, the B-52s and Pylon began to galvanize their own small community. In Louisville, the Babylon Dance Band anchored a committed punk stronghold. Alan Betrock made contact with a group from Raleigh, North Carolina, called Sneakers, and would eventually take their leader, a guitarist named Chris Stamey, under his wing when Stamey relocated to New York and the band morphed into the dB's.

Another of Andy Schwartz's hires at *Rocker*, in charge of advertising and circulation, was a New Jersey native named Glenn Morrow. An occasional contributor brought on board by Betrock, Morrow had tried to get a job at a record distributor and arrived at the windowless *Rocker* office fresh from another interview and dressed in a suit. He was close to taking a position as a legal proofreader, but Andy hired him. When the office moved to the second floor, Glenn even got his own desk. Glenn Morrow was the reason Ira Kaplan first went to Hoboken. But that wasn't uncommon. He was the reason a lot of people first went to Hoboken.

Glenn Morrow's train delivered him from the north, through the Meadowlands, and into the crumbling grandeur of Erie Lackawanna Station, where the stained-glass Tiffany skylight was painted black. There, only briefly glimpsing the rushing edge of downtown Hoboken, he hopped to the PATH train under the Hudson River to lower Manhattan.

Riding the PATH one day en route to a summer class he was taking before transferring to NYU, he ran into a classmate who mentioned she lived in Hoboken, and he began to ponder the idea. It was certainly cheap. Morrow and a high school friend looked at a few places, including one whose most recent tenants were evicted drug dealers.

They found a six-room railroad apartment at 1118 Hudson Street on the fifth floor of a six-story walk-up across from the coffee factory, just behind the *x* in the Maxwell House sign. Rent was $65 a month. The city seemed bleak, and it was. A television news segment had recently aired called "Nobody's Laughing at Hoboken Anymore," though that may not have entirely been the case.

Morrow and his friend took up residence in early 1977. The apartment was next door to Morrow's NYU classmate, whom he soon started dating. There wasn't much to do. "It was a vibe like *Stranded in Canton* by William Eggleston," he observed later, an abandoned grace that settled over the city when the light hit it just right. Morrow's girlfriend was friends with some older hippies who lived around town, a group of Memphis transplants who had once centered around the Insect Trust, an experimental jazz-folk outfit featuring future *New York Times* music critic Robert Palmer.

Much of Hoboken, including the city government, was mob-controlled. In large part owing to an intricate system of local patronage that was often rooted in Old World Italian townships, it was hard to find real estate one could buy even if you wanted it. Gradually, though, the city's east side—Hudson, Bloomfield, Garden, and Park Streets—became attractive to a few dozen people who saw an upside to Hoboken real estate. The streets were tree-lined and the two- or three-story houses usually had small backyards. The city's central artery, Washington Street, ran down the middle, through much of the old Elysian Fields.

After graduation, Morrow spent a summer working as a music critic for a local free weekly on the Jersey Shore. When he returned to town in the fall, he had a brief stint doing polling for *The New York Times* and joined a band who called themselves, simply, a. Playing Talking Heads–influenced punk, they gigged occasionally at the Showplace in Dover, a sometime strip club and occasional hard-rock venue. The a bassist, Rob Norris, slightly older than the rest, had played in a post–Lou Reed incarnation of the Velvet Underground.

Morrow sold his bandmates on Hoboken and soon they occupied the Hudson Street apartment, along with a second guitarist, Richard Barone, a hyperactive pop songwriter recently arrived from Florida who looked like a young Paul McCartney. In the former dining room, Barone leaned his sunburst Rickenbacker against a black Fender amplifier. The rockers had landed.

Another high school friend who ended up in Hoboken got a waitressing job nearby. A new family had bought the bar just around the corner, at Washington and Eleventh, and were looking to make some changes. "They want bands!" Glenn's friend told him.

"We were shocked," Glenn said. When he stopped by to check the place out, two of the new owners stood in front of the jukebox, deep in debate. The elder of the pair, Mario Mazzola, was boggled that the machine's selection included no Frank Sinatra. This was the city of Sinatra's *birth*, where Ol' Blue Eyes often occupied the *entirety* of a jukebox. To the younger man, a kinetic and warmly flamboyant twenty-four-year-old named Steve Fallon, no Sinatra was exactly the point.

Though they would retain the establishment's previous name, Maxwell's, it would be a new kind of bar, something different from the beer-and-shot joints that dotted Washington all the way to the Erie Lackawanna. Steve stocked the jukebox with singles by Television, Patti Smith, Plastic Bertrand Band, and the Hollies.

Steve and Glenn hit it off immediately, and he gave Glenn money to get more singles for the jukebox. Besides Bleecker Bob's, there weren't many places to buy underground 7-inches in New York. Village Oldies had some. Discophile on Eighth Street sold predominantly hi-fi equipment and carried a small selection of records. Musical Maze, ditto. Not that there were many to get yet. Steve had seen Patti Smith well over a dozen times. An excited music fan, he was happy to hear what Glenn brought back.

Raised in nearby Paterson, Steve Fallon and his brother Michael had attended prep school in Jersey City. After college, Steve lived in Jersey City and worked with his father at Murray Street Electric. He designed lighting for lower Manhattan restaurants as well as many new clients in the World Trade Center, which rose over the southern tip of Manhattan Island a few blocks south from where John Stevens's ferry once landed.

"I was a frustrated twentysomething," Steve reflected later. "My brothers, my sister Anne, and my brother-in-law [Mario Mazzola] were all involved in restaurants. We realized Hoboken was priced right at the time we were looking. The buildings were run-down. There were a lot of bars for sale at the time."

One such property the four saw listed was located at 1039 Washington, a twenty-minute walk from the PATH station. The former owner, Andrew McGovern, had died, and Mary was ready to sell. "When we were deciding what to buy, we went to Hoboken ten weekends in a row," Steve remembered. "And it was like, 'Why couldn't the bar ever be open?'"

They called Mary to clarify the bar's operating hours. "During the breaks," she told them.

"Breaks? What breaks?" The bar—Maxwell's Tavern—was only open for four hours a day, based around the shifts of the nearby coffee factory: one hour at noon, one hour at six p.m., one hour at midnight, and one hour at six a.m. When Steve finally saw the interior, he knew the place had seen better days. "There was a window on one side where it said 'Max,' but 'well's' was missing. It wasn't a very clean bar," he said. "There were two barstools. There was a lot of dog hair on the restaurant equipment." Though it was dirty, the front room had a gorgeous white tile floor beneath the soot.

The Fallons purchased the bar and building from Mary McGovern for $67,000 in early 1978 and began a restoration. Steve and his sister Anne moved in upstairs, where one of the previous tenants was paying $55 a month. The bar and restaurant opened in July with a revamped menu of comfort food, not long after Glenn showed up. In one corner there was a baby grand piano, played at Sunday brunch and occasionally during dinner. They used the back, the old adjoining storefront with a narrow passage from the main dining room, for storage.

On Halloween in 1978, Morrow, Barone, and their band, a, set up in the front corner of the bar. As they played, they lived out a great rock cartoon cliché as the music vibrated beer glasses off a shelf behind the bar and they fell and shattered onto the floor.

The rest of the Fallon family didn't see eye to eye with Steve on the club's rock-and-roll angle, preferring to own a more grown-up establishment. Still, Steve gave Glenn a meal a week, sent him to Bleecker Bob's for more records, and started advertising in *New York Rocker*. It was the kind of relationship based on goodwill that Steve Fallon thrived on. He also asked Glenn to help bring in some more groups to play every Thursday, next to the baby grand.

Between teetering stacks of back issues in the rear of the *New York Rocker* office, a couple of bands carved out a practice space they could use after hours. Information featured art director Chris Nelson, a punk with a deep absurdist streak who edited a zine of his own, *NO*. Founded with some NYU friends to document the wild, harsh variations punk had bloomed into, for *NO*'s final issue, they dropped uncollated pages into envelopes along with oddball items, including a piece of pizza and an assortment of pills. They recorded spastic bursts of noise-song and organized the release of a multi-band cassette, *Tape #1*.

"There was some sort of Spanish-Christian cult next door," Nelson remembered. "We always used to go smoke pot in their space. For some reason, we had unfettered access. They had some strange imagery on their walls, and they were obviously some sort of cult, although with ties to Christianity. During that era, it seemed like a typical place you would find yourself smoking pot while in rehearsal."

The dB's, the other band that practiced in the office, set up a Teac reel-to-reel four-track, and used the office stereo speakers behind Andy Schwartz's desk for monitors. A quartet of North Carolina transplants devoted to smartly constructed guitar pop, all four of its members would play quietly pivotal parts in Yo La Tengo's future.

Their guitarist, a short guy with neatly combed hair and prodigious skills, already had a reputation. Glenn Morrow, for one, had noticed him around NYU, not to mention playing in a few clubs. Chris Stamey had been at it for a few years already in his native Raleigh before he moved north. As a teen, he mastered violin, double bass, and cello before rotating through local rock bands. Mainly, he focused on Sneakers, cofounded with elementary school pal Will Rigby on drums and Mitch Easter on bass.

The lightbulb had started to go on for him when small pressings of 7-inches such as Patti Smith's "Hey Joe" and Television's "Little Johnny Jewel" began to trickle south. "I'd go to the Record Bar, the one record store in Chapel Hill, and they'd have all five underground records, and I'd *buy* all five underground records," he said.

But he didn't figure it out fully until, as a high school student, he spent time working as an assistant for local producer Don Dixon. One day, they recorded a bluegrass act who brought the tapes to a Nashville pressing plant and came away with a stack of singles. "It was kind of a revelation that you could give them money and they'd give you these records," Stamey said. "I didn't realize you could do that." So he did, and released a Sneakers single on his own Carnivorous Records, soon shortened to Car.

Operating one's own record label was exactly as difficult as it had ever been. Major labels had their own distribution chains of warehouses and contracted with trucking companies to move product across the country. Beyond that were nationwide networks of smaller outfits, such as the New Jersey–based JEM, or Pickwick, near Minneapolis, which covered large regional territories.

These networks had existed in different forms since the early days of the record business. Some fiercely independent labels such as Syd Nathan's King Records in Cincinnati developed its own branch system throughout the South to distribute early sides by James Brown and the Delmore Brothers. In New York, the Istanbul-born Ertegün brothers, Ahmet and Nesuhi, worked their node of the indie system—Atlantic Records—into a multinational conglomerate, building impressive coverage with regional distributors before selling the company in the '60s.

Though there were plenty of artist-founded labels, few flourished. Indeed, Chris Stamey's Car Records didn't last terribly long. He sent the Sneakers EP to *New York Rocker*. Alan Betrock became an instant fan and featured them in the fourth issue. By the time Stamey transferred to NYU and moved in downstairs from Alan Betrock in the fall of 1977, the label was pretty much finished.

Betrock hired the meticulous young songwriter to mix a new Blondie demo that he'd produced, for a song called "Heart of Glass." Stamey also got a gig playing bass for Alex Chilton when the former Big Star guitarist came up from Memphis to play a Valentine's Day show and stayed for a year. Quickly, Big Star's three early '70s albums had entered the still cozy canon, their covers-loving leader Chilton becoming a beloved figure despite his frequent self-sabotage. Glenn Morrow had seen Stamey play with Chilton during the residency and had been intrigued by the young bassist with the braces.

Two of Stamey's North Carolina friends, Sneakers drummer Will Rigby and bassist Gene Holder, rejoined him in New York in June 1978 as Sneakers transformed into the dB's and were joined a few months later by guitarist Peter Holsapple. They holed up at the *Rocker* office, recording on their four-track. Another religious group—Brazilian, chanting—was in the loft upstairs, but they never made it to the tapes.

Glenn brought Information and the dB's to Maxwell's, and they played in the front room, the glasses now secured on the shelf behind the bar. The Fleshtones, a pumped-up garage band from Queens, played several times too, bringing their equally pumped-up reputation with them. To passing police officers, the show seemed more like a bar fight than a rock gig, and they stopped the performance. Audience members threw cash at the officers, trying to convince them to let the Fleshtones continue.

Meanwhile, a, Glenn's band with Richard Barone, split up. Glenn moved in with the girl next door, leaving his former bandmates to themselves. Like Morrow, they found jobs through Maxwell's. Drummer Frank Giannini worked as the cook. In Maxwell's they also found a place to practice. With Steve's permission, Glenn and others pushed aside the supplies and unused neon beer signs in the bar's back room and set up some gear.

It wasn't just Morrow and his former bandmates playing in the back room. Peter Holsapple of the dB's and Mitch Easter of Sneakers joined a few times, as did Jeffrey Lee Pierce, then the president of the Blondie fan club who was soon to cofound the blues-punk Gun Club. Rob Norris, the former bassist for a, brought his Cerwin Vega rehearsal PA into the back. Barone and his roommates became the Bongos. Glenn and guitarist Jon Klages became the core of the Individuals. "I almost dreamed the whole thing," Morrow said later. "Putting pieces together, giving Steve singles, booking bands."

Around this time, sometime in early 1979, Glenn noticed another new arrival at the *Rocker* office. He recognized him from a Richard Lloyd show at Mudd Club that he'd gone to with his boss from his brief stint at *The New York Times*. She'd pointed out her ex-boyfriend Ira in the crowd. "She maybe said something about them having a Grateful Dead cover band in college," Glenn remembered.

Contributing to *SoHo Weekly News* and *New York Rocker* didn't yet qualify as making a living, even if Ira did get to go hang out at the *Rocker* office. Ira took a job as a publicist for the new label ZE Records, cofounded by Michael Zilkha, who had briefly handled advertising for Alan Betrock. Everywhere, the lightbulbs were flickering over the heads of subcultural entrepreneurs, from the thrown-together first hip-hop single "Rapper's Delight," a hit the previous summer for the Sugarhill Gang, to the metalheads who organized Shrapnel Records in California. All aimed to fill niches they felt were ignored, whether for fun, art, or profit.

Launched with big-budget flare, ZE's plan was to bring New York's confrontational No Wave scene to the post-disco masses. Their first release, the debut by James Chance and the Contortions, did not take off, and Ira was brought aboard for their second big project, the debut solo album by scene fixture Lydia Lunch. It did not go smoothly either.

"My hands were full," Ira remembered of a trip to the West Coast with Lunch, the cofounder of Teenage Jesus and the Jerks who'd once beat her bandmates with coat hangers at a rehearsal. "She could be really friendly and really not-friendly, depending on the mood of the moment," Ira said.

One of their first stops was Rhino Records in Los Angeles, a record store that had recently started to distribute records from its flagship storefront. When they arrived to the sound of Lunch's new album playing over the store's stereo, she chose not-friendly. At the end of the appearance, during which Ira also met critic Richard Meltzer for the first time, the store's manager invited Lunch to take a free record. She grabbed a whole stack, sending the store's staff into a tizzy until her manager paid.

In San Francisco, Ira skipped two of Lunch's three Mabuhay Gardens performances altogether, including one with the Dead Kennedys. Instead, he headed across town to catch shows by the Flamin' Groovies, the volatile psychedelic garage heroes who'd crunched on since the '60s. They were independent, too, and had self-released their 1968 debut, a 10-inch record called *Sneakers*, and had briefly managed the Fillmore Auditorium. Before Ira had split to see the Groovies one of the nights, he'd made the brief acquaintance of a manic fan who'd hitchhiked from Idaho to see Lunch.

Byron Coley had first mistaken ZE's young publicist for *Trouser Press* editor Ira Robbins. "He disabused me of his identity," Coley remembered. They didn't have much time to talk. But it wasn't long before Ira saw Coley again.

Within weeks, seemingly, Byron Coley was a fixture at *New York Rocker*. Office manager Janet Waegal arrived at work one morning to find him alone behind Andy's desk, flipping through records, and he never really left. He contributed to *Rocker* beginning with an account of following Devo on tour, flexing an obsessive mind and a gonzo personal style with prodigious chops.

"In a very drunken state, he once had crawled around the stage amongst the feet of Devo while they were playing at Max's Kansas City, and did so long enough that everyone took note," remembered art director Chris Nelson. "He was sniffing their feet or something and probably making funny noises, as he was wont to do. I think Devo thought, 'Well, there's New York for you.'"

Coley had discovered underground music as a preteen and, "apart from a few personally totemic artists, I more [or] less turned away from commercial music at that point in my life." Expelled from the unusually permissive Hampshire College for being "a negative influence on the mood of the campus," he headed for San Francisco, where he played guitar and bass "without knowing how to play either" in his own noise band, the Kahunas. In Los Angeles, he hung out at Greg Shaw's Bomp! Records, reading through his zine collection, and crashed in the offices of *Slash*, the punk publication founded a few years earlier that had quickly launched their own seminal label. And, in New York, Byron found his way to *New York Rocker*.

"You couldn't miss Byron," said Chris Nelson. "He was a very voluble, very exciting personality. He was the loudest person in the office, certainly, and I say that with a good deal of admiration."

Byron became a resident at *Rocker*. The office couch was a reliable place to crash when not occupied by Peter Holsapple of the dB's, or Glenn Morrow, recently broken up with his girlfriend and exiled from Hoboken. "Everything was Naugahyde," remembers Byron. "The sofa, the La-Z-Boy. In the summer, you took your shirt off, and you'd just peel yourself off it in the morning."

They fought about who'd get stuck with the La-Z-Boy, which sometimes didn't matter anyway. Byron regularly stayed up all night behind Alan Betrock's desk, hunched over index cards, carefully annotating the complete series of *Crawdaddy!* Founded by Paul Williams in 1966, it was the first publication devoted to serious rock criticism. "There was a lot of information in those kind of magazines, but nobody had made it trackable," Coley remarked.

Andy paid Byron $5 a day to sweep the office, deliver promotional issues of the paper to uptown record companies, and handle other duties in addition to the stream of copy he produced for the paper's pages. Occasionally he DJed at Tier 3. "It was a very reasonable time to get by," Byron observed later.

Byron plotted a version of the Kahunas East. He acquired a bass with a warped neck, which he decided he could play with a slide. Hanging out at the office or somewhere, he'd heard Ira had a guitar and drafted him into his fantasy band. The younger sister of one of Byron's Hampshire friends had just gotten a drum set and she would play that. They didn't even need to practice.

Information was putting together a gig—a party called Phenomenal World—and at Byron's urging added the Kahunas East to the bill. The day of the show, Byron Coley got stage fright and called in sick. The theoretical drummer was a twenty-year-old Manhattan native named Georgia Hubley. "She was so disgusted," Byron recalled.

CHAPTER 3

At Home with the Maypos

The workings of the family business had slowly made their way into routine by the time Georgia Hubley learned to walk. She was the last of four, and all of the kids would be drafted into service. The Hubley home and animation studio, in a pair of apartments blocks apart near Riverside Park on Manhattan's Upper West Side, were held in an equal balance of films and children, and—over the years—the work of each house would flow back to the other as the occasion called for it.

Faith and John Hubley embraced the raising of a nuclear family with an all-encompassing progressivism. While the kids were at school, the Hubley parents worked together at the studio. There were museum trips, and they spent time together sketching. John played a bit of guitar, Faith the cello. There were two pianos in the house, and all took lessons. Georgia and Emily shared a room.

The living room came fitted with a five-foot screen on which the Hubleys showed films borrowed from the distribution company that handled their own work, a few catalogs, and a permanent collection that the family grew to know by heart: the Marx Brothers' *Duck Soup*, Orson Welles's *The Magnificent Ambersons*, the W. C. Fields vehicle *It's a Gift*.

There were family drawing classes too. Emily remembered sessions near their country house in Montauk, on Long Island's East End. "We'd go to the seaport to draw boats or be freezing out on the beach in the middle of winter, drawing, like, a stick on the beach. You'd have all the sand blowing over your pad.

"Our parents' stuff would be all beautiful and we'd all stomp back to the car going, 'Mine really sucks!' Everyone would be in a horrible mood 'cause they hated their pictures. Then we'd have to do the critique. We'd put them up.

"'Got a good line there, good movement.'

"'*Can we go now?*'"

John described the lessons to *The New York Times* in a piece about the family published in 1967 as "a great relaxation . . . like peace."

"I remember feeling happy that they were doing something that I was remotely interested in," Emily said of her parents. "When they finished a movie or something, you'd be interested in seeing it, and it had things in it you could talk about. You could just understand, unlike a lot of [parents'] jobs, where they just disappeared and then came back [in the evening]."

"I couldn't really explain exactly what they were doing," Georgia told *chickfactor*. "Because they weren't literally drawing every single picture. After awhile I finally grasped it."

Usually, they watched the films at home on the living-room projector, but there was the time when Faith and John brought the girls to a local theater, where they saw their animated selves on the big screen, stars of an eight-minute movie titled *Windy Day* for which they'd recorded voice-overs one afternoon at the studio, when their parents put them under giant headphones and prodded them gently with questions. By the time they got a usable take, Georgia was all but ready to go home.

But on-screen, their animated selves transmogrified into princesses, giraffes, kangaroos, and multi-eyed green beasts. *Windy Day* was nominated for an Academy Award, though lost out to *Winnie the Pooh and the Blustery Day*, a short with an oddly similar name released by John Hubley's former employers at the Walt Disney studio. There surely would have been some at least part-melodramatic grumbling that night—not because of the Oscar loss necessarily, as it would have been the Hubleys' fourth award, but because of whom they'd lost it to. Walt Disney and his mouse's looming cartoon ears cast a long, complex shadow in Faith's and John's lives.

There was an air of normality about it, but in the twenty years since they first met, the Hubleys had legitimately established themselves as independent filmmakers, a hard-won stance that wound through every aspect of their family and career. John and Faith had become international ambassadors of animations, their films in constant circulation in schools and art houses. The Hubleys' commercial and experimental work provided an unceasing schedule of deadlines as teams of young animators and collaborators passed constantly through the studio, working under Faith and John's direction. Sometimes, Georgia's parents brought her the few blocks to the rooms filled with art supplies, where she and Emily played, talking on the intercoms and exploring the light tables.

Public School 17 in Midtown Manhattan was progressive, and there was no one more eager to progress than Faith Elliot, born in 1924. The daughter of a Hell's Kitchen dentist, a Polish-Russian immigrant who expected Faith to follow in his footsteps, she very quickly developed other ideas. This may have been in large part because of PS 17. The environs could not have been more integrated, in every sense of the word.

There were white students, Asian students, and black students. Only a minority spoke English, amid French, Italian, and Greek youth. Besides that, PS 17 was an early experimenter with John Dewey and William Heard Kilpatrick's new concept of integrated curricula, which seeded the phrase "learning by doing" into the national consciousness.

"[We] had wonderful teachers there," remembered Faith.

"Everybody was very poor. I remember that one student was a prostitute. Our teacher said, and I'll remember this until the day I die, 'None of you be cruel to her. She had no choice. Her father's an alcoholic, her mother's an alcoholic. . . .' I used to walk with her, I was proud to walk with her, and I guess my father saw me doing that and thought I was a prostitute because I was showing solidarity with her. That's how we were raised at PS 17."

Her family life deteriorated rapidly. "I think my parents perceived me as their meal ticket. If only I would become a dentist, I could take over my father's practice and support them in their old age." Affairs boiled, in Faith's phrase, to a "hilarious pressure." Faith had radicalized as a teenager and when she finished high school, her father—also her dentist— refused to sign her hygiene certificate, and she was refused her diploma. Faith went to work at the New Theatre League, where she booked concerts for Woody Guthrie and others. She tried various means of escape from her parents, including a failed marriage. When she turned eighteen, she went to Reno for a divorce and kept driving until she got to Hollywood.

She spent her twenties working as an editor of scripts, film soundtracks, and films themselves. For a time, she oversaw continuity on the Three Stooges' improvisation. "I was a lucky girl who grew up in Hollywood," Faith remembered when she was in her sixties.

During the postwar years, she was almost constantly social, rubbing elbows with a community of left-wing émigrés. In addition to her myriad studio jobs, she studied screenwriting and taught Marxism to elderly neighbors in Fairfax, California. Two months into the class, her students presented her with a bottle of perfume. They elected a spokesperson. "Darling, we didn't understand a word," the woman told Faith. "We only speak Yiddish. But you're so nice. Every week you came, every week you talked to us."

At a Hollywood gallery, Faith helped organize a film series. She and her friends borrowed a projector from a local college, rented prints from the Museum of Modern Art in New York, and ran pictures by the pioneering independent documentarians of Frontier Films, French avant-gardists including Dimitri Kirsanoff, and left-wing staples such as King Vidor's *Our Daily Bread*. Old-world Hollywood luminaries like directors Billy Wilder and D. W. Griffith (who lived six blocks away at the Knickerbocker Hotel) watched in the dark with Hollywood's avant-garde, including Oskar Fischinger, Kenneth Anger, and Man Ray.

The House Un-American Activities Committee (HUAC) hit the West Coast in a big way in 1947, and Faith saw her corner of Hollywood erode immediately. "I owed the world something," she said. She bought a one-way ticket to Poland to attend the Marxist-organized World Conference of Working Youth.

"I had pledged to work on a reconstruction brigade one day. And at the end of this conference, they asked, 'Does anybody want to work on a railroad in Czechoslovakia?' and I raised my hand. We dug trenches and we laid railroad ties for three weeks.

"I got a medal for bravery," Faith said with a laugh. "Because the average age for girls on this international brigade might have been seventeen. I felt very maternal. We were working in a valley surrounded by huge hills. I saw this boulder coming down the mountain toward the trenches and there was no stopping it and not enough time to jump out of the way. I saw this young girl who was going to get hit by the boulder, and I threw her aside and put my body between her and the boulder. I got hit and I still have the scar. After they cleaned up the blood we sang anthems. They gave me flowers and awarded me a medal."

Other adventures included a trip to Prague, a trip to Rome (spinal meningitis, four months in a clinic, near blindness), traveling the Italian countryside ("bopped around with a friend of mine"), doing a screenplay about the Mafia with the Sicilian director Basilio Franchina, and a stay in Paris (four months, a peace conference, and a steady diet of films and books). In 1950, as her money ran out, Faith returned to New York and got work as a film editor. There she saw an old Hollywood friend for the first time in years.

She'd met John Hubley in 1944, when she was a script supervisor and John was an animator on an educational short called *Human Growth.* He animated the menstrual cycle "just beautifully," Faith remembered. "Kind of like a Georgia O'Keeffe painting of the horns of a bull in the desert."

One day in the late 1930s, when John Hubley was a young animator working for Walt Disney, Frank Lloyd Wright visited the hivelike studio on Hyperion Avenue in Silver Lake. He brought along a modern Russian cartoon that Disney wanted to see by director Ivan Ivanov-Vano, and a screening was arranged for Disney and a crew of animators, including John.

The score, Wright told Disney, was by Shostakovich.

"Who the hell is he?" Walt barked.

At the end, Wright stood up. "Walt Disney, you too can be a prophet!" he declared majestically.

"Jesus Christ, you want me to make pictures like that?" Walt replied.

But John was transfixed. "It was very modern, with flat backgrounds, highly stylized characters, modern music," John remembered, still enthralled many years later. "It was very exciting."

Born in Marienette, Wisconsin, in 1914, John Hubley had been plucked from art school and brought into Walt's expanding hive during the Depression. Faith later called it a seduction. They deposited John in their apprentice program, and he progressed from animator to art designer while they pumped out film after film, beginning with *Snow White and the Seven Dwarfs* and eventually including *Fantasia*, for which John designed the sequence set to Stravinsky's *Rite of Spring*. His life merged with Disney; John married a woman in the painters' corps and rose through the ranks as he started a family.

Disney, thirty-four years old at John's 1935 hiring, spoke with the same kind of extreme Midwestern earnestness that would characterize the public manner of John himself. "We have but one thought, and that is for good entertainment,"

Disney said at the time. "We like to have a point to our stories, not an obvious moral, but a worthwhile theme."

While Disney's mind closed, John's opened. During a fiery and cataclysmic artists' strike, John was on strike because of the company's creative direction as much as anything else. He jumped to United Productions of America (UPA), creating the popular Mr. Magoo based on an uncle, and designing the Oscar-nominated *Rooty Toot Toot*. During the war, he was given the ceremonial uniform he was wearing when he first met Faith on Hollywood Boulevard. It was extremely creased, Faith remembered, and buttoned wrong. The two became professional acquaintances and worked together on occasion.

Making army training films, John discovered an ability to concisely visualize abstract concepts, a skill that led to peacetime industrial work. One he helmed for UPA on behalf of CBS was a hit, in its way, and CBS hired a distributor to handle screening requests. The Swiss design journal *Graphis* praised the advertisement, which visualized sounds via the objects that made them, for moving "very far into the domain of abstract sign language."

With plenty of left-wing ties, John's job at UPA quickly evaporated after HUAC's arrival. A few years later, he would be hauled in front of Richard Nixon. "I am an artist," he told the junior senator from California. "I have a right to say what I want. And I have a right to say what I don't want." It helped, as well, that by then John was making $18,000 for a typical minute of on-screen commercial work. Disney had paid him some $18 a week twenty years before.

Eventually using a frontman to dodge the blacklist, John established Storyboard, Inc. They specialized in the anti-ad, making fun of the product it supposedly advertised. In one Hubley-produced spot, archetypal anti-pitchman Stan Freberg repeatedly mispronounced the word "Worcestershire." When he could, John got work for his favorite jazz musicians. A spot for Philip Morris went out of its way to identify the musicians (Shorty Rogers and His Giants with Shelly Manne). He made spots for Bank of America and Ford. Though the spots paid better than Disney or UPA ever did, the constant negotiation with clients was far more emotionally taxing.

When John saw Faith in New York for the first time in nearly a half decade, "he had started to gain as much weight as he was making money," Faith noted. "Probably because he was unhappy. He was buying expensive clothes and he looked like hell. Here was this really good-looking, wonderful-looking man—now he was fat and overdressed and drinking too much and miserable."

In 1954, John signed on for the production of *Finian's Rainbow*, a feature film based on the Broadway musical whose voices would include Frank Sinatra, Louis Armstrong, Ella Fitzgerald, and Mr. Magoo himself, Jim Backus. There would be dance and ballet numbers involving "anthropomorphic wash from the clothesline" as well as an "abstract sequence of Boy and Girl symbols dancing with the moon."

Faith joined the crew as an assistant. "He wasn't sure I should come to Los Angeles, because we both knew that we had controlled our friendship for ten years and, after all, he was a married man with three kids. But we decided I would take the job and so I went to Los Angeles again."

With the dialogue and soundtrack recorded, the production collapsed. "We went out to lunch one day and came back and there was a padlock on the door. That was it. The official word was the blacklist. They said it was because of Johnny. But I think it had something to do with the power struggle among the backers."

Crushed and drained, Faith and John went to Europe and came back a couple. They decided to marry and wrote wedding vows. They would make one independent film a year and always eat dinner with their children.

The new client requested what first seemed like the usual anti-ad. But Heublein, Inc. wanted more. They wanted Faith and John to go as "anti" as they could dream. Money talked, for sure. But sometimes—in the case of Heublein's expensive and entirely tax-deductible advertising campaign for a food product they hardly cared about—it also whispered absurdly.

Heublein owned A.1. Steak Sauce, Grey Poupon mustard, a new aerosol-based barbecue sauce called Sizzl-Spray, and a company from Vermont called Maltex. Maltex, in turn, manufactured Maypo, nominally a maple-syrup-flavored breakfast cereal. By most accounts, it was utterly inedible.

The children had became part of Faith and John's work very quickly after they married in 1955. *The Adventures of* *, commissioned by the Guggenheim and a step closer to art film, starred a wandering asterisk as a stand-in for a newborn child. The film was scored by Benny Carter, a friend of Faith's from Los Angeles. It was Faith and John's first proper collaboration.

There was no dialogue, and they experimented together with texture, splashing wax with watercolors and double-exposing the film. Though she would later describe her role in the first decade of their partnership as a "pupil," for Faith, it was also a rebirth. "It was like being kids again," she said. When Maypo came along, it was a fairly easy decision to use toddler son Mark to anti-sell the terrible-tasting breakfast cereal. In Faith's words, the ad was a "one-minute documentary on feeding a child." Decked in an oversize cowboy hat, the newly dubbed Marky Maypo cooed cutely over the soundtrack and, in the end, delivered a scripted tagline conceived by a young adman named George Lois: "I want my Maypo."

Marky Maypo launched in the northeast in September 1956 and was an instant hit, especially during kid-friendly slots on weekday afternoons and Saturday mornings, and soon went national. The company redesigned the packaging to feature Marky in his cowboy hat, and the catchphrase slipped into the national vocabulary.

After the cereal box, John and Faith vetoed other tie-ins, growing more and more wary of the advertising industry, where they tried to take fewer and fewer jobs. Faith accepted a job as script clerk on Sidney Lumet's *12 Angry Men* to pick up the slack. The next year, the family settled into life on the

Upper West Side as Faith and John rechristened Storyboard as Hubley Studio, Inc.

But it was Maypo and other advertising money that financed more of the annual independent films. One was *Moonbird*, which starred Mark's and Ray's voices. "We heard the boys plotting to go to the park and find a bird," Faith recounted. "We all went to the studio with a birdcage, a bag of candy, and taped the soundtrack in three hours." Voiced by children, there was a natural sweetness to it, but it was also a serious foray into improvised dialogue and unself-consciously surreal narratives. It earned them their first Oscar a few months later.

More kids followed. First Emily, then—on February 25, 1960—Georgia. She was named after George Antheil, the modernist composer Faith had sound edited for on a murder mystery called *Spectre of the Rose*.

The same year, they made another Maypo spot, influenced by the experimental painter Gregorio Prestopino, a family friend and occasional houseguest whose landscapes sometimes morphed into Cubism. But John and Faith kept vetoing Maypo's merchandising and soon fell out with the company. It was an increasingly frequent occurrence.

"The last commercial I did, I can see the scene as if it were yesterday," Faith remembered. "We were making *The Hat* at the same time, with improvised dialogue between Dizzy Gillespie and Dudley Moore about world war, and it was very funny and very interesting. And these advertising people kept coming to the studio and saying, 'What, you're working on your own film?' And we said, 'Of course. That's our life.' Then they said, 'You like your film better than ours?' And we said, 'Well, of course we do.'"

Faith and John had been increasingly drawn to the art world, developing a personal language in their filmmaking that sought to transcend the simplistic fairy tales and slapstick surrealism that John had grown from and that most Americans associated with the medium. They became public champions of animation as a language beyond words, and John helped organize the American branch of the Association

Internationale du Film d'Animation (ASIFA). The Hubleys soon became regulars on the international film circuit. There were independent animation studios and screenings throughout New York and, at times, the Hubley Studio began to act as a training ground for young animators. But none of it sat well with the agencies that hired them to make commericals.

"They started to punish us," Faith said. "They just wouldn't approve a goddamn thing. They punished everybody. We used some of our jazz friends to do the score, partly to help them get some big money and partly because they would be good. Shelly Manne, the drummer, did percussion, and at four a.m. we were up to take 103, and we thought it was just bullshit. Shelly and Johnny and I looked at each other, and I made up my mind that we would never do it again.

"Fortunately, Johnny was a very gentle person, and not given to profanity, but at the last screening, where they requested another series of changes, Johnny just said, 'Go fuck yourself!' I had never heard him say that sentence! I burst out laughing, and the vice president—I forget which ad agency it was—said, 'You'll never work on Madison Avenue again, Mr. Hubley!'

"We looked at each other and said, 'Really? Goody! We're liberated!'" Faith laughed. "It was such a wonderful feeling."

By the time Georgia and Emily were teens, their parents' animation studio had transformed into a place of employment. Georgia connected with the careful graphic work. The magic markers were intoxicating. "They were so alcoholic, there was no texture," she remembered. "They'd just spread across the page as a flat color, so you wouldn't have to worry about gradation."

John had found replacements for advertising agencies by doing high-profile commissions, as well as shorts for the newly founded Children's Television Workshop, which was then launching *Sesame Street*. Much of the girls' work was for the new show, and all of it was on the books, so naturally Faith made them join the Animation Guild, as she did all their employees. John and Faith, as employers, were not members.

Like their brothers before them, the girls attended the Friends Seminary downtown. It wasn't long before they could thread the living-room projector. School friends came over for viewings, all often awakening later to the *thwack thwack thwack* of a run-out film reel.

Georgia's father didn't mention Disney much. "To get him to talk about that stuff wasn't very easy," she said. "Being independent didn't stop him from being bitter," Georgia remarked of her father in later years. When Georgia was nine, Disney rereleased *Fantasia* with a brand-new psychedelic marketing campaign. Georgia's friends wanted to go, but her father just sneered.

As the '60s bloomed. Faith and John remained as free-thinking as ever, though never when it came to the decade's libidinous aspects. They were martini drinkers, not pot smokers. They were also absolute music fans. Faith took Emily to hear Charles Mingus once, arriving hours ahead of the event to get a front-row spot.

When Mingus came by their table, a cigarette fell out of Emily's shirtsleeve that she'd been planning to sneak off and smoke. "Does this belong to one of you ladies?" the bassist asked. Emily tried to wave him off. "No, it's OK; you can smoke," Faith said, waving back, ever tolerant.

Though they played the kids plenty of jazz, rock infiltrated Georgia and Emily's shared bedroom by way of Mark and Ray's collections, as well as a free supply of releases on A&M Records, owned by John's recent collaborator Herb Alpert. Their father hated any kind of country music, which is perhaps why the post-Byrds twang of Gram Parsons and Chris Hillman's Flying Burrito Brothers and Richie Furay's Poco appealed so much to the Hubley sisters, especially Emily. (Georgia, in fact, found herself at the same 1972 Poco show at Wollman Rink that Ira attended.)

Other early staples included the Beatles and the Monkees (the sisters being fan club members of both), and the singer-songwriter folk of James Taylor, Carole King, and Joni Mitchell. Georgia had what she recalled as a "really major Stones thing."

Faith and John brought the kids out to the movies as often as might be expected of parents who were also experimental filmmakers, once dragging a teenage Georgia to Luis Buñuel's *The Discreet Charm of the Bourgeoisie*. Too young to grasp Buñuel's work, she was disturbed by the lack of a happy ending, and wished she were home watching television. In time, she became a lifelong film fan anyway.

Her parents continued their one-film-a-year pace and had begun teaching a storyboarding class at Yale when Faith was diagnosed quite suddenly with terminal lymphoma.

All four of Faith and John's children gathered to join the Hubley Studio team to work on *Everybody Rides the Carousel*, a one-hour special for CBS based on the work of psychologist Erik Erikson about the cycle of life. It was the first production in which Faith's design work reached the screen untouched by John, who had only recently begun to share full collaborative credit with his wife. When they were finished, they screened it at a small theater on Cape Cod. Faith cried in the dark next to John as the last horse exited their on-screen carousel.

It was a near total surprise a year later, then, when Faith was declared cancer-free and John, having a routine operation after a small heart attack, died unexpectedly on February 21, 1977—four days before Georgia's seventeenth birthday—at Yale–New Haven Hospital. The memorial was held at the Beekman Theatre at East Sixty-sixth Street, where many of John and Faith's films had made their debuts.

Recently expelled, but still hanging around the Hampshire College campus, the effervescent Byron Coley soon befriended Emily Hubley, who had enrolled there over John's objections. When she returned home from school, she was armed with new music, much of it courtesy of her new "music advisor." Not long after, Coley visited the Hubleys in New York. After John's death, Faith and Georgia moved out of the apartment near Riverside Park and into a place on Park Avenue.

Georgia used the former dining room as a painting studio, taking as naturally and seriously to graphic arts as one would expect from a child of Faith and John's. She had taken her father's death particularly hard and struck Coley initially as "the crabby sister." When she smiled, she looked like both her parents at their most delighted.

That summer, Emily planned a road trip to California in her Dodge Dart Swinger to make a short film; Georgia bailed at the last minute. Byron was in San Francisco and agreed to join Emily if she sent him a bus ticket to New York. Georgia regretted the choice, and spent the summer falling in love with *Shake Some Action* by the Flamin' Groovies, the San Francisco psych-pop stalwarts that Ira had skipped out on Lydia Lunch to see.

She met Byron Coley again when he and Emily passed through Baltimore, where Georgia had enrolled at the Maryland Institute College of Art. In late 1978, Byron had taken it upon himself to follow Devo as they toured down the eastern seaboard, which would soon be the basis of his first *New York Rocker* feature, and Emily had volunteered to drive part of the way. The pair befriended the band and brought Georgia along to a gig in Georgetown.

Georgia didn't last long in Maryland. She'd brought her cat, Shauna, with her. While she was there, Georgia decided Shauna seemed lonely, so she adopted another cat, whom she named Egon. All three headed back to New York, where Georgia spent a few frustrating weeks at Parsons School of Design, before taking classes at the New York Studio School of Drawing, Painting, and Sculpture, where she continued to paint.

Around that time, Georgia went with Emily to see the Who's *The Kids Are Alright* movie. "That guy's having so much fun," Emily decided. "Who wasn't in awe of Keith Moon?" Georgia said later. "I know I was." She soon decided to try drumming.

Playing on practice pads at home, she worked at the rudiments. The biggest revelation came when she realized that the drums needed to be arranged differently for a left-handed person. Sporadic, "very, very casual" lessons with friends followed—sometimes entertaining, occasionally traumatic. One friend chain-smoked endlessly while he showed her the basics. A jam session with another was "total torture; it probably set me back a few years."

At the Studio School, Georgia befriended a model in a drawing class. "It was very much the New Wave era," she noted. "She was a New Wave model." And the New Wave model was starting an all-girl band. At a subterranean practice space on the Lower East Side, Georgia played on borrowed drums before the girls in the band drove to Long Island with her and helped her pick out a cheap Slingerland set of her own. There was a big blue stripe down the middle of the floor tom. "It was a nice kit," Georgia recalled, and she would play it for years. She wasn't long in the band, which went on to gig as Dangerous Curves. Still, it was "a fun, good way to mess around and gossip for an hour."

Following the completion of a *Doonesbury* television special John and Faith had agreed to direct—and that would earn them their eighth and final Oscar nomination—Faith moved Hubley Studio into an office building on Madison Avenue. Though she ran a much smaller company, she tried to remain a union shop, even when it was cost prohibitive. "Faith would have arguments with the general manager," recalled Emily. "It was such great theater." At night, Georgia set up the new Slingerland there.

She drummed along with Stones records and her mix tapes, filled with the bands she had started to see regularly at Max's Kansas City. Faith received a call from the manager of the Carlyle Hotel across the street, saying that the playing was disturbing their guests and—in Faith's version—offering a bribe to stop.

"No, no, no, no," Faith told him. "She's pursuing her art and she has the right to do that, and we don't need your money." She didn't tell Georgia.

When Emily graduated from Hampshire in December 1980, she and Georgia moved into an apartment on Bleecker Street, in the heart of touristy Greenwich Village. "It was such a stupid place to be," Emily chuckled later. Byron dubbed it "the corniest corner." It was a short walk to CBGB, though. Georgia (and Egon and Shauna) took the front room.

The Hubley sisters became staples at shows around New York. Occasionally, they were recognized for the films they were in as children. They inevitably had the same reactions: Emily, an enthusiastic smile. Georgia, a groan.

Often they ended up at Tier 3, a new TriBeCa club, where they fell in love with the dB's. Though Emily had gone to Hampshire with the intention of studying writing, animation had proved too natural a pull. She volunteered to animate a film for the *New York Rocker* house band.

She set up a bulky light table in her room on Bleecker Street and worked by herself for a few months. *Big Brown Eyes* featured a world transforming with primitive surrealism around a pair of anthropomorphic eyes, a logical continuation of her parents' own personality-filled work. The video followed a few months after the dB's Alan Betrock–produced debut, *Stands for Decibels*, and just missed the debut of MTV.

It took a year for the fledgling music station to catch on. When it did, it was helped in large part by a network television advertising campaign that starred Madonna, Sting, and others, who exhorted viewers to call their cable providers and demand, "I want my MTV." The campaign caught on like wildfire. The station spread to nearly every cable-subscribing home in the country, perhaps owing partially to its tagline's inborn resonance. Its creator was George Lois, the man who coined "I want my Maypo."

CHAPTER 4

Music for Dozens

"I keep up with rock and roll, I get *New York Rocker*," ran the jingle. "All the music I can hold, I read *New York Rocker*. Interviews, local news, Boston, LA, London, too! I keep up and so can you, if you read *New York Rocker, Rocker, Rocker, Rocker, Rocker . . .*" Recorded on a four-track with pep to spare by dB's guitarist and sometimes *Rocker* couch resident Peter Holsapple, it would play perfectly over a montage of life at the publication's office.

"I wasn't that social a person," Ira has said about his early years in New York, but the lure of the *Rocker* headquarters was too great. "For all the misgivings I have about my writing life, the paper—not necessarily my contributions to it—is as fond as I get. A word I don't toss around that often, I'd say that it was probably *influential* on me. Especially as it went on, the broad range of music that it covered." Many of the people Ira first encountered at the *Rocker* office became friends and eventual collaborators. The office itself was a remarkable melting pot.

"To put it mildly, I was a very loose boss," remembered editor/publisher Andy Schwartz. "My main concern was being an editor, trying to get to the printer on time and avoiding financial meltdowns and so forth. If people were going to snort speed or smoke pot in the office, or live on the couch for a few weeks, I didn't really care that much."

True to his plan when he bought the magazine, Schwartz regularized *Rocker*'s publication at ten issues a year. Securing national distribution through Charlton Publications in Connecticut, almost 35,000 copies per issue spread the gospel of new music from the heart of the scene to the farthest reaches of the country and sometimes beyond. "There was a high pass-along factor," Schwartz said. "Multiple people reading one copy."

Some made it as far as New Zealand, falling into the hands of Hamish Kilgour and his brother David, who would soon form one of their country's first punk bands, the Clean. Other copies made it to Uniontown, Maryland, where another set of brothers, Jad and David Fair, dreamt their own group, which they would realize on their family's relocation to Michigan. When they pressed their first single under the name Half Japanese, they sent along personalized copies for the staff at the *Rocker* offices.

The mood was jovial and heady. One afternoon the pope drove by in the Popemobile, level with the second-floor offices. The staff waved. Musicians from different circles flowed in and overlapped. The meticulous popsters from North Carolina, Chris Stamey and Mitch Easter, helped engineer sessions by Information. The dB's Holsapple tracked a version of Gene Vincent's "Time Will Bring You Everything" with the tall, skinny Zantees frontman Billy Miller, who pressed the recording onto acetate and presented it to his new girlfriend Miriam Linna for Valentine's Day. Both had contributed to *Rocker*, and soon launched *Kicks*, which was devoted to the rediscovery of old rock and roll, as well as garage-rock-loving contemporary acts like the Lyres and the Dictators.

Commuting from Hoboken, Glenn Morrow, meanwhile, was playing with a new band called the Individuals. He kept his own name on the masthead as the publication's advertising director but retained the nom de plume Greg McLean for much of his coverage. That way he could skewer bands and still sell ads to their record companies with a straight face. Ira trekked to Maxwell's to see the Individuals play and seemed to keep finding himself on that side of the river.

He visited the Bongos at their apartment next to the Maxwell House factory ("the Bongos are proud of their hometown") on behalf of his *SoHo Weekly News* column, but increasingly *New York Rocker* was his home. In the fall of 1980, Ira convinced Andy Schwartz to let him take over the paper's frequently disorganized record reviews. As he assigned and edited more than a dozen contributions each issue, Ira stayed in touch by mail and phone with a small crew of writers scattered around the country. Many were active in their own cities, where they booked shows, played in bands, and published their own zines.

Though he didn't officially have a desk at the *Rocker* office, he often occupied one anyway, especially at deadline time. "It was hard getting copy out of Ira," recalled Glenn Morrow. "He was slow and meticulous about it. He wasn't cranking it out. Ira would show up really cranky. You couldn't talk to him for the first hour. He wasn't a morning person."

"I never liked writing," Ira said. "I enjoyed editing. That was fun." Ira became a staple at the paper's monthly late-night layout and paste-up sessions, where he helped shape *Rocker*'s knowingly referential captions and headlines. It was a good medium for studied precision and, for Ira, a total blast.

Byron and Ira, meanwhile, had connected as perhaps only two deeply obsessive fans could. "I had a few clashes with Ira," Byron remembered. "There was a huge blow-up over the first Robyn Hitchcock album. He was convinced it was that good because it was so vocally oriented, but that it was nowhere near the last Soft Boys album. I was convinced it was as good as the last Soft Boys album. We had a huge debate about whether music or lyrics were more important."

"I very much remember meeting Ira in the *New York Rocker* office," Emily Hubley recalled. "I was meeting Byron to go somewhere. I was nervous. They were being so serious."

The staff grew infatuated with records, played on repeat on the sole turntable, located behind Andy's desk, like Prince's 1981

Dirty Mind, which spun over and over and earned the twenty-two-year-old auteur from Minneapolis a spring *Rocker* cover.

As the staff cemented their friendships, a new rock economy formed in the city around them, following the boom at CBGB. The music known as New Wave was now big-time. Studio 54's exclusive door policies had trickled down to the rock venues. The Mudd Club installed a velvet rope. Larger venues like Hurrah (on Sixty-second Street, near Ira's freebie apartment) and Danceteria sprang up, as well as the reopened Peppermint Lounge in the middle of an unreconstructed Times Square. Several clubs installed giant video screens. Synthesizers were the thing. You could catch the PATH train to Hoboken a block west of the *New York Rocker* office and be across the river in as little as fifteen minutes.

Downstairs was a mob-owned pizza shop. Upstairs was a dump. The apartment had two rooms and a small kitchen. "The kitchen was uninhabitable," Ira remembered. "Only cockroaches could live in the kitchen."

"Essentially no furnishings whatsoever," noted Ira's new flatmate, dB's guitarist Chris Stamey. "We each had a room and mattress on the floor. His room was full of manuscripts he was copyediting and a lot of books. He had a Stratocaster in the corner that he wasn't playing very much, but it was an old one, and a really good one."

Stamey eyed the sanded-down Strat, interested—perhaps— in taking it off the hands of its not-frequently-musical owner. He took it upon himself to clean it up, regardless of whether Ira would part with it. Ira wouldn't.

They were a few blocks down Washington Street from Maxwell's, and that was pretty great. Maxwell's was different. There was no door policy. There was no coat check, simply a coat rack. And, when Steve Fallon moved the live music into the back room in the spring of 1979, there was a consistent place to play.

Bongos bassist Rob Norris had set up his PA back there for jamming and that became the house system. Steve started to book weekend shows from the pay phone by the kitchen door. He was a warmly rambunctious bar owner, emitting a charismatic stream of catty insults and one-liners. Members of Hoboken's musical community often found themselves with jobs, nicknames, gigs, free drinks, or all four.

Steve remained locked in perpetual battle with his family about the music. Though the bands drew steady customers, the rest of the Fallon clan was content to simply own a restaurant. But they could only look after it for so long. In the evening, when Steve came down from his upstairs apartment and took over, the place transformed.

On nights when bands played, Steve got DJs. More free drinks. In addition to becoming a hangout for Hoboken's ever-increasing population of musicians, the restaurant and main bar became a significant gathering point for the city's new creative class, with an overlap in its growing gay community.

Hoboken's gentrification didn't always sit well with the locals. Jim Testa, raised in Weehawken, was one of the few Maxwell's regulars native to the area. "There was a good bit of resentment," he remembered. "Townies would scream 'fag' at you as you went in."

A small strata of bands emerged. The sound was jangly, occasionally outright plinky, and a marked step back in intensity from what got played at CBGB. Some, like the Bongos and the dB's, crossed classic guitar-pop with a hyperactivity not unrelated to New Wave.

Another frequent headliner was the Feelies, who, along with their numerous side projects, came to best symbolize the venue in its heyday, at least spiritually. Led by guitarists Glenn Mercer and Bill Million, the Feelies were fussy types. They loved playing music but didn't have much tolerance for anything else. From nearby Haledon, about twenty miles northwest of Hoboken, after a few years in the New York trenches they started to decide that playing in Manhattan didn't suit them. "We don't go to New York much. We get real bad headaches going through the tunnel," Million told *Rocker*.

"You just can't breathe," added Mercer, whose intensely

blank-faced deliveries were betrayed by his twitching, spinning performances.

The two formed the Feelies back in 1976, after seeing Jonathan Richman and the Modern Lovers open for the New York Dolls. In late 1978, they headlined Max's Kansas City with Alex Chilton, played to an empty room, and scored a mention on the cover of *Village Voice*. Critic Robert Christgau soon declared them the best band in New York.

Their high-strung combination of tension and psychedelic jangle was infectious in the same way as Talking Heads, but they wore the Velvet Underground influence far more proudly. And whereas David Byrne turned the part of a regular guy into a character, the Feelies were actually *from* the suburbs—Million and Mercer met up to jog every day—and authentically low-key. "We're seasonal thinkers," Glenn Mercer once observed.

They wrote their first batch of songs in 1976 and tinkered patiently. "Songs that are a couple of years old are totally different songs," Mercer said in 1980. "We change the parts so much that they're not really the same songs. To me, they seem like new songs. A lot of times we felt the guitars were competing with each other, so we'd have Bill play percussion and we found that intriguing."

"There were other times when the drums would compete with the guitars," Million observed. "Sometimes the cymbals would hit this one frequency and all three would be canceled out. So we took away the cymbals and we had to replace them with something, so we added a percussionist." Million painted the interior of his house white, floor to ceiling, and cleaned obsessively. The first song on their 1979 debut, *Crazy Rhythms*, was fittingly titled "The Boy with the Perpetual Nervousness." The band fussed over it endlessly, and the ultraclean direct-input guitars sounded little like the Velvet joy they exhibited on stage. Despite the fact that they played the same songs in the same order at every gig, neither Ira nor Georgia ever willingly missed them.

But the Feelies neither gigged much nor practiced a lot. "I

don't think music plays that important a part in our lives," Million admitted. "We just feel real comfortable doing what we're doing. We pretty much approach it like we can take it or leave it."

The Feelies' normality was extreme but approached being genuinely normal nonetheless: why put one's self through any kind of wringer when the pleasurable thing was simply to play music? *Crazy Rhythms* received praise and even good distribution via Stiff Records, the well-established British punk label. The band headed to England for two shows, playing on rented equipment, to mixed reviews. They balked, though, when Stiff asked them to take part in that old British pop tradition, the package tour.

When they did play New York, they brought their own coffee maker, once spilling an entire bag of beans down the stairs at Irving Plaza. Other times, they mixed crazy fruit concoctions, which they spiked with chlorophyll to put oxygen in their blood and pep in their music. "Besides the Meat Puppets, no band's van was ever so filled with pot smoke," one *Rocker* writer noted. They became legendary for their multi-hour soundchecks.

Doing a day of endless press when *Crazy Rhythms* was released, they encountered Ira for the first time. "He was asking all this stuff like he'd read the liner notes," remembered Mercer. "You should have come in earlier," they told him.

After their falling out with Stiff, the Feelies retreated to their hometown in Jersey and focused on making abstract instrumental music. Drummer Anton Fier departed. They hung speakers around the bar across the street from Mercer's house, queuing quadrophonic tapes of chirping birds. If they felt like playing anywhere outside of Haledon, Maxwell's was the place to see them.

The Feelies implanted themselves deep in the DNA of what would become Yo La Tengo. After an offhanded joke about Feelies gigs being celebrations, the band began to intentionally book gigs on holidays. There could have been no more appropriate occasion for Ira Kaplan and Georgia Hubley to meet than when the Feelies played Maxwell's on Independence Day weekend in 1980, where *Rocker* office manager Janet Waegal introduced them. They'd seen each other before, through the small crowd at some show somewhere, but had never spoken.

The Rainbow Theatre was gigantic, cold, and British. It held three thousand people, but a fraction of that was spread out on the floor—a far cry from the sell-out crowds that had crammed the balconies to see the Who a few nights before in their first performances since the death of Keith Moon. The theater's management had removed the seats for the Who show, which added to the emptiness.

The Bongos went first. Richard Barone watched his breath come out of his mouth as he sang, sweat nearly freezing to his body. "I'm sure I was visibly surrounded by a misty halo of evaporating frost," he wrote later.

"The only thing that went wrong with the Rainbow show was the show itself," Ira would note in his coverage. He'd convinced *SoHo Weekly News* to handle his expenses, and he stayed with his aunt. The night seemed primed to be something momentous.

The initial idea to showcase the new New York bands in London belonged to Ruth Polsky, talent buyer at Hurrah. Somebody slapped it with a name, "Taking Liberties from New York," and the event took on a momentum of its own. The Bongos, the Raybeats, and the dB's had all recently signed British record deals, and the Fleshtones, Bush Tetras, and Polyrock filled out the bill, booked for early February.

Stiff Records, ever eager to pull together a package and just a few months removed from the Feelies, decided to record the show and rush release a live LP with the fabbest new sounds from the Big Apple. *Time Out* fed the hype, devoting their cover to it the week before.

"We thought it was like the Crusades," Glenn Morrow remembered, whose Individuals played a send-off at the Ritz. "We were all like, 'Farewell! Godspeed!'"

The trip hadn't started auspiciously. "You can bet The Bongos were surprised when an *NME* writer chided them for calling the music rock 'n' roll," Ira noted in his chronicle of the trip, "In a Sense Abroad." "They were informed that the term is currently out of vogue in English new wave circles because it conjures up overbearing macho attitudes."

The dB's did a warm-up gig at the Hope and Anchor, the night of Peter Holsapple's twenty-fifth birthday, but nothing could get anybody warm enough for the Rainbow. The *Rocker* house band went second.

"The whole place was like a big unheated cavern," Holsapple remembered. "Also, the PA company that had been contracted to do the show backed out the day before, and the road manager we had, Dave Boxall, spent all day cobbling another sound system together." The only food available in the backstage of the giant, cold theater was ice cream.

After the dB's set, Stamey collapsed onto the floor of the massive shared dressing room, falling asleep in the midst of the chaos. "When he finally arose," Richard Barone would write, "his image remained in the steaming frost for hours, like an eerie police outline of a murder victim on a sidewalk. For the rest of the night, everyone whispered about 'the shroud of Stamey.'"

"The English simply slammed it," said Glenn Morrow. One paper titled its review "Dead Scene Scrolls."

"I didn't bother asking how many people showed up," Ira reported. "It could have been 300 or maybe up to 1,000. But it certainly wasn't enough to keep the 3,000-plus capacity hall from looking anything but empty. And when you realized how many New Yorkers were there, it began to get a bit laughable."

Georgia had flown over for the show too, a few days shy of her twenty-first birthday, and it was in London that Ira and Georgia got to know each other, at the dB's Hope and Anchor gig and elsewhere. At the Rainbow, they explored the backstage, amid massive sets for Bow Wow Wow's coming residency, during which Malcolm McLaren would turn the theater into an indoor theme park, replete with roller coaster and cotton-candy stands.

The two spent as much time as they could together, doing what they might do back home: catching the Fleshtones at Dingwalls, and even returning to the Rainbow to see Bow Wow Wow, who featured a new singer named Boy George. Georgia extended her stay in London.

When they came back, Georgia and Ira were Georgia and Ira, a nearly inseparable couple. In short order, Georgia and Emily and the cats moved into a house at 719 Garden Street in Hoboken, a quick walk to where Ira had moved in above Peter Holsapple. The building on Garden Street was owned by Richard M. Smith, a *Newsweek* editor who lived next door. Georgia took the room across from Emily on the second floor of the narrow twelve-foot-wide building, and painted.

In Georgia, Ira had found somebody to match his enthusiasm, and the two went to shows constantly, sometimes traveling to Boston to catch wild sets by Jeff "Mono Mann" Conolly's bands, DMZ and the Lyres. NRBQ was another shared favorite worth leaving town for.

One of their roommates, Danny Amis, who played guitar with the surf-punk band the Raybeats, practiced in the basement. After complaints from the neighbors, he built a small interior room, bracketed with drywall and insulation and a particularly low ceiling. Ira and his record collection moved into the house soon thereafter. "We called them an affinity group," the landlord remembered.

Rocker launched a pro-American music campaign. After the drubbed show at the Rainbow, Glenn Morrow said, "We hated England. Some early Rough Trade stuff was OK, the Raincoats, the Slits, the Swell Maps, Gang of Four. But then they became like a fucking factory, regurgitating these perfect images of rock 'n' roll. Spandau Ballet and shit." The *New York Rocker crew* was not entirely on board with the new dance-oriented rock. They'd recently devoted a special issue to the Velvet Underground, an allegiance they continued to wear proudly.

Over the summer, the *Rocker*'s editors split the cover between four of the paper's favorite bands and ran an uncredited editorial titled "Demons of DOR"—dance-oriented rock. Joy Division's "pioneering efforts have led to the unbending electronic rhythms of Spandau Ballet who sound like Echo & the Bunnymen who sound like Teardrop Explodes who sound like Bauhaus who sound like U2 who sound like a happy version of Joy Division."

There was great homegrown music everywhere, the paper argued. "Look again at this cover of *NY Rocker*. Here are four American bands that don't fit into the endless dance trance: the immaculate, heartfelt pop of the dB's; the angry fire of Mission of Burma; the innocent wacko smarts of Half Japanese; and the political punk riot of the Dead Kennedys."

That spring, Andy Schwartz published a list of critics for national publications who covered independent American music. He excluded *Trouser Press* but sketched out a small network of writers, including his own reviews editor, Ira. In many ways, it was the moment American indie rock asserted its won parallel course to the sprawling scene that had emerged in the United Kingdom after designer Malcolm McLaren had borrowed Richard Hell's image for the Sex Pistols some half decade earlier. Though there would be crossover, separate infrastructures emerged on opposite sides of the Atlantic, each driven by its own country's particular geography and culture.

Despite *Rocker*'s best intentions, the new British music crept into Maxwell's, where a few Brit-obsessed DJs provided the majority of Ira's exposure to the new sounds. The leaders of the British post-punks, New Order, had made their American debut on Washington Street in September 1980. The *Village Voice* ad for the show clarified, parenthetically, "formerly Joy Division." That band would have made its American debut at Maxwell's too, earlier in the year, were it not for the suicide of frontman Ian Curtis days before the band's scheduled departure.

But Georgia and Ira increasingly had to leave Hoboken for music anyway. Not long after the New Order show, Maxwell's was in trouble. The 1980 subway strike had cut into business, and the crowds just weren't coming. Steve suspended the weekend gigs. "The space is tentatively slated for remodeling as an addition to the front dining and bar areas," *Rocker* reported in the spring of 1981. "The new furnishings will be modular so Fallon can redesign the room on short notice if he resumes booking shows, which he may do on a reduced basis in September." It would be years before they replaced the scalloped and crumbling ceiling tiles, which one could use to identify Maxwell's photographs for years. The heater stayed on the stage.

"It remains, without a doubt, the best place available to hear bands," Ira noted in *SoHo Weekly News* when the venue reopened in September. In the same column, Ira also marked the arrival of a "stunner" out-of-town act, one who pledged allegiance to the Feelies and the dB's, even. "Wistful minor chords, jangling Byrds guitars, vocals reminiscent of Shoes, but pitched lower and tougher," Ira wrote. "By all means, check R.E.M. out live."

And while some would dismiss American "record collector rock," as if there were something wrong with treating rock as a continuum, R.E.M. presented a decided alternative to the alienated and melodramatic vibes of post-punk England. "They're level-headed, well-managed (by themselves) and seem more interested in developing a solid grassroots base than taking the next train to NYC," Vic Varney offered approvingly in an Athens scene report in *Rocker* not long after the band's formation.

"In fact, R.E.M. are holding off pursuit of a record deal for the time being, to concentrate on being a live act," Varney continued. "I don't know long they'll stick to their guns about this, but it's a neat idea. I loved the Beatles in Hamburg." They played lots of covers. Their appearance in *Rocker* was important for another reason: it was R.E.M.'s first appearance in national print and allowed them to establish a trademark on their name over a few other bands that also used it. They bought some ads, too.

The Athens quartet rolled into Maxwell's in January 1982. As they did to everyone, R.E.M. charmed the bejeezus out of Steve Fallon. And as Steve Fallon did to everyone, he charmed the bejeezus out of R.E.M. Steve and guitarist Peter Buck became close friends. They made pals at *Rocker*, too, especially new photo editor Laura Levine.

R.E.M. crept across the country like a charmed and charming Southern vine, a mysterious force jangling through college towns, clubs, and out of the broadcast towers of university radio stations.

When Black Flag came to Maxwell's, Steve was lying in his bed on the second floor on the other side of the building when the band began soundchecking. "Yeah, you're going to have to lower that," he thought.

Hardcore music had never really found a home in Hoboken. A biker bar called Mile Square City briefly booked Saturday matinees, but when a show ran long the bikers and hardcore kids overlapped. "It erupted into a full-on John Wayne brawl with bottles over the head and bodies flying down the bar," remembered Jim Testa, soon to found the *Jersey Beat* zine. Not much other music ever came to Hoboken anyway.

But hardcore was difficult to ignore. A churning mass of teenage energy and rigid guidelines about breakneck tempos, it was clearly another branch of the punk spawned at CBGB. In parallel to R.E.M.'s college-town cartography, hardcore bands had begun to assemble an all-ages, do-it-yourself touring network of their own based (it is said) on Black Flag bassist Chuck Dukowski's phone book. *Rocker* provided coverage, although not nearly as much as the hardcore kids' own zine network.

Ira came to love some of it, and penned liner notes for the debut release by Bad Brains, an all-black act from Washington, DC, but remained puzzled by much of it. "I go just as agog in the face of a gang of music lovers (say, those on the NYC hardcore scene) that waves the flag of anarchy with one hand whilst giving the raspberry to any band that doesn't play by their (new, improved?) rules," he wrote.

Proudly suburban, the hardcore kids held the mainstream (and much of everything else) at a defiant arm's length, among the first to encode independence as a vocalized choice rather than an egalitarian necessity. With few major labels interested in something seemingly small and intentionally abrasive, it was an easy choice to make.

It was from those ranks that a new Boston correspondent arrived in the pages of *New York Rocker*. Ira and Georgia had met him on an earlier trip to Massachusetts to see music. Gerard Cosloy was something of a boy wonder, as Georgia called him later—a teenager with an encyclopedic grip on the new sub-underground and possessed by a curiosity that reached far beyond. To say that he liked to provoke was a mild understatement.

Despite being a teenager, Gerard Cosloy put on shows of his own, DJed on the Boston College station WZBC, and ran a hardcore zine, *Conflict*. Born Christmas Eve 1964, his father an employee of Wang Laboratories, and inspired by the college stations he picked up out of Boston, Cosloy turned out *Conflict*'s first issue to mark his fifteenth birthday in December 1979.

Hand-typed, sometimes bound by three staples down the side, sometimes by one quickly dashed into the pages' top-right corner, *Conflict* was as its name implied, and got around New England with remarkable speed. Deeply set punk attitudes, a sharp mind, and a raging drive for new music splashed across 8-by-11 sheets in ever-denser boxes of highly biased reportage punctuated occasionally by Xerox-scorched photography.

Quick-witted if thin-skinned, the articulate Gerard Cosloy made enemies quickly as he became a local legend. But he made friends, too. Originally from Wayland, twenty miles outside Boston, Cosloy attended high school at Concord Academy, where he'd reviewed Mission of Burma's debut for the school paper under the headline "Art Is a Hammer." In turn, Burma hid the underage Cosloy, who wore Elvis Costello–style record-collector glasses, behind amplifiers when bouncers came around to check IDs at Boston clubs.

He got some assignments writing for *Take It*, a Boston publication edited by Byron Coley, who also passed along the book review column to Ira. Andy Schwartz had kept up the fight too, absorbing hardcore into the spectrum of new American music covered by *Rocker*, but it was just one more kind of music to listen to. Cover subjects in 1981 ranged from Prince to the Fleshtones. Laura Levine shot rapper Grandmaster Flash with Talking Heads' Tina Weymouth. Black Flag's Henry Rollins appeared with Bad Brains' H.R.

In a piece called "Anglophilia," which came out near the end of the year, Schwartz observed that major labels were happy to provide one-off distribution for potentially hot British acts like Adam and the Ants but were uninterested in doing the same for domestic imprints like the Minneapolis-based Twin/Tone, who boasted the recently formed quartet the Replacements. As a division of A&M, only I.R.S. offered an outlet for American post-punk bands with any kind of real distribution. R.E.M. signed nearly as soon as they could.

In early 1982, Gerard Cosloy, too, began to contribute to *New York Rocker*, filing a live report on British punks Anti-Pasti and Boston acts Gang Green and Ice Age. As it quickly turned out, he was as much a willful champion of American music as Andy Schwartz.

"The current local punk scene *wasn't* inspired by [Anti-Pasti] or any other British hard-core band, but by other American ones ... how many other cities can make that claim?" Cosloy asked, quite reasonably. He turned on the *Conflict* charm for the kicker: "So if sub-par Limey punk bands come to your town, steal their equipment before they can finish playing."

They weren't sure what music they wanted to make, but at some moment the idea of making it at all seemed attainable. Ira played guitar. Sort of. Georgia played drums. Sort of.

Certainly, they were surrounded by music and the musicians making it. Dating for less than a year, a not-uncommon excursion was a trip they took to Saugerties in early 1982 with *Rocker* coeditor Michael Hill and his girlfriend to visit with NRBQ and tour the inner recesses of their infamously deep record collection.

Byron Coley had moved to Los Angeles and then Boston, keeping up with Ira and Georgia via a cassette exchange. Sony's Walkman had taken off around 1980, turning what had been common among music obsessives into a lingua franca. "I was always making them mixes, of singles and compilation cuts," Coley remembered. "I was serious record scum. There were lots of tapes floating around. Prizes were [John] Peel sessions, with weird arrangements and songs that hadn't been released, Alex Chilton demos, unreleased Velvets stuff."

He riffled through thrift stores, garage sales, and bargain bins—a world of past music as vital as the present. One of Coley's spots, Sun Music in Northampton, Massachusetts, also fed recordings to NRBQ, themselves an important node in the distribution of left-of-center music.

In the meantime, being a full-time man-on-the-scene New Wave journalist had ceased to interest Ira. There was more interesting music to listen to without having to keep up with the absolute latest and shiniest. He'd even given up his *SoHo Weekly News* column in late 1981. "I felt there was less interest in the kinds of things I wanted to do," he said, "and more interest in maybe flashier types of things. The coverage of the Plasmatics was, I always thought, a little more than what was warranted. But I could be wrong."

MTV spread from local cable network to local cable network and, in the next years, would become the dominant force in the music industry, altering sales in nearly every market where it aired. Mainstream pop stars like Hall and Oates and Air Supply seemed further away with each passing season, but Hoboken grew more bearable. Both shy about their music-making ambitions, Ira and Georgia had talked about playing together, and finally one day did it.

They borrowed a car, loaded in Georgia's drums, and drove to Croton and Woodybrook Lane, where they set up in the familiar confines of the playroom where Ira had once spent hours in the grip of records. They jammed a little bit, and had no conscious designs beyond that. Nobody quite remembers how Peter Holsapple knew that Ira and Georgia had been playing. But he was in charge of entertainment for *Rocker* photo editor Laura Levine's birthday party and invited them to join.

Georgia and Ira met up with Holsapple in the dB's new sixth-floor room in the Music Building, a sixty-studio practice space and teeming microcity across from the Port Authority Bus Terminal, and ran through a few songs. It went well enough.

Laura's birthday was on May 1 and fell on a Saturday. On a sad and strange note, the rock critic Lester Bangs had died the night before, accidentally overdosing on Darvon and Valium. "I don't recall how we all found out," Laura remembered. "But I assume we must have found out during the party. I'm sure that must have added to the intensity of the partying that night." Curtiss A, who Andy Schwartz knew from Minneapolis, played in the early part of the evening.

The dB's, now minus Stamey, who split to focus on solo ventures and producing, did some songs in their Slipcovers lineup (Holsapple: "as in, we're gonna slip some covers into the set for you"). Also playing were all four members of Morrow's Individuals, Michael Paumgardhen of Lydia Lunch's 8 Eyed Spy, and others. Possibly Steely Dan's Donald Fagen was there, but that might have been another party.

At some point, Georgia and Ira rotated into the ensemble. Though Laura had spent the day gathering equipment with Holsapple, she was surprised to see Georgia and Ira among the backing band for the revolving cast of singers.

It was a small step, to hang out with friends at a party and play cover songs, but it was also enormous, to go from not playing music to being musicians that some people enjoyed watching. They backed the birthday girl on the dB's "The Fight." Glenn Morrow, who'd quit *Rocker* the year before to focus on the Individuals, arrived fresh from a photo shoot for his band's first album and sang "Johnny Carson" from the Beach Boys' *Love You* with the dB's Holsapple and Rigby. Though gone from the office, Morrow was never far from the *Rocker* fold. His soon-to-be wife, Elizabeth Van Itallie, had taken over the art director chair.

They finished the keg just before "She's Got Everything," a 1969 Kinks B-side, and the night ended shortly thereafter with an extended all-star version of Flipper's "Sex Bomb," a recent *Rocker* fave. Janet Waegal took multiple turns at the mike, screaming the "sex bomb baby, yeah!" chorus.

Over the summer, *Rocker* marked the performance with a small picture of the "Sex Bomb" chorale, including Waegal, Holsapple, Michael Hill, and others, with a caption: "Photo editor Laura Levine celebrated her 24th by inviting her weirdo friends to speel beer on the NYR office and play some dubious 'music.'" For Ira and Georgia, the experience was nothing short of electrifying, and they thought about ways to do it again.

CHAPTER 5

Georgia and Those Guys

One afternoon, Ira, Georgia, and a group of friends met a band of freshly arrived Hobokenites en route to the ball field off Hudson Street, just inland from where the Knickerbockers once tramped from the ferry to McCarty's. They recognized one another from Maxwell's, which had returned quickly to having weekly shows. The two groups joined, picked teams, and established a Sunday softball game that would survive for well over a decade in some form or another, a feature of life in Ira and Georgia's extended circle.

The Hoboken game settled semipermanently in a lot near the corner of Sixteenth and Madison, past some factories and under the bluffs in the farthest northwest corner of town. The players dubbed it Dioxin Field. The group of new arrivals included two Ohioans, Dave Schramm and Fred Brockman, who had migrated east together earlier in the year and established their country-tinged band, the Kinetics, in Manhattan. They became regulars at the ball field, and quickly fell in with the rest of the Hoboken music world.

The game included members of the dB's, the Individuals, Human Switchboard, and other local bands. One player was

Bob Bert, the new drummer in Sonic Youth, then getting established across the river. In right field was Jim Testa, who played off the Liverpool weekly *Mersey Beat* with his new *Jersey Beat* zine.

Invented a half century after baseball, softball in part returned the rules to their Elysian casualness. Stymied by Little League pitching, Ira had discovered softball as a freshman at Sarah Lawrence and would later score the winning run in a dramatic 15–14 victory over nearby Concordia. "A women's liberal arts college, there was really no better way to crack the lineup," he noted. Not far removed from his brief collegiate career, he remained an enthusiastic and surprisingly competitive shortstop. Georgia pitched.

Ray Hubley came around for a while. Emily was a regular too, and it was on a Dioxin Field Sunday that she first met her future husband, Will Rosenthal. When they showed their children the spot two decades later, there was a sign warning of hazardous materials in the ground. Chemicals or no, Hoboken was a nice place to live.

The games lasted well into the autumn until it was just Ira, Dave Schramm, and a few others playing stickball. Sunday nights in winter, most of the same crew trekked to Bowlmor Lanes in Manhattan to roll together. One addition for the winter games was Bill Ryan, the curmudgeonly and beloved Maxwell's bartender who had cofounded Pier Platters, Hoboken's first and only record store.

Opened in late 1982 by Ryan and fellow Maxwell's bartender Tom Prendergast (with some help from Steve Fallon), Pier Platters quickly became a destination shop in *New York Rocker* circles and far beyond, one of the few places whose sole focus was to stock a reasonably complete selection of current independent singles and LPs. The availability of imported 7-inches from New Zealand not withstanding, gentrification was upon Hoboken.

Rent on four-bedroom apartments had nearly octupled since Glenn Morrow found his Hudson Street apartment just five years earlier. One-family brownstones that sold for $20,000 in

1972 were now worth around $130,000. "The new residents can be seen on the streets wearing designer jeans and driving foreign cars," *The New York Times* reported in the first of several dispatches. "Plants hang from macramé in condominium windows. Häagen-Dazs ice cream and *Tax Shelter Digest* are sold at the Hoboken Daily News store. Those who liked 'the old Hoboken' say it may already be too late. The first croissants have been served." Another *Times* piece featured the apartment shared by Glenn and Individuals guitarist Jon Klages. Glenn moved out the next day.

The Maxwell House plant down the block chugged along, spitting roast into the air every Monday as the factory decaffeinated it out of the Sanka. "You could sense the entire town buzzing," the Bongos' Richard Barone once noted. It was a feel-good PR spin too: the caffeinated bands of Hoboken. Several doors down from Maxwell's, the Elysian Cafe remained a hangout for factory employees guzzling 35¢ beers. "We seem to get a new crowd in Maxwell's, a new influx of cosmopolitan people, every few weeks," Steve Fallon observed.

Maxwell's buzzed too. Steve's upstairs apartment served as the deepest inner sanctum, a crash pad for hundreds of bands, and the birthplace of another venture: Coyote Records. With a logo designed by Maxwell's DJ, Guy Ewald, of a coyote howling in a bathtub—something Steve had found himself doing one night—one of the first releases was by Georgia and Ira's 719 housemate, Danny Amis.

Hoboken got its own recording studio, too, in Water Music at Second and Grand. Cries guitarist Rob Grenoble had gotten hit by a drunk driver en route home from CBGB. He invested the settlement money in gear. Chris Stamey, liberated from the dB's, was the first to record.

In buzzing Hoboken, Ira and Georgia started to get over their shyness when it came to making music. "We were drawn to each other because we could recognize the same certain shyness in each other," Georgia said in 2000. "We both really wanted to get over that, but it was very hard at first. It still is sometimes."

They continued to experiment. A trip to Feelies guitarist Bill Million's white-painted house and basement studio in Haledon yielded a decent cover of Donovan's "Hey Gyp," with Million on e-bowed guitar and Ira singing for the first time. In November, they hosted a session at 719 with Emily on organ; Danny Amis on bass; and David Bither, another *Rocker* writer, playing sax. A preadolescent named Jesse Burke screamed along on "Louie Louie" and Flipper's "The Way of the World," while Georgia and Emily sang backup on Danny's cover of the Barbarians' "Are You a Boy or Are You a Girl?" from *Nuggets*.

For musically inclined twentysomethings, Hoboken became an extended version of what urban theorist Ray Oldenburg called a "third place"—the elusive spot beyond home and work where community emerged. Between Maxwell's, softball, Pier Platters, backyard barbecues, and occasional house parties, Hoboken had a lot available in the mix.

Across the river, the rock economy continued to boom, but punk didn't seem cut out for the big-time. Danceteria and other rooms paid bands good money, often up to $1,000 a night. "No one was there to see them," observed Gerard Cosloy, the teenage zine writer who had begun to contribute to Ira's *Rocker* review section as well. "They'd all just be in the other room dancing. The band was the sideshow, communicating with no one. It was like a grant system, only instead of the NEA they were funded by the Ritz. What bands should have been doing was getting out of town, or making records or something."

Danceteria was home to a pioneering fusion of dance music and downtown culture, and it was there that a pre-fame Madonna Ciccone approached Glenn Morrow about working together. (Morrow declined.) Hip-hop forebear Afrika Bambaataa made regular appearances there after outgrowing the Mudd Club downtown as rap began to carve a place for itself in popular American culture.

But for the new rock groups still wielding guitars in the wake of New Wave and frowning British outfits, it was an uncomfortable match. "I always felt like we were just interrupting people!" Mission of Burma's Clint Conley remembered.

"They'd be dancing to the latest sounds from England, and we'd come in and make a big mess, and then they'd go back to their fun."

That fall, *New York Rocker* folded. "It was breaking even most of the time until it wasn't," Andy Schwartz said. It all happened very quickly. The final issue—#55, dated November 1982—appropriately featured Hoboken on the cover. "Bands Across the Water: Exploring a Model Pop Community," it read above Brady Bunch–style portraits of the Bongos and the Individuals. In coming years, both "New York" and "Rocker" would come to mean very different things.

Though she was mostly working for Faith, Georgia had started to contribute to the paper too, most recently collaborating with Ira to review Robyn Hitchcock's *Groovy Decay* as a ten-panel comic strip. To Ira, the closing of *Rocker* was "a shattering thing." The twenty-five-year-old journalist wasn't at a loss for assignments, and he picked up the odd piece for *Creem* or Robert Christgau at the *Village Voice*, but was less and less interested still. "Hustling for work—I certainly wasn't good at that," Ira reflected. "To this day, I have a very good relationship with [*Creem* editor] Billy Altman. I've always enjoyed his company, I think the reverse is true, but it wasn't like I was rocketing to the top of the *Creem* reviews section, and rightly so." Ira had never considered himself a great writer, which would make him one of the few to fail at music journalism only to succeed in rock music.

Meanwhile, a friend from college got a job at a cheap paperback house and started to pass Ira some proofreading assignments, which suited Ira extremely well and soon turned into copyediting jobs. An organized mind if an infrequently organized housekeeper, he could slot the work into what became an increasingly full schedule. Thanks to Steve Fallon, he'd picked up a new gig that kept him equally close to the action.

"Danny had a houseguest who was driving us crazy and we kept hoping he'd leave," Ira recalled. "But he stayed for a really long time and then announced he thought he was going to get a job doing sound at Maxwell's. Then we thought, 'Oh, man, now he'll *never* leave.' So I went to Steve and said, 'Don't hire him, hire me!' I didn't know anything about it at all, but that's how I got the job." Georgia began a Thursday night DJ slot there, and was only once—during a Feelies holiday spectacular—relieved of her duties for not being festive enough.

The two were fixtures in the small sound booth, a low and tiny platform crammed in the back corner of the back room as the local world blended seamlessly with the growing network of acts from around the country who found the free meals and enthused regulars at Maxwell's to be most pleasant. Ira mixed bands from the dozens of entwined indie circuits, from growing national names like R.E.M. and the Meat Puppets to local favorites like The Scene Is Now, Mofungo, and the Feelies' many projects.

Somewhat naturally, Ira and Georgia found a reason to trick themselves onto the Maxwell's stage. They signed on to play a birthday shindig for Maxwell's bartender and Pier Platters honcho Bill Ryan. The ever-pithy Steve Fallon inadvertently christened the new party act when he penciled them down as "Georgia & those guys," a half-joking (and lowercase) dismissal for the ensemble's only member worth remarking upon. They were all too happy not to have to think of a name.

Rehearsals commenced in the low-ceilinged practice space in the basement at 719 Garden Street, where they came up with a list of songs they were reasonably sure that party attendees would know well enough to jump on the microphone and deliver vocals for. Certainly neither Ira nor Georgia was quite ready for that. Jim Testa, a Dioxin right fielder, made mention of the new band in the eighth issue of his recently launched *Jersey Beat*. They were a product, he wrote, of "the new fad among local scenemakers . . . tribute band syndrome."

But while they may have been playing covers, Ira came up with a rule, a small caveat that began to describe the vaguest shape of an assembling band that was doing more than goofing around: they wouldn't repeat songs from performance to performance. It was the sort of tiny but thorough gesture that came to define the act taking form in Ira and Georgia's passive hands, rounding their choices of action down from things they *wouldn't* do.

Nearly stubbornly, they learned a whole new repertoire each time out. Over Georgia and Those Guys' yearlong existence, Ira, Georgia, and a revolving cast learned around a hundred different songs that ranged from Velvet Underground obscurities ("Sweet Bonnie Brown") to songs by their friends and New York contemporaries like the Individuals and the Fleshtones. They tackled recent faves like DMZ and the Meat Puppets; half-ironic FM fare including KISS and Cheap Trick; and deep cuts by Buddy Holly and the Beach Boys, including Bruce Johnston's pre–Beach Boys "Summer Means Fun," a song that went to #72 in 1964. It was a canon far from closed.

Bill Ryan's birthday yielded what many regard as a major highlight of Georgia and Those Guys' meteoric career. dB's drummer Will Rigby decided he'd like to sing "I'm All Right," a Bo Diddley tune covered by the Rolling Stones; and Richard and Linda Thompson's "Wall of Death," particularly the outtake arrangement produced by Scottish songwriter Gerry Rafferty. "It sounds like a Fleetwood Mac version," Will remembered.

"Whatever happens, don't stop playing," Will told Ira just before the band started.

As "Wall of Death" progressed, Will removed the mike from the mike stand and began to drag bar stools onto the stage. While the band played, he stacked the stools atop one another and, as he sang the final verse, ascended. On the last phrase—"wall of . . ."—Will and his wall toppled in a terrific spectacle to the floor. *"Death,"* he gurgled from under the pile. The band stopped.

"I'm all right," Will croaked into the microphone, his Southern twang in full effect. Ira looked on in surprise as Will stood up and brushed himself off. "I'm all right," he repeated. Hesitating for a second, the band swung into "I'm All Right."

The living room smelled like hairspray, perhaps sold in more quantity per capita in 1983 than during any other era of the American epoch but nonetheless an uncommon odor for 719 Garden Street. Georgia made fake gagging sounds as she led the new bassist to the basement. The odor's source was the band crashing at the house for the week, in town from Minneapolis on behalf of Ira's new venture in far-off Manhattan, near the corniest corner of Greenwich Village, where Georgia and Emily had briefly lived.

Just before *Rocker* closed, managing editor Michael Hill received a call at the office from Folk City, the venerable West Village venue. They wanted to book a regular night of "new" music, an increasingly common catch-all term for firmly committed fringe acts, be they off-kilter rock, free jazz, avant-garde folk, or idiosyncratic post-punk. Hill volunteered his services and invited Ira to join him. Ira named the series Music for Dozens. It was a comfortable smallness.

Advertising THREE BANDS FOR $3, 10 P.M., SHARP!, Music for Dozens opened with three consecutive nights at Folk City starting on November 17 and settled in for Wednesdays thereafter. There were lots of Feelies and dB's and Information spin-offs, local bands plucked smartly from various undergrounds, and a constant flow of national talent, culled from Ira and Michael's contacts at *Rocker*.

They fell into a weekly routine. Georgia designed flyers, usually the Tuesday night before Ira had to get them out to their small mailing list to advertise the following week's gig, and experimented each week with different combinations of collage, primitive line drawings, typography, and design. Michael xeroxed them at his day job with the phone company and, with Ira, hung them around town. If they scored a *Times* mention, they could fill Folk City's back room with nearly nineteen dozen, 225 legally.

In early December, psychedelic punks the Meat Puppets topped a bill that also featured the new quartet Sonic Youth along with Hose, an NYU hardcore band that included future producer and industry mogul Rick Rubin. The hardcore crowd taunted Sonic Youth's No Wave–influenced songs and retuned guitars, chanting, "Play faster, play faster!" Sonic Youth guitarist Thurston Moore had been a regular at Feelies gigs, too.

The band crashing on the Garden Street floor a few months later was Ira and Michael's biggest score yet, despite the hairspray. Scheduled for a major feature in the unpublished fifty-sixth issue of *Rocker*, it had been Ira and Michael's idea to book the Replacements' New York debut to begin with, and the shambolic Minneapolis quartet built a tour around it, which helpfully aligned with fifteen-year-old bassist Tommy Stinson's spring break.

Heavily hyped, their second album, *Hootenanny*, a few weeks from release, most of the Replacements arrived for their show at Folk City typically late. Ira suggested that songwriter Paul Westerberg do an acoustic set. Westerberg demurred and the owners turned on the houselights. The rest of the band arrived eventually and the show went on. Over five gigs in the New York area, including a night at Maxwell's, the band's booze-soaked punk-pop blew minds. Glenn Morrow, for one, was so inspired that he almost immediately disbanded the Individuals.

Bob and Tommy Stinson stuck around Garden Street for a few days while the Replacements gigged in the area. They were almost utterly sedentary houseguests, opting to spend their first trip to Manhattan in front of the Garden Street television set, leaving only to play shows and get pizza, which is where they were as Georgia and Those Guys convened for their next rehearsals.

The new bassist was Terry Karydes, who had recently followed her boyfriend Fred Brockman to New York and met Ira and Georgia during Sunday bowling. The latest idea had manifested itself earlier that spring after Ira's Dozens partner Michael Hill sang with the band during a basement house party: a Modern Lovers cover act fronted by Michael that could compete at the upcoming battle of the tribute bands at Danceteria. Ira had it all figured out. He just needed to ask Michael, which he did promptly, and subsequently organized the performance down to the setlist.

Renamed the Astral Planes for the occasion, Georgia and Those Guys trekked to Manhattan for their April 22 show and established another characteristic of the new band. "They liked to go eat before the show," Terry noted. "That was the main focus: *What kind of food are we going to get and where are we going to get it?* Before the Astral Planes show, they had the place all scoped. It was a rib joint. It was great. Just the kind of food you want to eat when you're nervous."

With Danceteria's four floors and giant video screens, the evening's bill was an odd collision of kitsch and fandom. "It was an ironic battle of the bands and a very serious battle of the bands converging in one night," Georgia remembered. The last act—covering a mishmash of Pat Benatar and other current pop—provided the percussion. "It was a massive kit with like eighty drums," Georgia said. "They had weird skins and everything. I could not even fathom what to do with them."

"We literally couldn't see Georgia behind all the drums," Ira said. "We had to strike some. We were difficult right from the start."

The Astral Planes set went fairly smashingly. The songs snapped into one another and Hill was engaging with the crowd. "Got any requests? OK, we'll do 'em all!" he announced as they jumped into a New Jersey–centric rendition of "Roadrunner." They skipped "Government Center," which they'd played at the house party, which would have been a shoo-in for any other new band who'd already gone through the trouble of learning a song. But a rule was a rule. They sent a tape to Byron later.

Afterward, with a Suicide tribute act between, Georgia pulled her second shift of the night in a Shaggs cover act led by performance artist and singer Ann Magnuson. "She made us wear African dashikis," Georgia pondered. "I didn't quite get the connection." Around that time, Georgia played another gig with them doing oddball covers under the name Black Lieutenant Uhura.

The drummer grew bolder in joining other musicians, and her drumming started to get better. Terry thought Georgia "fearless," but it didn't grow any easier at first. She and Terry became the rhythm section in Fred Brockman and Dave Schramm's latest version of the Kinetics. They played a house party in a Hoboken basement.

"I went into the closet to swig some Maalox out of my coat pocket," remembered Terry, who—like her bandmates—was petrified about playing in front of people. "Georgia came up behind me and said 'What're you doing?' She probably thought I was swigging from a flask and I was trying to hide it. When I showed her, she said, 'Oh, give me some!'"

The ever-polite Michael was generally the amiable face at the door of Folk City. There was no guest list at Music for Dozens, a fact they were adamant about. Though more established booking agents began to handle some of the bands that had debuted in a Wednesday-night slot, giving them access to an ever-fuller network of clubs, that didn't stop Ira and Michael from keeping the old, weird Village spirit alive at Folk City.

One night, on a bill anchored by avant-garde turntablist Christian Marclay, a percussionist lit a window frame on fire with lighter fluid and began to play it with a hammer. "The Folk City people were like, 'Make that stop, *now*,'" Michael recalled.

By Hill's estimate, Ira did two-thirds of the booking, though Michael had connections at Slash Records in Los Angeles and more mainstream quarters of the indie world. The Replacements weren't the only band to make their first Manhattan area appearance at Music for Dozens. Just a few weeks earlier, the Minutemen—the punk-socialist trio from San Pedro—had played there, along with Violent Femmes back in January, who packed the room and signed a record deal with Slash.

The bills continued to mix the obscure, the more obscure, and the occasional act that was right about to break. Hüsker Dü, another powerfully original band from Minneapolis, came to town and played their first non-hardcore show in New York on a bill with Men & Volts, led by oddball music archivist and zine editor David Greenberger. For Ira, booking shows was a fun pursuit, maybe more fun than journalism, but still not quite what he wanted to be doing with his time.

Byron Coley remembered the series fondly. "In 1982, the difference between [underground folk guitarist] Michael Hurley and Sonic Youth was unbridgeable," he noted, and Music for Dozens made it look easy. It wasn't every fan who was into both wild noise and idiosyncratic acoustic guitar slingers, and no catch-all existed to describe the connection, except that they didn't register on bigger radars. Ira and Michael worked as far in advance as they could, although they often found themselves scrambling for last-minute fill-ins. Sonic Youth was dependable in that category.

Folk City's management was never entirely fond of their Dozens. "They wanted us there, but they didn't want to deal with really doing this," Michael said. "Their sensibility had nothing to do with ours." Most nights, the club dealt in the remaining tendrils of the folk scene that the venue's original proprietor, Mike Porco, started booking back in the early '60s. (He was most famous, perhaps, for once acting as Bob Dylan's legal guardian on Dylan's first professional contract.) A typical week at Folk City circa 1983 might involve appearances by Rick Danko of the Band, Ramblin' Jack Elliott, Dave Van Ronk, or the Clancy Brothers.

"They would get annoyed with us and treat us like children," said Michael of the owners. "They wanted us to paint the dressing room after somebody had trashed it. They insisted we repair things, like when the speakers broke."

From his position at the door at Folk City, Michael Hill

befriended Karin Berg, the vivacious A&R woman from Warner Bros. who had worked with Television and the B-52s, among others. Though there was no guest list, he would scan the line for her and make sure she got inside. Berg quickly offered Michael a job. In the next year, she would begin to assemble an alternative marketing department at Warner Bros., the first real attention given to the underground by a major label. Energies sapped by his new day job, Michael soon dropped out of Music for Dozens.

The series rolled on with eclectic authority. Steve Wynn's Dream Syndicate, products of Los Angeles's Byrds-loving Paisley Underground who had since gone noisy, appeared twice. The Replacements and Hüsker Dü and Sonic Youth all returned. Half Japanese visited from Maryland, and Peter Stampfel, cofounder of folk destructors Holy Modal Rounders, appeared.

Eventually, the neighbors complained about the noise. Scaled back to one quieter act and a movie (and projector) borrowed from a friend, the new Mumblin' Music for Dozens wasn't nearly as successful. The series concluded with a duo set by saxophonist John Zorn and guitarist Fred Frith. Ira booked a few shows at Maxwell's and spoke with the Bitter End, another Village folk-era holdout venue, about continuing Music for Dozens, but nothing came of it, and that was that for Ira the promoter.

The summer of 1983 held great promise in the basement of 719 Garden Street. In between the Dozens and late nights at Maxwell's, Ira hatched what seemed like an audacious scheme: to turn Georgia and Those Guys into an actual band. Terry Karydes and her Ohio friend Tony Blow, playing guitar, joined them in the cramped practice room, with a tape recorder perched on an amp. They acquired a new name, A Worrying Thing, after a quote from Baseball Hall of Fame spitballer Stan Covelski, and a new task: how to find a voice.

Earlier in the spring, Georgia and Ira had flown the $29 People Express to Boston to see the final show by Mission of

Burma. They couldn't find anyone to drive and, after Ira's shift at Maxwell's the night before, decided they had to go. They witnessed the frothing, stage-diving, all-ages Boston hard-core scene in full flight during the matinee. Ira had left his ID at home, a problem that posed no problems at the airport but required Burma drummer Peter Prescott to escort him into the late show, which wasn't all-ages.

Georgia and Ira's equally intense love of art-noise bands like Mission of Burma alongside perennial favorites NRBQ, the Kinks, and others, also underscored exactly the problem they had when they joined Terry and Tony in the basement. They were fans of too many bands to be attached to any one ap-proach to how music should sound. There was too much in their heads to embrace any one thing to the exclusion of all else. Plus, unlike most, they didn't need to be in a band to meet a potential mate. They just wanted to play music.

Once asked if being a female drummer had ever posed problems for her, Georgia replied, "If anything, it was being already 'grown up' and then deciding to be in a rock band that was an issue." Neither Georgia nor Ira seemed at first to pos-sess the usual fire required for a new group, and this quality—or its absence—resounded in their earliest music.

In addition to the hundred-plus songs rolling through their recent memories, A Worrying Thing continued to prac-tice covers. Ira and Tony attempted harmonies on the Kinks' "This Man He Weeps Tonight." Tony did the Dils' "Sound of the Rain," and they took on a batch of '60s pop obscurities, includ-ing Love's "A House Is Not a Motel," the Monkees' "The Door into Summer," the Rascals' "Find Somebody," Syd Barrett's "No Man's Land," and Everything Is Everything's "Witchi Tai To." There was also Parliament's "One Nation Under a Groove," soul songwriters Gamble and Huff's "Drowning in the Sea of Love," and a recent Waves B-side, "Hey, War Pig!" There was likewise a pair of songs popularized by the Weavers, Ira's Hudson Valley neighbors: a funkified run at "Darling Corey," and a similarly tarted-up version of the left-wing anthem "If I Had a Hammer," written by Pete Seeger and Lee Hays.

There were even the makings of a few original songs in the jangling folk-rock mold. One fragment was based on an appealingly cycling riff, its title later lifted from a typo when Ira had spotted an extra "o" in an advertisement, "Three Blocks from Groove Street." Most of their original efforts didn't distinguish themselves nearly as much. Ira continued to try.

"Once the originals started coming, they started coming pretty fast," Terry remembered. "Ira never ceased having ideas. We were learning how to play better and, together, learning how to sing and play at the same time. Ira started singing at the mike more. Georgia would sing a bit, but she was really quiet. I remember Ira sometimes encouraging her, sometimes nagging her, to sing."

The band practiced throughout the summer while Terry's new job at the sci-fi/fantasy paperback house Tor provided both Ira and Georgia with copyediting work. They played at Maxwell's on August 27, opening for the Cyclones, and again a week later amid the giant screens at Danceteria with Fred Brockman and Dave Schramm's Kinetics.

Ira would later dismiss A Worrying Thing as "timid folk-rock," but his brother Neil remembered it fondly. To Terry's dismay, the set also included all nine minutes of Bob Dylan's "Lily, Rosemary and the Jack of Hearts." Ira didn't miss a verse.

Fred Brockman disbanded the Kinetics within a few weeks after A Worrying Thing's first shows, and soon broke up with Terry. Feeling overwhelmed, Terry dropped out of A Worrying Thing too. And so after the first bassist, the first search for a bassist. Ira and Georgia asked Emily Hubley if she was interested. She went into the basement and tried to play along with a disco tape but couldn't get through a song.

They kept looking for ways to play. A brief dalliance came with Jon Klages, a softball friend who'd recently quit his post as guitarist for the Individuals. He'd toured with former Television guitarist Richard Lloyd and wanted to lead a new band of his own. They gigged a few times, again at Danceteria and Maxwell's, with Dioxin Field third baseman Dave Schramm on bass, and backed Klages on an EP for Coyote Records, *In a Dream*. *Jersey Beat* described it as "white soul" and noted the softball connection.

Perhaps owing to the return of the softball season, the musical lineup didn't last. Klages booted Ira and Georgia from his band, with Schramm moving into the guitar chair. It was not a clean break. Emily and friends were shooting a movie at 719 Garden Street called *In the Light of My Renaissance*. Jon Klages played the lead. Georgia was in it too, including a scene with Klages, to whom she was no longer speaking.

Byron Coley recounted, "To solve this problem, the filmmakers filled a burlap bag with dirt and when either Georgia or Jon were supposed to be talking to each other, the bag would be held just off-camera so that they could talk to it."

Back at square one, still without collaborators and unsure how they wanted to sound, Georgia and Ira took desperate measures. In a move that Ira later described as "closer to stand-up comedy or a Don Novello bit than a real attempt at finding musicians to play with," they placed an ad in the *Village Voice*: "Guitarist & bassist wanted for band that may or may not sound like the Soft Boys, Mission of Burma, and Love."

It was little wonder Gerard Cosloy was ready to escape the local hardcore scene. "[I] got the impression that you've outstayed your welcome in Boston," Andy Schwartz noted in a letter to his young correspondent, and advised the *Conflict* editor to head for college. Cosloy hadn't lasted at the University of Massachusetts, though, and by the spring of 1984, wound up behind the counter of Newbury Comics, Boston's main independent record shop. At nineteen, too, he was finally old enough to get into most local bars without hiding behind amps.

Many days, he put in time at Radiobeat, the small label founded by Lou Giordano and Jimmy Dufour, where Gerard helped with promotional mailings to zines and college radio stations. The label's Kenmore Square studio became a hub for local acts, including Gerard's friends in Deep Wound, a hardcore quartet that Cosloy fell in love with immediately. The night he moved into his Amherst dorm in September 1983, Gerard had justified his doomed presence on the campus when he met fellow freshman Joseph Mascis. Known as J, he was the introverted local longhair drummer for Deep Wound.

As biting in person as Gerard could be in print, the two became friends and Gerard began to feature the band regularly in *Conflict*, even managing them for a time. "He was fascinated with J's whole thing and he wrote about it really well," Deep Wound guitarist Lou Barlow observed to music journalist Michael Azerrad.

At Amherst, Gerard got a slot on WMUA and tried putting on concerts in the area, but a Flipper show ended in disaster when they were seven hours late. More than anything, the sole semester for the future dropout had been an interruption of an already busy life devoted to an all-abiding enthusiasm for music. Among the slowly linking Dozens, Gerard Cosloy's sometimes vitrolic glee had turned into a massively connective force and would only continue to be so.

In the months that had immediately followed his spring graduation from Concord Academy, he had spoken at the New Music Seminar (on a panel with rap producer Rick Rubin and Gerard's caustic zine-writing counterpart in Chicago, Steve Albini), booked Sonic Youth's first Boston show after reading about them in *Rocker*, continued to DJ on WZBC, and published the thirtieth issue of *Conflict*. Nearly as a matter of course, he flunked all of his courses and dropped out of UMass nearly instantly.

Radiobeat proved a far more useful education, as Gerard Cosloy absorbed how records got made, from the recording to printing and assembling the jackets. "They explained the process in really simple terms," Gerard said, and the label soon commissioned the *Conflict* editor to make a compilation of local bands, which Gerard did readily.

Released in the spring of 1984, that compilation, *Bands That Could Be God*, sewed together Gerard's local obsessions— favorite acts "not being picked up on by the movers and shakers of the Boston rock scene, not being chased by management, and not being booked." Others barely existed at all. One, Beanbag, was a "conceptual prankish high school art band with maybe two actual gigs under their belt." Another, Christmas, introduced traces of high kitsch into post-punk.

Gerard's sights were set far beyond the tempo- and rule-obsessed hardcore kids. That spring, Deep Wound had disbanded too, soon reforming as Dinosaur with Mascis on guitar and vocals, playing music that reflected the music Gerard had hipped him to from Los Angeles's Paisley Underground, such as True West and Dream Syndicate. That season, *Conflict* offered coverage to expected favorites like Hüsker Dü and the Replacements, but also post-jazz guitarist Fred Frith, Feelies spin-offs, and—like everybody else—R.E.M.

Available for $5 mail order and at local stores, by summer *Bands That Could Be God* had sold more than 1,500 copies and entered the Rockpool chart at #25. "'Bands' means bands," noted hardcore zine *Flipside* of Gerard's new compilation, not really sure how to describe it. "This is not a thrash compilation, there are slow bands, arty rock bands and at least four bands . . . that I would consider fast."

"Incredible as it may seem, certain grudges and squabbles (many of which existed only in the mind of your editor) will cease to occupy this magazine's space," Gerard promised in the editorial to *Conflict* #36. "What will change is the overall meanspirited and hateful nature of the past few issues," he vowed. *Conflict* had recently received national distribution, via the new zine distribution wing of Dutch East India Trading on Long Island, and it was time for a change.

The seriousness of the promise was slightly undercut when, on the following page, Gerard devoted a solid text column to lobbing insults at local reviewers who'd slighted *Bands That Could Be God*. "Most of these mental midgets seem to write the same review; 'most of this LP is hardcore, two of the bands aren't' as if that tells anyone anything about how the bands <u>sound</u>," Gerard wrote. But, on the other hand, it would also be more than a year until Gerard published *Conflict* #37. In the late summer, he found exactly his ticket out of Boston in the unlikely form of a Long Island man named Barry Tenenbaum.

Only in his late twenties when he hired Gerard Cosloy in the fall of 1984, Barry Tenenbaum seemed much older. In many ways, his company Dutch East India Trading resembled what "independence" had meant in the record industry up through at least the punk era, if not still: sort of fly-by-night, entrepreneurial, and decidedly off the map of the broader culture. Dutch East's origins lay in Lord Sitar Records, which the then-fourteen-year-old Barry Tenenbaum precociously established in order to import Beatles LPs from the United Kingdom and resell them to local record stores. He expanded the business as he schemed to acquire British pressings of domestically released albums and undercut their American distributors. When this practice was banned in 1976, he kept his record-store network intact and began to license albums he could sell exclusively to them, creating Homestead Records for this purpose in 1983.

Sam Berger, a former Boston scenester, ran the imprint at first, and connected Dutch East with Reflex, the new Minneapolis label operated by Hüsker Dü. He organized a zine distribution enterprise as well, which helped spread *Conflict* far beyond the Boston area. Eventually, he recommended Gerard as his successor, a position Gerard accepted enthusiastically.

In the fall of 1984, the not-yet-twenty-year-old Gerard Cosloy moved to Flushing, Queens, not far from Shea Stadium, and went to work for Barry Tenenbaum. He discovered later that four people had turned the job down before him.

At Maxwell's one night, Steve Fallon introduced Georgia and Ira to a new couple who had just moved to Hoboken from Kentucky and played bass and guitar. "You guys should start a band together," he told them.

Which was perhaps true, except that Tara Key and Tim Harris had just started one, and had played their first show as Antietam only a few weeks earlier at CBGB. As members of

Louisville's leading punk outfit, the Babylon Dance Band, they'd organized shows and built a local following but felt ready to make the leap from their hometown. After a few triumphant gigs at Maxwell's, not to mention a *Village Voice* cover story, Key and Harris moved to Hoboken in early 1984. They were married at City Hall by the mayor.

"Our wedding literally took forty-five seconds," Harris remembered. "He was about to say the vows when somebody started yelling from out in the hallway, 'Fuck you, Cappiello, if you don't open the door, I'm going to come in and kill you.'" The mayor excused himself, locked the door, and finished the ceremony.

The band Key and Harris assembled in Hoboken that summer was already powerful and unique. "Tara was just a force of nature," *Jersey Beat*'s Jim Testa recalled, "just this tiny thing with long hair and such an amazing, amazing guitar player." Her playing was underscored by the unexpected rumble of the double basses of Harris and Wolf Knapp, another Louisville expat. Tim and Tara joined the weekend softball games. Tara pitched while Tim took over at first base and fielded throws from Ira. The two couples would become lifelong friends, but Georgia and Ira were still without bandmates.

The *Village Voice* ads yielded a handful of responses, which in turn yielded a series of awkward jams in the Garden Street basement. "Most fall blissfully out of your head—until years later when somebody feels the need to remind you of their audition," Ira would later write. It had been a demoralizing few months when a pair of Long Island friends made their way to Hoboken.

Dave Rick and Jerry Smith had placed their own ad too: "Don't call if not into Void, Sonic Youth or Burma." When Rick spotted the name "Ira" and a Hoboken phone number in a *Voice* ad for a guitarist and bassist, he correctly guessed who was behind it. "I was excited," he said. "Ira had written the liner notes for the Bad Brains tape." Not only was Dave Rick a *New York Rocker* subscriber, but as a teen his walls had been plastered with images cut from its pages.

A recent dropout of SUNY Stony Brook, he was living in his VW bug, working at a photomat, and perusing the *Voice* for possible collaborators. With Dave on guitar and Jerry Smith on bass (through Ira's tie-dyed bass cabinet), the quartet ran through some songs—a slowly unwinding riff draft of Ira and Georgia's known as "Crispy Duck," and probably a Neil Young cover.

"They took our timid little folk-rock songs and ran them through their Void/Sonic Youth/Burma [filter]," Ira would write, "and the result was easily the most 'musical' thing we'd hear in our songs for months to come, but also too much for our timid folk-rock souls. Dave, sensitive fellow he, grasped the situation immediately and told us confidentially that he thought he could play the bass in the manner we were looking for. We said we'd keep him in mind."

Faith moved her animation studio into her new Bronx apartment in 1984, and Emily had just the thing. With a grant writer, the elder Hubley sister had written a proposal for an ambitious film called *The Tower* to be animated by her and Georgia, and had received $10,000 from the National Endowment for the Arts to make it. The girls raided their mother's supply closet and built the film with tools and paints that were about to be tossed.

Georgia and Emily holed up on the second floor of 719, where they spun a surreal story from Georgia's idea for a traditional cat-and-mouse cartoon. *The Tower*'s surreal plot turns and hand-drawn mood referenced *Cockaboody*, a 1973 Hubley production based on a recorded dialogue of Emily and Georgia that was made a year or so before *Windy Day*. The two spent months at work, listening to music and inking cels.

The girls' collaboration belied complex perspective changes and a variety of classical cartoon techniques while extending the whimsical dialogue of the family project. They held a screening at the Squat Theater in Chelsea, the New York home for many years to cosmic jazz bandleader Sun Ra, but didn't pursue distribution.

Georgia continued to paint, as well, showing her oil paintings at the Sidney Frane Gallery when Faith held a show. In the same way that Ira's natural instincts had led him first to journalism and a variety of other related music-obsessive jobs before taking up music himself, Georgia's visual gravitations would eventually fall by the wayside. But her very practical graphic skills and sensibilities learned from a lifetime as a Hubley, combined with an increasingly confident aesthetic sense, would shape her and Ira's new band—and life together—in cool, quiet ways.

Most immediately, she designed the new logo for Egon Records, a label the two formed that year. Georgia's subtly handwritten *EGON*, surrounded by two black rectangles, seemed of a piece both with Black Flag's iconic four-bar emblem and the '50s pop sensibility of her parents' commercial work. Named for Georgia's black cat, it was her and Ira's turn to get into the DIY-label game. By then, it wasn't too uncommon a move, the paths of distribution mapped out roughly by the forerunners Ira had been keeping track of for years.

Their first signee was the Raunch Hands, a garage act whose leader, Ben Vaughan, had played Music for Dozens. Titled "Stomp It!," depicting the band leaping into a giant pile of manure on the cover, the single featured a B-side cover of Ray Charles's "I Got a Woman." The Egon bosses had the record mastered at a place on lower Broadway and paid extra to watch the engineer cut the disc.

Guitarist Michael Mariconda worked at Venus Records on Eighth Street, where the single sold "by the bucket." Ira and Georgia got a list of zines and radio stations and did promotional mailings.

"Raunch Hands was a dream," Ira remembered. It was an uncharacteristically auspicious start. But the auditions for their own project weren't getting much better, and Ira and Georgia continued to look near and nearer for solutions. They asked Will Rigby if he wanted to front a new group. He demurred.

Still unable to find a bassist, Ira and Georgia remembered

the kid from Long Island. "Unfortunately, though we remembered what he wore the night we played with him—a Häagen-Dazs Rum Raisin T-shirt—we forgot his name and lost his phone number," Ira wrote. They crossed paths with Dave Rick again at Maxwell's and invited him back to 719 for more practices.

The first show was on a Sunday: December 2. Antietam played too. Being an off night, it was another party at Maxwell's, but it wasn't for somebody's birthday. Later, nobody could quite remember the occasion. Just as likely it was in celebration of the new band. Antietam's Tara Key made a flyer on a brand-new early Macintosh at the Columbia University library, where she worked. She made sure to spell Ira and Georgia's new band's name correctly: Yo La Tengo.

Dave Rick had been the spark, or at least the consistent bassist, they'd needed. Every weekend, he drove his yellow 1970 VW bug over the Williamsburg Bridge, through the Holland Tunnel, down the Observer Highway, and into Hoboken.

"It was a miraculous thing, a surprising thing, that Dave Rick came along," Ira remembered many years later. "He was the first person we'd met that we understood on a musical level. Looking back, it's kind of hard to believe that he could figure out what we wanted, because I'm not sure we could. So how did he know what we didn't?"

Getting ready for the show, Ira and Georgia were "very nervous." But Dave, who looked far younger than his twenty years, was a seasoned pro, relatively speaking. With chops to match his nearly manic outgoingness, Dave was—like Ira—an utter music obsessive. Unlike Ira, he'd played with everybody he possibly could from middle school on, doing originals with a group called the Four Noses and four sets of covers a night with a party band on occasion. As a *New York Rocker* reader, they shared plenty of common ground. Another upside was that Dave was also short enough to fit comfortably in the low-ceilinged basement.

"Ira didn't love being the only guitarist," Rick admitted, but his aggressive bass lines filled in a lot of gaps, drawn from a love of hard rock unshared by Ira, who asked Dave to explain Led Zeppelin to him. "Maybe Zeppelin were too sexy for them?" the bassist wondered. They differed on hardcore, too. Ira had loved the first Black Flag single, but couldn't stand them after Henry Rollins joined.

Yo La Tengo went on first. The back room was nearly full, filled with the cast of characters with whom they had unconsciously surrounded themselves. They opened with an instrumental by UCLA art-punks the Urinals, "Surfin' with the Shah," and followed it with the new original they'd tried with Dave and Jerry Smith a few months before, which is when Ira—briefly—found himself paralyzed. He got over it, and the band made it through the first set intact.

"By the second set, I was less petrified," Ira said later. "I learned very quickly that the notion that it'd be easier to play for your friends than for strangers was one hundred percent incorrect." But it was friends they had, and friends they would rely on.

There were a few more originals, too. "The Evil That Men Do" gave Ira a place to flail at his guitar a little bit—not quite soloing, and not quite building up a full wall of noise yet either, but taking a dramatic step past timid folk-rock. They kept at that, too, though, with the slow, chiming "The Pain of Pain." "The Forest Green" and "Another Carrot" both found places of their own on the spectrum, occasional dabbling in surf-rock sparseness.

Naturally, they covered the Kinks, with "Big Sky." Later in the evening, they were joined by Glenn Mercer of the Feelies, Dave doing a quiet fanboy freak-out, for the Psychedelic Furs' "Pretty in Pink" and the Velvet Underground's "White Light/ White Heat."

Though it was only their third gig, Antietam had it slightly more together, and via Steve Fallon they'd scored a plum slot opening for Hüsker Dü a few weeks later. It was the first of two shows at Maxwell's for the Minneapolis band, including New

Year's Eve. The trio was becoming something of a staple in Hoboken, helped by Steve's close friendship with Hüsker guitarist Bob Mould.

"We played Maxwell's in Hoboken [last night] and it's a two o'clock club," Mould told a zine writer earlier that fall. "We got out of there at quarter to seven in the morning. We stayed up all night with the owner and got plowed. We did shots for about four hours. I quit drinking last night. One of those nights."

In a few months, Hüsker Dü would ink a very respectable contract with Michael Hill's new boss, Karin Berg, at Warner Bros., and become the first band of the American underground to sign with a major label. They paved the way for many to come. Seeing Tara Key and Tim Harris open for the Hüskers at Maxwell's in December, Gerard Cosloy caught Antietam at their most primal and approached them that night about recording for Homestead.

For the time being, Yo La Tengo would go unsigned. They were hardly ready for that anyway. But Georgia, almost twenty-five, and Ira, about to turn twenty-eight, had a band. It was nerve-wracking, but it felt right. They planned more gigs.

Flyer for first Yo La Tengo show, with Antietam at Maxwell's, December 2, 1984 (Courtesy of Tara Key)

CHAPTER 6

Yo La Tengo

Ira convinced Steve Fallon to donate a month of otherwise unused Wednesdays to the cause and, in March 1985, Yo La Tengo and Antietam took up residency. They charged $1, alternated sets, and took turns manning the door. Audiences were sparse, but there was a regular crowd.

Emily Hubley scored nearly perfect attendance. "I would enjoy it and feel mad at the people who would walk in and walk out, come in from the main room and check it out, and walk back out," she remembered. "I felt very protective, then wouldn't understand what their problem was that they'd be so judgmental or close-minded."

"Antietam were pretty raw," remembered Craig Marks, Ira's competition for shortstop at Dioxin Field who worked with Gerard Cosloy at the Dutch East India Trading. "They never *weren't* raw, but they were really raw those days. They were pretty jagged. Yo La Tengo were a traditional rock band in a lot of ways."

But Yo La Tengo were plagued by traditional rock-band problems too. And for the new band, even normal rock-band nervousness seemed exaggerated to near traumatic effect. For all his time spent around bands, Ira had failed to observe the handiness of securing a backup guitar. "Yeah, they were awful," remembered Jim DeRogatis, a teenage contributor to *Jersey Beat*. "The whole show would break down every time Ira broke a string, and he'd have to sit on the lip of the Maxwell's stage to change it."

Gerard Cosloy caught at least two of the shows and would wonder if Ira and Georgia "had any sort of grip on their instruments." "I was hardly the sort of person to be nitpicky," he said later, "but the level of musicianship was not exceptional at that point in time." Which was also the point of the shows—to find some chops and get some footing.

By the time of the residency, Georgia and Ira's setlist was composed of more than half original songs for the first time. It was the beginning of a long road, each new tune another small step, looking for a corner. Bands from Hoboken were hardly a new fad, and—to the outside observer—that is all Yo La Tengo were in the spring of 1985, another act born from the thriving scene around Maxwell's with midtempo rock songs that jangled when needed, melodies that spurned easy hooks, had clever lyrics, and a diffident singer who occasionally stirred himself into a small frenzy while writhing around with a guitar.

But in lives where shows and new releases marked time, the past spread out in tangled histories of the musicians they adored. Georgia and Ira now had their own adventures to go by, like when they played at a retro-style diner in Passaic, owned by friends of the Feelies, and Dave Rick had to sit in front of Creeping Pumpkins drummer Dave Weckerman's kick drum so it didn't slide away. They debuted in Manhattan at CBGB on March 30 (advertised in the *Voice* as "Yolo Tango"), and ventured tentatively as far as New Haven and farther into New Jersey for the occasional show.

Their repertoire of originals grew slowly throughout the spring as Ira changed the setlist with an obsessive fan's compulsion, keeping track of what they played at each show. "Looks may be deceiving," Ira insisted to zine writer Dave Sprague in a *Matter* feature that summer about new Hoboken acts, their first national press. "We're not the most slap-happy band on-stage, but we do like it a lot more than it looks."

If anything, they sometimes seemed to be taking their new band too seriously. For people who liked things to be *right*, the toughness had a tendency to spiral. "It was like paying to see my sister's first dance recital," Charles Aaron wrote in the *Village Voice* a few years later. "Hubley's hands were shaking so much she played a paradiddle every time she laid down her sticks."

The band didn't have to transport their gear far to record, just a few blocks southeast to Hoboken's own Water Music, the studio funded by injury settlement money from a drunk-driving accident. It had quickly become a requisite stop for nearly every local band. Perhaps predictably, Steve Fallon's hands were in it peripherally, going in with the Water Music guys, Chris Stamey, and Antietam on a top-of-the-line Scully 100 2-inch tape machine à la EMI's Abbey Road. Antietam traded their share for recording time for their first album.

But like the stage, the studio proved to be a worrying thing for Yo La Tengo when they entered Water Music to record their Egon Records debut, even with friends around. When Mofungo drummer and former *New York Rocker* art director Chris Nelson showed up with his trombone to add horn parts, Ira was flustered to discover that Nelson didn't actually know how to play the instrument, despite performing with it regularly onstage.

"Well, Ira, it's nice of you to invite me, and I'm happy to be here," Nelson told him, "but I can't do anything other than what I do, which is to just start blowing into the trombone. I don't know where any of the notes are."

"Oh, gee," Ira replied. "I don't think I'd take up an instrument if I didn't know where the notes are." With the Raunch Hands' Mike Tchang on saxophone, the two somehow worked out a horn part for the single's A-side, "The River of Water," a piece of concise folk-pop somewhat reminiscent of Dylan's *Blonde on Blonde*. It was packed with melody, though had no chorus to speak of other than an elliptical refrain about "the little lies of time."

Nelson's and Tchang's presence was the product of a needling urge to tinker that defined Yo La Tengo's working methods, a daily piece-by-piece mulling over of how one was to find a correct and musically appealing expression of his or her self. Songs were scrapped, revisited, tossed, and revised again. It would be nearly a decade before they set down "Crispy Duck," in a wholly transformed setting. And it would be long after that before they worked with horns again. It wasn't that they were tentative as much as careful.

Another studio experiment was far more satisfactory: the addition of softball pal and former Kinetics guitarist Dave Schramm, a brilliant player whose country licks instantly colored Ira's changes with inventive new phrasings. "Just to sound like a band was very exciting," Ira remembered. "Dave had a way of making us sound better than we were."

For the flip, they recorded Arthur Lee's "A House Is Not a Motel," from Love's *Forever Changes*. The gnarled false-ending jam became the band's first outlet for noise, and the one spot in the band's stage show where one might sense that Ira Kaplan was, in fact, enjoying himself. Though not ready to solo yet, he'd become comfortable enough onstage to let himself go, attacking his Stratocaster as he bent and straightened his mild frame in a motion that more than one person compared to the incessant pecking of a desktop drinking bird.

At first, it seemed like Egon Records had another success on its hands. Will Rigby had shared some recordings he'd made in the dB's practice space, where he was living at the time, with Ira and Georgia. Emboldened by the reception they'd had with the Raunch Hands single, Ira and Georgia asked a surprised Will if they could release his recordings as an LP.

With the drummer from a hot—or at least known—New York band, stores ordered a number of copies of Will Rigby's

Sidekick Phenomenon. Georgia laid out the cover. They placed ads in *Matter*, a Chicago zine that had relocated to Hoboken and gone national, an increasingly common move in the concise and unequivocal world of indie rock circa 1984. Ira picked up some copyediting work from them. They planned for more Egon releases.

But the end of Egon Records came comically. One day, copies of *Sidekick Phenomenon* started showing up in the mailbox at 719 Garden Street . . . and didn't stop. "We literally didn't know about returns," Ira said, "and unsold copies *flew* back. That was a real lesson."

Perhaps expecting something more like the dB's, few who heard *Sidekick Phenomenon* reacted positively. "Funny shit," read the entirety of one Spiñal Tap–like zine review, "but shit." Yo La Tengo would sell *Sidekick Phenomenon* alongside their own merchandise well into the 1990s, and songs from it quickly entered the band's repertoire, which never ceased to take on new covers. They scrapped all future Egon plans save their own single, which was about ready to go.

"The River of Water" 7-inch disappeared down the pipes of a few distributors, including Important and Dutch East, and did moderately well. It scored a blurb in *Spin*, John Leland noting the band's transformation of "an almost tangible Big Star obsession, a slide guitar, and way too many words into a sharply unaffected pair of rockers."

Pleased with how they sounded with Schramm's sea-foam green Stratocaster and lap steel, they officially asked him to join the group. He agreed. His Midwestern reserve and dry humor fit nicely next to Ira and Georgia, and—besides lead guitar—his soulful and polished playing provided something else the pedal-less Ira couldn't yet muster, for lack of gear, chops, and confidence: atmosphere.

Ira inherited a hand-me-down Buick station wagon from his parents—brown, wood paneling—and booked the band's first proper out-of-town weekend in Boston in mid-June. The Friday gig with the Turbines was fun enough. The band got carded onstage and Ira and Georgia crashed with Byron Coley. The next afternoon, Schramm and Ira caught the Red Sox–Blue Jays game at Fenway Park.

When Ira compiled a list of the twelve worst Yo La Tengo shows for a *Rolling Stone* piece, he would stress that the worst gigs were the ones that slipped from memory, the boring nights that added nothing to their lives. He ran chronologically through his setlist collection and stopped before he escaped the 1980s. Raconteurs with broad senses of fate, Georgia and Ira found some value in even a miserable gig, as anecdote or edification.

Their second show in Boston, at Down Under in Government Center, would be the first entry on that *Rolling Stone* list. There were Jonathan Richman jokes to make, but both other acts canceled. The band played badly. Dave Rick missed a cue and messed up a song. It rained on the way home and Ira yelled at him.

As was his signature, Dinosaur's J Mascis set up his towering amps on the Maxwell's stage and turned them up beyond belief, his voice and increasingly classic rock–sounding songwriting drowned in a wall of distortion while his long hair obscured his face. During the soundcheck, Ira grew exasperated. "You guys have really good songs," he told the band. "You really should turn down. You can't hear anything you're doing."

"They were wearing earplugs!" he noted later. "I didn't realize that was an option! Obviously guitar amps turned up to that volume sound amazing. If I had known I could have worn earplugs, we would have gotten along better." Gerard Cosloy had brought them in, and they would sign to Homestead quickly. Steve Albini's Big Black was on the bill too. Ditto Dave Rick's new band, Phantom Tollbooth. He'd dropped out of Yo La Tengo a few months earlier, tired of the commute to Hoboken and ready to pursue the band he and Jerry Smith had wanted all along.

Maxwell's saw the cream of the new bands, Ira behind the soundboard. The Minutemen came through again. From Seattle came Green River, the new Homestead signees who would eventually spawn Mudhoney and Pearl Jam. It was all an impressive bubble to exist inside of, removed from the pressures of anything resembling the real music industry.

It seemed like an eternity since Blondie had topped the chart three times in one year, between April 1980 and March 1981, the period during which Ira and Georgia met and got together and New York rock's last gasp at a pop breakthrough. But it had been four years. What small amount of guitar-oriented music appeared on the chart in 1985 was, with few exceptions, so far removed from what was going on at Maxwell's as to seem like caricature, no more so than when Ira's teenage favorites Jefferson Airplane morphed into the barely recognizable Starship and scored a #1 hit with "We Built This City"—a song about rock and roll that sounded nothing like the rock and roll that happened a few nights a week at 1039 Washington.

Steve Fallon ran the place with manic energy, fueled by booze, coke, and the buzz of the new rising bands coming through. The cameras came to Washington Street and for a time, at the end of the summer, Yo La Tengo was in heavy rotation on MTV. Or Georgia was anyway. For a millisecond.

Local filmmaker John Sayles had brought Bruce Springsteen and the E Street Band to Maxwell's back room, rearranged it entirely, and shot a hit video there for Springsteen's "Glory Days." Georgia and Ira were extras in the crowd, and one frame caught Georgia in the same shot as the Boss. Tim and Tara captured a video still and printed it out for them. It sounded a little more like rock and roll as recognized at Maxwell's—after all, Springsteen was a regular at Max's Kansas City—but not by much.

Then, a local television station, WNYW, sent a crew to shoot a half hour news segment on the scene featuring Maxwell's, Water Music, and a montage of musicians crediting Steve Fallon. Chris Stamey put forward the caffeine-in-the-air-making-everyone-peppy theory. Also featured were the Feelies. Gradually, the abstract instrumentals turned into songs, and they decided to start singing the old Feelies tunes, as well. They never quit with the Velvet Underground, Television, and Brian Eno covers. They became the Feelies again and started to record and tour.

"At its worst, the business part of bringing new music to the mass market can burn through bands in bunches," alliterated the mustachioed WNEW reporter. The program was called "The Hoboken Sound."

"Some groups jump right into that big-time dream machine, only to discover a world of magnetic madness that can scramble everything from their music to their molecules, if they'll let it. But here in Hoboken, the feeling seems to be, 'Hey, it's only rock and roll, and that's good enough for me.'" There was no sign of Yo La Tengo in the program.

Late 1985 marked the last major burst for the Hoboken music world that had started at Maxwell's. The Bongos released their second and final album for RCA, while Glenn Morrow assembled a new band, Rage to Live, whose self-titled debut became the first release for a new label called Bar/None, which had sprouted in the Pier Platters basement.

The attention and activity was a microcosm of what was going on nationally with indie bands and indie scenes. Both the Replacements and Hüsker Dü made national television appearances. MTV aired *The Cutting Edge*, a video show funded by I.R.S. Records and hosted by Fleshtones frontman Peter Zaremba, and was itself preparing for the early 1986 launch of *120 Minutes*, a program that would radically alter the landscape for what was increasingly being called "college rock" for the home it found on university radio stations. R.E.M. toured incessantly. So did Black Flag, who sold some quarter-million records through their SST label, which was pumping out classics—including double LPs by the Minutemen and Hüsker Dü on the same day—but also endless, unmarketable vanity projects.

Steve Fallon's Coyote Records, too, had big news: a distribution deal with Twin/Tone. The Twin Cities label had been cofounded by Peter Jesperson, the former manager of Minneapolis's Oar Folkjokeopus, where *Rocker* editor Andy Schwartz had once clerked and which anchored the thriving local scene led by the Replacements and Hüsker Dü. The label shared an office building with both bands and had figured out strong routes into the US market, selling some 42,000 copies of the Replacements' *Let It Be*. A *Rolling Stone* article that summer estimated Twin/Tone's gross at some $300,000 a year, although they were undeniably in the red. Their involvement with Coyote would bring Maxwell's house label to far more stores nationwide. Steve passed the day-to-day operations of Coyote over to Glenn Morrow, who found an office in Manhattan.

The first release of the new arrangement was a single by Dreams So Real, an Athens, Georgia, band produced by R.E.M.'s Peter Buck. In the fall came a new compilation of Hoboken music, appropriately titled *Luxury Condos Coming to Your Neighborhood Soon*. The album featured the latest crop of Hobokenites—*New York Rocker* refugees (Glenn Morrow's Rage to Live), Feelies and dB's spin-offs (the Trypes, the Jacks, Mr. Bonus), Yo La Tengo roommates (Peter Moser, drumming with Myra Holder), and two Egon recording artists: the Raunch Hands, and Yo La Tengo themselves, the latest signees to Coyote.

They contributed their leftover song from the Water Music session, "Private Doberman," and received the now-requisite typo when the LP's sticker listed it as "Private Dalmatian." In the gatefold, they lean on a car on Garden Street, Dave Rick looking like a kid.

The search for a bassist this time was short. His name was Mike Lewis and he lived across the street. But the process was already routine. It was an existential grind that Ira and Georgia would endure into the next decade, pieces moving in and out of a band not quite on the cusp of making it.

For his part, Mike Lewis had always dreamed of playing in

a band where he wouldn't have to lug anything by train, bus, or car to get to practice. In Boston, he had played in DMZ and the Lyres, two explosive garage-punk bands that Ira and Georgia loved, led by the fanatical record collector and (in Lewis's words) "difficult at best" frontman Mono Mann Conolly. Lewis's preferred style of music was dance-driven R&B, the type championed by Mono Mann, the Fleshtones, the Raunch Hands, and Billy Miller and Miriam Linna's A-Bones, whom Lewis also joined on his recent move from Boston to Hoboken.

"The few gigs we got were total lunacy," remembered Lewis, who maintained a day job as a pharmaceutical chemist in central New Jersey. The offer from Ira to play across the street was too good to pass up. After "the sheer disorganization and thuggishness that characterized Boston through the late '70s and early '80s," Yo La Tengo was Lewis's dream come true.

"Ira was really organized. That was shocking to me. Not only did I not have to do anything organization-wise, I just had to play bass, but things actually happened on time. That, too, was a real shock to me. I never played with people who could do that. Georgia and Ira were really tight. There was no undercurrent of that political crap that usually happens in bands."

Another surprise for Mike was Yo La Tengo's willingness to take on garage-rock songs. A knock that Yo La Tengo would sometimes receive in later years was their lack of commitment to specific sound and dalliances with many. But for Yo La Tengo, it became second nature, a flexibility built in an unplanned way from an ever-rotating cast of players.

Mike also got a firsthand look at another characteristic that defined Yo La Tengo: their sheer wholesomeness. "Because I was across the street, I was always early for practice, and I'd end up talking to them. Many times, I'd get there, and Ira and Georgia would be eating their dinner and watching *Wheel of Fortune*. They were really into puzzles and games, and they'd just eat dinner and be able to really quickly guess the answers, much quicker than what I could figure out what was going on."

Dave Rick had attended a party at 719 Garden Street

around the time of his tenure in the band. "They were playing charades," he remembered.

Sometimes, Mike Lewis would wander the house. For all their trepidation about being in a band, Georgia and Ira had built themselves a comfortable life. "The walls were covered with records," Mike said. "There was no wall space; it was just floor to ceiling. I remember wondering if the walls could support the weight of the records."

The road was still another story as the band pushed (slightly) westward during a weekend in Pittsburgh and Columbus. The Pittsburgh show—at a skinhead club called the Electric Banana—made the all-time-worst-gigs list. "Cognoscenti could challenge this show's appearance on the list," Ira wrote, "because at no time did the owner pull a gun on us."

Ira's brother Adam landed in Hoboken after college and inquired nearly daily at Pier Platters about the arrival of *Luxury Condos*. He'd met Georgia for the first time at the softball game, which he joined, awestruck by the musicians. "There were a lot of cool sunglasses," he remembered. Late summer in Hoboken was always filled by the Feast of Madonna Dei Martiri, which involved copious fireworks in the streets.

"For three days, it was like bombs exploding," Adam said. "You'd kind of get battle fatigue. It was window-rattling. Every year around that time you'd have yuppies writing letters to the editor of the *Hoboken Reporter* saying, 'This has got to stop,' and you'd have the locals writing back saying, 'Well, go away, this is our culture, we didn't ask you to move here.' You know, '*Fuck you.*'"

Adam also scored a brief, disastrous job at Dutch East India Trading, where Homestead Records had fast become a portal between Hoboken and the world at large, on par with *New York Rocker* as a place that collected soon-to-be insiders. Barry Tenenbaum had moved to a warehouse in Rockville Centre, and hot new imports, product from dozens of tiny American labels, and bushels of zines towered outside the small office where Gerard Cosloy operated Homestead. If there were literal nerve centers to the new independent music in the United States, they were places like Dutch East, ready to redistribute the work of hundreds of bands on dozens of tiny labels and fire new music across the continent.

With a year under his belt at Homestead, Cosloy revived *Conflict* and got around to reviewing the *Luxury Condos* compilation with typical flare. "A mixed-bag all the way around," he made sure to note, "which I can respect even 'tho much of this album only has me shaking my head as to HOW ANY-BODY W/ AN OUNCE OF BRAINS could tolerate some of this, in partic., tracks by Gut Bank ('bout as emotionally gripping as any Jimmy McNichol movie) . . . cool stuff however from Yo La Tengo, the Trypes, Raunch Hands and the previously unknown-who-the-fuck-are-they Deep Six."

In the cramped Homestead office, Cosloy was joined by Craig Marks, who'd been playing softball so competitively at Dioxin Field that he once had his arm broken in a home-plate collision with the Kinetics' Fred Brockman. Marks doubled in the sales department upstairs, where a crew stayed in touch with record stores around the region, convincing them to stock Dutch East product. One account that didn't need much argument was Pier Platters and, a few times a week, Marks stacked records in his car and dropped them off en route home.

"There was nothing not modest about the entire operation," Marks remembered of the office's decor and attitude. Barry Tenenbaum's father, "this doddering accountant guy," worked upstairs with his son, too, and maintained the Beatles mail-order business, Lord Sitar Records, that started it all. On each record sleeve there appeared a small notice of possession— "℗ LSR Records, Inc."

Though he barely lasted the summer, Adam Kaplan fondly remembered the afternoon Gerard was left to write notes for the sales department about the newest records. "They were total Gerard-style, why a record was a piece of shit." Adam laughed. "Very well-written, fast, cantankerous, smart. The head of sales was not amused that this is what we were given to work from. I feel like he missed the point. If you were smart, you could take Gerard ripping something to shreds and completely get the information you needed about who would want it in their stores."

It was one of the first signs of an adversarial relationship that developed within Dutch East between a staff of record collectors and an upper management that seemed like grownups from another planet. On the back end, signs of sketchiness emerged from the upstairs office. "My favorite retarded trick is he would make the numeral and literal amounts of the check different, so our bank couldn't cash it," remembered Big Black's Steve Albini, an early signee with the label. "It was like dealing with a small child who's trying to hide cookies under his pillow. I'm sure it did earn him a small aggregate profit, being so duplicitous about everything. But it seems like so much work to be that devious about small amounts of money. You can't have a mistake on every single statement without it being intentional. It's impossible. Just by chance, you'd get one of them right, you know?"

Gerard released the first Dinosaur LP and Sonic Youth's *Bad Moon Rising* (and booked their first national tour on the side). Homestead put out discs by New York gloomsters Swans, post–Mission of Burma Boston rockers Volcano Suns, Kentucky noise precisionists Squirrel Bait, Australian mainstays Nick Cave and the Bad Seeds, and Seattle ground zero outfit Green River. Cosloy and Marks were the label's only two employees, and they dealt with the administrative and marketing duties. Gerard etched music critics' names into the run-off grooves of promotional LPs and checked the used record stores in Greenwich Village to see who was selling them back.

"I guess I was trying to document the entire national scene as it was at a certain time, and how I thought the sounds were all interlinked," he would observe. "To my mind, there was this overlap between all the bands who just created themselves and weren't influenced by what was currently on radio and television. They were bands who had a traditional rock lineage but that was a little hard to trace . . . that fit in some thin gap, as it were, between Ray Davies and Thurston Moore."

As winter came on, Yo La Tengo loaded the Buick and headed twenty minutes into deeper New Jersey for their first radio appearance. Naturally, the engagement came via Maxwell's. Frank O'Toole, a bartender there, had been a student at Upsala College in East Orange, twelve miles west of Hoboken, and got a slot on the student radio station WFMU. Ten years later and long after his graduation, he was still on the air. WFMU was like that.

The appearance on O'Toole's show was hardly memorable. They were one of a cavalcade of local bands that passed through, but it was the first tendril of what would become a unique and fruitful relationship with the station over the coming decades. At the time, it signified something even more immediately important to their success: their entrance to college radio.

During "The Hoboken Sound" news segment a few months earlier, radio personality Pat St. John, introduced as a "top jock" and sporting a transcendent walrus mustache, explained why bands from Hoboken didn't get played on WPLJ, one of Manhattan's biggest stations that was completing its transition to the contemporary hit radio format at the time.

"The things that get on the air are gonna be big hits," St. John said. "And if it doesn't look like they're gonna be, they're not gonna be on the air very long, that's it." He shrugged and offered a half smirk. "We're there to play hits. It's great to give a break to whoever you can, but you can't do it, just, like, 'I like you, I'm gonna give you a break'; it's not like that.

"It's what's gonna *make it*, and what the public's gonna like. Hopefully they'll make it, 'cause they're making some good records, but again, there's all kinds of stuff that goes into it. From record sales to research. What goes into it, it's incredible."

What St. John meant by "research," probably, was the so-called indie promoters who had evolved out of tip sheets like Kal Rudman's *Friday Morning Quarterback* and functioned as middlemen in a system of payola that had CBS Records alone paying out an estimated $8 to $10 million annually. Even without the bribery, though, it is hardly a stretch to say that the avid Maxwell's goer would snicker right back at St. John and argue that the ideal world is one in which DJs played songs because they liked them.

By the mid-1980s, college radio had developed into a nearly de facto promotional outlet for the post-punk underground. In turn, the *College Music Journal*'s charts—as well as their annual summer conference—ballooned in importance. Just a few weeks before Yo La Tengo's appearance on WFMU, MTV telecast CMJ's New Music Awards from the uptown Beacon Theatre. They hosted Andy Warhol and U2, and honored R.E.M. for *Fables of the Reconstruction*, which had just broken all college radio chart records. The Athens quartet performed at the end of the night, joined by two of the Bangles and dB's guitarist Peter Holsapple.

If Yo La Tengo was to find any success, the path would almost unquestionably include college radio. And WFMU was, for all intents and purposes, the local college station. It had started as exactly that, going on the air in 1958. For its first decade, WFMU hummed along like a pleasant radio station at a pleasant Lutheran university, broadcasting six hours a day, five days a week. At least until November 1967, when an Upsala student named Vin Scelsa secured an all-night Saturday slot, in Scelsa's words, "without really anyone's permission."

He played folk, rock, and whatever else he felt like. At the end of May 1968, while students elsewhere rioted and held sit-ins, the Upsala campus remained conveniently empty and WFMU became the first full-time freeform station on the East Coast. The first fund-raising Marathon followed immediately to raise $3,000 so the station could stay on the air during summer vacation.

"Find some outrageous people in New York who are doing really interesting things," Larry Yurdin, a producer at WBAI for freeform pioneer Bob Fass, told Scelsa. "You don't have many college kids on the air anyway; it's just whoever wanders in. There's no reason not to recruit amazing people. They'll work for free—they'll take the public-service bus out to Jersey— because they can build a following for whatever it is they're doing."

"Freeform essentially means breaking down the boundaries of music, which the musicians themselves are doing," Scelsa told the *Upsala Gazette*, "so that there is no longer anything called jazz, folk, or classical. It's all being molded together. So that a 'new progressive rock group' may be influenced by the music of Bach. It may be influenced by the Indian music of Ravi Shankar. It may be influenced by old ragtime music."

By 1969, the station reached—according to a contemporary estimate by Scelsa—around 60,000 listeners. Other DJs included Lou "The Duck" D'Antonio (a comic holdover from the pre-freeform days), as well as Bob Rudnick and Dennis Frawley. The latter two named their Friday-night show *Kokaine Karma* after their *East Village Other* column, and soon relocated to the MC5's Trans-Love Energies commune in Michigan. Danny Fields, the Warhol associate who acted as "company freak" at Elektra Records and helped sign protopunk bands the Stooges and the MC5, held a slot five nights a week. Iggy Pop's 1969 visit to WFMU was later depicted in their "Great Moments in WFMU History" trading-card set with the title "Raw Power All Over Scelsa's Shoes."

But, the revolution being what it was, Scelsa and D'Antonio— who feared administration takeover and the demise of the counterculture—shut down WFMU in August 1969. Ten months later, the station was back on the air. Eventually it moved into a phase of—in one account—"experimenting with tape loops, political speeches, and six-day Marathon readings of *The Lord of the Rings*."

Tuning in to the station in 1974, local teenager Irwin Chusid, who remembered WFMU's halcyon days, "couldn't believe how awful it was. I mean, it was just *atrocious*. What I heard on FMU were a bunch of guys in the studio at once, four or five guys with one mike. One of the guys would be on the mike and he'd be carrying on a conversation with other people in the room, but you couldn't hear what they were saying. You just heard, 'Yeah, so, what'd you think of that concert we went to last weekend?'

"'Helwjekwhehe.'

"'Yeah, yeah remember?'

"And then, 'Youhdlhdsa.' It was like that. A lot of that. It was embarrassing."

In his last act before he stepped down, station manager Bruce Longstreet gave Chusid a DJ slot. Chusid went on the air in February 1975. "I was committed to taking advantage of programming liberty from the start," he said, and aired music by microtonal inventor Harry Partch, exotica bandleader Martin Denny, Miles Davis, spoken-word poet Ken Nordine, blues singer Moses Allison, Leonard Cohen, and British odd-ball Robert Wyatt. He played children's records, old 78s, and "found audio artifacts, obscurities, oddities, and abnormalities."

"I disregarded categories and dispensed with consistency. The show was programmed in real-time, with no advance planning. I did longer monologues and read articles and short stories on the air, and hosted the occasional live guest."

Chusid thought it time for another revolution. He entered what he later described as "preemptive propaganda mode— get to new staff before old staff got to them" and distributed memos. In one, written in June 1978, he wrote, "It behooves me to scream out once and for all what free-form radio—in fact what the medium of *radio itself*—is not. It is not *Music*, however varied and intelligently programmed. Radio, especially of the free-form variety, certainly *includes* music. But contrary to what 'progressive' radio folk would have you believe, there isn't much creativity in just playing recorded music. Any laboratory ape can do it with varying degrees of appeal."

By 1980, Chusid estimates the blend of comrades and straights at the station was "half and half," and changing fast. Some DJs, like Frank O'Toole and the noise-loving psychonaut

William Burger, were Upsala students. Many more weren't. New station manager Ken Freedman arrived from Ann Arbor's WCBN in 1983 and quickly bonded with Chusid. He was twenty-six years old when he started, but within a decade Freedman's hair would turn completely white.

Though major labels had tried to advertise to college radio during the "enlightened capitalism" rush of the late '60s, they virtually abandoned it over the next decade. In 1980, some even began to charge college stations a subscription fee in order to receive promotional records, all but dismissing their ability to break new artists. "The trick is to 'sell' your college station to the record companies, student broadcasters attending the Nov. 14–16 Loyola National Radio Conference learned," *Billboard* reported that year.

Around the country, commercial radio playlists began to standardize. Old standbys crumpled. In 1979, KSAN in San Francisco abandoned freeform, and Infinity Broadcasting purchased WBCN in Boston and shifted it to become more commercial within a few years. Many stations adopted Selector software, invented by Andrew Economos in 1979, to determine what to air based on tempo, performers, and local Arbitron ratings. Soon enough, the company branched into automating the stations themselves.

Like pregentrified cities, college radio stations were places where independently produced music stood a fighting chance in the hands of whatever motley crew had fallen into life around the campus DJ booth.

By the time Yo La Tengo descended into the basement at Froeberg Hall for their first session on WFMU, more significantly, they had songs worth playing. The work the band was putting in began to pay off. Dave Schramm had a few numbers of his own. Ira had a few more, including "The Asparagus Song," with lyrics by Emily, and "Did I Tell You," soon to be Yo La Tengo's first straightforward love ballad, just as soon as Ira finished it.

Performed for the first time at WFMU, Ira had completed the song's melody, but it took a bit longer to get the words right. His stand-in nonsense lyrics would last for over a year, and the up-tempo arrangement even longer, but it was the sole original of the band's early repertoire to survive well into the next century.

Boston was cold. All but Mike Lewis, a Boston native, stayed with Byron Coley and his girlfriend. Byron made them "a strange rice dish," as Dave Schramm remembered it. He'd been living there for a few years, coediting the dense and essential *Forced Exposure* zine, which would soon evolve into an important music distributor itself, and kept up with Yo La Tengo by cassette. By day, Yo La Tengo headed to Newton and its White Dog studios, nestled in the basement of a stand-alone suburban house, to record their first album.

Clint Conley was as helpful as could be. The former Mission of Burma bassist had all but retired to a life as a public television producer when Ira called and asked if he wanted to oversee Yo La Tengo's debut full-length for Coyote. He visited them for a practice at Garden Street, where he helped them choose a Kinks cover to include ("Big Sky" over "God's Children") and corrected the chords.

And when Coyote couldn't pony up the money for the studio bill on time, Conley was able to help out there, too. "They were clearly new musicians," he recalled. "I had no idea what a producer did. We were very polite with each other, gingerly walking the territory, making sure we weren't doing anything too offensive to the other party."

There was almost zero reverberation on the drums, a remarkable rarity in an era when kits were made to sound like they were in stadiums. They paid tribute to the Feelies with a cover of "The Empty Poor" by Coyote labelmates Yung Wu, a Feelies iteration led by percussionist Dave Weckerman. *Ride the Tiger* was, in some ways, the sound of good taste alone.

What the songs lacked in distinction, the band made up for in creative and tactful arrangements. For the first time, Georgia sang, adding backing vocals to "Big Sky" and "The Pain of

Pain." "I wanted Georgia to sing more; I loved her vocals!" producer Clint Conley remembered. "Just getting her to sing background on one song was really, really difficult. She didn't want anybody to look at her."

Eventually, they found a screen and put Georgia behind it. Singing incredibly quietly and later turned up in the mix—but not too much—she began to fit her voice into Yo La Tengo. Dave and Ira traveled back to Boston for a second round of overdubs. The day of the *Challenger* spacecraft disaster, seen on Byron's television, burned itself into Schramm's memory.

The pair returned to Hoboken in the Buick in a bitter freeze, the shotgun passenger's feet on the dashboard to keep warm. When they pulled onto Garden Street, Ira ran inside so quickly he didn't notice his wallet had fallen into the street, where they found it the next day when they moved the car.

Clint Conley, who hadn't played bass since Mission of Burma's disbandment in 1983, had agreed to join Yo La Tengo for a gig at CBGB in late February. He'd added bass to the last few tracks they'd recorded, after Mike dropped out of the band between sessions in Boston, needing to devote more time to his day job. This time, Gerard Cosloy got it. "We find Yo La Tengo on the brink of something pretty awesome," he noted in *Conflict* a few weeks later.

"Some songs here the likes of Dumptruck 'r the Neats would slay their parents to be able to write. Despite the absence of a fulltime bass player (temp. fill-in Clint 'flannel' Conley did OK considering he had a mere one rehearsal under his belt) this bunch are as loose and confident onstage as anyone's got a right to be . . . while Yo La Tengo may not exactly be gushing w/ stage presence, there's enough personality between 'em to keep me plenty interested. Volcano Suns and Antietam also played pretty well tonight, but I don't know if it was karma or what 'cause Yo La Tengo outclassed both of 'em (no easy feat)."

Georgia designed the new album's cover, using a favorite bit of clip art of a saber-tooth tiger skeleton she'd featured on a Music for Dozens flyer. There was another laudatory *Conflict* notice and polite write-up in *Jersey Beat*, but the rock press devoted little ink to *Ride the Tiger*. "The type of rock 'n' roll that gets you all fired up to proofread some copy," Rob Sheffield later wrote dismissively in *Spin*.

Bassist number five was tall, skinny, dressed in black, and Swiss. He wore his pants high and played his bass high as well. He was also nearly silent, his six-foot frame folded into the backseat of the Buick as Yo La Tengo drove south for their first real tour. They had a booking agent now, Frank Riley, who set them up for a two-week loop down to South Carolina opening for Camper Van Beethoven, through Nashville, and home by way of Ohio to promote *Ride the Tiger*.

"He didn't speak much," Ira remembered of number five, whose name was Stephan Wichnewski. "Once in a while, he would get drunk and talk a *lot*. Sort of a drifter, darkish personality."

Stephan had been dating the Swiss-born bassist for the Wygals, led by former Individual Janet Wygal and her siblings. "The couple lived in Williamsburg, which at the time was a scary place, and neither one of them had any visible means of support," Wygal remembered.

"About all I knew about them was that they never seemed to shed their black leather pants. And that she claimed to have been born under a camel. I also seem to recall that in lieu of a bed, they slept on an old door. I'd been around Stephan a bit, and he appeared to be an agreeable sort—despite his and her requisite European insouciance—but he was literally the quietest person with the known capacity for speech I'd ever met. I'm guessing now that perhaps the problem was simply that his English was shaky and he was shy about using it."

"*What is puddle?*" Emily Hubley remembered Stephan asking quizzically.

"He was a very angular fellow," observed bandmate Dave Schramm, who found himself sharing the backseat of the Buick and rooming with the sometimes-befuddled Swiss man. "He played like that too." Though Stephan could barely fit into the Garden Street practice space, he gelled well, adding an odd but sympathetic touch of propulsive Euro-pop to Georgia's drums.

The Buick wasn't built for real touring duty. They turned the air-conditioning off as they drove through hundred-degree temperatures in Georgia with the windows down, hoping not to overheat. They looked for college radio gigs and, it being summer, failed entirely. On the plus side, there were a few more Minor League ballparks to check out, including the Mets' class-A team in Columbia, South Carolina.

Despite the lack of radio appearances, there were still places to stop by that might prove beneficial to a young band. Along with zines and the underground press, venues, independent labels, distributors, and record stores, one could fairly refer to the users of this finite network as "indie." It was now firmly in place—an alternative America laid out over the map, ready for Yo La Tengo. A lot of the time it was purely practical. In North Carolina, they visited the Record Exchange, clerked that summer by home-for-break NYU fan Phil Morrison, who offered up his dad's place to crash.

And even empty shows resulted in important out-of-town contacts. Earlier in the year, they'd traveled to Chicago for the weekend and caught a Pirates–Cubs game on a gorgeous afternoon at Wrigley Field. Playing the West End, they met up with people like talent buyer Sue Miller, who would book Yo La Tengo shows at a range of Second City venues over the years, as well as Rick Rizzo and Janet Beveridge Bean of the band Eleventh Dream Day, who became lifelong friends. With each stop, their already-wide circle widened even more.

Even so, living in Hoboken, they were often reminded that things were different elsewhere. "We had to set up in front of other bands' gear before and have set up in front of other bands' gear since," Ira wrote of one gig that year. "But only on this night did we set up in front of two bands' gear—both including exclusively electric drum kits."

A recurring issue was Georgia's left-handedness, and

specifically that she was often unable to share a drum kit with an opening act unless there was a complete breakdown of the kit between bands. Another issue was sheer lack of audience. In Nashville, ex-roommate Danny Amis joined the band on stage for a surf number, and the crowd dwindled to none.

But during that tour through the South, Georgia and Ira initiated a practice that got them, perhaps more than anything else, through their lean years: really good food. Armed with a soft-backed, well-thumbed, and eventually coverless copy of Jane and Michael Stern's *Roadfood*, the band hunted barbecue with an aggression that often saw them plan—and capably stick to—earlier travel departures to allow time for various meat-related adventures. They began to return to Hoboken with bottles of favorite sauces, filling the refrigerator at Garden Street.

It was six thirty in the morning when Ira and Georgia awoke to a transcontinental call from Stephan, who informed them that he'd missed his flight from London and would be unable to make the CBGB show that night. This was particularly worrisome. To cancel this CBGB gig would mean a lifetime ban from the venue.

Despite its fame, owner Hilly Kristal maintained the venue as a stubbornly local place, and it remained important for bands of Yo La Tengo's size in Manhattan. National network of indie rock or no, Yo La Tengo found themselves mostly among a group of close-knit New York bands, one of whom had gotten them into this particular predicament. Specifically, that band was Mofungo, featuring former *Rocker* art director Chris Nelson.

"We had a kind of working-class perspective that only a middle-class person can have," recalled Mofungo bassist Robert Sietsema, who doubled as a local photographer. "Partly bogus, partly genuine. We were always in conflict with Hilly Kristal. Despite the fact that he owned—or his wife owned—

the club we loved the best, he was an impossible pill. He was always playing these weird angles, trying to get bands to make deals with him.

"Sometimes, he made the band pay all the employees out of the door, so there'd be a deduction for the soundman and a deduction for the guy at the front door. And, that time, we were pissed because he kept adding more and more bands per evening, meaning that the door was further decreased and you got paid less despite the fact that there were more people in the club. We'd come to him with a show we'd put together, and then we'd find out when the *Village Voice* came out that there were a couple of more bands added. Our dream was to control the means of production, to create shows out of bands our friends had." So they declared a strike.

"There was nothing those guys liked more than a strike," Ira recalled. "*'We should not play the show.'* So we're like, 'yeah, all right, let's not do it.' And so CBGB's said, 'If you ever want to play here again, you'll start with this next show.' They broke us, I'll admit it."

It had been a particularly turbulent year. Even before the tour the previous summer, they'd had Big Dipper's Steve Michener in for a few gigs, and then Mike Lewis agreed to play for a few weekends. Not wanting to tour, Dave Schramm split the band too, a move that seemed inevitable but which nonetheless bummed out Ira and Georgia pretty hard, though they kept playing softball every weekend. With each move came a tinkering, more time spent in the basement practicing.

The band played its first wedding, for Byron Coley and Lili Dwight, and reverted to Georgia-and-Those-Guys mode to learn an entire batch of songs by guests they expected at the reception. "Big Black's 'Kerosene' was my favorite cover," Byron recalled. "That was fucking great. With Albini standing there. He reacted with *disgust*. I picked him up by his feet and swung him around. His hat stayed on." It was a kind of discovery, and as much a vindication as any of Yo La Tengo's other quiet accomplishments to date: they were the kind of band that could play weddings. Lead guitar duties that night were handled by Michael Cudahy of Christmas.

For the CBGB gig with Mofungo they'd recruited Dave Rick, who had returned a few times on lead guitar to give the band a hard-rock flare they rarely possessed before or after. Sometimes Chris Stamey filled in. And it was Stamey who answered his phone early that Friday morning and agreed to play bass for the absent Stephan. The show went on, Dave Rick shredded, and the ban was averted.

The band received another invitation to perform at a wedding reception, this time for Craig and Diana Marks in the back room of Maxwell's. It was a tradition Steve Fallon had unknowingly continued from the Ambrose Chius days a half century earlier. The band jumped into another songbook that overlapped slightly with Byron and Lili's and learned music by artists who recorded for Craig's employer, Homestead. Great Plains drove from Columbus to perform. En route from the ceremony to the reception at Maxwell's, Diana's father suffered a fatal heart attack. Yo La Tengo didn't play.

They made another last-minute lineup switch for a show in Albany. It was out of town, so if it didn't work out, it wouldn't be a big deal. "It was like being thrown into a swimming pool," Ira noted of the night he'd acted as the band's sole guitarist. They'd existed as a trio for a few months when they started, but he'd vehemently disliked it.

Seasoned guitarists like Dave Schramm, Dave Rick, and Chris Stamey hadn't needed to practice in order to prepare for fill-in gigs with them, so Ira had tried his hand at it in the 719 basement during rehearsals, doing his best to fill the spaces between verses. When they opened in Albany with a pumping rock arrangement of Neil Young's banjo dirge "For the Turnstiles," the B-side of a new 7-inch they'd recorded with Chris Stamey, it turned out Ira was fine.

At first, he even overcompensated with too many notes, a

manic cross between the two Daves' twang and speed-noise. Toned down slightly, the style went well with the face-contorting screams on new songs like "The Story of Jazz," a tale of a surreal night on the town, soon couched in the abruptly autobiographical first line, "Georgia left me alone last Wednesday night."

They even had a built-in guitar workout to play, with a tenminute Grateful Dead–style segue between Love's "A House Is Not a Motel" and a new arrangement of "The Evil That Men Do," both extended with noisy jams. They closed with "The River of Water" and earned an encore. "Five Years!" somebody shouted for Schramm's tune from *Ride the Tiger*.

"Sorry, we can't do that," Ira responded. "The guy who wrote that isn't here."

The same audience member requested two other songs that they couldn't play without Schramm, including the Kinks' "Big Sky."

"Sorry, that guy's not here either."

Making the best of their own means of production, they opted for two songs that didn't require solos: a quick blowout of the Urinals' "Sex" and the hush of Bob Dylan's "I Threw It All Away." Their encores, too, became a means of expression, pulling from their ever-replenishing well of covers. With that, the band drove back to Hoboken, at least one problem solved.

CHAPTER 7

Road Food, Good Food

The ceremony was at City Hall. For the reception, they imported barbecue from South Carolina. So, on April 16, 1987, Kaplans and Hubleys met on the tiled floor of Maxwell's front room. Not that Faith, Abraham, Marilyn, and their progeny were ever strangers to hometown Yo La Tengo gigs.

Will Rigby organized the band. Dave Schramm played guitar, Sue Garner from Fish and Roses played bass. They changed Van Morrison's "Gloria" to "Georgia" and dug deep into the marriage canon, coming out with Ernie K-Doe's "Mother-in-Law," Otis Redding's "Don't Mess with Cupid," and Chuck Berry's "You Never Can Tell."

For their honeymoon, Ira and Georgia headed for Jazz Fest in New Orleans, where they stayed with Ira's youngest brother, Jeremy, who'd recently moved there. Longtime favorite Alex Chilton was a resident too. He'd relocated from Memphis in the early '80s, worked menial jobs, and occasionally played R&B standards with a Bourbon Street cover band. During a Jazz Fest gig, Ira and Georgia took a picture of actor Harry Shearer watching "Alex Chitlon," as the Big Star singer was typoed on the stage-side sign.

Back up north, Maxwell's was almost more a home than a home base. "They'd wake up, they'd come into Maxwell's,"

Steve Fallon recalled. "They were just sort of family members." He'd committed Coyote to the next Yo La Tengo record, to be titled *New Wave Hot Dogs* after an enterprising advertisement on a local wiener truck, and they self-produced it that spring at Water Music.

The narrow house at 719 Garden Street included new roommates, too. An occasionally boisterous mainstay of garage-punk record-collector circles, Todd Abramson had taken over Ira's Wednesday-night slot at Gerde's Folk City, and—when that venue closed in early 1986—took over booking of Maxwell's from Steve.

With Abramson's residence, 719 became an outright social place from time to time, a late-night post-Maxwell's hangout as much for bands on tour as for Hoboken friends. Late sleepers both, Ira and Georgia were only sometimes irked when their new housemate cranked records before noon or woke them with drunken living-room wrestling matches with A-Bones guitarist Bruce Bennett, who would then inevitably play the marimba Ira and Georgia had set up there.

Emily Hubley married too, moving out of 719 and in with her husband, Will Rosenthal, whom she'd met at Dioxin Field. In her place came Gaylord Fields, a friend of Todd's from the Upper East Side. About to begin a career as a writer and editor, as well as being an occasional record clerk, Gaylord was a soft-spoken black man with equally obsessive and far-reaching musical tastes. "It was like *The Mod Squad*," said Abramson. "Except Ira was the one with the Afro."

One night, Todd and Gaylord came upon a pair of beauty-parlor chairs with vast Plexiglas domes. These need to be the chairs in our kitchen, they decided, and dragged them back to the house. Several years later, they would find a third matching chair, and gleefully added it to the collection while Georgia and Ira were on tour. "We can't wait to see the looks on their faces," they recalled thinking, and the setup paid off when Georgia and Ira pulled back into town after an all-night drive to find their housemates "electrically awake" as they prepared for a friend's wedding, the catatonic musicians rubbing their eyes in surprise at the new addition. Georgia groaned. She eventually took a hammer to one of the chairs, although not before featuring it on the cover she'd designed for the *Human Music* compilation that Gerard Cosloy put out at Homestead.

Although everyone had their own phone lines, it could be chaotic. If bands didn't have a place to stay, they often ended up at 719.

Gaylord Fields held particularly fond memories of a visit from Fugazi. The flagship band of the powerful Washington, D.C., scene, Fugazi became a taxonomically exemplary paragon of the do-it-yourself movement. All releases on guitarist Ian MacKaye's Dischord Records were $10, postage included. Shows were all-ages and never more than $5. *Always.* And there was, as well, the matter of straight-edge. A doctrine of substance-free existence and much more, straight-edge was distantly derived from the forty-six-second song of the same name performed by MacKaye's former band, Minor Threat. The Washington, D.C., rendition of punk radiated outward like a suburban religion.

"They brought in a case of Evian water, when no band drank Evian water," Fields remembered of the houseguests. "We stayed up talking about Washington, D.C., soul radio and classic soul DJs. They couldn't have been nicer. In the morning, all the beds were made, the bottles were put back into the case for recycling, and they left a thank-you note. There's a band that practices what they preach."

Other times, more hijinks ensued. One night, Ira and Georgia headed into the city to see Christmas, a Boston art-punk band they'd grown friendly with over the years, led by another guitarist-drummer couple, Michael Cudahy and Liz Cox. "We returned [at] threeish and were greeted by our two cats, normally a scenario we enjoyed, except this time they were outside our house, on our front doorstep," Ira remembered.

"Confusion and annoyance quickened our pace into the house, where we bumped into our living-room sofa bed in its bed position. Our roommate hadn't warned us we'd be entertaining that evening. Georgia turned on the overhead light and two groggy rockers raised their heads. 'Who are you?' she barked. 'We're Mudhoney.'"

The only other time Mofungo had toured, they'd ridden to Minneapolis in the back of a sedan with their amps on their laps. This time they determined to do it in style, renting a mobile home and hiring a soundman, who happened to be Ira.

In addition to bread-and-butter copyediting, the occasional freelance assignment for the *Village Voice*, and mixing bands at Maxwell's, Ira took a few traveling sound-engineer jobs. He did local work with Camper Van Beethoven, took a trip to North Carolina with Redd Kross, and even did some shows for the ever-fussy Feelies. "I really didn't know what I was doing," Ira admitted. "It was more that what people liked about me was that I wasn't going to make the bass drum sound too loud.

"I knew how their songs should sound. It didn't mean I was capable of doing it. But some of the egregious club sound . . . I made different mistakes. The Feelies walked off a few times because of monitor feedback I couldn't control." He did get to mix the night Lou Reed sat in with the Haledon heroes for some Velvet Underground covers at Club Babylon on Long Island, though.

As always, Ira brought *Roadfood* with him for the week-and-a-half run to the Midwest and back with Mofungo. Robert Sietsema, Mofungo's bassist, took notice. Already adventurous—indeed, the name Mofungo itself was a slight mutation of "mofongo," a plantain-based Puerto Rican staple—Sietsema had never seen *Roadfood* before.

"Ira would convince us to go way off the road to seek out these amazing things to eat," he remembered. "I've got to credit him for turning me on to a different way of looking at food. I obviously already had those sorts of ideas, or we never would have done those sorts of things, but he was the culinary ringleader of the trip."

In Cincinnati, they ate chocolate-laced chili. In St. Louis, they sought snoots: deep-fried pig snout. "We pulled up outside this place and we all knew that snoots were the most exotic item on the menu, but nobody really wanted to commit to the snoot lunch," Ira remembered. "So we all ordered other things and we're sitting in the motor home, and we're still there. And Robert said he would pay for it if somebody else would go get it. So somebody else walked back and got one order. Everybody professed to liking snoots, but the four of us couldn't finish the order. It was so overpowering." As they traveled farther and farther from Hoboken, Ira and Georgia became world-class eaters, their palates as methodically well mapped as anyone's.

Inspired by his experience hunting snoots and other delicacies with Ira, as well as by the array of titles available for browsing in the new East Village zine store See Hear, Robert Sietsema launched a publication of his own, *Down the Hatch*. "I decided to make a food zine, using the same technology, stealing xeroxing from the people I worked for and putting it on colored paper. Initially, the zine was directed towards other musicians, because it used to be that you would do a soundcheck at four or five in the afternoon after the load-in, and rock shows were even later. A lot of clubs didn't start music till ten or eleven, and you might not start until one or two. In the space between when you did your soundcheck and when you played your set, you had all these hours with nothing to do other than find a cheap place to eat.

"The whole zine was dedicated to finding cheap places to eat, once again influenced by Ira's *Roadfood* book. I wasn't looking for Americana classics like a pie cooling on the windowsill. I was looking for ethnic food, which was what New York had in abundance at cheap prices, so I'd be sending people all over Brooklyn and Queens to eat this cheap, amazing food." It was the beginning of a food-writing career that landed Sietsema at the *Village Voice* in 1993 and eventually *The New York Times*.

The zine world had swollen in every direction. Zines were everywhere. Early home computers gave publishers an easy new tool, and the layouts grew incrementally more slick. And with titles like *Down the Hatch*, the ideas of modesty and scale around indie music began to spread to other areas of culture.

At the counter of See Hear was a zinester who'd become an enormous Yo La Tengo fan, an NYU student named Mike McGonigal. He'd bought a copy of "The River of Water" single as a Miami teen, reviewed it in the second issue of his *Chemical Imbalance*, and soon included Yo La Tengo's cover of Fleetwood Mac's "Dreams" on a 7-inch with the fifth issue, topping an A-side that also featured a rare Big Black cut.

McGonigal became part of a slowly but steadily increasing crowd just older than himself at Yo La Tengo shows "It helped give shows a sense of a cool scene," he said. "This is one of the things the cool older, smarter people were into." Gerard Cosloy was a regular now, along with members of Fish and Roses, Mofungo, Stan Demeski of the Feelies, and a crew of students from NYU, including zine editor McGonigal and aspiring filmmaker (and new Coyote intern) Phil Morrison. The shows grew longer.

Though Yo La Tengo would remain friends with people at all levels of the music-writing world, Ira's career as an active rock critic ended formally after a final *Village Voice* piece for editor Robert Christgau in the fall of 1987. Fittingly, it was a review of a bootleg LP of Jonathan Richman demos. "*Route 128 Revisited* is available at fine illegal stores almost nowhere," he wrote.

A few nights into the tour, a miserable show in Philadelphia brought to mind the time Ira saw Monty Python perform live. "The ticket was expensive," he remembered, "but [Bonzo Dog Band/Rutles songwriter/Python collaborator] Neil Innes was with them and the chance to see Neil was really overwhelming.

"He's playing while Carol Cleveland does this dance that's completely unrelated. She finishes while he's still singing and the audience claps like crazy. She resumes dancing. He finishes and leaves while she's still dancing. The audience was fixated on her. I was not fixated on her, I was watching Neil Innes."

JC Dobbs in Philadelphia was long and narrow, with a bar down one side, above which a TV showed game seven of the World Series. Ordinarily a topic of interest for Ira, who made good-natured banter about it between songs, the bleak inconsequentiality of it got to him. "There'd be no reaction to what we were doing and then, in the middle of a song, people would start clapping. We felt belittled."

Afterward, they made a decision and found a theoretical path out of the malaise. "The next time that happens," they decided, "let's just jam."

Two days later, they arrived at the Blind Pig in Ann Arbor, Michigan, set to open for Boston pals Volcano Suns, and discovered their inclusion on the bill was neither advertised in advance nor even listed on the club's marquee. They played a forty-five-minute, three-song set, consisting of "A House Is Not a Motel" and "The Evil That Men Do," followed by Ira's love ballad "Did I Tell You," and earned an encore.

Later that night, R.E.M.'s Peter Buck—with his own band on a night off between Columbus and East Lansing—turned up to see Volcano Suns. "What're you doing here?" he asked Ira.

"We're the opening act," Ira replied.

"I called the club!" Buck said, frustrated. "I even asked who was opening!"

The band played that three-song set several times throughout the tour, and—despite the adversarial circumstances that may have caused its original deployment—none of the nights would earn an entry on Ira's Worst Shows list. November 3 at No Bar and Grill in Muncie, Indiana, did, however. "Always August shows up for their date a whole week early, are added to the bill, and outdraw us."

Then: triumph. A European tour playing to audiences primed and ready not just for American indie rock, but Yo La Tengo. It started four shows in, at Club Vera in Groningen, where the

crowd cheered the band through eight songs and forty minutes' worth of encores. "It felt weird at times," Ira admitted.

But it was a welcome start to the monthlong tour, seventeen shows in twenty-seven days, beginning in mid-November
1987. The Netherlands-based Paperclip Agency had recently
not only convinced the Feelies to tour Europe but had pulled
it off with aplomb and thus began to cultivate a dedicated
audience for small American acts across Germany and Holland. The agency "booked some fifteen hundred shows a year
throughout Europe, most of those for North American bands,"
remembered Paperclip's Rob Berends. "The London-based
agents did not even acknowledge the club circuit we were using until years later." In years to come Paperclip would book
the first European shows for Nirvana, Soundgarden, and many
others.

If Yo La Tengo's late-November shows weren't completely
overflowing, the audiences were beyond enthusiastic. "It was
never that clear how much it had to do with us specifically,"
Ira said with a shrug.

"People knew the material," insisted Craig Marks, who escaped the Dutch East warehouse to join the band as roadie
and driver in return for a plane ticket. "They weren't just
showing up in Tübingen for the heck of it. They were fans. For
a lot of bands in those days, the fervor of the fans in Europe
was much larger than what they experienced in America. It
was so much more pleasurable touring Europe than touring
America that touring America wasn't even close."

Marks drove "a diesel van that could barely break sixty on
the Autobahn" and, after a few pre-departure lessons from Ira
at the Maxwell's soundboard, arrived ready to mix sound, too.
"Every venue would have its own sound guy, and I would make
sure that the sound was to Ira's liking, which just meant no
vocals and lots of guitar. All I had to learn was to push the guitar pot up and I was fine."

It was the beginning of a new system of friend-roadies
that Yo La Tengo began to employ, in Georgia's words, "because [if] we're going to be stuck in a van with this person for

what seems like an eternity, we better have someone we want to be around."

"We would travel to Europe and just bring a friend of ours to help instead of a professional soundman," Ira remembered. "It's amazing how clueless and kind of self-destructive we were in that regard in our naïveté."

But the clubs were small, and the fans were zealous. The band earned quadruple encores in Hamburg. "I just love the way you speak English," one German fan told Ira.

"Oh, uh, thank you."

"*Ja*, you know Dream Syndicate?" another asked Craig.

In the small east Dutch city of Nijmegen, Stephan took the afternoon off and Ira and Georgia set up with an acoustic guitar, small drum setup, and organ at Waaghals, a local indie record shop. They'd played in this configuration once before, just before departure, at Rocks in Your Head in New York, and debuted virtually an entirely fresh set of music—almost all covers—that became the basis for a new acoustic version of the band with an ongoing parallel repertoire.

And in this version of Yo La Tengo, ready for living rooms, record stores, college radio stations, and the world, Georgia Hubley sang. Her voice was beautiful, full, and expressive and a soft couching for Ira's occasional nasalness. She sounded as if she had known great sadness. Though she still didn't sing lead, their new weary harmonies distantly recalled the Weavers. But instead of old blues from the American South, Yo La Tengo repurposed songs from their own underground and called out sweet, buried melodies.

The new repertoire included tunes by the Who, Volcano Suns, the Velvet Underground, and a thrillingly aching duet on the Flamin' Groovies' "You Tore Me Down." They even covered Yo La Tengo, Ira singing Dave Schramm's "The Way Some People Die." On John Cale's "Andalucia," Georgia added simple sustained organ, evoking the sad winter of Cale's lyrics with droned chords somehow both warming and evocative of the cold outside.

More than even finding an audience in Europe, the arrival

of Georgia's voice and deeper musical presence in Yo La Tengo was a giant step, both audibly and ineffably. Sometimes given to defeatism, giggling or otherwise, the slow turn of Georgia's creative self-confidence was perhaps the most important thing to happen to the band since they'd started playing together five years earlier. Her drumming grew better and more creative as well, a solid tether for Ira's increasingly unhinged solos and a real part of their slow torrent of new material. Another layer of self-deprecation vanquished, Yo La Tengo quietly passed into a new place.

Where they could be, they were adventurous eaters. In Antwerp, they tried "this ham-and-cheese casserole, and inside the casserole was an entire leek and an entire banana," Ira remembered. "Stephan's mother used to make them all the time. I think he ate all three of them."

Sometimes, Hoboken seemed impossibly far away. Georgia felt it hard. "We learned a valuable lesson about homesickness," Ira said. "You can't give into it. You have to fight through it, no matter how much you might crave a hamburger in a place where you don't belong. We got a hamburger that something was crawling out of."

It didn't stop them from an investigation of the pancake houses they spotted around the Dutch countryside. "We discovered hilariously that 'pancake' means something completely different to them," Ira said. "It's dinner, so they didn't open until four. We thought, 'OK, we can go without eating until four.' So we were there first thing in their day. The menu was divided into savory pancakes and sweet pancakes. So the notion of having a pancake with blueberries and bacon, which didn't seem that outlandish to Americans"—and, more specifically, to a homesick Georgia—"seemed truly impossible to them."

They made one to order just for Georgia, though, and the cook emerged to watch her eat it. For once, it did the trick. "It was good!" Georgia said. "It was pretty much what I was expecting!"

Sometimes, however, Europe reminded them a little too

much of home. "London was like being back in the States," Craig groused of the tour's second-to-last gig. "It was such a brutally abysmal show. Not that anyone was there to be bothered or excited by it." The venue was Dingwalls in Camden where, eleven years earlier, members of the Clash, the Sex Pistols, the Damned, and others had seen the Ramones' second UK show and sped up their own music accordingly. Yo La Tengo was booked for a showcase set.

"The house soundwoman, seemingly convinced that Georgia is claiming to be left-handed merely to make extra work for her, refuses to set up drum mics," Ira wrote. "Our scheduled 20-minute set clocks in at a minute and a half, 40 seconds with the DJ's record still on. I know, because I have a tape of it."

Byron wanted to release it as a single, *Yo La Tengo: Live in England.*

The Southwest was cold and bleak with, in one account, grumpiness to go around. Yo La Tengo barely escaped it. Ten days out from home in a rented minivan, they'd driven into a freak blizzard in Dallas, played for eight people in an unheated club, did the "House Is Not a Motel"/"Evil That Men Do" set, and earned an encore.

"That whole part of the tour was pretty rough," assessed Phil Morrison, the Coyote Records intern, NYU fan, and generally enthusiastic friend who'd joined the band as a roadie for the trip. "I was tuning guitars and changing strings," Phil remembered. "I was diligent, and I cared, but I had no talent for it. I was doing it to the extent that any non-dummy could do it, but no more."

The month-and-a-half-long tour was the longest to date, in large part because of a new booking agent back home, Bob Lawton. Though they were trying years for Yo La Tengo, the late '80s were some of the most charmed years for bands of their ilk, in large part because of tacticians like Lawton, who helped build an infrastructure to support the hundreds of like-minded acts now crisscrossing the country.

College radio boomed. The dB's called it quits in 1988, and Peter Holsapple signed on with R.E.M. as an often-uncredited fifth member. The band broke through ceiling after ceiling. In early 1987, *Life's Rich Pageant* passed the 500,000 sales mark and earned them a gold record. Later that year, they scored a top-ten single with "The One I Love." By the time Yo La Tengo drove through the gray desert toward Albuquerque, *Document* had sold to more than one million record buyers. The major labels scrambled to get their records on the college airwaves in an effort to mirror the success of R.E.M. and started to bolster their alternative marketing departments with former college DJs.

While it was hard to tell by the endless highway miles, empty clubs, or stewing band members, the environment was suited perfectly for Yo La Tengo, who continued their slow mull on the road. The wryly humored Lawton, who'd relocated to New York from Boston at Steve Fallon's urging, was the perfect match for the band, who began a daily ritual of checking in with him from the road via pay phone.

After inheriting Yo La Tengo from Frank Riley, Lawton added Sonic Youth to his roster and established himself in the Cable Building in Manhattan. Like the Dutch East warehouse or a modern version of the Brill Building in Times Square, the six floors of offices at 611 Broadway became a place that one might point to as the embodiment of indie rock. The building housed at least two dozen labels (including Rough Trade's American headquarters and the cassette-only ROIR), booking agencies, and other music-affiliated outfits.

Lawton himself shared a seventh-floor office—desks pushed against one another in classic New York fashion—with three labels, each with a profound Yo La Tengo connection. One was Coyote, where they were signed, which was now managed by Steve Daly. Another was Bar/None, born in the basement of Pier Platters and run by Ira's former *New York Rocker* comrade Glenn Morrow. The last was What Goes On, who specialized in imports, managed by Ira's younger brother Adam. The only music the whole office could all agree on to listen to,

Adam Kaplan remembered, was a Pixies demo making the rounds. If Yo La Tengo had a home base besides Hoboken, it was there.

There was plenty to recommend the three-year-old band by this point. The turn away from folkier colors had served them well, and they had legitimately begun to build themselves a small following. Ira's confidence and creativity as a guitarist grew daily, almost in direct proportion to each pouting noise jam, the ultimate staging of which came in Albuquerque, four days after the Dallas snowstorm, at the appropriately-named-for-all-occasions Fat Chance.

The "house soundman decides we're not heavy enough for a soundcheck," Ira wrote. The stage was a small platform several inches off the ground. When the band finally set up, Ira placed the base of the microphone stand on the floor to give himself a little bit more room on the small stage. The soundman grew livid.

With utter venom, he pointed down at the ground. "*THIS IS THE STAGE*," he told Ira, growing red in the face. "*THIS IS THE DANCE FLOOR*."

As the band started, the monitors began to feedback loudly. "Things were bad, and we were blaming each other," remembered Ira. "More specifically, I was blaming Georgia."

And in the middle of the set, Georgia split. "I deserved it that night," Ira admitted. She stormed off to the club's bathroom, slamming the door.

"I thought, 'Well, now what happens?'" Georgia remembered. "It's not like there was a back door." She eventually returned to the stage. The band resumed, and so did the feedback.

"I managed to get a hold of myself in that regard and stopped taking it out on people who were innocent and started taking it out on people who weren't," Ira said.

"Your guitar is too fucking loud!" the soundman screamed at Ira.

"I think that's why we needed a soundcheck!" Ira screamed back.

"No," the soundman retorted. "*You* needed a soundcheck."

The band turned their backs and started Love's "A House Is Not a Motel," and continued with their longest version of the "Evil That Men Do" pairing yet, extended to nearly forty-five minutes.

Afterward, Ira went outside, buzzing and light-headed. ("Denver gets all the press, but Albuquerque is just as high altitude," he noted.)

"How *dare* you do that?" a man screamed at him.

Meanwhile, another man approached Ira, "sort of a street dweller." It was unclear if he had seen the show or merely listened from outside. "That was the *best* concert I have *ever* seen," he proclaimed. "You are *better* than Ace Frehley," he continued. "You are *as good* as the Eagles."

The joys of the road presented themselves as needed, and carried Yo La Tengo from city to city—a chain of stories born through the faith that they were doing the right thing. At a barbecue stop in Oakland, Phil found a strange soda. He offered some to Ira, who politely refused. "Ira, this stuff is *so weird*, you really should try it." Ira shook his head again. "Why won't you try it?"

"I'm not ready for the taste of this barbecue to leave my mouth," he told Phil.

The first time Stephan Wichnewski quit, just before a tour, they recruited ex-Antietam bassist Wolf Knapp. The former Maxwell's doorman had only a few days' warning before being dragooned into service with Yo La Tengo. "I have no doubt that the rehearsals were tense," Ira said. They had time for three practices.

Ira presented Wolf with a list of nearly thirty-five songs to learn for the eight shows, and Wolf was kind of annoyed. "There was a Stones song, and all Stones songs sound the same to me," he complained. He'd left Antietam a few years earlier and had recently done a tour with Christmas. "Is it in 6/8?" Wolf asked several times.

"I could see him having a panic attack," Wolf remembered. "I bet he was thinking, 'This is a Rolling Stones song; it's the easiest thing in the world to learn,' and I didn't know the Stones. I just didn't feel the Stones. His shoulders went up and his face got tight. I had never played any covers in my life," Wolf said. "I had a crappy ear and I didn't care about it, and Ira and Georgia did care about it."

Though presumptuous, having a big available repertoire was an indicator that Yo La Tengo was different from other bands. "The approach we used was that we never did something as mundane as learning to play a reasonable number of songs," Ira said. "We were changing our set from the very beginning and, given that situation—short notice and everything—it would have made more sense to just shorten the list, which is ultimately what we did."

In Wolf's memory, although other witnesses' accounts differ, another rehearsal was cut short when Wolf saw something he'd witnessed at the occasional Yo La Tengo show. "Ira was being pouty and recalcitrant," Wolf said. "I'd seen Georgia do this onstage: she throws the ride at him and walks off. He ducked, and it just missed me."

Despite the pre-tour tension, the Buick made it to Dutch-Amish country in time for lunch at a *Roadfood*-approved restaurant open only a few hours a day. "I don't think anybody was too happy with it," Wolf noted. "Seemed like comfort food without much distinction." And then it was off to Chicago, for a gig at the Cubby Bear with Sapphires. The show went all right, and the meal was one of the highlights of the run, on the linen tablecloths of Carson's Ribs Steaks and Chops. "The gigs started fine and got better," Wolf assessed. The Buick's speedometer got stuck, and the band had no idea how fast they were driving. "We only got pulled over when we knew what speed we were going," Ira noted.

Tempted back into the band by a plane ticket to Europe, Stephan returned for some summer shows, including a scorching night at CBGB that wound up on tape. Combined with Ira's deeper forays into abstract noise guitar, which had evolved from reactionary jamming to showstoppers, the band seemed finally to be coming into themselves. They headed back to Europe for another half dozen shows. Then Stephan quit again.

Mike McGonigal videotaped Georgia and Ira at Garden Street singing Dion and the Belmonts' "A Teenager in Love" and Buddy Holly's "Everyday" for a VHS edition of *Chemical Imbalance*. Georgia's hair is in a bob and her polo shirt is shapeless. The thirty-one-year-old Ira's arms poke skinnily from a red T-shirt, the video degradation blurring his already young-looking face into timeless adolescence.

Neither band member spends much time looking at the camera, Georgia staring downward into a towel-muted snare drum, Ira singing with eyes closed. Georgia sings too—wordless *ahh*s behind her husband.

"Good job!" a commenter posted many years later on YouTube. "You should do 'I Wonder Why' by Dion!"

No visual markers suggest that the two are anything other than a pair covering songs in a living room. In fact, there is something wholly universal, bordering on generic, about the performance of the '50s hits, oddly well-known selections by the standards of Yo La Tengo in 1988. But the music is simple and unfussed-over. The effect is sleight-of-hand, all the parts plain and visible: Georgia and that guy, a guitar, and a drum. As she slides on her four-note backing part in "A Teenager in Love," it emerges between them, a far-off melancholy.

They'd been listening a lot to the debut LP by California songwriter Barbara Manning, *Lately I Keep Scissors*, especially Georgia. Manning's deeply personal songs became a favorite. "I think her singing really made me think it would be good to sing more; it would be OK, it wouldn't sound bad," Georgia said.

They played a matinee at CBGB with Peter Stampfel, Half Japanese's Jad Fair, and former dB's drummer Will Rigby, who was playing in a duo with his wife, Amy. Georgia joined Ira at the front of the stage, drumming on a small kit while standing up, and—for the first time outside of record stores and college radio stations—singing.

She bowled over the NYU gang instantly. "It was like, 'What the fuck?' 'cause she could clearly sing really well but seemed so hesitant and nervous and that made it even better to our precious little Beat Happening–loving selves," Mike McGonigal recalled.

They covered their friends (Will Rigby's "Tail of a Star," The Scene Is Now's "Yellow Sarong"); underground heroes (Peter Stampfel and Antonia's "Griselda," the Ramones' "I Can't Make It on Time"); obscure kitsch (Rex Garvin's 1963 single "Emulsified"); and ancient pop (Shirley & Lee's "That's What I'll Do," the Chords' "Sh-Boom"). Two-part vocal arrangements plus the addition of Georgia's vocals to Ira's new songs gave Yo La Tengo another powerful tool in an ever-growing bag.

Bob Lawton booked a tour for just the two of them to the Midwest and back in the Buick. Without the specter of noise, the experience grew comfortable enough to talk onstage, the first glimmers of a charming public rapport. In Chicago, Ira joked about tuning his guitar like Sonic Youth's Lee Ranaldo, and Georgia asked if they might do a Sonic Youth song.

"As you know better than anyone here, we could," Ira responded.

"As *you* know better than anyone here, we could," she shot back.

"As I know better than anyone here, we won't."

The next time Stephan rejoined Yo La Tengo was one of the few times he voiced his opinion about anything, and it was to present a demand: that they find someplace else to practice. The ceiling in the Garden Street basement was just too low. They found a rehearsal space downtown, next to Water Music, and moved.

"He was very quiet and kept to himself," Ira remembered. "We didn't know what he was thinking."

It's possible, too, that Stephan often didn't know what his bandmates were thinking either. "We bonded over being the only ones who weren't Ira or Georgia," recalled Chris Nelson, the friend-roadie on one tour and, by default, Stephan's roommate. "He felt that he was somewhat of an odd duck because Georgia and Ira were a duo and he was experiencing some issues with that. He was a little inscrutable."

To outsiders, which was nearly everybody, Georgia and Ira could be inscrutable too, their silences and intricacies easy to misread. "They could be difficult at times, to be diplomatic," remembered Gene Holder, the former dB who'd signed on to produce and play bass for a session at Water Music just before Stephan's return. To Georgia and Ira, the studio was just as bewildering and defeatism inducing as ever.

"I think pretty much everybody that they dealt with wanted to give them a more refined sound," Holder commented. "I think they had a bit of a problem with that, and rightfully so. They were making records in the '80s when the '80s were all about the big drum, kick, and snare sound. They were going for the exact opposite of that. They were going for a smaller drum sound. That was the result of hearing the snare drum really big with crazy gated reverb on it. Anytime you'd put any kind of effect on it, Ira's eyes would bug out of his head."

More important, perhaps, was Holder's encouragement, urging them to record something representative of their most recent tours as a duo. In response, Ira finished "Alyda," where the atmospheric trick of Georgia's vocals made its first appearance in a Yo La Tengo original.

Two versions of "The Evil That Men Do"—a noisy incarnation recorded live at CBGB with Stephan, and a surf-rock take contrived for the jam-hating Craig Marks—dotted the sides. It began with "Barnaby, Hardly Working," a third-person rocker that borrowed Ray Davies's wide-screen sweep and brimmed with cinema both in lyrical content and song arc, and ended with a cover of Bob Dylan's "I Threw It All Away."

To Holder, despite Georgia and Ira's obvious discomfort, it seemed like "they had a vision and knew exactly what they wanted." And despite their insistence that they only knew what they *didn't* want, *President Yo La Tengo* made the first complete image of the band—a mysterious figure emerging from the negative space around it.

And it was back to the road for six months, the Swiss bassist in tow. "I saw them fighting to work with Stephan, and sometimes the result of that was great, because he had this kind of bouncy and jazzy vibe to him that was nice at times," remembered Mike McGonigal.

"Vaguely Teutonic," assessed Byron Coley of Stephan's playing. He raved in a feature for *Loaded*, the Dutch East house zine, about the band they had turned into. Songs were "wedges of pure meat that'll dog-dive smoothly into the ear-pockets of unsuspecting listeners everywhere" and Georgia and Stephan's rhythm section created "seamless blends of steamroll urge." Coley also observed, "Ira's finally getting as cocky about his guitar playing as he should be."

For Stephan, American culture could still come as quite a shock. On the road in Missouri that spring, a friend from a local band brought them to a nearby diner for a post-show meal. One specialty item was a massive four-omelet dish, free to any customer who could complete it, or $14 otherwise.

"Wait! You can get free food just for eating it?" the Swiss bassist asked. They called over a waitress. "Yes, can you drink coffee wis' dis'?"

"Honey, you can drink or eat anything you want along with it, s'long's as ya finish her," the waitress told him. Stephan ordered.

Georgia, Ira, and the late-night college-town diner crowd cheered him on as he calmly attacked piles of eggs and fillings. He punctuated his eating with cups of coffee and methodically soaked up omelet with bits of toast. Georgia or Ira pointed out that he maybe didn't have to eat *every* last bit of food. "I'm *wery* hungry," he told them sternly.

As the band finished their meal, Stephan ordered another cup of coffee, took a short walk, and made the final ascent up the mountain of omelet. Memories differ about whether he completed it, but as the rest of the party paid for their meal, the rest of the diner erupted into laughter as a patron spotted Stephan through the window, vomiting the omelet into the bushes outside—a process that would continue through the night.

Though the Buick caught fire in Florida (Ira: "a trifling"), the band received tangible signs of approval for their work, as *President Yo La Tengo* ticked for the first time onto CMJ's top 30. Perhaps small beans compared to R.E.M. or the Pixies, whose *Surfer Rosa* debut on 4AD had sold a half million copies worldwide the year before and whose *Doolittle* would double that in 1989, the chart entry was a banner accomplishment for Yo La Tengo.

While one could still purchase a copy from behind the bar at Maxwell's, aiding the sales too was Yo La Tengo's gradual climb up the distribution ladder, from the first self-released single (which Ira had personally brought to Venus Records) to the Steve Fallon–run rendition of Coyote through that label's deal with Twin/Tone. Most recently, Twin/Tone had entered into a new distribution agreement with A&M Records—which, in turn, after some quarter century of large-scale independent operation under the aegis of John and Faith Hubley's one-time collaborator Herb Alpert, had that year been absorbed by Polygram, itself owned by Koninklijke Philips Electronics N. V., the Dutch megaconglomerate. Yo La Tengo's music was now available in many, many places.

Because it seemed like they needed a manager, Yo La Tengo hired Steve Fallon. The Feelies had enlisted Steve's laid-back managerial services too, their condition in signing formally with A&M for 1988's *Only Life*. The bigger label was all too happy to have Steve as well, paying him some $15,000 a year to recommend bands. But they laughed when he suggested they sign Sonic Youth, whose relationship with a major label would soon change the indie game permanently.

After another trip to Europe for Yo La Tengo—Chris Nelson counted thirteen songs of encore one night in Germany—Stephan quit the band again, one final time.

CHAPTER 8

Fakebook

The strange, moralless adventure began after an acoustic set during the tenth edition of the New Music Seminar. It was almost by chance that the Japanese delegation caught Georgia and Ira in their acoustic-duo lineup, on a bill with Gene Holder's wife, Myra. Going to see a show billed as Yo La Tengo (or any of the still prevalent typos) in the year after Stephan's departure, one might find oneself seeing any number of bands. Most lately, they'd played duo shows with both Ira and Georgia on abrasive electric guitar.

By the summer of 1989, the New Music Seminar had grown to about five thousand attendees paying $295 a ticket to see 270 bands—a maelstrom of collegiate tourism and business that descended for a week into Manhattan's already busy clubs. CMJ and the NMS traced their origins to the college radio conventions of the early '80s, and the twin annual gatherings in New York were platforms built atop the distribution and touring networks that spread (and generated) commerce and information by and for the youth of America. It was indie, all right, but a good deal more organized than it had once been.

At panels and shows, the ever-growing population of professionals could manifest themselves for a few days of partying, networking, and buzz making. In some sense, it was the transactional landscape of Maxwell's writ large, the caffein-ated ambition of Steve's regulars prototyping indie's emerging business class. But in other ways, although Maxwell's helped picked bands for the New Music Seminar and even hosted shows, the festivals remained removed from the neighborhood hangout, booked by Todd Abramson from the venue's pay phone. Despite its gentrification, Hoboken could never become Man-hattan.

In the chaos of the New Music Seminar that July was a Japanese party working on behalf of JBL Panasonic, there to take in the sights, sounds, and smells of American indepen-dent music. It was an increasingly boundary-less tent, as evi-denced by the three bands they narrowed their search to. One act the Japanese delegation considered was 24-7 Spyz, an Af-rican American heavy metal group they caught a few nights earlier at the Rapp Arts Center. Another was the New Orleans swamp jammers, the Subdudes. But the band they picked to send back to the other side of the world was Yo La Tengo.

In Steve Fallon's memory, the party from JBL Panasonic—who soon contacted him—sought to see how fast they could popularize an archetypal American college rock band in Ja-pan. Working with CMJ, they dispatched five plane tickets to Hoboken. The Japanese received the electric trio Yo La Tengo, Robert Vickers on bass. Formerly of the Go-Betweens, the Australian-born Vickers was a softball friend. At band prac-tices, Ira had found it hard to play without Stephan's bass lines, which—despite their creator's own flightiness—had be-come oddly permanent parts of the songs.

Steve took the fourth ticket. Also along for the ride was Phil Morrison, in his mind, as a reward for the misery of the bleak trip through the Southwest the year before. They boarded a flight for Tokyo just before Halloween 1989.

Their first show was an afternoon showcase for a group of Japanese businessmen in suits who—in Steve's words—were "trying to figure out what they were going to do." Ira responded with what Steve called "the debauched noise"—an increas-ingly prevalent strain in Yo La Tengo's songwriting that Steve in particular hated, extended screech-outs like "Mushroom Cloud of Hiss" and "The Evil That Men Do." The businessmen all but stared blankly.

There was also a press conference, where the band sat behind a table while a half-dozen reporters hurled questions and took photographs. Throughout the trip, Ira fielded endless questions about "Haber-san," CMJ founder Robert Haber.

"I had a crazy dream I was floating across the room," Steve said when he woke up the first morning.

"Did you read about the 7.4 earthquake last night?" Georgia and Ira asked him.

"Oh, is that what happened?"

The gigs were scattered around Tokyo and included an appearance on JCTV's *Space Shower* program and one outdoors on the campus of Waseda University. At a radio station, the band was practically force-fed Chicago-style hot dogs, a cultural faux pas their Japanese hosts couldn't possibly grasp.

One evening, the band informed their JBL Panasonic representatives that they would be checking out a karaoke bar. The company first insisted that they assign individual translators but eventually relented.

At the karaoke parlor, a group of students studied Yo La Tengo with interest. True to form, the band remained too nervous to sing. Finally, a reluctantly elected student approached Phil. He pointed carefully at himself. "May I?" he asked. "Sing with?" Then he jabbed excitedly at Phil: *"Me!"*

Embarrassed, Phil first pretended not to know what he was being asked, though he soon joined the student onstage. Eventually everybody sang. Georgia duetted with Phil on Cyndi Lauper's "Girls Just Want to Have Fun."

"After the four days of shows, the last one was attended by quite a few people," Steve Fallon said. "There was a core of kids who knew who they were." Having made a small reputation in Japan, the experiment in commodification concluded and, perhaps still unsure what to do with them, JBL Panasonic sent Yo La Tengo back to Hoboken. An early indicator of strange things on the breeze for indie rock, it had been a small whirlwind for Yo La Tengo. But that was that.

Gerard Cosloy moved to Manhattan's East Village and started carpooling to the Dutch East warehouse with two employees slightly younger than he was, Patrick Amory and Chris Lombardi. "We were always late, but they couldn't fire all of us," said Lombardi, who knew of Gerard as a local legend while attending boarding school outside Boston. Amory, a fiendish collector who had contributed to *Conflict*, was good at finding imported singles in the corners of the Dutch East warehouse worth buying wholesale and reselling to local record stores.

The past few years at Homestead had proved extraordinarily frustrating for Gerard. Both Sonic Youth and Dinosaur, bands with whom he had made early friendships, split Homestead for Black Flag's überhip SST. Though it would fray his relationships with those bands for several years, it was nothing personal on the musicians' parts. Nothing personal toward Gerard, anyway.

Sonic Youth had visited the Homestead offices on Long Island to meet with owner Barry Tenenbaum. Then-drummer (and Hoboken softballer) Bob Bert suggested they record the meeting to have a permanent record of it.

"It wasn't like we were trying to sneak the tape in and record the meeting," guitarist Thurston Moore remembered. "We were going over some brass tacks with Barry, who's a totally old-school business dude. . . . Talking to this guy was like talking to the parents in the *Peanuts* cartoon. It was all '*Wah-wah-wah*.' I could see the look in his eye when he saw the red light on the Walkman. He was completely freaked out by it. He made us turn it off, and the mood in the room just turned nefarious."

"He's portrayed as a villainous figure," Gerard Cosloy said later. "He was never that sinister. He was actually a friendly guy. His social skills may have been worse than mine, but he was not an unfriendly or nasty person. He didn't set out to rip anyone off."

Nonetheless, bands continued to jump ship as the label's debts piled up, and Gerard didn't feel good enough about Homestead to sign bands he actually liked. There was no shortage of acts he was keeping tabs on via *Conflict*, and he continued to use his publication as a pulpit to praise Yo La Tengo.

"Yo La Tengo have quietly managed to become one of the best bands anywhere any style and sometimes any lead guitar player they happen to have," he gushed in a review of the "Asparagus Song" single. "The ability to write and perform non-goofball pop material convincingly is a rare enough feat. Perhaps if this band was from a town other than Hoboken and on a label other than Coyote, this magazine's readership would take them a bit more seriously (ie. we don't print every letter we get) . . . in other words, if we told you Yo La Tengo were on [New Zealand label] Flying Nun you'd be on your way to the record store right now."

While still at Homestead, Gerard landed "a very nice no-show job" with Island Records that was similar to Steve Fallon's arrangement with A&M. "They paid me a respectable sum to meet with the president, play him things, suggest acts," he remembered.

The president he reported to was soon replaced by Mike Bone, the flamboyant former head of Chrysalis who was later subject to sexual harassment suits. "He was very nice to me and indulgent of my crazy ideas," Gerard said. "He didn't think any of them would sell, but I think he thought, 'Let's listen to what he has to say, he's entertaining,'" and feigned enough interest in Yo La Tengo to invite Ira, Georgia, and Gerard in for a meeting.

"I don't know what Mike's usual meetings with bands were like," Cosloy said. "I'm sure he probably had so many thousands of meetings with bands in his life that there's a certain rote manner in which you do these things. Chances are, I've handled things as poorly myself on a couple of occasions. He's introduced to Georgia and Ira, and goes into an explanation of

Island's market share, and who the top acts on the label are. It's not the kind of thing that's going impress somebody like Ira or Georgia. 'Oh, wow, you guys have U2? I was not aware of that.' Then we sat there, and he asked, 'Any questions?'"

Ira responded, plainly, "Well, yeah, why do you want us on your label?"

A look of annoyance grew over the executive's face and he pointed sharply at Gerard. "Because *he* said it was a good idea."

After Ira and Georgia left, Bone turned to Gerard. "Boy, I liked her," he said.

"She didn't say anything," Gerard replied.

"Yeah, that's *right*."

A half decade into their career, Yo La Tengo was part-time work for its members. Some income came from playing shows, but copyediting, proofreading, soundman jobs, and DJ gigs continued. "Proofreading and copyediting was more of a desk job," Ira said. "But luckily we owned a desk." In their two rooms on the second floor at Garden Street, Georgia and Ira alternated turns, spreading out unbound manuscript pages, character lists, and a dictionary. Especially while on deadline, one would often work while the other slept. During daylight hours, it was a profitable way to pass time while listening to records.

"It was a pretty substantial aspect of income," Ira said. "I probably wasn't doing it as quickly as I could have been, it certainly paid better than Maxwell's, but I was pretty lazy about it." Janet Wygal, the former Individual who'd become a production editor at Random House, kept plenty of musicians fed over the years by giving them the work.

The titles were "hilariously bad," often nonfiction war books, postapocalyptic survival dramas, and the occasional self-help volume. "They were written so quickly and so poorly that they were completely riddled with errors, so you really had to be on your toes," said Ira. One series traded in "bawdy old Western tales," one of which yielded a Yo La Tengo song title. "Sleepily correcting some softcore, I misread the word 'crown' as 'cloud' and corrected the typo in the phrase 'The mushroon crown of hiss penis,'" Ira wrote later. He missed the extra "s," but came away with a good phrase: "Mushroom Cloud of Hiss."

The rent stayed cheap, though, and every time they lost a bassist, they either doggedly resumed the search for the next or figured out something to do until they found one. Frustrations aside, it remained a worthwhile and mostly enjoyable path, an existence of constant transience and surprising transition.

They recorded a John Cale cover in the basement with Tara Key, featuring Shauna the cat on backing vocals. Ira joined Phil Morrison and booking agent Bob Lawton in Double Dynamite, a party band thrown together for a set at Maxwell's to celebrate their shared birthday. But Yo La Tengo bookings were so few that the ordinarily scrupulous guitarist failed to record the dates in his log of the band's gigs. One of note came at the Middle East in Boston.

"I think they were expecting us to do an acoustic show, since we do that a lot," Ira said. "I had the idea that we both should play electric guitar, and that should be the show. So we weren't going to do anything remotely acoustic. Instead, it was pretty abrasive." This latest willfully contrarian gesture marked another significant turning point in Yo La Tengo's development. Ira and Georgia created an almost entirely new set of music and crossed another bridge. "'Songs' might be overstating what we wrote, they were sort of *pieces*," Ira said, but they were the pair's first collaboration on original music.

In the next months, they kept working at the material, fitting instrumental sections together in new settings until they became songs far evolved from their origins. Through constant editing, one would eventually yield significant sections of "From a Motel 6," "Mushroom Cloud of Hiss," and "The Summer"—songs realized, respectively, as a soaring indie-pop number, a noise vehicle, and their most lapidary composition yet. Each took a while.

The problem of identity was rarely one to bother Yo La Tengo, except logistically. Others grew more frustrated with their implausible switches, each with its own worried-over logic and conclusion about whether it was the right thing to do at that particular moment. Not long after they returned from Japan, Steve Fallon brought some A&M executives to see Yo La Tengo at the Knitting Factory, where they were booked to play an early show and a late show. In the spirit of Television's two-set performances Ira had seen at CBGB, they'd decided one would be noisier and one more accessible. Steve and the executives arrived for what Steve hated most, more of Ira's "debauched noise." Exasperated, Steve and the executives walked out. It was a well-practiced independence.

But the time was uncharacteristically right for Yo La Tengo when they convened for a few days at Water Music with Dave Schramm, returning on countrypolitan guitar; producer Gene Holder; and Dave's friend Al Greller on upright bass. As the dB's, R.E.M., and others had tamed punk's wildness into music that was potentially and actually commercial, a kinder, gentler landscape grew in the ether, paved in the far-off distance by MTV's new *Unplugged*. College radio was as huge as ever, and collegiate audiences had *always* been hungry for acoustic music, going back at least as far as the Weavers.

The resultant album of covers, *Fakebook*, drew from the acoustic repertoire Yo La Tengo been working on for more than two years. It featured the usual Yo La Tengo twist, too. Despite the covers concept, the album was fully one quarter originals, especially after Gene Holder nixed a ten-minute version of Gram Parsons's "A Song for You" and urged them to include more of their own numbers. Though, to be even more contrarian about it, several of *those* originals were covers of versions recorded earlier by Yo La Tengo. And to be triply contrarian, the album itself began with one that wasn't.

They had every good reason to feature these songs, too. "The Summer" was the band's first bona fide classic, sung in hushed duet by Ira and Georgia, holding a fragile moment for two and a half well-edited minutes. Though traditional in its form, "The Summer" had evolved out of Ira and Georgia's two-guitar repertoire, its jewel-like guitar melody fixed into song after song until it worked. "Barnaby, Hardly Working" and "Did I Tell You" recast favorites, as well. Along with the alternately jangly and noisy versions of "The Evil That Men Do," *Fakebook* instituted an era where nearly every Yo La Tengo song existed in one or more doppelgänger arrangements.

The sessions went smoothly. By now, Georgia had specific instructions for how she wanted to be presented, still framed in terms of a negative, but more clear about what she wanted the result to be. "I don't want it to sound like the snare drum and its little friends," she told Gene Holder. Schramm contributed his usual perfect lines. Peter Stampfel of the Holy Modal Rounders joined on "The One to Cry" by the Escorts, but not "Griselda," the song on the record's flip side on which he *did* originally perform.

When WFMU relocated its East Orange base from the Froeberg Hall basement to a house in the middle of the Upsala campus, records were filed everywhere, including under the sink. In the attic was the Alan Watts Rejuvenation Chamber, named for the late Buddhist philosopher whose lectures the station often broadcast, as well as a ratty futon for DJs to crash on. "When we were in the house, it was like, 'Wow, we can sit out on the lawn! We can have a barbecue out back! We shovel the driveway when it snows!'" remembered DJ Irwin Chusid.

"It was a home. We had keys to the front door. People would sleep there. You'd go there and hang out, much more than you did at Froeberg Hall. FMU became a warmer place to be and more of a community."

With Ken Freedman at the helm and an increasingly expert crew of DJs, WFMU had by the mid-'80s earned a national reputation as a home for off-center music that included indie rock but absorbed much else besides. For the next five years running, *Rolling Stone* would name WFMU the best radio station in the country before disqualifying it for having won too many times. Even as major labels ramped up their college radio marketing programs, WFMU remained "unworkable, which was fine," according to Karen Glauber, a onetime Hoboken resident who headed up promotions for A&M.

One day, while DJ Nick Hill, host of *The Music Faucet*, was on the air, he received a surprise call. Even without the playlist systems that more and more college stations began to adopt, the Texas singer-songwriter Daniel Johnston had become one of WFMU's most-played artists. Released on cassette in small batches by a friend, his helium-pitched Beatle-folk was touched with a very real emotional rawness, a manifestation of Johnston's own increasing mental distress. The twenty-nine-year-old Johnston arrived with a mythical but absolutely true backstory: he'd joined the circus, worked at McDonald's, and rotated between mental institutions and his parents' new home in suburban West Virginia while creating guileless home recordings and surreal comic drawings.

"He had many boosters here and may have been trying to reach someone specific," Hill remembered. "But the call seemed more random than that."

The year before, Johnston visited the Manhattan area at the behest of Sonic Youth. Homestead had released a double-LP collecting Johnston's cassettes. The trip ended in disaster, when—during a gig at Pier Platters, Ira and Georgia in attendance—Johnston had a psychotic episode. He ranted about Satan and eventually disappeared into the wilds of a Manhattan flophouse. Eventually, Sonic Youth's Lee Ranaldo and Steve Shelley tracked him down in a motel on the New Jersey side of the Holland Tunnel.

When Johnston rang WFMU during Nick Hill's show in late January 1990, he was back in West Virginia. Hill had a second-anniversary show planned for the following week and invited Johnston to appear. Also appearing were Yo La Tengo, who, coincidentally, had recorded Johnston's "Speeding Motorcycle" only weeks before for their new album—a fact Hill may or may not have actually known when he suggested they collaborate with Johnston via phone.

With Dave Schramm along, fresh from the sessions and a gig in Brooklyn the night before, they played most of *Fakebook*. And when the band's set finished, the phone rang promptly in studio A: Johnston calling from his parents' West Virginia bedroom. Without warning, Johnston launched into an hourlong homemade radio special filled with fake interviews in which he provided the voices of fans, managers, and critics. Johnston collaged four-track recordings with made-up ad jingles for his next album, and—in the dead middle of it all—suddenly addressed the stunned crew in the WFMU studio.

"I heard you got a band there," he said.

Yo La Tengo, still set up and listening on headphones, sprang to attention. Hill tried to introduce Johnston to the band. "Hi, band!" Johnston replied, and without counting off, launched straight into his own "Speeding Motorcycle." Though there is almost no way he could have heard the band over the phone, Johnston managed to stay in perfect time with the trio in the studio. They did two more songs, neither as successfully, and Daniel took some calls from listeners. It was the kind of thing that could only happen on WFMU.

Also a Maxwell's bartender, Nick Hill was likewise the cofounder of the Singles Only Label with Steve Fallon and ex–Hüsker Dü guitarist Bob Mould, who had recently moved to Hoboken. Distributed exclusively through Dutch East, as all their discs were, SOL released a 45 of the WFMU "Speeding Motorcycle" that gave Yo La Tengo another legit college radio hit. What's more, it was a hit without a formula, requested ad nauseam by fans in years to come.

Johnston returned to Austin that spring as a cause celèbre at a new indie-oriented industry convention held in his home city dubbed South by Southwest. As he had in New York, Johnston went off his medication to give an edge to his performance, and the excitement frothed him into a manic attack. Flying back to West Virginia in his father's small plane,

Johnston wrestled away the controls and crashed into the woods below. Both walked away miraculously unscathed, but Johnston was institutionalized. While still confined, he would become the subject of a major-label bidding war.

At Homestead, Gerard Cosloy finally got fed up. The situation had deteriorated even further. It wasn't merely cooler labels like SST that he had to worry about anymore. Sonic Youth had recorded two albums for SST before discovering they were no better at paying its bands than Homestead, and jumped ship there, too. By the summer of 1989, they were being eyed by DGC, the latest imprint run by the baby boomer mogul David Geffen, and one of seemingly dozens of big labels who'd started to open their pocketbooks to underground acts. Sonic Youth's lawyer Richard Grabel, a former *New York Rocker* contributor who had given R.E.M. their first international press via his column in the *New Music Express*, negotiated a five-album deal with Geffen estimated at $300,000.

For Gerard, Homestead was an obvious dead end. In the summer of 1989, he received the self-released debut 7-inch by a new band from Stockton, California, whose guitarist was a regular reader. At the first chance he got, he reviewed Pavement's *Slay Tracks* EP as enthusiastically as possible. "Genuine songs buried underneath mountains of dust and soot, absolutely perfect," he wrote. "Blindfold test would've had me guessing something on Xpressway or K, and since I mistook the label name for that of the band for over a month, there's no need to believe any of this if you're skeptical."

But Homestead was no place for them, and it was no place for Gerard either. In early 1990, Craig Marks accepted a job editing CMJ's monthly music magazine. "There was too much work for one person to do," Gerard said. "I realized Barry wasn't going to replace Craig. It was only going to get worse, and the idea of doing it solo was exhausting."

Gerard and Craig presented their boss with their notices at the same time. Barry Tenenbaum didn't say a word.

The van was windowless. It wasn't so bad, but it was still hard to believe that it had been the reason they'd signed with Bar/None Records when they did. Talks had stalled when Yo La Tengo landed a spot on a cross-country tour supporting the Sundays, a British quartet who had achieved a sudden buzzy success. With a new four-person lineup featuring upright bassist Wilbo Wright and guitarist Kevin Salem, a van was a necessity. Carrying Yo La Tengo across the country and to their first national success, the long, lightless rides were a rite of passage.

Life in the "tin-can van" was agreeable for Salem, an avowed stoner at the time, who noted that "nothing goes better with pothead than people looking for crazy things to eat." The band added new songs to the proverbial fakebook nearly every night, a sharp contrast to the tour's comparably green headliners who mustered a barely changing setlist of a dozen tunes.

The *Fakebook* party remained in good humor even when the Sundays tour was canceled after a two-day haul from Minneapolis to Denver. A representative from the club pulled up next to the van on a motorcycle and delivered news of an illness in the Sundays' family. On the way home, Ira joked about the appearance of the mysterious rider: *I bring you word of the Sundays*.

Even as they piloted the Bar/None cargo van back east, their new label boss was preparing for *Fakebook*'s release. Founded in the basement of Pier Platters, Bar/None's first record had been by Rage to Live, led by former *New York Rocker* editor and Individuals songwriter Glenn Morrow. It hadn't panned out. In addition to managing Bar/None, Morrow spent some time writing quick-and-easy rock biographies under a pseudonym. He pumped out a good-selling paperback about Michael Jackson and found himself with some money.

After Bar/None had a surprise hit with They Might Be Giants—their video for "Don't Let's Start" found success on MTV's *120 Minutes* and college radio—Morrow offered to buy the label with his Michael Jackson book earnings. It was a natural match for Bar/None to sign Yo La Tengo, if hardly a lucrative one. It was also the first deal Yo La Tengo made with anything like a real contract. Still acting as their manager, Steve Fallon urged them to hire a lawyer. They didn't.

Though Bar/None's advance for *Fakebook* was modest, they did put up money for—and insist the band make—a music video. Originally intended to be shot in the intersection outside of Maxwell's, Phil Morrison filmed a baroque performance short for "The Summer" with Georgia and Ira near his Grand Army Plaza apartment in Brooklyn. More than ever, it seemed, Yo La Tengo was at odds with the broader culture that summer, bursting with hard rock and gangsta rap. It aired a few times on MTV's *120 Minutes*, fitting not uncomfortably into the program's college radio–influenced mix.

As a way to get critics to listen, Morrow sent out advance cassettes without a track listing, and promised prizes to any who could identify the songs. Only Fred Mills, music editor of Atlanta's *Creative Loafing*, answered correctly. *Fakebook* was received with open arms by a surprised rock press.

"Wholly wonderful," wrote Jim Greer in *Spin*. "I don't think there's ever been a more welcomed package from home," Jim DeRogatis observed in *Jersey Beat*, unemployed and homesick in Minneapolis.

In the months that led up to *Fakebook*'s release, Ira and Georgia had already started to hit college radio stations hard, following the model set by the trailblazing R.E.M. Over the next year they spent promoting *Fakebook*, the pair made more than fifty on-air appearances, sometimes two or three a day in addition to their club shows. Later Ira would credit Georgia's new enthusiasm for singing as something to do to avoid awkward interviews.

Fakebook made #18 CMJ as they hit Europe, where it was one of the first releases on a new German label, City Slang. Despite the success, Yo La Tengo continued to switch at will between acoustic and electric billings, but it was the four-piece with Kevin Salem and Wilbo Wright that spent the late summer and early fall back in the windowless Bar/None van, finishing out the rescheduled Sundays dates and continuing up and down the East Coast for a few months afterward.

In Yo La Tengo's absence, changes were afoot in Hoboken. Maxwell's had recently been appraised at some $1.2 million, and the time seemed exactly right for the rest of the Fallon family to cash out. Within the year, helped by a credit assist from R.E.M.'s Peter Buck, Steve Fallon bought the building and the club. And in June, as Yo La Tengo headed out with the Sundays for the first time, General Foods announced the forthcoming closing of the Maxwell House plant. Costs were lower in Florida, they said.

Though not always clear what, Yo La Tengo were doing something right. It was around this time that Ira and Georgia noticed that more than half of their income was derived from playing music. In the end of 1990 and the beginning of 1991, the band's unceasing activity made them two new connections that would radically alter their career. The first came in the stands at Shea Stadium. There, Ira and Georgia ran into Pere Ubu leader David Thomas in the company of his manager, Jamie Kitman.

Also steering the career of Bar/None's flagship act, They Might Be Giants, Kitman had quit a job at a high-priced law firm before he had even started. Instead, he chose to write about expensive cars, beginning with an assignment that involved driving a Corvette to the 1986 American League playoffs in Southern California. Glenn Morrow had tried to put him in touch with Yo La Tengo previously, but it didn't take until they crossed paths at Shea.

"Without him, it would be easily arguable that we wouldn't exist," Ira later said of Kitman. "We started taking ourselves more seriously because he did. He instructed us to buy a van, instead of renting them all the time, and to set ourselves up as a business. He was good at doing things that captured the tone correctly."

The van purchase itself was another milestone. "That was really the first time we promised anyone—in this case, a bank—that we'd continue to be a band for the next four years and pay off this loan," Ira said. A decade later, they were still driving it.

The second connection came via dinner. Before a February 1991 show at Club Babyhead in Providence, Rhode Island, Ira and Georgia dined with their friends in Christmas, themselves no strangers to needing a third member. Ira and Georgia kvetched about their usual problems. Offhandedly, between mouthfuls of food, Christmas's latest bassist volunteered for the job.

CHAPTER 9

And Suddenly . . .

James McNew was from Charlottesville as much as he was from anywhere. Born in Baltimore on July 6, 1969, he spent his first decade in motion. His father, Jim, worked for State Life Insurance, and moved the family to Florida briefly, and then throughout northern Virginia. "All the towns that begin with A," James would say.

"Moving didn't bother me so much," remembered James, who became easily adaptable. It seemed all too normal. The family would move, James would make new friends, State Farm would reassign Jim, and the family would move one more time. James rarely saw the friends again. "It sounds horrible now, but I really never thought about it," he said. His parents were his most frequent company.

His mother, Elaina, was a quick-tongued font of happiness, possessed of an easy good cheer that she would pass on to her only child. Wherever they lived, there were long car trips to visit grandparents in Queens or Baltimore, and endless hours of delicious radio to absorb. Jim liked the Stones and James Brown. Elaina favored Bob Dylan and Joan Baez and had a nylon-string guitar in the closet. They happily indulged James's love of music, and bought 45s of his favorite radio hits, like Paper Lace's "The Night Chicago Died." Soon he discovered Elaina's guitar.

When James first tried playing it, he was disappointed when it didn't sound like the guitars that had intrigued him on the radio. But he continued to play, and—around the time the McNews settled in Charlottesville—began to take lessons at a local music shop from an overly laid-back teacher. An electric guitar followed, an imitation Les Paul. "Why don't you bring in a song that you like and I'll show you how it goes?" the instructor suggested. James brought in Cream's "Badge" and the instructor happily complied. Next up was a Van Halen record. "I do remember his face at the first note," James recalled. "It was like seeing a grown man cry."

But Eddie Van Halen—or playing like him, anyway—didn't quite suit James either. "I sort of had the premonition that taking lessons was on the line between *this is fun* and *this is school*." James resisted anything when it became too organized. "Johnny Ramone isn't Van Halen and he's great," James recalled thinking, a magical revelation. For his tenth birthday, Jim and Elaina gave him a *Rolling Stone* rock encyclopedia, which James devoured. Somewhere, sometime, he'd inhaled the spore too, and eventually there was almost nothing but music.

Unlike his future bandmates, it came easily to him. He quit taking lessons and discovered he could hear songs and figure out the correct key and chord changes. Soon enough, James had a band of his own: four guys with guitars, no bassist, "and access to a drum kit."

They named themselves after "ME-262," by Blue Öyster Cult, which they tried to learn. At home, James discovered how to use adjacent cassette decks to create primitive overdubs, and again tried to play "ME-262." "That was a big hit around my room," James recalled.

Browsing the magazines at the 7-Eleven near his house, James picked up an issue of *Creem* with Van Halen's David Lee Roth on the cover. Inside was a story about Pere Ubu. Though hardly the *Creem* of the rollicking Lester Bangs years, the magazine's humor pulled James in and he soon became a regular reader.

During his freshman year of high school, his English teacher spotted him with a copy of *Creem*. "Do you read that magazine?" Mrs. Hull asked. "My husband writes for that magazine."

Mrs. Hull's husband—Robert "Robot" Hull—happened to be the chief music critic for the *Washington Post* and a longtime contributing editor at *Creem*. He'd moved to Charlottesville to teach courses in pop music at the University of Virginia. His wife, Susan, brought in Lenny Kaye's two-LP *Nuggets* compilation and the Velvet Underground's *White Light/White Heat* and loaned them to James. He recounted the moment happily later in life: "All right, bye! I appreciate this! I'm sorry I won't be paying attention to class anymore." He was hooked in every way.

James participated in the school's new Rock Album Critics Club, but it was through *Creem* and *The Bob*, a Delaware music magazine, that James discovered R.E.M. and, soon thereafter, bands like the Feelies, Mitch Easter's Let's Active, Camper Van Beethoven, Dream Syndicate, and other exponents of American indie rock. Like his future bandmates, "I was never interested in British stuff, ever."

In early December 1985, R.E.M.'s never-ending tour circled through their native southeast for ten shows, with a handful in Virginia college towns. "They knew where their bread was buttered," James observed. He attended nearly a half dozen, collecting autographed 7-inches along the way. The opening act was the Minutemen, fronted by the kinetic and rotund D. Boon. James, hardly a skinny teenager, was entranced.

"*There's a guy who looks like me!* I'd never seen a guy who looks like me making music," James remembered. "*There he is! Pogoing! And he doesn't give a fuck!* I was completely self-conscious growing up as a weirdo in this conservative part of the country and . . . *look at that guy!* Everything fell away at the moment."

The young rock fan's instant identification with the outsider San Pedro trio could only have been confirmed when the Richmond crowd booed off Boon and company, and were subsequently admonished by R.E.M.'s Michael Stipe. Boon was killed in a car accident only weeks later, the Minutemen destroyed at their peak.

The entry to the Corner Parking Lot was narrow, no more than an alley between buildings with the attendant's booth at the back end. It was there, in late 1987, that James McNew "began life from zero" as a parking-lot attendant after one miserable semester of higher education.

Bridgewater College was an hour northwest of Charlottesville, near the base of the Appalachians. Though close to home, James hadn't known anyone else heading there, a situation exactly by his design. "I never wanted to see any of the people I'd grown up with again," he said. "While I was there, my parents split up for a while. I was in a horrible relationship. I kind of had a nervous breakdown and dropped out of school."

The parking lot itself was triangular, bounded on one side by train tracks and just removed from the college-bar bustle of University Avenue. It was a fairly meditative job, collecting tolls, operating the gate, doing light cleaning, and—in James's words—"dealing with people for the first time and studying something that I couldn't apply to anything I knew." Plan 9 Records was just down the alley to the left.

In the particular conditions of Charlottesville, jobs at the Corner Parking Lot had become a sustaining occupation for local musicians, its booth a center for the city's burgeoning indie rock scene. Much of this had to do with Maynard Sipe, the music obsessive who had gotten James his job there, and the kind of local scene maker who could only have emerged in the mid-1980s.

James had first encountered Maynard in high school. After seeing the Minutemen, he'd started a new cover band. Unaware of the New Jersey act by the same name, James and his friends dubbed themselves the Smithereens and had gotten a gig at a local party where Sipe was in attendance.

Maynard had arrived as a UVA first-year in the early '80s, secured a late-night slot on the 600-watt WTJU, and made himself into the city's first beacon on the indie rock map. He published a zine called *Live Squid* and began to book national acts around town. Intermittently, he dropped out of school and worked shifts at the Corner Parking Lot. At least one touring band would come to refer to the promoter in each town as "the Maynard." He also kept an eye on local talent.

"I always tried to do all-ages shows, which was quite a struggle back then," Sipe said. "There was a handful of high school kids who attended, including James. He came by the Parking Lot and dropped off a tape. He was a junior, I think. I was impressed by them." In Maynard Sipe, James found a mentor when his collegiate career burned.

James moved in with Sipe's friend John Beers, a fellow Corner Parking Lot employee and a possessor of nearly a hundred back issues of *Conflict* and *Forced Exposure*, the massive and dense zine Byron Coley had spent much of the '80s editing. Each of the latter "took a month to read to figure out what the hell they were talking about, if they liked the records or not, trying to decipher Byron. With Gerard, you at least knew what he meant. Byron was more obscure." James inhaled the texts in the Parking Lot booth, soundtracked by hundreds of cassettes copied from vinyl. He temporarily "got real macho about the long reads" and tackled James Joyce's *Ulysses* and Thomas Pynchon's *V.*

James's new roommate, John Beers, was six years older than he was. He'd occupied the midnight-to-two-a.m. Friday-night slot on WTJU, just before Maynard, and was a member of the Landlords, Charlottesville's first hardcore band. They'd debuted at a local Holiday Inn and lasted all of three and a half minutes before the bar's management cut the power and threw them out. Hardly doctrinaire about hardcore, the Landlords—like goofier Feelies—mutated into a half dozen other incarnations.

Big Foot had Beers and bassist Eddie Jetlag playing through a telephone. The Jazz Deacons played lounge music with free-form freak-outs. There was the Mel Cooley Fusion Project; the Rock and Roll Brothers; and finally, Beers and Charlie Kramer's Happy Flowers, whose spastically improvised juvenilia grew more popular than the still-existing Landlords. They landed two tracks on Touch and Go's high-profile *God's Favorite Dog* compilation and played an album release at CBGB. Gerard Cosloy complimented them after their set.

"You wanna sign us?" Beers asked.

"Send me a tape," Cosloy replied, which Beers took for a blow-off until Gerard called him in Virginia wondering where the tape was. Homestead released Happy Flowers' *My Skin Covers My Body* in the summer of 1987, a flagship band for the ever-fertile WTJU scene.

The new station manager that year was a drummer from Rochester named Bob Nastanovich, and the DJ roster included a history major from California named Stephen Malkmus, as well as the tall, heavily drinking poet David Berman. All three played in Ectoslavia, a basement noise outfit that used massive oil drums for percussion. Nastanovich also worked at Plan 9, which sold *Conflict* and the latest underground sounds.

The Corner Parking Lot was an eclectic space, filled with the kind of outsiderness that can only come when one's job is to attend to one's peers. The eight-hour shifts were deep zones that could become transcendental for James, who permanently associated the opening of "Wouldn't It Be Nice" with a clean spring morning, sweeping the alley while listening to *Pet Sounds* on the booth's boom box. He flyered for Maynard and helped load gear at bigger events, like the Replacements.

Amid a friendly cast of regulars, James saw an almost mathematically perfect slice of humanity: former high school classmates, and a man who seemed to sleep in his car (though not in the parking lot itself). He was even witness to a man's death. Shortly after Beers quit, he was at the lot with James when a man paid his toll and exited the alley toward the street.

James and John heard a crash, and found the driver slumped at the wheel. James called 911, but the man had died of a heart attack seconds after he'd paid for his parking. The lot shut down for several hours.

"At the time, that was the closest I had been to anyone who had passed away," James remembered of the "amazing weird afternoon." "I think I was still too young to have been to the funerals of my relatives. That was my first brush with it and it was a pretty heavy contemplative day or two at work after that. It had a strangely almost dignified feeling to it. The guy died doing something everyday, a mundane transaction, and it was peaceful. It caused me to think very deeply for a while."

Boom box staples included New Zealand rock bands like the buoyant garage-punk of the Clean, their Dunedin neighbors in the Chills, and the home recording Tall Dwarfs. James blasted Lou Reed's *Metal Machine Music* one afternoon, took in Japanese noise rock, and, at Beers's suggestion, "nearly turned a tape to dust" listening to John Lennon's *Plastic Ono Band*. He became a rabid fan of the first few Black Flag albums but didn't follow hardcore's tenets any deeper than the music.

Soon enough, thanks to John and Maynard, James picked up late-night shifts on WTJU that began at two a.m. and ended with a six-a.m. sign-off. He played Corner Parking Lot favorites and sometimes auditioned curiosity-piquing LPs from the station's library live on the air. "It was just me in a room by myself playing records, having the time of my life," James said. "The time would fly."

It was left to James to tell Christmas that their show was canceled. Robyn Hitchcock had called in sick. James had been excited when Maynard had added them to the bill. The Boston oddball punk band had become one of his favorites lately. They'd been driving all day and Maynard paid them anyway. They were happy to hang out with the enthusiastic fan, who interviewed them in their van for his zine.

Not long after he returned to Charlottesville, James had started to contribute to *And Suddenly . . .* , a zine started by some high school friends. "One liked to write, one liked to draw," James said. "I saw it for something else. Once I convinced them to lose interest, I took it in my own direction."

James poured a lot of energy into *And Suddenly . . .* and took months to assemble his first issue in the Corner Parking Lot booth. Frustrated by the denseness of zines like *Maximumrockandroll* and the endless typos in *Flipside*, he borrowed pleasantly from *Conflict*'s cynicism and worked hard to represent *And Suddenly . . .* as more than a local publication.

His interview with Christmas was a score. They'd eventually repaired to a local bowling alley. Afterward, he stayed in close contact with Michael Cudahy. "James had the tiniest handwriting of anybody I know," the Christmas guitarist would recall later.

James interviewed other bands that Maynard brought through town, including Sonic Youth and B.A.L.L., an indie supergroup that included Gumball guitarist Don Fleming, Sonic Youth's Kim Gordon, producer Kramer, and former Yo La Tengo bassist Dave Rick. He solicited top-ten lists from many, including Calvin Johnson and Gerard Cosloy, and struck up mail correspondences with a number of his favorite musicians and writers.

He enlisted John Beers, whose spelling skills he trusted, to retype articles from handwritten notebook drafts at a UVA computer lab. Maynard's occasional job at the copy shop next to the Corner Parking Lot allowed James to camp there after hours, shrink the text to spec, and lay it out with rubber cement. He distributed the 125 copies as best he could, by hand and via Plan 9. A copy made its way to Dutch East, who offered to distribute the next issue.

James sent fifty copies to the Dutch East warehouse on Long Island. From there, *And Suddenly . . .* made its way into the nooks of the underground, including Pier Platters in Hoboken. Through the zine, James continued to make friends around the country, including a fellow *Conflict*-inspired zine editor in New Jersey named Tom Scharpling, who ran *18 Wheeler* and became a regular mail correspondent.

During his last year of high school, James had started to make four-track recordings of his own, which he eventually played for the Parking Lot gang. A new band, the Maynards, played a half dozen times, with their namesake on the drums.

Around this time, James ended up in the basement of the Red House, the infamous party residence frequented by WTJU's David Berman and Bob Nastanovich where they and Malkmus practiced with Ectoslavia. James joined the rotating cast temporarily, a brief and incompatible tenure of which most parties remember little. The incompatibility did not seem to be uncommon. Berman soon fired the rest of the band.

James was also excited when Maynard brought in Yo La Tengo for a show in early 1988 (bassist: Stephan Wichnewski) and helped flyer. He saw them again opening for the Feelies in January of the following year (bassist again: Stephan). He knew *New Wave Hot Dogs* and *Ride the Tiger* "backwards and forwards," but didn't meet the band. It wasn't that unusual. James had a lot of favorite bands, a product of both his relentless enthusiasm and his terrific memory for music.

He volunteered his Ford Escort station wagon for one of Happy Flowers' rare out-of-town trips to D.C., New York, and Boston, and earned the name Mr. Surrogate Roadie in the process. In New York, the band stayed at Gerard Cosloy's East Village apartment.

Scared, James asked Beers what Gerard was like before the trip. Beers told him not to worry. "He looks like Elvis Costello," he said. In *Conflict*, Cosloy referred to his new digs as "The Cave."

"One room was a massive record collection, and no order to it," Beers remembered. "You could ask him where something was and he'd just reach over and grab it."

"His cats climbed all over us," James remembered. "I was terrified of him, but he was really nice." Happy Flowers shared a bill with Gerard's new roommates in White Zombie.

Back in Charlottesville, James plotted the next issue of

And Suddenly...in the Corner Parking Lot booth. It would feature the result of a long correspondence with Tall Dwarfs' Chris Knox in New Zealand. James prepared to return to school, as well, and took an intensive summer school class in Japanese—a topic that actually interested him, and no more so than when a mysterious package showed up at the post office for John Beers, postmarked from Osaka.

When they got the package home, John and James discovered a bundle of apparently hand-pressed records with jagged edges. Also included was a note, barely in English, from a group of Happy Flowers fans in Japan led by Tetsurō Yamatsuka, known by the stage name Yamataka Eye. He had once driven a backhoe through the wall of a club and now led a violently noisy outfit called the Boredoms. "We are from Osaka," the note read. "We make our own records."

One afternoon, James received a phone call in the Parking Lot booth. He'd never received a call there before. The phone itself was new. Michael Cudahy had somehow found the number and was on the other end. Christmas had been on tour, opening for the Bangles, but the tour had crashed. Cudahy and Liz Cox were in Boston working on songs and, once again—Cudahy explained—without a bassist.

He invited James up for a weekend. The twenty-year-old James McNew had never played bass before, but he got there as quickly as he could. The weekend went well. A month later, Cudahy called again and invited James to join Christmas full-time at their new home in fabulous Las Vegas.

"Boston is kind of a pugnacious place," Michael Cudahy once said. "It's really one of the meanest cities in America. I got pummeled all the time, walking down the street. One time, I was at a party where I thought I was safe with my wimpy punk-rock pals, and some drunken guys from Quincy—tripping, thuggy guys—sort of clocked me. I was in the hospital for nearly a month and nearly died. That shit went on pretty often."

Cudahy affected what he described as a "Jerry Mathers/

Don Knotts, least-likely-guy-in-the-crowd-to-have-a-gun" look and followed his "strong belief that unless somebody was bleeding or something was broken it wasn't a good gig." Gerard Cosloy loved Christmas, going out of his way to not apologize for writing about them (and Yo La Tengo) too much in *Conflict*. They briefly hired him as their manager. "He was underage, but he was tenacious," Cudahy remembered.

By 1988, they were ready to exit Boston and, with unsurprisingly perverse humor, had chosen Las Vegas. Cudahy calculated that it was within commuting distance of Los Angeles, and "the least likely place to live for a rock band." They'd passed through earlier that year while on tour with Hüsker Dü, and Cudahy marveled at the giant, kitschy suburb in the desert.

The band found a house off Fremont Street, a short walk to the old Strip. Built in the '50s, the house was ancient by the standards of Las Vegas's contemporary expansion. Cudahy drove to the edge of town to look at the "cookie-cutter houses, like the houses in Monopoly. Go another block, and it'd be houses under construction, and then in another block, it'd be desert. If you came back a few months later, it'd be another mile before you hit the desert." On maps of the city, he noticed streets named for *Star Wars* characters. Elsewhere in the town, there were the Knights of the Round Table. The city had expanded so fast that it had run out of street names.

With its cheap rent and strange local conditions, Las Vegas seemed like an outsider bet for Hoboken-style gentrification. Cudahy envisioned the potential result as something bizarre and wonderful: boho kitsch. Christmas knew one or two other bands in town. There was one hip record store. They'd connected with psychobilly novelty songwriter the Legendary Stardust Cowboy at a gig in Boston and he visited them occasionally at their house for barbecues and backyard Pictionary.

They rented a space in a vast rehearsal complex to write songs for a long-overdue second album for I.R.S. The band's neighbors were local heavy metal combos, including one (never encountered in person) who left a drum set with a triple kick drum on the corner. They saw Sammy Davis Jr. perform a few times, but drove to Los Angeles many weekends. Their latest bassist had split in the middle of the year.

They'd been charmed by James's tales of the Parking Lot in his letters. Earlier in the year, they'd shared a bill with James's band the Maynards in Charlottesville, where they covered Bobby Brown's "My Prerogative"—a song Christmas had been covering of late. Michael thought James might be a good solution.

James put in notice at the Corner Parking Lot and told his parents. All agreed it was a fine idea. He boxed up the unpublished issue of *And Suddenly . . .* , moved his records into his parents' place, and left Virginia with $150 and a bag of clothes. In Las Vegas, he crashed on the floor of the band's tiny house and lay awake, looking forward to practice the next day.

The feeling didn't dissipate during his three months in Nevada. "They had not that many records," James said, "so I'd memorized every detail of what little they had done. A few impossible-to-find 7-inches and two LPs."

"James was a really good fit," Cudahy assessed. "He totally got where we were coming from. We weren't into writing things by jamming, but he would always come up with the perfect thing. It was like, 'Wow, where have *you* been?'"

James's easygoing, accommodating demeanor slotted in comfortably around Michael and Liz. Though they had long since broken up, old fights flared up occasionally. "Liz and I were like an old married couple," Cudahy said. "And James would get freaked out when we would bicker." James was a quick study, though, and learned to navigate the ins and outs of band/couple dynamics—an oddly specific skill set in the indie rock world that would prove useful very soon.

Band and bassist gelled, a partnership that produced nearly twenty songs in a matter of months. In the warm desert autumn, it was a joy for James to be there. He explored what was left of the old, seedy Las Vegas and wandered the bad-smelling remains of Glitter Gulch, the Golden Nugget, and the Big Cowboy.

Several times, he found his way into local pawnshops and thought he must be dreaming. "Everything was there," James said. "Everybody had hit hard times. There were banks of Vox speaker cabinets and old Orange amps, organs, keyboards. I wished I had some money." In Vegas, James played on Michael's brother's bass. He'd been in Christmas too.

Life in a rock band wasn't as exciting as James thought it would be. Christmas finished the demos swiftly and made "the rational decision" to move back east. They chose Providence, Rhode Island, partially because it was close to Boston without being Boston, and partially because Michael's girlfriend lived there.

James passed through Charlottesville, got his stuff, and joined Cudahy and Cox in early 1990. They headed to Brooklyn to record their new album. Dave Rick—experiencing success with King Missile, whose novelty hit "Detachable Penis" had earned them some renown—joined them on guitar for one song. They crashed with Gerard Cosloy.

The new bassist was eager to delve into the band's back catalog and play shows, but Cudahy and Cox weren't as keen on it. "For a guy to join a band with people who'd been in a band for almost ten years and were discouraged and confused . . . ," Cudahy said later, sympathetically.

In March, the McNew-era Christmas played their first gig, a Music for Choice benefit in Boston with Sonic Youth and Yo La Tengo. James enjoyed Yo La Tengo immensely (bassist: Gene Holder) and was all the more surprised when Georgia and Ira launched into a cover of Christmas's "Junk," a song they'd been doing occasionally since the year before. James met them afterward and talked briefly about nothing in particular. He got a few vocal spotlights in the band's occasional live shows too, including prominent backing vocals on the Osmonds' "Yo-Yo," which blew away Adam Kaplan, for one, at an NYU gig.

But it wasn't really enough. In addition to rarely playing gigs, Christmas didn't practice too much either, so James

The Hubley family at home, mid-1960s
(Sam Falk /*The New York Times*)

Andy Schwartz, Glenn Morrow, and Ira at late-night paste-up
session at *New York Rocker*, 1982 (Photo by Laura Levine)

Georgia and Ira back Will Rigby and Peter Holsapple of the dB's at Laura Levine's birthday party, Michael Paumgardhen and Randy Gunn on guitars, *New York Rocker* office, 1982. (Photo by Laura Levine)

Ira and Georgia back the "Sex Bomb" chorale, *New York Rocker* office, 1982 (Photo by Laura Levine)

Ira and Byron Coley,
early 1980s
(Courtesy of YLT)

Ira and hospitality
spread, Europe, 1987
(Courtesy of YLT)

Ira and Bill Million of
the Feelies, c. 1989
(Courtesy of YLT)

Ira in the Buick, Hoboken,
1980s (Courtesy of YLT)

Detouring America with
Georgia, early 1990s
(Courtesy of YLT)

Copy editors abroad
(Courtesy of YLT)

Ira and Georgia record *May I Sing with Me*, 1991 (Courtesy of YLT)

Roger Moutenot, mid-'90s (Courtesy of YLT)

"May I Sing" with Phil Morrison and Ira, karaoke in Japan, November 1989 (Courtesy of YLT)

James at Maxwell's,
Hanukkah 2010
(Photo by Liz Clayton)

Ira, Maxwell's, Hanukkah 2007
(Photo by Liz Clayton)

Yo La Tengo and Alex
Chilton, Hanukkah 2007
(Photo by Liz Clayton)

Georgia, Ira, and the Clean's Hamish Kilgour at
Maxwell's, Hanukkah 2010 (Photo by Liz Clayton)

Yo La Tengo and Bruce Bennett slop up some requests,
WFMU Marathon, March 2011 (Photo by Jeff Moore)

Ira, Georgia, and James, February 2003 (Photos by Jack Chester)

dusted off his four-track, often at the band's practice space, and continued to accumulate recordings of new originals and obscure covers he'd begun in Charlottesville.

In Providence, James moved in with friends of Michael's girlfriend, guitarists Ric Menck and Jeffrey Underhill (né Borchardt) of the newly formed power-pop band Velvet Crush. He got a job at a coffee shop at Providence Station, opening the store at five thirty each weekday morning and working until two.

Nights and weekends, James took hours at In Your Ear, a record store on Thayer Street near Brown University, the only record-store gig for any of Yo La Tengo's three primary members. "It was a constant, entertaining battle," James remembers. "You could kill a whole day just by putting on [the Byrds'] *Sweetheart of the Rodeo* and starting an argument."

And always more recording. "Solitary bummed-outness is the unifying concept among most of it," he concluded. He drew a small cartoon bunny as a logo. "My roommate had another group called Honeybunch, and they sounded like they would be called Honeybunch," James remembered. "I reacted so violently to that name and everything about it that I thought, like, 'What's the opposite of that?' and came up with Dump. It's short, right to the point, it's really negative, and it makes me laugh. I can stand by that."

Late in the year, I.R.S. rejected Christmas's new album, which they'd titled *Vortex*. "They told us to go back and rerecord," Cudahy remembered. "Their criticism, at the end of 1990, was 'This sounds too much like a Sub Pop record.'" The nearly broke Seattle label was less than a year away from its redemption at the hands of Nirvana, at that exact moment the subject of an intense multilabel bidding war that would change the face of indie rock forever. But to Christmas, it was just a huge bummer.

Yo La Tengo rolled through town with their own woes shortly thereafter, stopping off at Liz Cox's place for dinner. They had an electric tour of Europe planned for the spring. Like Christmas, they had no label either, at least in the United States, where Bar/None struggled to make ends meet.

Christof Ellinghaus's Berlin-based City Slang had funded and was about to release an EP, *That Is Yo La Tengo*, but the band had no bassist to bring with them to Europe to promote it, and subsequently hadn't practiced. James—who'd taken to bass as easily as he'd taken to drums and nearly every other instrument he tried—suggested he could do it, and the meal continued. A week or so later, Ira called. "No, seriously, if you want to do it, it could be fun," he told James.

James listened to Yo La Tengo records over and over at work, learned the songs, and drove down I-95 to Hoboken to practice over a few March weekends. After the first, they repaired to Maxwell's and talked about *SCTV*, which seemed an auspicious sign. He returned to Providence each Sunday night in time to open the coffee place the next morning.

His first show was March 22 at Maxwell's. The next week, they played at Amherst in western Massachusetts and stayed with Byron Coley, whom James met for the first time.

"It was like staying in a museum," James remembered. "He was a great host. On subsequent visits, he would set things out. Something by Harry Crews, a limited edition of two articles and short stories that I'll never see again. Or a limited edition Captain Beefheart lithograph."

CHAPTER 10

Big Day Coming

Even before their dinner with Christmas, Yo La Tengo could almost sense something in the air. Just prior to James's debut, Ira and Georgia muscled onto a bill at Maxwell's for the express purpose of debuting a new song. Joining them for the night—number fourteen in the sequence of semipermanent and fill-in bassists—was Tim Harris of Antietam, who headlined. Six years after their first shows, the two bands remained tight. The year before, Ira and Georgia had hung out with Tim and Tara for a few weeks and helped produce a new album, *Burgoo*. For his gig with Yo La Tengo, Harris only had to play one note, albeit over and over again.

The new song occupied Yo La Tengo's entire twenty-eight-minute set and started with a chintzy keyboard loop-drone that cycled under Ira's slow-burn counterpoint. "Let's be undecided, let's take our time," Ira began. The words were unfinished as usual, but the first line, chorus, and sentiment were intact. Georgia played feedbacking guitar, building into cacophonous abstraction over the loop-drone. Some twenty minutes in, without being asked, Sleepyhead's Rachael McNally joined in on drums. It was a breakthrough on nearly every level, giving them a new way to play—a distinct blurring of loud and quiet—in addition to the quality of the song itself.

As Yo La Tengo hit the road with James McNew—number fifteen—over the spring and summer, Ira worked on the words. Nostalgic for the basement they'd recently moved out of, he slathered on the meta-detail until the song became an unadorned mission statement, love as music and vice versa. "Let's wake up the neighbors, let's turn up our amps, the way that we used to, without a plan. We can play a Stones song, 'Sittin' on a Fence,' and it'll sound pretty good till I forget how it ends."

The chorus that followed was almost accidentally journalistic, but Ira was nothing if not a prescient columnist. "There's a big day coming, I can hardly wait," Ira sang, more wistful than enthusiastic. The year would prove utterly transformative for both Yo La Tengo and the world in which they existed.

Though in stores less than a year and a decent seller for Bar/None, *Fakebook* was already out of print. Restless, the label's distributor, had gone bankrupt and sent back boxes of LPs. "There are times when we're more a state of mind than a record company," Glenn Morrow told *The New York Times*. "It was like a plague almost, trying to cram stuff under desks," he remembered, and attempted to sell the label's albums directly to stores. "We were lucky enough to have *Fakebook*, which was selling by that point."

"While *Fakebook* was a towering achievement, Bar/None was clearly inadequate to the task," remarked Jamie Kitman, the band's new manager. "They were understaffed, undercapitalized, and unwilling to take big risks." Following a lead from Ira, via a fan and friend who'd gotten a job at a new California label, Jamie made contact with Alias Records.

They were, if nothing else, a sign of the times. The label had emerged seemingly from nowhere, a new California indie ready with plane reservations and deep pockets. Behind the label was Delight Jenkins, a character as singular as any that crossed paths with Yo La Tengo.

She was married to David Jenkins, a part owner of the San Francisco Giants. His father, George, had helped invent the modern supermarket. "Alias seemed to have the key to Fort Knox," remembered Stephen Hunking, a regular at Pier Platters and Maxwell's whose band Hypnolovewheel signed to Alias for 1991's *Space Mountain*.

Alias flew Hunking and his band to Los Angeles and treated them like rock stars. They put them up in a gated-in pool house in the big compound where the Jenkinses lived. One of the Everly Brothers had the mansion next door. "Delight was strange," Hunking said. "She was a sweet woman. She was this weird female Joey Ramone-y type, really tall. As I remember her, reddish hair and wearing psychedelic mini-dresses. She had a rock-and-roll house—custom couches, purple with red or pink trim, and a jukebox in the living room. She always had the refrigerator stocked with pizza and whatever nonsense twenty-four-year-old guys need or want."

The label maintained offices in Los Angeles and San Francisco, staffed by genuine indie rock fans who seemed somewhat at odds with their flamboyant boss. "She drove around in a brand-new Jaguar Roadster XJS, dark blue," observed Jamie Kitman, who still moonlighted as a car columnist.

Somebody at the label suggested Hunking put in a good word with Yo La Tengo to help ease the deal along. "I remember Ira asking me what I thought about Alias and, in my naïve youth, I said, 'Oh my God, it's the best label ever. They've got unlimited resources, and how can you go wrong? And when we go out there, we stay in this pool house, and we swim all day, and we get stoned, and they chauffeur us around and bring us to fancy meals and take us to local radio stations and cable outlets to do interviews.'

"In retrospect, it wasn't a lot of money, but compared to what other indie labels were able to come up with, it seemed like a major amount of money. I was blinded by the lifestyle."

Jamie Kitman was dispatched to the coast and negotiated a deal he estimated as worth nearly twenty times the amount Bar/None was able to offer for *Fakebook*. "I went to Los Angeles, made unreasonable demands, and they came remarkably close to them."

The world around them was changing. Over the summer, Georgia and Ira had traveled to California to play a few duo shows. They caught a few Mets games too, at Los Angeles's Dodger Stadium and San Francisco's Candlestick Park—paeans to New York baseball gone west, the long-held dreams of beloved local outfits shipped away. "We got to see them lose in L.A., which is quite a bit different than seeing them lose at Shea Stadium," Ira quipped. At Dodger Stadium, actor Alex Winter—costar of *Bill and Ted's Excellent Adventure*—recognized Ira at a concession stand. Probably.

When Yo La Tengo signed with Alias, they returned home for the first time on firm financial footing. Not long afterward, Ira and Georgia went on WFMU by themselves to promote a last-minute gig with the *Fakebook* lineup, their second-to-last as it turned out. Their host this time was Gerard Cosloy, who'd been asked to do a show by station veteran Irwin Chusid. They chatted sparingly about baseball, movies, and cable television.

"Are all your guests this talkative?" Georgia asked the *Conflict* editor.

"Usually they're not allowed to speak," Gerard said. "So this is an improvement."

Later in the summer, James moved to Brooklyn, taking up residence in the Park Slope neighborhood. Gerard Cosloy noted James's new position in the "lieslieslies" section of the fall 1991 *Conflict*. "Christmas bassist/*And Suddenly* . . . editor James McNew is now playing bass for Yo La Tengo," he reported, oddly without comment, perhaps so used to his favorite bands' ever-shifting lineups. It was Gerard's fifty-second issue, and his last.

His tenure at WFMU ended around this time too. "Gerard's show was a disappointment, having been familiar with him and *Conflict* in general," station manager Ken Freedman admitted. "His sense of humor didn't become apparent until his last show, which he got kicked off the air for.

"His nastiness and wit finally came out because he was being attacked by crank callers—*Finally, this is Gerard Cosloy!*—and he announced one of the crank callers' phone numbers on the air. David Newgarden was program director at the time and, for that, David fired him. I thought it was an overreaction." It didn't matter anyway. Gerard's new gig was a far better mouthpiece than a zine or radio show could ever be.

Chris Lombardi would call the Cable Building "the indie rock ghetto." But it was on this well-established terra firma that he and Gerard Cosloy found themselves with their new enterprise, Matador Records. Glenn Morrow and Bar/None were there too. The twelve-by-twelve Matador office was a mess. They shared the space with a woman who sold wholesale fax paper and toner from a desk in the corner.

"Inside that office was a separate office, which had a window," Lombardi remembered. "Neither Gerard nor I would take that office, because we didn't want to feel superior to the other one. It was so stubborn of us. We all sat outside. And this office, which had this great window, became the cardboardbox room. It was a total waste of space."

Lombardi had started the label almost as a goof. In early 1990, Gerard had booked the Australian band H.P. Zinker at CBGB's Record Canteen. He introduced them to Chris, who'd worked in the Dutch East sales department. Lombardi hit it off with the band and partied into the night. Somewhat spontaneously, Chris decided to put out the band's yet-to-be-recorded single and booked them almost immediate studio time.

As the 7-inch went to press, Lombardi needed a name for his new label. He'd just seen Pedro Almodóvar's 1986 film *Matador*, and that was it. Several months later, the records accumulating in his TriBeCa apartment, Chris invited Gerard aboard, recently liberated from Homestead Records. After a few months and with a loan from Lombardi's father, they moved to the Cable Building.

They hired Rusty Clarke to do sales. "We knew her because we'd seen her at shows all the time," Gerard said. "Every good gig, you'd see Rusty down front. She had a great record collection. She was completely up on things. She was a good talker. She possesses an amazing work ethic. But at least to my knowledge, Rusty *had no prior experience* in sales or the professional music industry. We just thought she was awesome." Two decades later, she still works for Matador.

Matador tried to create the opposite of the "music hater" environment of the super-square Dutch East office. "We thought we could make some sort of difference," Gerard remembered. Using a boilerplate contract borrowed and modified from Homestead, the new company tried to stay aboveboard. When Superchunk guitarist Mac McCaughan received his first royalty statement, he was surprised to see how traditional it was.

Midway through the first year of Matador's existence, sales picked up with releases by Superchunk and Teenage Fanclub, a Scottish pop outfit Gerard hadn't been able to sign to Homestead. The company had trouble printing enough to meet demand. Chris hit on a solution to ensure the continued flow of income by establishing Matador Direct, a mini distribution service. He arranged buy-ins on records and publications from other labels and used the relationships he'd built with record stores in the sales department at Dutch East to sell zines and albums from Drag City, Merge, and others alongside new Matador product. Office shelf space shrunk, but the amount of available funds grew.

Chris and Gerard's new label distributed their product through the usual outlets too, including their old friend Dutch East India Trading. "I think Barry paid us half of what he owed us," Chris remembered. "But we never went exclusively with one distributor. We didn't want to get fucked if one went out of business." It was something they'd seen happen time and time again.

They ran full-steam ahead with Gerard's backlog of albums he couldn't conscionably release with Homestead. There was *New York Eye and Ear Control,* a thirteen-song set of bands that frequented the Knitting Factory and other experimental-minded Manhattan venues. And there was Pavement, a quartet with deep roots in the same Charlottesville scene that produced James McNew. Georgia and Ira had met a few of the band's members when they played in a weekend softball game Gerard organized in Jersey City, where he was living for a time. Pavement's laid-back abstraction was fully in place as they recorded what would become their debut LP for Matador following a self-released single and a pair of 7-inches for Chicago's Drag City.

Within a year, Gerard Cosloy finally grew tired of zine writing and discontinued *Conflict* in the fall of 1991 after nearly eleven years. "There was an element of self-parody creeping into it," he said. "It was not something that excited me as much as making records and dealing with it from that end. I got burned out on a lot of the peripheral stuff, the level of invective going in and out." The end of *Conflict* didn't mean Gerard ceased to voice his opinion, however. He filed columns for *CMJ* and abused Matador's fax machine. "Dude, this is getting *insane*," Chris told him. The office-supply distributor had moved out. "I told Gerard he had to cut out the fax wars because fax paper was expensive. I went out every other day for a thirty-dollar roll. He would write some long fuck-you, print it out, then fax it. He always had to have the last word." Chris recalls "a guy at Alias who seemed to have a bone to pick with Gerard."

Even though he was as massive a Yo La Tengo fan as ever, Gerard didn't give much thought to signing them to the new label, only a few months old when *Fakebook* was recorded and far less capitalized than Alias when Yo La Tengo went looking for a deal. "Matador was in no position to be talking about approaching a band from Bar/None or Alias. We had no track record, no distribution, and no money. The idea would be ludicrous."

One song they taught to Number Fifteen was one they'd worried over for a long time. They'd shown the changes to Dave Rick when he came to audition at the 719 Garden Street basement and probably a half dozen of the other bassists since 1984. It was the one Ira almost couldn't sing at the first Yo La Tengo gig. It was now called "Five-Cornered Drone (Crispy Duck)," and they'd finally grown comfortable with it and slated it for recording on their Alias Records debut. James had a number of songs to brush up on.

They'd given up on finding a permanent bassist, but they'd never stopped working, tinkering endlessly with songs. Despite—or perhaps because of—*Fakebook*'s success, or perhaps merely a backlog, the new songs veered toward the band's noisier side. But they'd also started to move slowly beyond that, into atmospheric music that somehow folded in their earliest folk-rock jangle, *Fakebook*'s warmth, and Ira's peeling guitar. Beyond "Big Day Coming," there was "Swing for Life," which had spare instrumental lines over spare drums, a noise solo, and a hypnotic vocal by Georgia, now ready to sing outside of the acoustic gigs. She and Ira sang together too, the far-off melancholy blending into harmony atop all their other new tricks.

Even after James had joined, Yo La Tengo continued to operate as two bands, and still booked the odd show for the *Fakebook* lineup, even learning one final batch of songs with them for a wedding. But on tour in the Midwest earlier that year, Yo La Tengo found they got along well with Number Fifteen.

"James was pretty mellow, which was pretty essential, because Ira was not so mellow," observed Jamie Kitman, who was in daily contact with the band from his office in New Jersey. James had little trouble with the pit stops for barbecue and records. Even in a down mood, he was quick to laugh.

Also on board from the Christmas camp was Joe Puleo, who would move slowly but surely from the friend-roadie slot into an indispensable and salaried part of the operation. Puleo was another piece of the puzzle they hadn't realized they'd been missing—ready to travel and able to assert the band's very particular particulars to venues. With each passing tour, he assumed more duties but, more important, became an instant confidant.

At first, Ira and Georgia made the college radio appearances without their touring bassist, as they'd learned was easier over the years. But James was different, and enthusiastically adapted to the band's acoustic songbook. He could sing, too. By the end of the first tour, they'd written their first piece of music together, a mostly formless jam born from ten-minute introductions to "No Water," which was soon titled "Sleeping Pill."

"We had this much more spontaneous repertoire than I'd ever really thought about," James said, who took to it as happily as he did every new task. "I didn't know bands did that. If I didn't know a song, I'd follow along.

"I'd never been to the Midwest, period," he remembered. "I was just a little kid." When he moved to Brooklyn, they'd made him keys for the practice space. Nobody said anything otherwise, and James figured he was in, which he was. He'd just turned twenty-two.

Not long after the final gig with the *Fakebook* band, Georgia, Ira, and James met Gene Holder in Boston for a quick recording session to set down the first of two discs guaranteed under the deal memo they'd signed with Alias. "It was not an easy record," remembered Holder, the former dB's bassist who'd worked with them regularly since *President Yo La Tengo*. "The songs were really good, but there was a lot of tension, and I don't necessarily think it was on the technical side. I think it wasn't coming out the way they wanted."

Named *May I Sing with Me*—the question that the Japanese student had asked Phil Morrison in a Tokyo karaoke parlor—the album featured songs written mostly before James joined the band. There were debauched guitars in "Mushroom Cloud of Hiss" and "86-Second Blowout" (the title a tribute to a Peter Holsapple B-side). There was a new Georgia ballad ("Satellite") and a catchy single with Georgia and Ira singing together ("Upside-Down") that, despite borrowing Kinks lyrics, would do little to dispel the now-persistent Velvet Underground comparisons.

"I think this album was recorded the same year I threw a drumstick at Gene Holder and kicked Ira in the shins," Georgia wrote years later. "Somehow, [engineer] Lou Giordano got away unscathed." They insisted on live takes. Nothing came easily. For "Mushroom Cloud of Hiss," they'd had to duct-tape a pair of headphones to Ira's head so they wouldn't wobble off mid-solo.

Things had been afoot for some time. While in school, Karen Glauber had gotten a college radio promotions job at A&M and, after graduation, moved to Hoboken. She dated Adam Kaplan briefly, and her twin sister, Diane, married Craig Marks, Yo La Tengo's first roadie and later an editor at *CMJ*. But Glauber's work with college radio stations soon evolved into an A&R gig at Warner Bros. She helped put together a deal to land Seattle's Soundgarden, a longhaired and often shirtless quartet on Sub Pop who'd released a single and an EP.

To make it look like they weren't selling out, at least straightaway, Glauber engineered a stopgap LP on the then-flailing SST. Founder Greg Ginn had overextended himself like Homestead and other indie labels of the time. Sonic Youth and Dinosaur Jr. (forced to add the diminutive after a legal notice from the Dinosaurs) had both left Gerard Cosloy and Homestead for SST a few years earlier; both bolted from SST as soon as they could. "I like Greg Ginn and stuff, but they wouldn't pay you," Dinosaur's J Mascis noted.

Released appropriately on Halloween 1988, a major-label record dressed as an indie, Soundgarden's *Ultramega OK* only further illustrated the distance between the bands that were about to break out of college radio and the underground they were leaving behind. Somewhere, the term "alternative" had been coined to describe the music not generally played by commercial radio, and it caught on.

"It was a fake indie deal," Glauber admitted of Soundgarden's debut LP. "It was the most rock thing I'd ever dealt with. I was used to Suzanne Vega—more palatable stuff. Soundgarden changed the game in a lot of ways: to have a swagger and be so rocking, and be such a college radio band. It was a pretty sexless format before that." Indeed, Soundgarden's punk fell just short of heavy metal, an unhidden influence on one of their Sub Pop labelmates, Nirvana.

In April 1991, David Geffen's DGC—run by the '70s record mogul and owned by MCA, in turn part of Japan's Matsushita

Electric Industrial—concluded its bidding for Nirvana and snatched the Olympia-based trio off Sub Pop for $287,000, with an agreement to feature the smaller label's logo on the back cover of the next Nirvana album. Based on the 118,000 units Sonic Youth's *Goo* had moved the previous year, DGC pressed 50,000 copies of Nirvana's *Nevermind*, which they released on September 24. The album entered the *Billboard* chart two weeks after its release at #144, and the trio got affixed with its very own buzzword: "grunge." "Smells Like Teen Spirit" went into rotation on MTV in November, and everything blew up from there.

R.E.M. had long ago gone multiplatinum, and the infrastructures of indie had, for an equally long time, helped shepherd bands from various punk undergrounds into the mainstream. But Nirvana's success came on an unprecedented scale. "We saw an incredible number of kids returning the CDs their parents had given them for Christmas, and buying *Nevermind* in exchange, or using money they'd gotten as a present to buy the CD," reported one Bob Zimmerman of Tower Records. In January, the record went #1, displacing Michael Jackson's *Dangerous*.

The record saved Sub Pop, who received $2.50 for each copy sold. In the end, *Nevermind* topped $80 million in sales. The reverberations were felt at every conceivable level of the music world, from practice spaces to boardrooms, from scrawls on high schoolers' notebooks to the way independently recorded music operated in the global marketplace.

"Regular studios, engineers, producers, mastering engineers, et cetera, still did not figure out the punk 'voice' until they had to, after Nirvana got on the radio," observed Joe Carducci, the writer and onetime co-owner/house producer at SST. Fashion designer Marc Jacobs premiered a "grunge" line. The indie world exploded. The rush was on.

One afternoon, with their repertoire in good order and no particular shows to get ready for, Yo La Tengo plugged in an Ace

Tone Phenix organ that had been lying around their practice space. It belonged to one of the bands they shared the room with. *May I Sing with Me* was about to come out and, with James's move to Brooklyn, Yo La Tengo had shifted into a five-day-a-week practice schedule. After ten years of playing together, Georgia and Ira's work-happy ethic finally manifested itself in an unquestionably full-time band.

With Ira on keys, the band ran through "roller-rink versions" of the songbook, originals and covers. "A half hour into practice, we realized it was something," James remembered.

"A practice like that could've never happened unless it was a *band* practicing," Ira later declared. "Everything kind of grew out of that day." The transformation was subtle but undeniable.

Billing themselves as Sleeping Pill, the trio played a January Friday at CBGB and featured the Ace Tone prominently on a pair of new songs, notably a seventeen-minute jam piece called "Sunsquashed." The full-time addition of the organ to Yo La Tengo's setup—played at some point by each of the three band members—began to transform the band's complexion from a guitar-driven trio into something with far more possibilities and a slowly growing confidence.

May I Sing with Me came out in the spring of 1992, and the band stayed on the road until the end of June, finally finding a comfortable rhythm on tour. They passed through Europe with My Bloody Valentine, the Irish band who had elevated guitar distortion to actual ear-damaging levels. But *May I Sing with Me* failed to break through. It sold more than *Fakebook*, but even in a marketplace suddenly looking for new sounds, it wasn't the post-grunge coming-out anybody had hoped for. "We were figuring out how ineffectual Alias were," Ira said.

The mood at the label had turned "very bad," according to Hypnolovewheel's Stephen Hunking. "They hired this guy who was a lawyer, and he was kind of just a douchebag. I say he was a douchebag, but he was probably trying to bring the label down to where an indie label should be. Like, manageable. We heard all these horrible rumors about him when he'd worked at other places. When he came in, the gravy days very much came to an end."

It was an attitude that transferred to Yo La Tengo as well. Alias requested that the band write a song they could release as a single. The band presented the label with "Sunsquashed."

"Ira, it's twenty-four minutes long," Jamie Kitman told the guitarist.

"Yes," Ira replied. "But it only feels like it's seventeen." It became the centerpiece of the five-song *Upside-Down* EP, the band's first CD-only release, for which the band also did consent to a (theoretically) more radio-friendly remix of the title song.

"They could do some shows that your grandmother would love and do other shows that would scare eighty percent of the people out of the room," Jamie said. "Even at those shows, I can remember Ira's parents would be there, and his mother practically being in the speaker. But they looked like accountants. It was a funny familial thing." Despite developing no particular affinity for rock music, Marilyn and Abraham Kaplan remained regulars at Yo La Tengo shows. In New York, Yo La Tengo still played CBGB, but now they were headlining, and the room was consistently full.

Kitman reaped wonders for the band on a professional level, negotiating high fees for song licenses, including twice in movies by indie filmmaker Hal Hartley: "Always Something" for 1992's *Simple Men* and "Drug Test" in 1993's *Surviving Desire*. But affairs between Ira and Jamie had begun to grow contentious.

For the first time, the copyediting work went by the wayside, and Yo La Tengo became Ira and Georgia's full-time occupation. In large part because of how seriously Jamie took to the task of managing them, they had only recently started to think of Yo La Tengo as a real job worthy of equivalent attention. While appreciative of the hardworking manager, for Ira, that meant staying actively involved with the small print of the band's growing business.

"A lot of bands are smart enough that they could be their

own managers, their own lawyers, their own record companies, if there were only enough hours in the day," Kitman remembered. "Negotiating a Yo La Tengo contract took longer than most because they could really sweat the details. Ira could read contracts like a lawyer to the point of being incredibly persnickety about deal points that were so tediously irrelevant, and could get totally incensed by them.

"Ira was concerned about royalty rates, what was recoupable and what wasn't. You could imagine him putting his green eyeshade on and getting out his slide rule and his abacus and crunching numbers on whether this happened or that happened, and how it would impact them. Some of it was really esoteric. I've never seen anybody get as deep into the theory of it."

IRA IS AN UPTIGHT FAG read the graffiti over the studio door. It was at the end of a long, disgusting hallway. THIS IS ART read another proclamation scrawled elsewhere on the wall. AXL ROSE—GAY, another. Down the hall was Sleepyhead, a slew of metal bands, and a single shared bathroom "that definitely was the bane of Georgia's existence," in one recollection. Sonic Youth practiced next door.

While Yo La Tengo was on the road, Lyle Hysen—whose Ace Tone organ the band had borrowed from the corner and not returned—had fixed up the room as a functional budget recording studio. "The point wasn't quality recording," said Fred Brockman, the onetime Dioxin Field center fielder who joined Hysen in the endeavor. "There was no way you could do that under those circumstances. It was sitting in a room holding a microphone up, basically."

Working five afternoons a week while the space's other leaseholders took on recording projects in the evenings, it became Yo La Tengo's second home as they eagerly began to assemble new songs in a far more collaborative manner than ever before. Increasingly, James's bass lines pulled surprising melodies from Ira's noise-heavy progressions and gave them powerful new shapes, his natural ear an ever-useful asset in their day-to-day work. Brockman often stuck around to help them demo new songs and offer occasional input.

Georgia brought in a new ballad, "Nowhere Near," she'd worked out at home. "From a Motel 6" was sourced from Ira and Georgia's two-guitar lineup. There was a quiet version but also a rushing, electric one, Georgia now comfortable enough to sing inside a noisier squall. They hadn't put "Big Day Coming" on *May I Sing with Me*, and played it for Fred. He was mystified that they played such an accessible number so slowly. They were mystified at his suggestion of turning it into a rock song. They humored Fred and tried it a few times unsuccessfully and put the loud version aside.

Which is not to say that everything was hunky-dory. The new album would eventually take the name *Painful* and, as every member of Yo La Tengo long continued to point out, the process was exactly that. "The very painful sessions," Georgia groaned almost twenty years after the fact.

"We had never had a band that rehearsed all the time," Ira said. "We rehearsed every day, and we were working really hard. There were lots of arguments within the group, knowing something was possible but not knowing how to get it." Gradually, they did, but the tension would remain an element of their creativity for a long time to come. Though their deal memo with Alias stipulated at least one more album, they hoped to avoid that, especially as they got further into the process of writing new songs.

"[Alias] had no idea how to market their product," noted Stephen Hunking of Hypnolovewheel. "They didn't understand who the target audience was. They didn't have credibility, and they just threw money at things."

Yo La Tengo's hopes for their unrecorded album were great, and they didn't want it to be left in Alias's hands. Through City Slang, the German label that had bankrolled the *That Is Yo La Tengo* EP the year before, Jamie arranged an advance. Coupled with some money borrowed from their families, the band continued to work without Alias as long as they could.

Their manager also made a suggestion that Ira agreed with: that they hire a producer outside their immediate and established circle of collaborators.

"We met with people," Ira remembered. "It took us into a world where we weren't comfortable." One of Jamie's suggestions was the New York–based Roger Moutenot. Raised in Cliffside Park, north of Hoboken, Moutenot had worked for Run-D.M.C. and the Beastie Boys, as well as the cream of the downtown avant-garde scene, including jazz musicians like John Zorn and Don Byron. Not to mention Lou Reed. What intrigued Yo La Tengo wasn't merely that Moutenot had worked for irascible figures like Zorn and Reed, but that both had chosen to work with Moutenot again.

Moutenot immediately endeared himself to the band when, reluctant as they were, he didn't return Ira's phone call. "He was the opposite of aggressive," Georgia observed.

The day in spring 1992, when the Matador staff arrived at 611 Broadway to ship the 35,000 copies they'd finally managed to print of Pavement's *Slanted and Enchanted*, they were met in the hallway by an armed marshal, a landlord's representative, and—most pertinently—the Cable Building's maintenance man, who went to work attaching a padlock to their office door. Matador was in sore need of income.

It was obvious that *Slanted and Enchanted* would go a long way toward changing that, but they cut it awfully close. The album was so hyped that *Spin* granted it a rave lead review some three months before Matador had copies to sell. "Not to wax transcendental or anything, but the first time I heard Pavement's new LP . . . all the little hairs on the back of my neck stood at attention," Jim Greer wrote.

Chris Lombardi dashed to the bank for a certified check, drawn from a combination of early earnings for *Slanted and Enchanted* and another small loan from his father. When he returned, he found the staff "laughing nervously" while the marshal explained to Gerard Cosloy "that if he didn't leave the office immediately, his college record would be seriously fucked."

In the next year and change, *Slanted and Enchanted* sold some 80,000 copies. Over time and with a 2002 reissue, the album would move more than 250,000 units. Though it would be a while before Matador could afford to relocate, "we were gonna have to change how we worked every day and stay on top of things," Cosloy said. "Because the sheer demand for *Slanted and Enchanted* was so much bigger than anything we'd coped with before. I mean, we didn't have a publicist for the first couple of years. I handled that shit myself." *Slanted and Enchanted* became nearly a full-time occupation. They spent so much time on it that in 1992 Matador released less than a dozen 7-inches and EPs and no further albums until autumn. The alternative boom continued around them unabated, its accidental figurehead, Kurt Cobain, already in and out of rehab several times.

MTV News that summer was devoted heavily to the second edition of the touring Lollapalooza festival, which rolled out across the country on July 18 for thirty-five dates in twenty-two states. Headlined by Los Angeles skate-funkers the Red Hot Chili Peppers, it featured rapper Ice Cube, as well as grunge staples Soundgarden and Pearl Jam. Dreamt up at the Reading Festival a few years earlier by booking agent Marc Geiger and Jane's Addiction drummer Stephen Perkins, with frontman Perry Farrell acting as ringleader, an initial 1991 tour featured Jane's Addiction, Nine Inch Nails, and Music for Dozens vets Violent Femmes. Like MTV's *120 Minutes*, Lollapalooza's 1992 rendition of alternative became an access point to the mainstream, taking in some $20 million as newspapers filed hyperbolic reports about the dangers and/or sociological significance of mosh pits, piercings, and dyed hair. It was a fairly gigantic tent, open to hip-hop, heavy metal, and even hippies, apparently, as when MTV's *Alternative Nation* paired Seattle's Screaming Trees with the Spin Doctors the following summer.

"For the first time in 150 years, bohemia can't be pinpointed on a map," C. Carr proclaimed in the *Village Voice*. In December, *BusinessWeek* ran a cover story about the 46 million eighteen- to twenty-nine-year-olds that represented an estimated $125 billion annual market. It was titled "Move Over, Boomers." Big business was coming for the underground, and Chris Lombardi and Gerard Cosloy were suddenly right in the middle of it all.

Recently named president at Atlantic Records, Danny Goldberg was a revered member of the classic-rock old guard. A onetime wunderkind press assistant for Led Zeppelin, his Gold Mountain management handled Nirvana, in no small part because they'd been recommended by Sonic Youth, another client. Thurston Moore and Kim Gordon befriended Goldberg, who asked the impeccably plugged-in couple who to look out for.

"Matador," they told him.

Plane tickets were dispatched to the Cable Building. Chris and Gerard traveled several times to meet with Goldberg in his Los Angeles office. He took them to Hamburger Hamlet.

Though long since transmogrified into a multinational corporate beast, Atlantic Records had begun life in a manner not dissimilar to Matador. Founded in 1947 by Ahmet and Nesuhi Ertegün, well-born sons of a Turkish diplomat and rabid jazz and blues fans, the brothers had promoted shows around the Washington, D.C., area and sponsored recording sessions, which they distributed in tiny, white-label pressings. They founded and discarded a few imprints before they settled on Atlantic and relocated to the west side Manhattan neighborhood known then as "Jukebox Row"—home to the city's growing number of independent labels a few blocks west of where the bigger companies made their Manhattan bases.

"The independent labels were like the ancient Judean tribes in the desert," the Erteguns' partner Jerry Wexler said later. "There were literally dozens of them. They're all gone now, except for Atlantic: they're the Israelites of the indies." By the time Danny Goldberg began his negotiations, Atlantic's indieness was a long time gone, too. The Erteguns sold to

Warner Bros.–Seven Arts for $17.5 million in 1967 and hadn't looked back.

One year into the alternative era, the Warner/Elektra/Atlantic group (WEA) took in an estimated $3.2 billion. Among others, Atlantic's college music roster boasted the Lemonheads and the Stone Temple Pilots, bands that seemed the opposite of Yo La Tengo in every way and were designed (and destined) to implode quickly and naturally. It was clear that nobody knew what to call the new music anymore. Danny Goldberg still wanted Matador, and badly.

"He courted us so aggressively," Gerard remembered. "He had Thurston and Kim lobby us, which was not the smartest move. I was actually very resentful that he did that."

Billboard covered the developing deal in November with an item titled "No Buy, but Matador Talking." The two labels were "negotiating ties," as the trade publication put it. The item had Atlantic's absorption of Matador as a veritable fait accompli: "A spokesperson for Atlantic, which recently purchased North Carolina indie Mammoth Records, had no comment."

"We are still involved in an ongoing discussion with Atlantic, but we're not negotiating a purchase of Matador," *Billboard* quoted Gerard Cosloy as saying, in a statement one imagines to have been scrubbed of profanities.

Two intense weeks kicked off when Yo La Tengo and Fred Brockman wheeled the gear next door to Water Music in late 1992. The remnants of a massive Nor'easter were blowing through for good measure. "It began with a couple of difficult days," Fred remembered. "It was concentrated hard work."

Jamie had gotten in touch with Roger Moutenot, who'd agreed to coproduce with Fred. As it turned out, he lived around the corner from Ira and Georgia in Hoboken. The first time they set Georgia up to sing, Roger thought the microphone in the studio was broken.

"You could hear the metal sound of the microphone working," Fred remembered.

"I walked out to the room, because I had the mike pre-cranked and I was still getting no level. I was like, 'What the . . . ?'" Moutenot told *TapeOp*.

"Could you sing for a second?" he asked Georgia.

"And it was literally like . . ." In his retelling, Moutenot made a high, whispering sound. His eyes widened.

"I thought, 'OK, now I get it.'"

Moutenot understood more than just Georgia's voice. Yo La Tengo had read Roger's reluctance astutely. "He's hardly a go-getter, which temperamentally matched us so well," Ira assessed. Most of all, Roger was patient, willing to help the band figure out how to translate themselves to tape.

"I have a vivid memory of trying to record 'From a Motel 6' and feeling that our voices weren't meshing right," Ira remembered. "The only way to hear Georgia was to make her way too loud. I remember Roger and Fred trying all these compressors, and really *listening* to us."

Each song required a strategy of its own, as finicky and detailed and idiosyncratic as its creators. On "Big Day Coming" Ira whispered along with the keyboard loop while the band built a wall of sound over which Ira . . . whispered along some more. "And you're talking about an eight-minute song that's very personal as far as the performance goes," Fred noted.

Another painful aspect of the *Painful* sessions was the legal negotiations the band found themselves in during the exact weeks of recording. Ira had heard about Matador's impending deal with Atlantic and contacted Gerard. The move was a massive gamble, and the first time Yo La Tengo had ever approached a label directly.

If Yo La Tengo could get out of its deal with Alias, would Matador be interested in working with them? Ira asked Gerard. For once, having a budget and a way to get their records out, Gerard Cosloy's answer was an unequivocal yes. It didn't take much for Chris to agree. But the even bigger gamble was how Alias might react.

"We felt we had a contractual way of getting out," Ira said. "Jamie and [booking agent] Bob Lawton were adamant about thinking it was a bad idea. Alias could tie us up." Lawton had seen it happen recently when a deal between Dumptruck, another band he booked, whose former label had subsequently blocked the band by court order from recording a new album. Alias had deep pockets, Jamie reminded them, and were quite capable of the same. But it still seemed like the move to make.

"No offense to Ira, but he was not knocking on our door in 1991," Gerard noted. "He was knocking on our door when we made a deal with a major label. I'm not saying he was attracted to being on a major label; I never got that sense. Certainly, from the outside, Matador seemed to be a more solvent, smooth-running operation, and that probably made us more appealing to a band who wanted to be on a label that wouldn't go broke or leave them stranded in an airport somewhere."

Quite coincidentally, things had also blown up with Jamie Kitman. "My then-wife did business affairs, and there was some merchandise deal and Ira was so horrifically rude about it that she told him to go fuck himself and, at that point, we sort of quit and they fired us in the same breath," he remembered. "They were both hotheads, but he was one of the hottest hotheads and, as a matter of familial harmony, I had to go, 'You're right, you can't talk that way to my wife, or anybody who works for me.'"

Their newly contracted lawyer, Michael Goldsmith, handled the bulk of the negotiations while the band continued work on their new album at Water Music. Fred Brockman observed that Roger Moutenot was a voice removed from the Alias and Matador unpleasantness. "He was very calm. He was very outside of it," Fred said.

They experimented with amps for the first time. Getting their music across successfully, they seemed to realize, was a problem of logistics. And solving thorny logistics problems was something Ira loved to do. One night, after James started the long trek back to Brooklyn, Ira and Georgia tried the faster version of "Big Day Coming" again and recorded it, leaving space for James to add a guitar part the next day.

The album would begin and not quite end with the song, a

veritable theme number in both of its finished forms. Both the tape-loop version and the guitar-rock iteration were filled with equally triumphant dreaminess, delivered in clean, direct prose. There was not a little nostalgia, the stairs to the basement as evocative as any path to Ray Davies's Village Green. It was a love song about love getting greater and a conflicted life getting better.

While Hoboken had largely been overrun by condo-buying stockbrokers and a decidedly non-hipster drinking scene that sometimes resembled a Midwestern university town, Washington Street still held some magic. The Tall Dwarfs played the United States for the first time, crashed with Adam Kaplan, gigged with Yo La Tengo, and witnessed the Maxwell's debut of Ira's mother, Marilyn, who sang "Griselda" at a Bill Clinton/Al Gore rally a few days before the 1992 presidential election.

Earlier that year, Ira and Georgia had celebrated ten years playing together. Some degree of success was finally upon them. The basement practice space at 719 Garden Street sat empty, but life at the house was a nearly miraculous preserve of the community Ira and Georgia had found when they crossed the Hudson in the early 1980s, and they continued to make roots within it. Maxwell's thrived, but somewhere it had started to lose a little bit of something.

"The social scene ended," Glenn Morrow observed. "It was like people went there and met and fell in love and that was that. It had all just been a mating ritual and they stopped going out and got a life." Yo La Tengo remained regulars.

At another show there around that time, Ira and Georgia invited their housemate Gaylord Fields to DJ between bands, a role he'd been occupying at the club lately that his housemates had once filled themselves. During one set, he was approached by Irwin Chusid, whose freeform gravitas had remade WFMU in the mid-'70s and who remained an active DJ at the station. "You know, Gaylord, you ought to be a WFMU DJ," Irwin told him. Several other station DJs, including music director Dave Newgarden, made similar comments that night. Like his housemates, Fields wasn't the aggressive type and didn't pursue it very hard. Not long afterward, Newgarden came to Garden Street to personally retrieve Gaylord's audition tape. When he put Gaylord on the air, WFMU became Yo La Tengo's neighborhood station in every way.

James continued his own activities from his *And Suddenly . . .* days. He edited the zinelike *Yo La Tengo Gazette* and released a self-titled Dump EP through 18 Wheeler, the label founded by zine editor Tom Scharpling, who soon secured his own WFMU slot. Gradually, the band added Dump tunes to Yo La Tengo's songbook.

"Big Day Coming" and *Painful* (despite its name) captured a good life. It was personal and private and absolutely worth holding on to. Why go through all the fuss otherwise? Nirvana had brought the gold rush to the larger world that Yo La Tengo occupied, but Hoboken was Hoboken. After ticketed admissions and salaries had turned nineteenth-century baseball into a professional sport, the city grid had collapsed around the Elysian Fields' dreaminess and what had once been special was lost forever under the concrete. The same threat now loomed vaguely around the edges of Maxwell's.

Early in 1993, the band had traveled from Hoboken to Electric Lady, the studio Jimi Hendrix built a few blocks south of the 9th Street PATH station in Manhattan, to mix *Painful*. James Taylor was at work in the studio next door and somebody introduced him to Georgia.

He told her to "persevere."

"It was practically a year ago, so the memory might not be totally fresh and maybe he said something else," the band noted when they recounted the anecdote on the "Big Day Coming" 7-inch.

CHAPTER 11

Hot Chicken

Nearly as soon as Chris Lombardi and Gerard Cosloy signed Matador's deal with Atlantic, they flew to England to meet with Mark E. Smith, frontman of the Fall, in a London hotel. Gerard had covered the confrontational punk band in *Conflict* almost ten years before, seeing them multiple nights at Irving Plaza in Manhattan and then City Gardens in Trenton. The young zine writer couldn't help but be drawn to Smith, a master provocateur who had been known to wear swastika armbands as a teen, take acid, and go to a local club. Within two years of the Fall's 1976 founding, Smith was the only original member left. As the first release to go through the Atlantic pipeline, the Fall's *The Infotainment Scan* sent an unambiguous message that Matador wasn't exactly going mainstream.

Gerard and Chris were all too giddy to wield their new power, and their new power was vast. In return for 49 percent of their company, Matador would release a half dozen albums through Atlantic each year, receive a $5 million annual operating budget, and remain free to issue whatever else they wanted on the side. Chris bought out his father and brother's quarter of the company and gave it to Gerard, making them equal partners. They escaped the indie rock ghetto of the

Cable Building, moved a few blocks up Broadway, and tripled their office staff to a robust half dozen.

Steve Albini, for one, would accuse Sub Pop (who'd negotiated a similar deal with Warner) and Matador of being "opportunist labels that sort of sold off their bands at the first opportunity." From Chris and Gerard's perspective, it was pragmatism. "We are of the opinion that no single independent (or major) distributor offers sufficient penetration into the various chains, one-stops, and mom-and-pops we depend on," they told *Billboard* in an official statement. "We believe that no single distributor can be counted on to properly represent a label with a diverse roster."

They continued to release records through their own channels, including the direct-to-stores connections Chris had carried over from Homestead. Atlantic Records was, in some ways, just another distributor, albeit one with a lot of money that could get them into a few new places, such as the various chains owned by the Trans World Entertainment Corporation.

By the end of the year, Gerard appeared in an *Entertainment Weekly* feature on the "101 Most Influential Power People in Entertainment." "I was in an airport men's room laughing at the list and I stopped laughing when I saw my own name," Gerard said at the time, noting, "I'm the only person on that list that hasn't made millions of dollars for somebody. Everybody else on that list completed some deal to sell TV dinners to Martians or something."

Around the time of the deal, Gerard received a cold call from a Chicago songwriter named Liz Phair, who had self-released several cassettes. He gave her a $3,000 advance to record what would become *Exile in Guyville*. The twenty-six-year-old Phair arrived at Matador with a self-described chutzpah that matched the label's new standing. "Are you ready for me to make you a millionaire?" she asked Gerard. For her, the big contracts and Calvin Klein ads would come later. *Exile in Guyville* went gold and was heaped with acclaim but didn't receive release through Atlantic, and barely dented the top 200. Instead, the second product that Matador sent out into the broader American marketplace via Atlantic was Yo La Tengo's *Painful*.

For Gerard and Chris, it was a no-brainer. Like the Fall, Yo La Tengo was a long-running concern that Gerard held dearly. And while the Fall had been a perverse choice, Yo La Tengo was a legitimately commercial one. "In our scatterbrained minds, these terrific, veteran, radio-friendly bands have exhausted the independent network and are ready to go *kaboom*," Cosloy remembered.

One day, Lyle Hysen was summoned to Manhattan. He'd assumed managerial duties for Yo La Tengo while continuing to operate the studio out of the Hoboken practice space. Trips to the company's midtown offices were always a bit strange.

"I went up there and had meetings with obvious non-fans," said Hysen. "Some of the bigger wigs up there. It was still way more old-schooly—dudes who looked like they were in Rush, saying 'Oh, yeah, I love Yo La Fungo.'" On that day, though, he'd been called in to see Atlantic president Danny Goldberg, who wanted to speak with him about the new Yo La Tengo video.

Atlantic had put all of their resources into Matador, and Chris and Gerard were frequent visitors to their offices. Label founder Ahmet Ertegün was still a presence, chiefly evidenced by the fact that Chris and Gerard could smoke cigarettes in corporate meeting rooms, where Ertegün visited them several times. "His teeth were really orange, probably from smoking," Chris remembered. "He was just, like, 'Hi, boys, good to see you! Good luck!'"

For Yo La Tengo, those resources included a budget to hire indie film director Hal Hartley to helm a video for "From a Motel 6." Together, they conceived a slow, dry joke that fit Yo La Tengo perfectly. Hartley's artful camera tracked the band as they set up their equipment, undramatically mimed to a few bars from the song's middle section, broke the gear back down, coiled their cables, and loaded out.

"I remember being there for that video," Chris Lombardi

remembered. "It was Hal Hartley and his full crew. We might have spent fifty thousand dollars. It might have been more." What followed was, in Chris Lombardi's conclusion, *insane*.

The label was behind "From a Motel 6," Atlantic assured Hysen, but they weren't behind the video. It was too arty, Danny Goldberg told him. But Atlantic would pay for a new one with a different director.

"He wouldn't shake my hand," Hysen recalled. "I thought, '*Huh.*' I didn't get a good vibe after that." Shot with David Kleiler later in the year, the band bit the bullet and remade "From a Motel 6" with a full lip-synch. Really, it wasn't so bad. If being able to make a video with Hal Hartley had seemed a luxury to begin with, then the ability to scrap it at the record company's whim was hardly worth the fight. It was certainly an improvement over the painfulness of the formal transition after Matador's buyout of their two-album deal memo with Alias.

It cost them significantly. Their former label retained the rights to *May I Sing with Me*. Likewise, there was a nondisclosure agreement, a type of document virtually unknown in Yo La Tengo's professional lives. But, if having Atlantic Records reject an expensive music video was the worst that might happen in their new relationship, then the worst was behind them in almost every single way.

Whether the top brass knew the difference between "Big Day Coming" and Hüsker Dü's "New Day Rising," the label's machinery swung into action for Yo La Tengo long before *Painful* came out. The band's new publicist was Ken Weinstein, a longtime fan who joined Atlantic's staff in the summer of 1993 as they prepared for the album's release. During his first marketing meeting, he learned that the Stone Temple Pilots' debut, *Core*, had sold 86,000 copies that week alone—a number it took most indie albums months to achieve, if they ever did. "Holy fucking shit," Weinstein thought. "New game. Where does Yo La Tengo fit into that? Where does *Painful* fit into that?"

Another new feature Atlantic offered to Matador was the retail promotion—"coming soon" posters and banners for

Painful sent to record stores nationwide. Well over a year after the initial demos, the very painful album made it to racks, and the band toured in much the same rhythm they had for the better part of the previous eight years. "I flew separately from Ira and Georgia, and it's too bad," James noted in a tour journal. "Ira told me how they wouldn't let him take the acoustic guitar on the plane and he got in a huge shouting match with an airline clerk, who, in the spirit of Halloween, was dressed in a bunny costume."

The band's ceaseless travel rolled by in a montage: Craig Marks scoring Ira a gig covering the Velvet Underground's reunion in Paris via his new job at *Spin* (where Byron Coley had also landed), "Speeding Motorcycle" getting longer each night (up to fifteen minutes by Dortmund), and Ira in a Santa suit in Berlin. In Enger, in the spirit of NRBQ, they honored requests for any song (by any artist) that they could reasonably try to remember and did numbers by Jonathan Richman, the Clash, Public Image Ltd, the Only Ones, the Beatles, and more. Joe Puleo sang Queen's "We Are the Champions." On New Year's Eve, the touring party crashed a black-tie soiree at the hotel where they were staying.

Back home, they had peak years for record collecting. In the era of the CD, vinyl detritus littered the land. "Those were heady times for snapping up cheap records," James recalled. "Almost everything on my dream checklist, I found. Silver Apples, eight dollars, with the poster? Check." In Lexington, Kentucky, they stumbled on a small stash of Sun Ra singles from the cult jazz musician's brief stint of producing pop songs. The band tucked their scores under the mattress in the van's loft, where they could lie flat and not warp.

Where the road had once vexed them, it was now something manageable, even enjoyable. They had their favorite spots, friends to visit, and places to check out in nearly every town.

With a few weeks off in New York, Ken Weinstein booked the band on *Late Night with Conan O'Brien*. On the air barely four months by the time of the band's appearance, the show's host was a green thirty-year-old and so far had neither good ratings nor good reviews. But, as Weinstein reminded Ira, "even if only a million people are watching, it's still a million people." The night before, James stayed up to watch O'Brien announce the band's appearance. "Coming up tomorrow night, we'll have Gregory Harrison, actress Martha Plimpton, and musical guest . . . Yo Lo Tengo!"

Their appearance playing "From a Motel 6" was over quickly. Behind the band, the Chroma Key screened *The Tower*, the film animated by Emily and Georgia at Garden Street in 1984. The show's producers enjoyed the film and arranged to use it again for other bands.

It was around this time too that building owner Rick Smith and his partner sold 719 Garden Street. Gaylord, Todd, Ira, Georgia, and Egon moved out. Ira and Georgia rented a condo a few blocks away, which they would buy a few years later. "It would have been smart if we bought it then," Ira said. "It would have been smart to buy that *house* then." The new place had a garage. Hoboken continued to change. Musicians remained around town, including plenty of people still active in Yo La Tengo's world, but there weren't any new Hoboken bands. The Feelies had broken up the year before too, this time seemingly for real.

The Feelies were successful by indie rock standards and still revered, but they hardly pulled the kind of stable income that might be expected in the suburbs they still called home. "I saw a lot of value in staying where we were at," Glenn Mercer said. "Like playing clubs. What if we go to the next level and play to a half-empty theater? Or you could play to a jam-packed club. To me, it was much more fun playing to a club to a jam-packed audience. But not everybody in the band felt that way and our manager [Steve Fallon] said 'now's the time to make that next jump.' So we booked theaters and what I figured happened, did happen."

The fragile balance that held together the Feelies finally snapped when Bill Million and his family moved to Florida without telling his bandmates. There was a job there he'd had to take. Glenn Mercer and Dave Weckerman kept playing every week in Mercer's basement.

In the summer of 1994, Ira flew to North Carolina for his third performance with Double Dynamite, the party band that only performed on July 30, the shared birthday of Yo La Tengo booking agent Bob Lawton and onetime friend-roadie Phil Morrison, who had worked for Lawton for a few years before becoming a video director. Lawton drummed and Morrison fronted the band with glamorous glee. Ira played guitar.

Besides being July 30, the occasion of the show was the fifth-anniversary celebration for the Durham-based Merge Records, founded in 1989 by Mac McCaughan and Laura Ballance of Superchunk, early Matador signees who'd found more success putting out their own records. Phil Morrison knew them from North Carolina, and Ira and Georgia had become friendly over the years. They'd recently signed a distribution deal with Touch and Go, the Chicago-based label that'd grown from a hardcore zine. "Merge Fest" featured the cream of their roster. Plus Double Dynamite, with Superchunk's Ballance on Moog.

Morrison had recently put Yo La Tengo in his Brooklyn bedroom to make a lively video for the fast version of "Big Day Coming." Among other setups, he'd dressed Ira in a red suit and had given him an old-style microphone to dance around with. He shot him sitting on the edge of the bed as well, doing a blank-faced lip-dub to the chorus.

The video was one final Atlantic-sponsored push for *Painful*. It'd sold more than any previous Yo La Tengo album out of the gate and continued to sell. But those numbers were barely a "blip on the radar" for Atlantic, in Gerard's words. The video barely aired.

"The time and energy Atlantic have to spend helping Yo La Tengo go from 25,000 to 40,000 is equivalent to the time and energy they have to put in to help the Lemonheads go from 300,000 to a half-million," Cosloy told an interviewer. "The math isn't hard to figure out."

Very few bands broke through at the numbers of Nirvana or the quadruple-platinum R.E.M. By indie standards, the 246,000 copies of Pavement's *Crooked Rain, Crooked Rain* that Matador sold on release qualified it as an instant classic, but the sales didn't do much to impress the brass uptown. There was trouble brewing at Atlantic, too. By midsummer 1994, an "executive civil war" (per *Rolling Stone*) at WEA ousted Danny Goldberg.

Still, around the industry, the big labels continued to experiment. As had happened when youth culture met big business in the '60s, major labels offered contracts to all kinds of unlikely bands, from the acid-soaked Butthole Surfers (Capitol) to Yamataka Eye and the Boredoms (Reprise), who'd sent hand-cut lathe records to John Beers of the Happy Flowers a half decade earlier. Occasionally, it paid off. Far away, on a different limb of the punk tree on the opposite coast, a California trio called Green Day released their third album, *Dookie*, through Warner Bros.' Reprise label, and sold eight million copies. Far more than Nirvana's *Nevermind*, *Dookie* permeated the country.

"When *Dookie* came along and all of a sudden punk was commercial, *that* was when tons of kids started fanzines," pointed out *Jersey Beat*'s Jim Testa. "All the labels had money to spend on ads. That's probably 1994, 1995. That to me was the heyday of the fanzine movement." Tower Magazines, an extension of the massive record retailer, became a dependable national distributor for hundreds of titles.

It was undeniably a bubble. But besides the shuffle from Alias to Matador, there was not much of an effect on Yo La Tengo's immediate world. They remained centered in a web of connections and fandom that stretched back to the *New York Rocker* office and continued to reward them creatively and personally outside of the alternative gold rush. Like dozens of other bands, Yo La Tengo carved out their own ways to thrive from their own set of circumstances, part of a new national firmament that had gradually replaced college rock graduates like R.E.M. Chief among Yo La Tengo's new contemporaries was Merge's flagship band, Superchunk, who'd sold 40,000 copies of *Foolish* on their own label.

At the time of Merge Fest, Superchunk's Laura Ballance and Mac McCaughan had recently split up—always a distant and mostly unspeakable threat for bands founded by couples. There were plenty in Yo La Tengo's circle and the indie world. Though they proved unfounded, predictions of Superchunk's imminent demise trailed them for a while.

Georgia surprised Ira and flew down for the second day of the Merge Fest weekend in time to see Phil lead Double Dynamite through songs by Queen, David Kilgour, Reagan Youth, and others. Ira told her about a great new band he'd seen the day before, one of the most recent additions to the Merge roster. Georgia caught Lambchop back in New York a few days later and introduced herself. It took a few more meetings, but the Nashville-based Lambchop would soon become as important in Yo La Tengo's world as the Feelies and dB's had been a decade earlier.

The Double Dynamite show was one of many extra-band situations that the members of Yo La Tengo began to throw themselves into. That summer, Ira also filled in with Eleventh Dream Day for a tour of Europe. In Olympia, he played in the Super Stinky Puffs with Simon Fair, alongside Nirvana's Dave Grohl and Krist Novoselic in their first performance together since the suicide of Kurt Cobain earlier that year. Georgia sang sometimes with Will Rigby's wife, Amy, as well as the local band Salmon Skin. Ira also served with Georgia as a backing player in a live edition of Dump, James's solo home-recording nom de plume. Over the previous three years, he'd produced a trio of singles, a 10-inch EP, and a full-length.

If there had been any question about James's status as a full member of Yo La Tengo, it was long gone. His voice was every bit as expressive as Georgia's, capable of a high, sweet falsetto that gave Yo La Tengo angelic and unexpected harmony arrangements with the male taking the upper register above his female counterpart.

James's guitar playing on "Big Day Coming" began to

democratize the band even further as instrument switching grew more and more common. His accommodating nature manifested itself even in his musicianship. When he got behind Georgia's drum kit on occasion, he didn't even have to rearrange it to play right-handed.

As always, Ira and Georgia went to the movies a lot, active filmgoers of both art-house and Hollywood fare. Sometimes, on the road, it was exactly what was needed. Once, on a day off in Phoenix during the *Fakebook* years, Ira had caught *The Freshman* and had been instantly transported back to New York.

When in town, they often went with Faith to the Film Forum downtown. Georgia's mother had continued her remarkable one-film-a-year pace with a series of spiritual and autobiographical shorts. Recently, Georgia and Ira (along with Will and Emily's son, Max) provided voices for a short called *Tall Time Tales*. For Georgia, filmgoing with her cinema-loving mother could be "a white-knuckle experience."

"My mom was a vocal spectator at the movies," she wrote later in an essay for Criterion. "Sighing, gasping, moaning, even uttering words of advice or disdain to the screen were not beyond her. It was often embarrassing. Even the most vapid milquetoast piece of crap could get a rise out of her."

Emily Hubley continued the steady production of her own animated films as well, and one of Georgia and Ira's many projects in 1994 was providing soundtracks for a few of them. At Water Music, they turned older material into spacious new instrumental configurations. To score Emily's film *Enough*, "Walking Away from You" became a fuzz-bass instrumental with a chorus of multitracked Georgias singing a wordless Christmas carol.

The week after soundtracking with Emily, back in their rehearsal space next to Water Music, all the outside work came to a sudden and decisive payoff when Jad Fair from Half Japanese came to visit. All three members of Yo La Tengo had worked with him before in various one-off projects, a medium that Fair had honed into a platform for art-goof spontaneity while championing an extreme form of naïve nonmusicianship and creation.

"Jad asked if we wanted to rehearse or just record," Ira said. "We went in with no songs. We just started playing, and would settle on something. Jad had a book of lyrics." The quartet hammered out sixteen bursts in one afternoon, words by Fair's brother and Half Japanese partner David. Few of the pieces were longer than two minutes, improvised atmospheres with very few sudden changes, but they were most definitely recognizable as songs, subtle shifts in Fair's dry cadences rolling with the arrangements.

The spontaneity enthralled them and by summer's end, Yo La Tengo discovered an ability to work quickly, grounded by a musical self-assurance they'd never before had access to. The editing process could still take a while. But despite an unceasing schedule, the band would produce an entirely new batch of songs ready to be recorded within a matter of months. It was a kind of flexibility.

Inspired by their recordings with Jad Fair, they began to tape jam sessions at the practice space with the intention of homing in on interesting sections to shape into songs. James took charge of the project, compiling cassettes to pass along to his bandmates. One afternoon, they fixated on a four-chord progression. "Ten minutes into it, I added the fifth chord," James remembered. "I definitely remember having that on tape, all of us *knowing* that it was on tape."

It took two years for Georgia to appreciate the fried chicken, which was fine. Yo La Tengo found themselves with plenty of reasons to be in Nashville. Once there, trips to the northern part of town and Prince's Hot Chicken Shack were well within reason. "Hot chicken is bright-orange pan-fried chicken, the color of a traffic cop," Georgia explained. "When you order it 'hot,' it's unimaginably hot." The band Versus had hipped them to the joint, but there was plenty to discover in Nashville.

Working on *Painful*, the band had loved Roger Moutenot's patience, ear, and no-bullshit demeanor. So when Moutenot relocated to Music City USA and declared with an admirable precision that he wouldn't produce any country music, it seemed wise to follow him. Roger knew of a bunch of cheap studios with killer gear.

Alex the Great, the studio Roger found, did exactly the trick. "The greatest thing about that place is that anything you want, all the guitars, keyboard, organs, Ace Tones, vibes, piano," Roger said, "if you have an idea, it's all there for you to use. The vibe is great and so is the rate." There was even room for James to crash there.

There was also a Ping-Pong table, a pastime Ira adapted to with an aggressiveness that surprised Roger. "It was amazing how Ira transformed from a mild player into a cutthroat, with the jones to annihilate anyone he could, at any time." Taking advantage of the cheaper rates, Yo La Tengo took their time.

There was only one day off during the sessions, and even that wasn't spent socializing, but they managed do some anyway. Ira and Georgia camped out with their former 719 housemate Danny Amis, who'd graduated from the Raybeats to Los Straitjackets, a Lucha-Libre-mask-wearing surf-rock outfit. They also reconnected with Lambchop, the band Ira had first seen at Merge Fest. Based in Nashville, they sometimes contained over a dozen members and didn't travel easily. Thankfully, they didn't require much validation from the outside world, either. Like Yo La Tengo, they'd taken a long time to find their form.

Lambchop had evolved, first, from a regular jam session organized by the employees of a local flooring company. "A lot of people came in and out of the basement or wherever we were getting together at the time," guitarist and singer Kurt Wagner recalled. "We'd pick a day and do it regularly. It was like poker night, Wednesday night or whatever. I was writing these songs, and since nobody else really was, that's what we played. We didn't really have a plan. We just wanted to make little records and record our progress as we got together."

The music had elements of folk, country, punk, R&B, and classic pop. Centered on Wagner's idiosyncratic, hyperarticulated voice, Lambchop was less indie rock and more the type of left-field anarchist folk combo that Ira might have booked at Music for Dozens. Wagner worked full-time laying floor, and if his ambitions were decidedly mellow, he remained enthusiastic about his band.

One member of the collective was Jonathan Marx, a college friend of Superchunk's Mac McCaughan who had taken up trumpet expressly to join Wagner and company. He sent some tapes to Merge and the band inched toward a professional career. They played often at Lucy's, a record store turned all-ages venue that became the center of a rich rock scene emerging in the shadow of country music. Through Marx, they shared bills with indie acts that passed through. The band's unwieldy size made them a cross-generational home base for an ever-shifting collective of musicians deeply embedded in their hometown. Wagner began to date the store's owner, Mary Marcini. In the summer of 1994, they'd gotten booked on a leg of the $26 million Lollapalooza behemoth, which is how they ended up in New York and met Georgia. It was their first tour.

"It was like we had sixteen new friends," James said. "They know their hometown backwards and forwards and were able to show us amazing stuff, really amazing restaurants. Especially through Jonathan and Kurt, we found out so much more about the history of the town and all the other incredible music that was made there besides the country stuff that everybody knows about—especially the soul stuff from the '60s and '70s. Those guys schooled me hard on that stuff. It was great."

Near the end of the sessions, they invited Lambchop and others to the studio for a party set of covers they'd worked up for B-sides, at least one of which—the Seeds' "Can't Seem to Make You Mine"—had been in the band's songbook since the Georgia and Those Guys gigs.

Songs were scattered between boho freak-outs ("Attack on Love"), some guitar jams ("Blue Line Swinger"), and new Georgia ballads. "Paul Is Dead" fell into the growing bin of songs that seemed a distant extension of Ira's music writing, and tested the band's new super-quiet three-part vocals. They added "Hot Chicken #1" and "Hot Chicken #2" as subtitles to "Flying Lesson" and "Don't Say a Word," respectively, simultaneously an homage to Prince's Hot Chicken Shack and the Flying Burrito Brothers. When *Electr-o-Pura* was released in 1995, songwriting credit would be attributed for the first time to the collective Yo La Tengo.

At the sessions, the members of Yo La Tengo also tapped into a heretofore unsuspected ability to relax. Getting ready for the trip, they'd kept a mess of song ideas in circulation, developed them as they felt comfortable, and even left some unfinished until it was time to meet Roger in Nashville.

One aggressive song they brought in had only two chords, and a bass part that descended into a chord change. They removed the guitar, reset the song to piano and organ, added lyrics, and it became "The Hour Grows Late." the five-chord jam they'd taped at the practice space became a four-minute pop song. Ira added lyrics concocting a new plot for British movie stars Julie Christie and Tom Courtenay. Both featured in some of Georgia's favorite films, including 1963's *Billy Liar*. Not coincidentally, both were likewise mentioned in the Kinks' "Waterloo Sunset," references and meanings that spiraled inward like a seashell.

CHAPTER 12

Electr-o-Pura

During the only full day off during the Nashville sessions, the band visited the Museum of Beverage Containers north of the city. "It ended up being this really remarkable place," Ira said. "It was like leafing through an old magazine, a history of packaging and typefaces." There, they spotted a bottle of Electropura soda, manufactured in Mexico, and found their album title.

It wasn't the only alternative-sugared beverage crossover in those years. Coca-Cola briefly marketed OK Soda, a beverage aimed at Generation X that had grown out of their two-year study of the global teen market. They determined, in the words of a *Time* report, that "the current crop of teens suffer, along with their twentysomething elders, from an acute sense of diminished expectations." And thus a soda and marketing campaign angled toward the mediocre and rendered with a citric note that recalled flat Coca-Cola. *Eightball* artist Daniel Clowes designed the packaging. The drink was test-marketed in nine cities, Hoboken not among them, and never distributed nationally.

Perhaps around the time Bud Dry began to advertise itself as "the alternative beer," it became clear the boom couldn't last much longer. But where one boom ended, others began. In the coming years, American popular music would turn its attentions away from indie rock. Meanwhile, though, in Northern California, the first wave of Internet companies was putting vast power in the hands of a generation of well-educated twentysomethings. Instead of labels, they launched start-ups and sprang across the cultural landscape the way college rock had only a few years before, and then far, far beyond, as they transformed the entire world—indie rock included—to the core.

The captains of industry came to increasingly resemble ruffled graduate students. Some of them even probably had record collections. Later, it was noted by none other than Neil Young that Apple founder Steve Jobs preferred vinyl. In this way, several hundred years of bohemian tradition would soon merge incontrovertibly with the dominant economic class. The going was good, especially if one could keep one's bearings and not be distracted.

In 1994, on tour in Tampa, Ira had been in a thrift shop going through records. "It was a huge stack and I kept pulling out one thing after another that looked promising," he remembered. "It was an untapped store. One record was called *My Little Corner of the World* by this guy Richie Van. It was really captivating, a weird fake lounge record with real applause after studio recordings, performed with a drum machine. He does 'Joy to the World,' which is way off, timing-wise. It's a very odd record in that try-to-read-the-mind-of-the-musician way. The last song on the record was 'My Little Corner of the World.' We listened to it a lot, and assumed he wrote it. We'd never heard it before. It was a signed record, even."

The record became a talisman for the band, even before the song made it into their repertoire. "I want to send this out to Richie Van, in his thrift-store corner of the world," Ira sang on "The Hour Grows Late," the song they'd mostly improvised in the studio. Like "Big Day Coming," it seemed to call back simultaneously to the basement at 719 Garden Street and the Kinks' Village Green. There was still plenty to connect them to the world they knew, but also plenty more spread out before them.

Sometimes, the proper response seemed to be to push back in some small, cantankerous way. When *Electr-o-Pura* was released in May 1995, the CD timings on its back cover bore no relation to the tracks within. For Ira, it was a simple gesture that described a meticulous logic.

"Like on the vinyl, for instance, the times are wrong on the cover but right on the vinyl," he pointed out to one interviewer. "We were sort of predicating it on the fact that your average CD player has the digital readout, so we didn't really think we were fooling anyone. It was right there, and all you'd have to do would be to press the Time button and you'd know. But at the same time, we have read enough reviews where it seems people just sort of reflexively pick out the longest songs and call them the worst ones. That didn't bother us. But these long songs sometimes have nothing in common except their length; how could they be both the 'worst'? So people have a tendency to look at the long songs and have a prejudice about it. We thought, 'Let's have them hear the record once without knowing where the long songs are gonna be. After that they can figure it out.'"

Before the album's launch, Matador issued a press release that wrote about *Electr-o-pura* as if it were a movie. The lede heralded the return of "three of independent filmmaking's mightiest and most uncompromisingly idiosyncratic talents," and went on to promise that "following its theatrical release this April, Hubley, Kaplan, and McNew will embark on an ambitious promotional tour—not only enduring a grueling interview schedule, but actually acting out large portions of the work in groundbreaking performance tableaus."

The joke sailed over the heads of many interviewers, or their assistants. "Someone told me you were dabbling in film?" Janeane Garofalo asked the band during their appearance on a syndicated radio show called *7-Up Listen Up!*, yet another soda-pop crossover.

"Not really," Ira admitted.

"So you're calling your record company liars, then?"

"Creative," Ira replied without missing a beat.

Elsewhere, it spurred conversation, as when the host of *Idiot's Delight*, Vin Scelsa, actually convinced Georgia to talk about her parents' films. Though the PR bulletin was tongue-in-cheek, and even printed the wrong release date, the subtext was there for any who cared to decode it: Yo La Tengo was a band too smart to fall for the what-I-really-want-to-do-is-direct syndrome that had gripped everybody from the Beatles to David Byrne. They were a rock group, and exceedingly happy to be one. On *Electr-o-Pura*'s release, they introduced a cover of Grand Funk Railroad's "We're an American Band" into their encores, much to Georgia's chagrin. The oddly self-confident message (and clonking cowbell) rang loud and clear.

The parking lots where the side stage was set up were gigantic and hot, but the Lollapalooza crowds were usually pretty good anyway. It was certainly better than playing to rows of empty seats in amphitheater pavilions, where the expensive sections often sat unfilled and many fans watched from the distant lawn.

When Yo La Tengo started their midafternoon sets, a frequently sighted bit of roadie's tape on the stage indicated one of its most recent occupants and his futuristic instrument: MOBY OCTOPAD. "He was selling twenty-five-dollar hemp vegan T-shirts," James remembered. "Gangsta's Paradise" rapper Coolio often played after him. It took a week into the tour, but the band was finally able to orchestrate a photo with their friend-roadie: the long-awaited meeting of Coolio and Puleo. It had been that kind of year.

A few months earlier, they'd entered into a most bizarre service, playing the surrogate Velvet Underground in Mary Harron's film *I Shot Andy Warhol*. "We knew that there would be no better way to cement the comparison, and that perversely became one of the positives in doing it," Ira said of the band's participation. With Antietam's Tara Key along for the ride, the band stepped through the looking glass and into a re-creation of Warhol's Factory, the whole set covered in silver shining Reynolds Wrap, just as the original had been. Ira was affixed with sideburns, James with a new, happening hairdo.

Various Factory regulars visited the set during the two-day shoot, including Billy Name and Velvet Underground bassist John Cale himself. Cale approved, but later noted the odd-looking band onstage. The bass player, he thought, looked like Tiny Tim. They were on-screen for just under a minute, though their "Sister Ray"–like instrumental soundtracked the full four-minute Factory sequence.

"The year that Lollapalooza broke, and not in a good way," Ira said later of their turn on the traveling megafestival. It was supposed to be indie rock's big summer, Sonic Youth set to close over Courtney Love's Hole. The Jesus Lizard, who recorded for Chicago's Touch and Go and was fronted by the confrontational David Yow, was on the bill. Even the Minutemen's Mike Watt was along for a few legs.

The year before, Pavement had been dumped from the lineup after Smashing Pumpkins leader Billy Corgan became displeased by Stephen Malkmus's abstract diss in "Range Life." In the summer of 1995, Pavement was back, with a substantially higher fee. They also insisted that Lollapalooza purchase them a Ping-Pong table and transport it around for the band's use. "It was the most luxurious thing I'd ever heard of," Ira commented. Though he had sharpened his skills during the Alex the Great sessions for *Electr-o-Pura*, Ira "got trounced at Ping-Pong by every member of Pavement."

Malkmus's band was heavily favored for success. "I kept imagining how 'Rattled by the Rush' was going to sound on KROQ," Gerard Cosloy said. In epoch-defining songs, Malkmus coaxed brilliant, stumbling melodies from knotted lyrics that recalled Dylan at his most surreal. "I was smoking a lot of grass," Malkmus said later. "They sounded like hit singles to me." In a rare convergence, Yo La Tengo even backed Malkmus for a few songs at a Seattle radio session just before the tour began.

One omen, mostly unnoticed, was a *New York Times* piece

by Neil Strauss that ran a week and a half before Lollapalooza's Northwest kickoff. "The revenge of the normal," Strauss said of the second sold-out show at the Jones Beach Amphitheater on the marshy southern coast of Long Island by Hootie and the Blowfish. The South Carolina band, Strauss wrote, represented "the return of the well-adjusted and the congenial to the rock world: it talks about sports onstage, dresses casually in T-shirts and seems to have neither a chip on its shoulder nor an ounce of artistic pretension." They loved R.E.M. and the Replacements. In a strange twist, one of the auxiliary Blowfish was none other than Peter Holsapple, who'd split with R.E.M., taken up with the Continental Drifters, and signed on with the touring company of Hootie.

Hootie's *Cracked Rear View* became the year's top seller. Not long before, Epitaph had sold more than five million copies of the Offspring's *Smash*, released the week of Kurt Cobain's death. Sales eventually topped 12 million worldwide, and it would remain the biggest-selling album ever for an independent rock label. By 1995, indie was gone from the charts, increasingly dominated by R&B, hip-hop, and country. Other nominally rock best sellers that year included the Eagles (*Hell Freezes Over*, five million–plus copies), Christian lite-metal rockers Live, the decidedly late Beatles, and *You Can't Do That on Television* alum/songwriter Alanis Morissette.

Electr-o-Pura's sales were slightly less than *Painful*'s, ultimately clocking in around 150,000 copies. Across indie rock, the numbers continued to climb, but barely scratched the surface of *Billboard*. Pavement's *Wowee Zowee* came out in April 1995 through Warner Bros., where Danny Goldberg ended up after his ouster from Atlantic.

Yo La Tengo treated Lollapalooza in the same way Matador did Atlantic's distribution network: as another outlet. "I have warm feelings towards how hard they were," Ira said of the gigs. "Many long drives and summer heatwaves. Gigantic parking lots with no shade. I just remember being drenched in sweat at all times."

Playing opposite Yo La Tengo was Irish pop singer Sinéad

O'Connor, whose career hadn't recovered after she'd ripped up a picture of the pope on *Saturday Night Live*. A few shows in, she announced her pregnancy and dropped off the tour. Organizers rescheduled Yo La Tengo opposite Beck and labelmates Pavement.

There was also the one-woman media storm of Courtney Love, whose melodramatic repertoire included a beef with former Bikini Kill singer Kathleen Hanna (Sonic Youth made peace between them) and, after that, turned her attentions toward Sonic Youth themselves. Love's spiraling cone of private paranoia spilled—by at least some design—into the public.

Though she was a female drummer who sang and played an equal part in the band's creative process, not to mention guitar and keyboards—and would soon manage the band's books—Georgia Hubley's role as a woman in Yo La Tengo was simply to be part of Yo La Tengo. She was as far from a riot grrrl hero as she could get. "We tried to consciously remain oblivious to her and the soap opera," said Georgia. The closest they got was a photograph James took of Ira posed with a black-velvet painting of Courtney Love somebody was selling in the concourse at Lollapalooza.

Besides the occasional Ping-Pong game with Pavement and a post-show movie expedition with Sonic Youth's Lee Ranaldo, Ira, Georgia, and James didn't associate much with their tourmates. The drives, in James's words, were "brutal, spectacularly brutal."

"There was no feeling about 'Gee, what a big break this is,'" Ira said. "We were on the side stage of a not particularly well-attended Lollapalooza. But it was really fun, under the circumstances." Indeed, tour revenues were far down from the previous outings, the most recent of which had been that year's top grosser.

"But the shows were awesome," James stressed. "We played in front of tons and tons of people who never would have seen us otherwise. It was all for the best. It was easy to get access to the main stage to watch other groups. I missed the day David Yow got arrested for taking his pants off in Indiana. I watched Sonic Youth a bunch, saw Beck once or twice, Hole a few times."

Sonic Youth played last, frequently to a small exodus of departing Hole fans. The band closed their sets with a new song, "The Diamond Sea," an often twenty-minute requiem of chiming guitars played to the summer concert sheds of America in the waning days of the alternative nation.

R.E.M. remained one of the few bankable indie-era acts in the grunge years. Their elegiac *Automatic for the People* reached #2 on its 1992 release and spawned a half dozen megavideos-cum-singles. 1994's more rock-oriented *Monster* didn't quite capture the masses in the same way as its predecessor, but it still went #1, quadruple platinum, and begat a multiyear stadium and arena tour. In August 1996, fifteen years after Ira's writeup of "Radio Free Europe" in the *SoHo Weekly News*, R.E.M. signed a five-album contract with Warner Bros. reportedly worth around $80 million.

The band had found its version of the good life. Bassist Mike Mills bought a house in the Hollywood Hills. Michael Stipe split his time between R.E.M.'s hometown of Athens, Georgia, and New York. Guitarist Peter Buck took up residence in New Orleans, Seattle, and Hawaii, where—that year—he hosted his old friend Steve Fallon.

One afternoon, Steve started to laugh for no apparent reason.

"What's up?" Buck asked him.

In between giggles, Fallon managed, "I'm watching a fucking film backwards."

The previous years flashed back to Steve in a long, streaked blur. He'd moved out of the apartment upstairs from Maxwell's and opted for a place nearby. With Peter Buck's aid, Steve had bought his family out of the building and the business in 1990, and resolved on-and-off twelve-year conflicts between siblings, especially with his brother-in-law. "There was a point when I threw a bowl across the front of the room at Maxwell's,"

Steve remembered. "He was by the jukebox, and it whacked him right in the head, perfect aim. That's how angry I could get with him. Probably alcohol had something to do with it. Later on, I regretted all that.

"They had a thankless job because they were unseen people and they *did* work hard. And they were done. And the market had skyrocketed." Steve's sister Ann and her husband, Mario, moved to Florida.

But in the post-Nirvana years, Maxwell's and the music world had become drastically less freewheeling, even without family members around. "Maxwell's has always operated in a quasi-socialist atmosphere, because the original investment was so small," Steve noted at the time, and it was harder than ever to keep the place afloat. The no-funning of indie seemed to be happening everywhere.

The first place Steve noticed it was in college radio. During the last years at Coyote, he'd watched as major labels took interest in collegiate stations. "They'd started wining and dining the DJs at these schools. They'd talk them into programming directors, they'd talk them into playlists by saying, 'This is what you're going to school for; here's how to be professional about it.'" College radio had always operated with a degree of minor payola, but it had accelerated to outright absurdism. Brian Turner, who became music director at WFMU in 1996, heard stories of prominent label reps who treated other program directors to lap dances at CMJ. Coyote Records faded into history.

Another place Steve saw the unfun in action was in Maxwell's booking. "Before, we called our own shots, but audiences stopped coming in for unknown bands," he said. "We were being controlled by the booking agents." One sold-out show that Steve resented was an appearance by soon-to-be rap-metal behemoths Korn. "It was a big crowd, but I'd never have them shit in my fucking toilet," Steve said. "The bass player gets off the stage and beats the living shit out of the bus driver. Ugh. It all disgusted me."

In December 1995, Steve sold Maxwell's—though not the building—to William Sutton, a self-described efficiency expert who told Steve he wanted to keep the club "the same." Ira and Georgia's former housemate Todd Abramson agreed to stay on as talent buyer. Sutton immediately decided to turn Maxwell's into a brewpub and installed enormous vats in a front window. One day, Abramson—who also operated Telstar Records—arrived to see a man about to wheel out the jukebox, filled with Todd's own record collection.

As it had a century earlier, the encroaching civilization threatened to swallow the peaceful spot in the middle, the old club by the site of the old ball field. The infrastructure that had nurtured Yo La Tengo rapidly changed. In 1995, Bill Ryan's Pier Platters closed. They'd opened an annex to cover CD sales, but their adherence to vinyl had been their undoing.

One major discovery came in Seattle in October 1995 in time-honored Yo La Tengo fashion: getting pissed off. "The club were just dicks to us, all night long, fighting us every step of the way," James remembered. "When we got offstage, security was ready to call it a night, and we were not ready to call it a night, and there were people there who were not ready to call it a night."

For an encore, the band played a quiet version of "Speeding Motorcycle" that didn't stop. "We didn't play loud, but our meaning was clear," Ira said. "We were carrying ourselves like a noise band. You can do the same thing by utilizing sounds that usually annoy but by making them come out very pretty and emotional. Some sounds are more flexible than they're given credit for being."

As the band played on, one of club's owners approached Sue Garner, whose band Run On was along for that leg of the tour, and a close friend since the Last Roundup practiced at 719 Garden. "Do you think they realize what time it is?" he asked.

"I think they *absolutely* know what time it is, yes," Sue replied. Earlier in the set, she'd walked into a backstage room to find Joe Puleo locked in a stare-down with a recalcitrant promoter. She backed away silently.

"It was the most beautiful, quiet fuck-you you ever heard," Garner remembered. "They don't cotton to being taken advantage of by anyone, and it's part of their wisdom to take it out musically. They're *fierce* when they get screwed over. They do *not* put up with that nonsense. I *love* that about them."

Eighteen minutes in, venue management flipped on the houselights. Six minutes later they cut the power. Later that night, an Ace Tone disappeared from the band's gear.

There was little time to practice, but the band's commitment to their instincts continued to result in new ways to expand their palette. In Europe, they experimented with an instrumental that was so skeletal they barely remembered performing it later. James played a tumbling eight-note pattern over a 4/4 backbeat that rose and fell like an M. C. Escher illusion. Ira noodled on organ. It wasn't so much a song as a groove, and there was nary a guitar solo—or, so far, even a vocal—in sight. Somewhere along the way it got affixed to the story about Moby's Octopad.

Around the time WFMU found itself alone on a dead college campus, Ken Freedman's hair turned white. It had already fought off one challenge when three stations, including Fordham University's WFUV, claimed the discovery of a twenty-eight-year-old clerical error that would reduce WFMU to 650 watts and deprive it of a potential 2.2 million listeners.

WFMU had worked hard to maintain an idyllic existence in the middle of the mostly benign Upsala College and weren't about to give that up when it suddenly appeared in the early 1990s that the college was about to go out of business. Especially since Gaylord Fields had gotten his weekly show, Yo La Tengo had been part of station life more and more often. Frequent tour pals Run On, who'd been there for the Seattle "Speeding Motorcycle," included WFMU music director Dave Newgarden. For a month on Newgarden's show, Yo La Tengo had hosted a "Sleeping Pill Radio Hour," jamming on the air with a two-drummer setup, lots of tape loops, and a few guests, including their old friend Phil Milstein, who'd founded the first Velvet Underground fanzine in the '70s and tracked down Moe Tucker and Sterling Morrison.

Using a third-party organization called Friends of WFMU, station manager Freedman created Auricle Communications, a nonprofit group of DJs and other WFMU community members. They held an emergency pledge drive and forked over the $150,000 required to purchase the station and broadcast tower from the college, who used the money to file its last payroll. Upsala College shut its doors and abandoned WFMU in East Orange. They were a college radio station no longer.

Before the college chaplain moved out, he bequeathed to Freedman a collection of five paintings on black velvet, including a Vampirella, "a bizarre nude," and a copyright-infringing depiction of *Star Wars* characters. "I thought you might like these," he told Freedman, who began a collection.

"It was weird, but I kind of still remember it kind of fondly, and I think everybody kind of remembers that period kind of fondly," Freedman recalled of their time alone on the campus. "I think it was weird, and dangerous. There was a lot of crime, a lot of fucked-up things happening. You know, people getting mugged, people's cars getting vandalized, people's cars getting stolen, bands' cars getting stolen from the front of the station. Attempted break-ins, shootouts between the cops and some drug dealers that ended on our front lawn. Gunfire way off on the abandoned campus, you know?" Freedman and company hatched a plan to buy a building in Jersey City and pull the station into some semblance of civilization.

Pledge drives at college and noncommercial radio stations had been an important tradition for many decades, and in the mid-1990s, as WFMU fought for its life, the stunts DJs acted out in return for pledges reached unparalleled heights. Freedman received a Hotel California tattoo on the air. Tom Scharpling, the *18 Wheeler* zine editor who'd issued a few Dump singles, ate prodigious amounts of blueberry pie. Others ran naked across the campus. Listeners received prizes, such as albums and various WFMU ephemera, including their

Catalog of Curiosities, spotted in Kurt Cobain's hands on MTV's *Unplugged* in 1993.

"The key to a WFMU radio stunt was that it was something you really didn't have to do, because it was radio," noted Gaylord Fields. "They were radio sight gags. But the meta part of it was that everyone actually *did* the ridiculous thing they said they were going to do." For the 1996 edition of the Marathon, Gaylord landed one of the most memorable recurring stunts in station history, this time involving Yo La Tengo.

One night, A-Bones guitarist and filmgoing buddy Bruce Bennett was on the phone with Ira when he heard Georgia's voice in the background: *"Ask him if he wants to do the FMU thing."*

"Oh, right," Ira said, and detailed his idea for a Marathon stunt to Bruce, who had been a fixture as an "Ed McMahon type" on a WFMU show hosted by station veteran Jim Marshall known on-air as The Hound. In return for pledges, Ira explained, Yo La Tengo—and Bruce—would play any song, by anybody, ever. Bennett thought, "involving me is the dumbest thing in the world," but he knew plenty of songs and was game.

The quartet met up for an impromptu rehearsal and tossed out song names. "It was really draining and difficult," Bennett remembered. "It turns out that Georgia knew all the words to 'No Woman, No Cry.' I'd give my pinkie for a recording."

The band took to the air on the evening of March 9, the news spread by the station in the preceding weeks. They laughed through more than twenty songs, including classics by the Monkees, a few by the Kinks, and a pair by Will Rigby from *Sidekick Phenomenon*. There were bubblegum obscurities (the Lemon Pipers' "Green Tambourine") and a song composed by Faith and John Hubley with Quincy Jones and being performed at the time by Dump, "So Sedimentary." Stumped by the fancy chord changes in "God Only Knows," they dipped into the station library, grabbed *Stack-O-Tracks*, a proto-karaoke release by Capitol in the '70s, and Georgia took a whack. "Wow, we're great," she noted as the backing tracks swirled in.

The stunt was a wild success, and it became an annual part of the station's pledge drives. Station manager Ken Freedman grew fond of bolstering WFMU fund-raising materials with vintage communist propaganda. EAT FLAMING DEATH, FASCIST MEDIA PIGS one T-shirt would read below an image of freeform soldiers, fists, tools, and eyes raised to a better tomorrow. The attitude was well earned, especially in the scheme of American radio in the 1990s.

In the wake of Nirvana's success, commercial stations switched rapidly to what was formally known as the alternative music format. Even Z100, Manhattan's venerable top-40 station, converted in 1994. But while mainstream radio burped former college stars into high rotation, its own business model rumbled into decline.

Just one month before Yo La Tengo's first WFMU Marathon appearance, the New York classic rock station K-Rock became a "ghost ship between formats," guided by a playlist-generating Selector program running in Los Angeles. The notion of a radio station with a live DJ grew increasingly threatened, even more so when the Telecommunications Act of 1996 allowed conglomerates to own up to six stations in a single market. The decision would more or less destroy traditional FM radio. In a backward way, there was no better time to be WFMU.

The new higher-ups were not amused by Gerard Cosloy's behavior of late. As promised, he had trimmed back on the fax wars, but simultaneously had discovered the Internet. He took to the early Usenet groups and message boards as readily as he'd taken to zines as a teenager and directly engaged indie rock fans on the intricacies of his company's business.

In one posting, he explained exactly why Liz Phair's *Exile in Guyville* hadn't been released through Atlantic. He likewise made sure to clarify that "most major label records are a pile of shit, that's why there's so much guilt in being associated with them. But I'm not sure there's anything great about 'indie' if it means stuff like the Supersuckers, Lucy's Fur Coat or the Drop Nineteens (sorry if anyone is a fan of those bands, I'm not)."

"We had so much fucking attitude in those days," Chris Lombardi remembered. "We didn't realize it, but the Atlantic folks would refer to our attitude as 'Matitude.' We tried to shield everybody from the people up there. They were in a totally different mind-set than we were. We thought they were a total bunch of idiots. And they weren't. Some were and some weren't. They were in a totally different world, and that's fine."

The Fall's Mark E. Smith had been as disastrous as billed. "I don't think he ever ate," remembered one Atlantic publicist, "just drank his weight in calories." The Dutch band Bettie Serveert seemed primed for a potential breakthrough but failed to sell. But those were hardly the only acts Matador concerned themselves with. There was still plenty of small-ball indie pop, which included YLT pals like the Shams, with Amy Rigby and Sue Garner, as well as *Vortex*, the rejected album James had recorded with his former band, Christmas, in 1990. Michael Cudahy and Liz Cox of Christmas would soon sign to Sub Pop and go on to success with Combustible Edison, where they built on the kitsch-pop vibe they'd chased to Las Vegas.

"That Atlantic money allowed us and the bands to seem bigger than they and we actually were," Chris said. "They lost a lot of money and they were happy to keep writing checks like crazy. We were just burning through the fucking money."

But Atlantic Records finally grew tired of Matador. A *New York* magazine profile of Chris and Gerard filled with appropriate smack talk didn't help, and Atlantic dissolved the relationship in January 1996, giving up its stake. Matador had never ceased to be itself. Though not as bad as getting locked out of the office on the eve of *Slanted and Enchanted*'s release, they forgot to pay the phone and electric bills as Liz Phair's *Whip-Smart* was about to go out, resulting in a candlelight shipping frenzy.

At some point, one of Gerard's *CMJ* columns provoked an angry Courtney Love to call the Matador offices. She reached the answering machine, which featured an outgoing message recorded by Chris "shouting the praises of Matador recording artists, U2" while the Irish megaband's "I Will Follow" played in the background.

Though removed from the bosom of WEA, Matador's cachet remained undiminished. One afternoon, Lombardi received a call from Mo Ostin, the longtime head of Warner Bros., himself recently ousted. "I'm in the neighborhood," he told Chris. "I was wondering if I could drop by and hang out. I've got an independent label now and I wanted to remind myself what an independent label looks like."

Matador wasn't homeless for long. Almost as quickly as the deal with Atlantic ended, a new bidding war started. Danny Goldberg got involved from his position as new president of Mercury. Ultimately, Capitol Records picked up where Atlantic left off and purchased 49 percent of Matador for what *Rolling Stone* reported as $20 million. "That is complete and utter bullshit," Gerard told them. "Who's the fucking source for that?"

Speaking of the original deal with Atlantic, Gerard later noted, "We didn't cash in personally. That didn't happen till later." Whatever the correct number, Matador made out well.

Once again, Matador would continue to issue the majority of releases through the normal independent distributors, and would send a few choice acts—Pavement, Liz Phair, Jon Spencer—into the pipeline via the space-age Capitol Records Tower on Vine Street in Hollywood. Yo La Tengo would not be among them. They were just not that kind of band, though this decision was more practical than ideological.

"Cosloy is a rare visionary," Jim Barber of Geffen was quoted as saying. "He has been consistently right since he was eighteen years old."

There was a show at Tramps in New York during Adam Kaplan's stint as Yo La Tengo's manager. He'd replaced Lyle Hysen, as strong a sign as any of the band's intentions of keeping affairs on a close, local scale. Not that Ira's younger brother was unqualified. Adam had spent the past decade working at record companies, including Virgin and Atlantic.

The show was sold out and people kept congratulating Adam. "You must be so excited," they said.

"And I realized that I was for Ira, and I was for Georgia," Adam said. "They were a band that deserved it, but it didn't have shit to do with me." He'd come on around the time of *Electr-o-Pura.* "In a lot of ways, my job was 'What do they want?' and I'd find out what they wanted, and then I'd go to Matador and say, 'This is what they want,'" Adam remembered. "I had a series of meetings at Matador where we said, 'This is what we'll do,' and I spent the rest of my time reminding them. And that was sort of my job.

"For me, Yo La Tengo was absolutely what let me know that I needed to leave the record business, without question," he said later. "I'd worked for all of these labels, and there were bands that I loved, but I'd worked lots of bands' lesser records, and I just didn't really care. So here I was, with family, and a band that I loved, and Ira would say, and I believed him, 'Look, we trust you, and because we trust you, we can relax, and we're a better band.' And I felt like, 'I believe you, but I don't feel it.'" It was a very Kaplan-like kind of independence.

"Band managers always say, 'We're in Boston on Tuesday.' No, *they're* in Boston on Tuesday. And if I wasn't going to feel it with them, I wasn't going to feel it." Adam went back to school, eventually to earn a PhD in clinical psychology. Soon Yo La Tengo decided to manage themselves, an almost inevitable decision in a career where there was almost no such thing as a no-brainer decision, every choice debated and analyzed. They remained in contact with their record company, booking agent, and lawyer, but—for the most part—made the decisions that needed making. Not that they didn't consult people.

"Take the money!" Faith Hubley told them when they asked whether they should accept a commission to soundtrack a surf-rock version of the Roto-Rooter theme. Though she hadn't in years, Georgia's mother was an old hand at supporting her own creative endeavors with the occasional out-and-out commercial gig. The Roto-Rooter spot never made it to the air, but it was the beginning of a new line of income for the band.

Not long thereafter, they contributed music to a Coca-Cola ad affiliated with the summer Olympics in Atlanta. At first, the band simply planned to rerecord the song the agency requested. But they stopped. Like everything else, if Yo La Tengo was to proceed into the world of advertising, there needed to be a rule. While they were OK with contributing to an advertisement, it would not be with one of their own songs. Those were just for them, they decided, though they would also be happy to create a new piece of music to order, perhaps even in the specific spirit of one of their existing songs.

But Coke was it, and the rule went into effect. "There would be something a lot easier about just licensing a song," Ira observed. "The positive is that you're keeping your song. The negative is that you end up dealing with the advertising people a lot more, which isn't always the most fun aspect."

A case in point came almost immediately with the Coke ad, but it was the first of many. The band comforted themselves in knowing they were to join a lineage that included Gary Lewis, the Left Banke, Los Bravos, and many others. "We spent an afternoon in New York's RPM studio, James, Georgia, me and some suits," Ira wrote on a band web page titled "Yo La Tengo Sell Out," illustrated by a photo of Georgia in a bathtub filled with beans, re-creating the cover shot from *The Who Sell Out*.

"There were some concerns voiced when the beginning of our composition was deemed 'too sad.' I made matters worse by pointing out that that section was in 3/4 time. That's the problem! was the response. You must change it out of 3/4 time. But we stood our ground. How, I no longer recall. Did someone suggest that the American team, however talented, was unlikely to win every single gold medal at the Olympics, and perhaps our jingle might remind people that, though sad not to take home first place in the Women's Kayak Slalom Singles, one might still reach for a Coca-Cola as if to say, 'Good try, Dana Chladek.' As I said, I don't remember."

The final spot was as concise an example as any of Yo La Tengo's newfound control, shifting in forty-seven seconds from a lilting guitar melody to an overdriven finale—indie rock in shorthand and made to order.

They learned the title song from Richie Van's *My Little Corner of the World*, Georgia singing lead, assuming they'd found a lost classic. After one show, Ira's mother complimented them on the song, saying it was one of her favorites.

Ira was astounded. "Gee, you love the Richie Van record too, Mom?" Soon thereafter, the band discovered the song's previous life as a hit for Anita Bryant in 1960, written by Bob Hilliard and Lee Pockriss, and covered by middlebrow pop singers thereafter. They kept it in their setlist.

William Sutton's changes at Maxwell's did not go well. There was a fire in the kitchen. And the brewing equipment didn't work properly. Steve Fallon, who still owned the building at 1039 Washington, was contracted to stay on as a consultant, and lived a few blocks away on Castle Point. Not long after Sutton took over, Steve received a call from one of his tenants upstairs from Maxwell's, who reported a horrible odor in the building. Steve returned to the familiar bar.

"When I opened the door, it smelled like horseshit," he recounted.

"I don't know what's going on," Sutton told him. "It's a Friday night and there's nobody here."

"Well, what the hell is that smell?"

"What do you mean?"

"Are you venting the brewing equipment?"

"We didn't get that done yet."

"You really can't be brewing beer without a ventilation system," Steve told him. He went to the basement, and saw yeast spilled on the floor. "Do you know what yeast is?" he asked the new owner. "That's gonna be all worms in about two days."

From longtime booker Todd Abramson's perspective, it went well for a month or two. "Nothing had changed," he said. "There was some good business and publicity. But things went south quickly. [Sutton's] family got involved, which made things worse. If there was a meeting, four of us would be there. Two of us were trying to talk sense into him and the fourth person would agree with everything he said."

When Abramson quit at the end of 1996, it was the last straw for Yo La Tengo too, their link to the club removed. They played a two-set New Year's show to close it out, and began with the intro to Don McLean's "American Pie" before shifting into the Stones' "The Last Time." Glenn Mercer and Dave Weckerman of the Feelies were on hand too, to cover a few of their tunes. They'd kept going in a new band, Wake Ooloo.

During the encore, the band played Sham 69's 1978 amped-up, wall-busting single, "Borstal Breakout." Ira flailed on drums, Georgia on guitar. James sang. They warned the crowd not to smash the venue's CD jukebox as they exited the venue, and then closed with "Did I Tell You."

CHAPTER 13

Rocket #9

Dropping the needle on *I Can Hear the Heart Beating as One* and listening to its opening instrumental, "Return to Hot Chicken," it is possible to hear a distant connection to the band that recorded "The River of Water" more than a decade earlier, were one still able to find a copy of the out-of-print single. On Yo La Tengo's debut, though, it was an atmosphere that seemed more an idea than a palpable feeling they could achieve as musicians.

By the time they rejoined Roger Moutenot in Nashville in the fall of 1996, the atmosphere was well within their grasp. Released the following spring to mammoth acclaim and excellent sales, *I Can Hear the Heart Beating as One* pushed the band beyond the boundaries of the underground jukebox and its familiar language of elegant fuzz and, simultaneously, right back into it, their work producing at least two songs almost assured to turn up on indie-era *Nuggets* sets of the future.

Plenty of Yo La Tengo's contemporaries had evolved in surprising ways over the years, but listening to the latest releases by bands like Sonic Youth and R.E.M., even as they entered their own respective experimental phases, one could easily hear the missions with which they began. But with "Moby Octopad," *I Can Hear the Heart*'s second song, Yo La Tengo turned yet another corner, one that had taken quite a while to come to. *I Can Hear the Heart Beating as One* also pushed the band, as gently as possible, out beyond the boundaries of the underground as a whole, its songs presented with an assured and accessible eclecticism and unobscured emotion that would bring them to an enormous new audience.

Music had come together naturally in their practice space as they continued to patiently refine songs from James's rehearsal tapes. They brought in a few from home, too. Georgia and Ira found a samba beat on a Casio keyboard and wrote a gentle bossa nova bounce called "Center of Gravity." James brought in "Stockholm Syndrome" nearly fully formed, and would become his first lead vocal on a Yo La Tengo LP. Its chorus was high and sweet, and Robert Christgau would compare it to Neil Young. But there was no looseness in the song, from its quick pickup into the first line to the tight few bars it left for an Ira noise solo. More than ever, though, the band felt confident enough to leave even more songs unfinished as they headed back to Nashville, which is how "Moby Octopad" had arisen.

They'd tried it in skeletal form live, a loping bass groove played over and over—no vocals—but it was veritably reinvented with Moutenot at the House of David studio in Nashville, affixed with a dreamy Georgia-and-Ira duet plus a swooping three-part chorus about falling asleep while watching a Mets game. Alongside the wordless Beach Boys–esque harmonies was a triggered sample from Burt Bacharach's "Bird Bath" and the chopped-up pedal steel of onetime Flying Burrito Brother (and Elvis TCB band member) Al Perkins, who contributed more audibly elsewhere.

More than anything, the song—and especially its gently droned first line, sung by all three Tengos: "locked in a kiss, outside eyes cease to exist"—established a mood of instant intimacy. There were rock songs on the album too, certainly. Up next was "Sugarcube," one of the album's two future "nuggets," and almost entirely predicated on deep, slashing fuzz. But everywhere was a sense of spaciousness and patient movement. On the front cover, in a photograph by Steve Thornton, cars streak through a busy intersection, shot from above.

Songs like "One PM Again" and "Center of Gravity" followed quiet, complex progressions. Other songs used surprising instrumental combinations to create unexpected shifts. On "Autumn Sweater," a love song that emerged fully formed in practice one afternoon after Georgia demonstrated the changes on the organ, James manned second drums while Ira played Farfisa. He quickly added lyrics that were, if not outright personal, then at least seeming to ring quite true about their singer: "I try my best to hide in crowded rooms," he sang. "It's nearly impossible."

Along with "Sugarcube," "Autumn Sweater"'s its rock-anthem *Nuggets*-y companion, Ira universalized neuroses into anthemic hopefulness. "I'm trying to be more assured," he sang on the latter, "I'm trying to be more right there, I'm trying to be less uptight, I'm trying to be more aware." Their confidence came across full blast, at whatever volume they were playing. In the slot for the noise solo in James's "Stockholm Syndrome," Ira's playing came out as all notes, a concise bit of melody that moved the song logically to the next chorus. The editing paid off.

The seriousness of the enterprise was compromised somewhat by the album inserts advertising fictional Matador releases like the Shitheels, *Heroin!* the musical (presented by Sir Christopher Gerard), and a trio of albums by the Condo Fucks. On the flip side of one of the sheets, there was an uncredited poem. "I see a beach . . . the waves pounding against the shore. A beautiful girl, her heart pounding against her breast. I see a tall, handsome man. Now I see it! Now I see! I can hear the roar of the Ocean. And finally I can hear the music of love. I CAN HEAR THE HEART BEATING AS ONE."

Day after day, the album took shape, pilgrimages to Prince's Hot Chicken Shack continued. As per habit, lyrics came last. Ira and Georgia stayed with Kurt Wagner of Lambchop and his wife, Mary, and usually the lyric writing got done there. They'd become close friends. The Wagners had celebrated their recent nuptials by loading into three minivans with a dozen Lambchops for an East Coast tour/honeymoon with Yo La Tengo.

Working on lyrics one afternoon, Ira amused himself with the idea of titling a song "We're an American Band." "It's too good a concept to leave to Grand Funk Railroad," he figured. "I thought we'd do our own road song with all the non-strippers-and-hotel-room-trashing things that happen in our road stories."

He recalled a night in Maryland, playing at Johns Hopkins University. The day had been shitty and the sound was terrible. They abandoned the setlist early in the night. In the crowd, Ira thought he heard someone shout for Sun Ra's "Rocket #9." They'd never played it before, but he called for the song anyway and threw his arm down on the organ. If it looked from the crowd like the band was in a bad mood, they were. James figured out the tune's main riff quickly. "Presto change-o, 'Rocket #9,'" Ira recalled.

It was a trick emblematic of Yo La Tengo. Acutely sensitive to being treated in a secondary way, Yo La Tengo had long been fond of giving their audiences what they neither expected nor necessarily wanted. There were always reasons. They had been ignored in some capacity for so long that when success came calling for them, it found the trio sometimes elusive, often indifferent to or distrustful of the attention. If an interviewer seemed genuinely interested, it wasn't so much of a chore, but as review copies of the new album made it out, there were more and more questions to answer. The less asked about their personal lives, the better. All Tengos remained cordial, though Georgia ducked out of interview duties whenever possible. But the questions seemed secondary. There was really nothing that needed explaining about their new album.

The music on *I Can Hear the Heart Beating as One* was no mere synthesis of influences, no matter how long the list, or how sudden the inspiration. At its one-beating heart, the sounds and creative choices on display were expressions of a deeper independence, arrived at by happenstance, choice, heritage, and creative toil—an American band to the core.

Before the album came out, the band rented a community college campus in Santa Monica for a two-day video shoot.

Phil Morrison had moved to Los Angeles and was making a living shooting television commercials. In New York, before he'd moved, he'd become a regular attendee at *Eating It*, a Monday-night comedy showcase at the Luna Lounge on the Lower East Side organized by Marc Maron and Janeane Garofalo that became a gathering point for a new wave of stand-ups. He brought Georgia and Ira with him a few times. With Joe Ventura, another *Eating It* regular, Phil and Ira conceived an ambitious video for "Sugarcube."

With *Electr-o-Pura*'s allotted budget, Phil had invented a daft scenario for "Tom Courtenay," in which Yo La Tengo were invited to open for a Beatles reunion show. The shoot had been a fun party, filled with Fab in-jokes. This time, the scenario was even more promising: Yo La Tengo would be sent to school to learn how to rock. Phil had a commercial shoot that week too, and they borrowed the equipment, but mainly they shot in California to secure the video's three co-leads: David Cross, Bob Odenkirk, and John Ennis of *Mr. Show*.

Yo La Tengo had staked their own connections in the comedy world too. Ira and Georgia had been in Los Angeles on vacation and read in the paper that Odenkirk, whom they were familiar with from late-night favorite *The Larry Sanders Show*, was scheduled to make a free stand-up appearance at a Borders Books in Santa Monica. He was about to begin the second season of *Mr. Show* and the article made clear that Odenkirk and his collaborators were serious music fans.

"He was *amazing*," said Georgia of the sparsely attended bookstore gig. After Odenkirk's performance, Ira "got up some courage" and introduced himself.

"This couple comes up to me and says, 'We're huge fans,'" remembered the comedian. "My assumption was, *he's* a comedy writer. But I ask him what he does and he says, 'I'm in a band.' He wouldn't tell me what band. Finally he says, 'Yo La Tengo,' and I fuckin' shit." Odenkirk had entered comedy through college radio at WIDB in Carbondale, Illinois, part of the new generation of comedians for whom music and comedy were entwined.

Odenkirk landed at *Saturday Night Live* for a few years in

the late '80s, where he wrote and appeared as an uncredited peripheral player, and then headed for Hollywood. There, he found a small alternative comedy scene based around the Sunday night Un-Cabaret shows booked by Beth Lapides, a major crossing point of its own. There, Odenkirk met David Cross, two years his junior, who had inhaled *Saturday Night Live* and *SCTV* episodes as a teen the same way others listened to records, which Cross did too.

In addition to the *Mr. Show* regulars and the members of Yo La Tengo, the "Sugarcube" video ensemble included Pier Platters' Bill Ryan, the band Refrigerator, and at least one former touring member of Poison, who they'd found via a pile of headshots. Calls on the two-day shoot were early, and James—at least—was asleep by nine on the first night. "That was a perfect day," he thought. "I don't want anything else to happen today."

The *Mr. Show* gang had "gone to town" on Phil, Joe, and Ira's "rock school" setups, and improvised gag after gag. The band did its best not to fall into hysterics as Cross (in a pink rooster wig) attempted to instruct Ira to play guitar with a violin bow, like Led Zeppelin's Jimmy Page. "Do you think that Mr. Beck got an all-access laminate backstage pass by *not* learning to bow his guitar or sample the bowing of a guitar?" asked Cross, getting in Ira's face, while Georgia barely contained herself in the corner of the shot. In one take, the *Mr. Show* star cracked before Ira did.

"That was my great triumph as an actor," Ira later noted.

As Cross, Odenkirk, and their *Mr. Show* costar Ennis improvised, subplots emerged (Georgia, glitter, eyewash station). Like "From a Motel 6" and nearly every Yo La Tengo video since, the few instances of miming to the music were set up with arm's-length self-referentiality. By the video's end, the new rock school graduates are unchanged from the shoegazing, monochromatic, WFMU-T-shirt-wearing stereotypes they played at the start. Never mind the song's greatness, the spot was a hit: nearly weekly play for the target audience on MTV's *120 Minutes* throughout the late summer and early fall of 1997. It was their final video.

The claim that "comedy is the new rock and roll" had first emerged probably around the 1975 premiere of *Saturday Night Live,* or perhaps with Neil Innes and George Harrison's associations with Monty Python. It surfaced again in conjunction with Bill Hicks and a crew of Texas funnymen in the late 1980s. As indie rock multiplied across the landscape in the '90s, though, it collided with comedy in so many places that they finally became culturally inseparable.

It wasn't unnatural for Yo La Tengo to come into the path of stand-ups. Another fixture at the *Eating It* comedy shows was Tom Scharpling, the *18 Wheeler* zine editor who'd put out the first few Dump singles. He had a slot on WFMU, but had recently begun to feel constrained by the song-patter-song format of traditional college radio. Humor had long been part of the twenty-seven-year-old Scharpling's appreciation of music. "I used to love *Conflict* the most," he remembered of his zine-writing days. "It was my absolute favorite. It really meant the world to me. It showed you could have an attitude and you could be funny and talk about music you loved. You could be mean to certain things, but you weren't afraid to love things wholeheartedly also and just have a sense of humor while you did it. It was a prime influence on me in a lot of ways."

Through *18 Wheeler,* Scharpling befriended the Merge Records crew. "Superchunk would play New York all the time, and I'd go see them. Everybody was friendly and trying to do like-minded stuff. I would talk to Mac about putting records out. Everybody was on board with the same thing, really trying to do stuff in their own ways. It was very exciting."

Superchunk drummer Jon Wurster became a regular caller on Scharpling's show. One night, he posed as Ronald Thomas Clontle, author of *Rock, Rot & Rule*, a simplistic pop music almanac he claimed to be "the ultimate argument settler." He took calls from increasingly angry listeners. One asked "Clontle" if he'd ever read the work of former *Trouser Press* editor Ira Robbins. "Is he in Yo La Tengo?" Wurster responded.

After a hiatus, Scharpling would return to the airwaves with *The Best Show on WFMU*, comedy fully in the foreground.

It wasn't that comedy was the new rock and roll, but they were about to entwine permanently. For Yo La Tengo, it made visible another quiet path to expression that they'd dabbled with over the years between Ira's and James's writing and their general demeanors as people. After all, they'd once called an album *New Wave Hot Dogs*. Mostly, comedy just seemed like a natural fit. Ira contributed a blurb for the CD release of the *Rock, Rot & Rule* broadcast, the first of many archival Scharpling/Wurster discs: "Do the math: Scharpling + Clontle = TOUCHDOWN!"

Alex Chilton was in one of his cantankerous moods when James caught him at the 1997 edition of the South by Southwest festival in Austin. James could relate. It was very hot out. "He led a trio through a set of swinging soul-jazz numbers in a tent while the crowd talked about post-rock or something," James remembered.

Founded ten years earlier, South by Southwest had gained a reputation as being a laid-back alternative to the Manhattan-centric festivals put on by the New Music Seminar and CMJ. But it was not Yo La Tengo's scene. Seventy-degree March weather and delicious barbecue were among the festival's incentives, but Yo La Tengo, ever the road-food experts, never needed an excuse to get barbecue, and knew the better pits lay some thirty miles to the south in Lockhart anyway.

Though the festival had started with hand-stapled schedules and a good deal of local music, South by Southwest had swollen quickly and earned a near-mythical reputation as a place to catch an express train to rock fortune. Yo La Tengo had made their first appearance there in 1995, promoting *Electr-o-Pura*, were scouted in a crowd by a booking agent, and were immediately contacted about a gig on Lollapalooza. The year before, soon-to-be teen-pop sensations Hanson performed on the street there and hounded every person who looked like a suit until a music attorney named Christopher Sabec paid attention and offered them a contract.

More practically, removed from Manhattan's economic

and social baggage, South by Southwest became the industry's de facto annual conference, filled with promotions, chaos, and networking opportunities. It was a deeply unrelaxing place. James described the experience as "having deafening, largely shitty music shot at you everywhere you go."

By the time James caught Alex Chilton's soul-jazz set, both were among an estimated seven hundred acts playing around Austin, the vast majority unaffiliated with any kind of major label. Approximately 5,500 people attended, representatives of a marketplace that pumped out some five hundred new releases a week. What had grown from a finite group of music fans into a small national subindustry had merged, beyond fad or contrarian avocation, into a regular part of the American economy.

Yo La Tengo played an hour-long show of their own at Liberty Lunch. "Lots of crowd noise" reads the caveat on one bootleg recording. If representative of anything at all, the show was one final push in a sequence of small nudges that had begun some thirteen years earlier. *I Can Hear the Heart Beating as One* was an unqualified success. Yo La Tengo's record sales up to that point tracked with the general interest in indie rock, but the new album more than doubled *Electr-o-Pura*. By a few years later, it had sold more than 300,000 copies, an indisputable commercial breakthrough. If any lesson could be drawn from Yo La Tengo's new success, it was that their moment came naturally, formed neither from youth nor major-label push.

There was nothing left to do but continue to nudge, moving forward in as many tiny ways as they could find. They continued to take chances onstage and carried on with their strategy of obsessive, incremental self-revision. There were always reasons to tinker, not the least of which was to make sure they remained unpredictable to both their audiences and themselves. One new tactic was to begin shows with a quiet song (such as Georgia's "My Little Corner of the World") or, more often, something abstract and instrumental, such as "Spec Bebop" or "Green Arrow," from the new album. Or abstract and not instrumental at all, in the case of "Rocket #9"— one of several tunes they'd introduced from the formidable catalog of the idiosyncratic modern jazz master Sun Ra. All were ways to set moods for the night, to establish their music-making as something more than just a band clattering in the corner of a noisy club. It was in typical Yo La Tengo fashion that they chose to make these statements in any number of ways that didn't consist of making a bang.

Though they still couldn't get "Moby Octopad" quite right in its live incarnation, there was plenty else to focus on in the spring and summer of 1997. Their stage setup now included a additional snare/hi-hat so James could play the second drum part on "Autumn Sweater," and the Feelies–like extra percussion served well for both abstract freak-outs and the occasional guest.

There was a drum-machine arrangement of *Electr-o-Pura*'s "Ballad of Red Buckets." A new obscurity in rotation was "Love Power," a psychedelic-era showtune from Mel Brooks's *The Producers* that gave Ira the opportunity to test his own improv comedy chops in a frenzied monologue that quickly became a surprising and hilarious show closer. Their newest forays into jamdom were "Looney Tunes" (a long, flowing take on the famous Warner Bros. theme) and on a pair of 7-inches released in Britain that featured "Rocket #9" b/w "Wig Out with Charley Dapper" (for Planet Records) and "Blue/Green Arrow" b/w "Watching the Sun Rise or Johnny Carson" (for Earworm). Anything to keep themselves from coasting.

If Yo La Tengo seemed happy with this performance strategy, it was with good cause. Until recently, they had continued to play many of the venues they'd first passed through in the mid-'80s. When they hit Minneapolis in June, it was to make their headlining debut at First Avenue, where Prince had shot *Purple Rain*. There'd been two nights at the 7th Street Entry the last time through, in late '95, and they'd been playing *there* since their first time through town in 1986, when they'd convinced Mike Lewis to rejoin them for a few shows in the Midwest.

Both venues had been indispensable stops on the indie map since the early 1980s. Oar Folkjokeopus, the record store where the local scene germinated (and *New York Rocker* editor

Andy Schwartz manned the counter) was long gone, and the Replacements had disbanded in 1991, Hüsker Dü in 1988 (Bob Mould had moved to Hoboken). Comparatively slow blooming, Soul Asylum—who they'd opened for at 7th Street Entry in 1986—had scored some MTV megahits in '93, and were on their way back to earth. Yo La Tengo played for a bit over an hour and a half, touching mostly on their recent albums; closed a six-song encore with a slow, feedback-and-shaker-drenched version of "Upside-Down"; got back in the two vans they'd recently started using on the road, with room for themselves and a small crew with a host of logistical benefits; and made for the West Coast and the tour's next leg.

In Dunedin, New Zealand, they stayed with David Kilgour from the Clean, whose trio with his brother Hamish and bassist Robert Scott was near and dear to all three Tengos since a 1986 Homestead collection of singles and EPs that Ira listened to obsessively on cassette. "I've spent more time loving The Clean in the last 25 years than any other band," he wrote later.

In New Zealand, Yo La Tengo hopped from university town to university town in a small prop plane, hitting the local equivalent of the college circuit that had nurtured the Clean and longtime favorites like Tall Dwarfs, the Chills, and many others, bands of music obsessives who'd derived their own particular conclusions from punk rock and exploded into a small array of acts.

"It was insanely thrilling to be there after obsessing over that country's music for so many years," James said. "We got to see an incredible show on a night off in Dunedin, featuring solo sets by Alastair Galbraith, Sandra Bell, and Peter Gutteridge." The Clean themselves had drifted Feelies-like into other projects, sometimes consisting of the same members, like the punning Great Unwashed.

The band visited Roger Shepherd's Flying Nun Records in Christchurch, the country's premier indie label, launched in 1981. Hamish Kilgour had worked for them, where he'd forged connections to local record stores the way Chris Lombardi and the Dutch East staff did in parallel on the other side of the planet. Tall Dwarfs' Chris Knox—a life-size cartoon cutout of whom hung on the wall at Yo La Tengo's practice space—acted as an informal field scout and producer for the label. "[They] let us go through their warehouse," Ira remembered. "We were kids and it was like Christmas for us." Yo La Tengo played a few shows in Japan en route home—thrilling for James, especially, who'd almost gone back to school to study Japanese before Christmas's call to join them in Vegas.

These were all swell benefits of *I Can Hear the Heart*'s success. The members of the Clean, too, would become close friends and perpetual collaborators. They soon re-formed, in large part due to Yo La Tengo's encouragement.

Another, even happier, surprise awaited at 1039 Washington on the band's return. New owner William Sutton had not worked out at Maxwell's, to put it mildly. "Today, it's microbrewed 'Alternative Pale Ale' and Blues Jams on Wednesdays," *Jersey Beat*'s Jim Testa reported. "Tomorrow, who knows? Jell-o shots and wet T-shirt contests, probably. The slow process of change that began when Steve Fallon sold Maxwell's in [1995] has accelerated weekly; it seems that almost every week, there's some new atrocity to make you shudder.

"First, the venerable singles jukebox was replaced by one of those shiny new CD jukeboxes full of Top 50 crap. A TV set went up over the bar. At the end of last year, Todd Abramson— who had booked bands there for ten years—quit. His replacement lasted about two and a half months. Her replacement is Rob Affuso, a former member of Skid Row. That's right, Sebastian Bach's old drummer is now booking bands at Maxwell's."

The situation, thankfully, was hardly tenable. "His brother-in-law was running the place," said Steve Fallon, who knew perhaps more than anybody in the world *exactly* what that meant. When Sutton finally defaulted, Steve—who still owned the building—called Todd. "Pay up his debts and it's yours," he told him. With Dave Post, the bassist and leader of Swing-adelic, and Steve Shelley, Sonic Youth drummer and Hoboken resident since 1987, Todd Abramson purchased Maxwell's from Steve. They reopened at the end of July 1998. Shortly thereafter, Yo La Tengo played four nights in a row, a booking move they'd tried at the WestBeth Theater in Manhattan over the previous Halloween. It was a Hoboken-style homecoming week in the back room.

Some gestures were endearingly predictable, like a first-night encore of the Kinks' "This Is Where I Belong." Others were almost entirely unexpected, as when Dave Schramm returned for the first time in eight years to join the band for an entire night of understated music that drew from the acoustic spirit of *Fakebook* but whose sweep now included the gentle bossa nova of "Center of Gravity" and the extrapolation of "Looney Tunes." Other nights saw guest appearances by Joe Puleo (singing "I Got You Babe" with Georgia) and Clean drummer Hamish Kilgour, on the ever-more-flexible snare/hi-hat setup the band had first brought on the road for "Autumn Sweater." In whatever weird world was to come next, at least there was Maxwell's.

The Simpsons called. After befriending staff writer Donick Cary, who'd introduced himself to Ira at the merch table a few years earlier, they recorded a psychedelic version of that show's theme, which aired in November 1998. "*The Simpsons* is our favorite show on TV, and this will finally be a way to get my mom to watch it," Ira told *MTV News*.

Midway through the *I Can Hear the Heart Beating as One* tour, they played an in-store at Tower Records' New York flagship on Broadway in Manhattan. When their former roommate Todd Abramson showed up, there was a line down the block. He snuck in. "They were about to stop me," he remembered. "I'm not even sure I was thirty yet, but the people lining up seemed like they were all twenty. I could see the guy doing a mental calculation: *This guy's too old, he just wants to buy records*, and I just walked in."

It was maybe hard to tell, but indie rock had reached a singular peak. In fact, the four-floor Tower flagship store near

Washington Square Park with an annex around back was a temple to the past half century of music, and the product of an industry that had recently matched and then surpassed its pre-disco heights. Everywhere, long-simmering music scenes exploded into national popularity.

When Nielsen SoundScan began to track retail sales in 1991, it was discovered that hip-hop and country accounted for a much higher percentage of the market than previously thought. N.W.A.'s second album, *Niggaz4Life*, released by the independent label Restless, entered the chart at #2. Every sub-culture from jam bands to heavy metal would develop parallel independent infrastructures of their own, both self-supportive and as pipelines to the mainstream. Vinyl sales had ceased to be any kind of factor around 1991 too, but people still wanted to buy music, and lots of it. There'd been a slight dip in con-sumer music spending over the previous few years, and it would shoot back up slightly before the turn of the century, but Tower Records in the summer of 1997 was a jewel in the music industry's half-century-old crown.

Across the street from Tower, the new store Other Music was two years into business. Opened in 1995, it focused hard on independent labels. Taking lessons from Pier Platters' re-luctance to stock CDs, Other Music embraced them, without losing track of the newest wax and releases by small imprints. It was still a small world. One owner, Jeff Gibson, had worked as a buyer at Dutch East. Another, Josh Madell, was the new drummer in Antietam.

The building that housed the band's Second Street practice digs was bought. They'd been there for almost a decade, since their long-departed Swiss bassist Stephan insisted they move to a place with higher ceilings. They packed up the life-size Chris Knox cutout and giant Yellow Submarine prop from the "Tom Courtenay" video and bid good-bye to the disgust-ing bathroom and IRA IS AN UPTIGHT FAG graffiti. Not quite para-dise lost, but still noteworthy: there was a scarcity of cheap practice spaces within Hoboken city limits. They found a spot in a giant warehouse complex beyond the big-box shops in the industrial park wastes between Hoboken and Jersey City.

The new place was anything but soundproof. Bruce Bennett remembered a practice before a WFMU benefit around that time. "There were people stacked in there cheek-by-jowl," he recalled. "The guy downstairs was a fine artist. He was sick of us slaughtering 'MacArthur Park' or whatever, and he starts cranking up the music, which was *Who's Next* by the Who."

"Why don't we just take his requests?" Ira suggested, and played their own versions over the distant sound of their neighbor's Who record.

Bruce described the scene. "I picture it drawn by R. Crumb, smoke coming out of his head as he cranks up the stereo to drown out the annoying band upstairs, and then they start playing the same thing."

And something else: loud songs boomed, echoed, and sounded terrible in their new practice space, and it took a little bit of time before they figured out the problem. It wasn't the only place they'd begun to get quiet. The band played a few more weddings, each with its own playlist. At one, Georgia played the church organ as the band covered Steve Miller's "The Joker," Carl Douglas's "Kung Fu Fighting," and Devo's "Gut Feeling." Or maybe they were self-conscious about the new neighbors. Things stayed quiet.

They couldn't help but notice that their old practice space had been demolished too, replaced with apartment towers branded for the century's end: Millenium Condos. The onetime copy editors couldn't help but notice, as well, that "Millenium" was missing an "n."

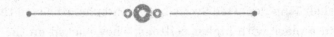

CHAPTER 14

Our Way to Fall

The person most accountable for what "indie rock" came to mean as the twentieth century turned into the twenty-first wasn't a musician, record executive, zine editor, or DJ. He was a sound engineer named Karlheinz Brandenburg and, like Yo La Tengo, he began his work in 1982, when Georgia and Those Guys played their first shows, the Mets floundered in last place, and the bogeyman of music distribution (and distributors) had barely yet appeared on Gerard Cosloy's enemies list.

The eventual birth of the mp3 on July 14, 1995—YLT was on Lollapalooza in Columbus, Ohio—was the most significant format innovation since Philips's introduction of the CD in 1979, and perhaps long before that. More than Sony's Walkman, released the same year as the CD and which had given a killer platform for the cassette, or even the ascendant music video, Brandenburg's invention redefined popular music. As was all too appropriate for its primary new use, the code was soon stolen.

"I think it was '97," Brandenburg remembered. "Some Australian student bought professional-grade—from our point of view—encoding software for mp3 from a small company in Germany. He paid with a stolen credit card number from Taiwan. He looked at the software, found that we had used some Microsoft internal application programming interface . . . racked everything up into an archive and wired some Swedish site, [and] put that to a US university FTP site together with a read-me file saying, 'This is freeware thanks to Fraunhofer.'

"He gave away our business model. We were completely not amused. We tried to hunt him down. We told everybody, 'This is stolen software, so don't distribute it,' but still the business model to have expensive encoders and cheap decoders [was] done." He might have been speaking of not only the music industry at large but the very place music occupied in society.

Though Gerard and others found the Internet a fine way to remain connected to fellow obsessives, its potential for music distribution seemed fanciful at best. By late 1998, barely a quarter of American homes had Internet access, and fewer still at speeds convenient for downloading media files. When the file-sharing service Napster was launched in June 1999, Gerard didn't see many reasons to worry. "I think I was initially not super freaked-out about file sharing because bandwidth/speed issues were such a stumbling block for so many, initially," he said. Besides, he got the sense that "the early downloaders/uploaders were hardcore music nuts who tended to buy more records than anyone else." That would soon change.

The Internet had already started to absorb the culture around it. With its low-bandwidth, text-only content, zines were among the first things sucked into the Internet's maw, especially after the introduction of the graphics-friendly World Wide Web browser Mosaic (later renamed Netscape Navigator) in 1993. For zine writers who didn't care for the rigmarole of collation, it wasn't a hard choice. Being on the fringe of popular culture anyway, and largely centered around college towns where Internet access was plentiful, publications jumped the divide quickly.

A nineteen-year-old from Minnesota named Ryan Schreiber went live with his site, *Pitchfork Media*, in 1995, first calling it Turntable. One of its earliest columns was titled "Three Blocks from Groove Street," after the *Ride the Tiger* track, and a 9.7 review of *I Can Hear the Heart* declared Yo La Tengo "the greatest band on earth."

One fragment they'd brought to Nashville was a fairly simple slice of hushed folk. Even before Ira added words, it transformed into a uniquely Yo La Tengo epic one afternoon when they kept going with it, jamming through the chords over and over until something happened. "We went in daring ourselves," said Ira of their latest residency in Nashville with Roger Moutenot, their longest yet. Per usual, they stayed with the members of Lambchop—Ira and Georgia with the Wagners, James with horn player Jonathan Marx.

In a process that began with *Electr-o-Pura* and continued with *I Can Hear the Heart Beating as One*, the band took, in Ira's words, "a more and more generous notion of what it means to write a song." What they came up with in their new practice space was quiet, even spare. Songs started with organ parts, drum machines twisted through guitar pedals, gentle bass lines, elegiac cymbal taps. Anything but rock, and sometimes without Ira at all.

The elongated strum grew and grew, an expanding mood abstracting into feedback and percussion atmosphere, changing internal configuration like the shifting moods of a sleepless night. It required the most complicated set of in-studio logistics yet. Recorded in a single live take that took two days to achieve, "Night Falls on Hoboken" was the inverse of one of WFMU's sight gags, as the band executed a nearly impossible sequence of unseen maneuvers to move between the song's sections while playing continuously. "Night Falls on Hoboken" would fill their new double-LP's final side.

"It was like a science experiment," Georgia remembered of the trial-and-error process. Ira began the song on acoustic guitar in the studio's main room with James and Georgia, his amp in the hallway beyond. The problems came when the song called for feedback. "I—and we—try not to wear headphones," Ira said. "So we needed to have the door open to have any notion of what I was playing during quiet parts, and then Roger had to close the door to keep the feedback from dominating every open microphone. To make the feedback I had to go *to* the amp, but still had to hear the drums somehow."

Another complication was that Ira moved to a second drum setup as the song ended. The full choreography required endless takes to figure out, each fifteen minutes of performance followed by a playback to determine if the mix was acceptable. "I used to get upset reading about the million-dollar budget for something like [Fleetwood Mac's] *Tusk*," Ira noted, "but I'm beginning to understand how you could do that." Elsewhere at the session, they wheeled out the studio's vibraphone.

"One of the things I like about Yo La Tengo is that we never brought in people," Roger Moutenot later commented. "There might have been a few guest appearances, but Georgia will play vibes. Georgia doesn't play vibes, but there's something beautiful about that. You don't have this guy that's just flowery on the vibes, you've got Georgia and she's just reaching for that C and is just an eighth-note behind. And that's character, and I love that."

A cover that struck an unexpected new mood was the disco-soul bounce of "You Can Have It All," penned by Harry Wayne Casey of KC and the Sunshine Band. There'd been a one-off of Sly Stone's "(You Caught Me) Smilin'" at the Knitting Factory a few years back, and a more regular slow jam on William DeVaughn's classic "Be Thankful for What You Got," released on the *Little Honda* EP in '98, but this arrangement was something new entirely, as Georgia, Ira, and James bomp-bomped in delirious (and difficult) doo-wop syncopation.

"When they work, you don't see them a whole lot," noted Kurt Wagner, who again played host to Ira and Georgia. "I remember there was a time for each record where they'd have to focus on words, and they'd each go off to their own places and work on that," Wagner said. "They'd have to find a place to sit and work on stuff, whether it was the bedroom or the coffee table. I remember them remarking frequently that it was their least favorite time."

Writing about and to Georgia was something Ira had done quite naturally since he had started to write lyrics, and was among a host of other word strategies that ranged from Ray Davies–esque character studies like "Barnaby, Hardly Working" to pop-as-metafiction exercises like "Paul Is Dead."

Like everything else, he got much better. Whereas early songs like "The River of Water" and "Did I Tell You" relied on endearing elliptical declarations and opaque melodies, the band's newest lyrics enjoyed a well-achieved terseness. Heard framed by the new quiet arrangements, they were direct statements placed tentatively but unquestionably into the spotlight.

Perhaps literally autobiographical, perhaps not, the lyrics of the new album—soon titled *And then nothing turned itself inside-out*—were real-life love songs set against an ongoing, complex relationship. Some read as period fiction, such as "Last Days of Disco," with metacriticism on the side. "And the song said 'Let's be happy,'" Ira sang, "and I was happy. It never made me happy before." Others, such as the Georgia-sung "Tears Are in Your Eyes," carried universal sentiments of resolution: "Although you don't believe me you are strong, darkness always turns into the dawn, and you won't even remember this for long, when it ends all right."

"What did I miss here? What can't you take anymore?" Ira asks in the beginning of "The Crying of Lot G," Thomas Pynchon by way of Newark International Airport. "You say that all we do is fight and I think to myself, gee, I don't know if that's true," he added in a midsong interlude spoken over softly shifting jazz. "Maybe I'm out of my mind. Maybe I'm blocking out the truth. But it seems like just a little thing, like you don't want to listen, and I can't shut up."

Few, if any, had asked Ira and Georgia about unison-sung lyrics like "dream a quiet place for us to fight" in "From a Motel 6," where they were slathered in feedback drone. But when the feedback had fallen away, Yo La Tengo made music as particular as they were. Without the pretense of trying to rock, it was hard to say what category the music on *And then nothing turned itself inside-out* belonged. Drums skittered into dubby echoes and organs hummed coolly over drum machines while astoundingly personal-sounding lyrics came whispering from the speakers when they weren't inventing new comic scenarios for Tony Orlando and Frankie Valli. Perhaps "alternative" was a correct label after all.

Though far fewer people asked about it than would inquire about Georgia and Ira's personal lives and lyrics, the album's title sourced from a 1973 live recording by Sun Ra, the jazz bandleader who claimed to be born on Saturn. Ra's Arkestra began to chant: "At first there was nothing." The calls changed, wordplay blooming to cosmic profundity. "And then nothing turned itself inside out and became something! Nothing turned itself inside out and became something!"

Matador Records celebrated its tenth anniversary in September 1999 with a pair of shows in Manhattan and London, where Gerard Cosloy had started to spend time as an increasingly dedicated cybercommuter. It had been a turbulent but triumphant period for the label. The year before had seen big releases by garage-noise bandleader Jon Spencer and fuzzed-out home recorders Guided by Voices, both on the tenth-anniversary bills along with Yo La Tengo. In London, Spencer joined Yo La Tengo onstage to roast Gerard and Chris during an extended version of Superchunk's "Slack Motherfucker," an early single on Matador before they'd founded Merge.

The label had expanded its sights considerably over the past few years. "We went through a weird transitional period around 1999 where we put out some different music [and] we got into underground hip-hop for some reason," Lombardi said. "[We] decided to give it a go. That was kind of a failure for us on a business level."

They put out albums by artists like Non Phixion and MC Paul Barman, as well as clever Japanese pop from the Shibuya-kei scene, including the brilliant Cornelius and the band Pizzicato Five. Chris and Gerard's instincts were far better honed on their home turf, even if some of the acts they signed didn't find success until they recorded for other labels. One such artist was the Portland, Oregon, band Spoon, whom Gerard first saw at a South by Southwest showcase in 1994.

Their stable included Scottish twee-poppers Belle and Sebastian (briefly) and Chan Marshall, who sang fractured soul-folk under the name Cat Power. But the high-price Capitol deal brought record-company bosses who demanded more from them than Danny Goldberg had. "With Capitol there was a little bit more pressure to make our year-end numbers," Chris Lombardi noted. "There was a big change in the music business at that point. It was really urban-oriented, and Capitol had not invested any money in that."

Though they had an enthusiastic supporter at the label in president Gary Gersh, Capitol grew "frustrated with the records we were turning in," Gerard said. "They were frustrated by our inability to whip certain artists into shape. It took forever to turn in that Liz Phair record [*Whitechocolatespaceegg*] they'd paid a king's ransom to acquire. It was like, *Why can't this record get done?* and, when it was done, *Why wasn't it a better record?* I think those are fair criticisms." As always, they remained remarkably successful by the standards of independent labels, but a drop in the bucket to an international concern like Capitol Records.

The Matador tenth-anniversary celebrations, then, not only marked a decade in the business but six months of brand-new independence. On April Fool's Day 1999, Chris Lombardi and Gerard Cosloy bought back Capitol Records' 49 percent stake in Matador. Their hard-earned access to the American independent distribution networks remained unparalleled. The press offices at Atlantic and Capitol had helped, but even before the latest split they focused on building a publicity department of their own and recruited artist favorite Nils Bernstein from Sub Pop.

Though Yo La Tengo were happy to help Matador celebrate, they were in no mood to look back. Over the two shows they debuted a handful of new songs and turned another corner. In

London, they introduced songs from their not-yet-released new album, including the fifteen-minute "Night Falls on Hoboken." At Irving Plaza in Manhattan, they were joined for an extended appearance by members of the free-jazz collective Other Dimensions in Music. Feeling expansive, Ira asked Steven Joerg—who'd worked for both Bar/None and Dutch East and now headed the jazz label AUM Fidelity—for suggestions as to whom they might collaborate with. Joerg introduced them to a New York coterie that revolved loosely around saxophonists Mateen and Daniel Carter, bassist William Parker, and pianist Matthew Shipp. The musicians had pushed away from even underground jazz's mainstream, staged guerrilla subway gigs and built relationships with New York's noise underground, fostered by Sonic Youth's Thurston Moore and White Out's Tom Surgal.

"It's like going to another city," reflected saxophonist Sabir Mateen about playing with Yo La Tengo. "The music is pure and good and sincere. There's no difference [between it and jazz], except rhythmically."

Together, they recorded a double 7-inch titled *Some Other Dimensions in Yo La Tengo*, James on the small second drum kit, Ira on organ, and Sue Garner of Run On on percussion, and released it on the band's revived Egon imprint.

"Before that, we had been limited to playing with people we knew," James remembered. "Those guys really opened our minds to collaboration. Here were these serious, lifer musicians, and we don't think of ourselves in the same way. I'm not qualified to carry this guy's case! The three of them were just not interested in that in the *slightest*. They were more interested in how we got along. That's what informed the music and the collaboration. We were able to find a common level and a vibe really fast. After that, it was off to the races. *We can ask anyone now!*"

The bus had to make regular stops. It was in the driver's contract. Mac McCaughan remembered one particular afternoon in the middle of nowhere. The Superchunk guitarist and Merge

Records cofounder was along on the tour as an auxiliary player, alongside David Kilgour of the Clean. Playing as a quintet was one of the factors that had justified Yo La Tengo's first tour bus. Factoring out the hotel bills, it could even be more efficient.

"It was a drive between two places that were far apart," McCaughan remembered, "and it was a stop that the bus driver legally had to make." So the ensemble walked down the highway. "We managed to find this great used CD store. They managed to find good places to eat and record stores in places where you wouldn't think those things existed."

The expansion of Yo La Tengo to a quintet for the tour behind *And then nothing turned itself inside-out* was typically paradoxical: more musicians to play quieter music. For the first time, as well, the band played for seated crowds. And if the venue didn't have seats installed, they were brought in for Yo La Tengo's show. Their choice in accompanists had as much to do with sociability as musical qualification. McCaughan and Kilgour re-created *And Then Nothing*'s myriad details on various guitars, keyboards, and vibraphone, an instrument neither had played much before.

They didn't practice until a week before departure, David Kilgour unable to get to New Jersey from New Zealand. For perhaps the first time in their career, Yo La Tengo didn't stress it. And indeed they were fine. The vibes filled out *And Then Nothing*'s songs with the same half-accidental grace they did on the album and added lush touches to older numbers.

"They have this faith in other musicians to be able to do the same kind of crazy stuff they can do," McCaughan remembered. "All three of them are just encyclopedic in their memory of their own songs and other people's songs. Their ability to play this stuff on the fly and have it sound totally great is kind of amazing. For some reason, they had that same faith in me and other people around them to be able to do the same thing. So when they say, 'Oh, you're just going to play keyboards,' and I'm saying, 'I don't really know how to do that stuff,' they'd just say, 'Oh, no, you can do it.' The whole tour was amazing. That was one of the best experiences of my life. The amount of trust they put into people around them is inspiring."

In Europe, they did the expanded lineup with former Spacemen 3 guitarist Sonic Boom; Soft Boys leader Robyn Hitchcock; and Neil Innes, leader of Ira's childhood favorites, the Bonzo Dog Band as well as avatar for the Rutles' songwriting team of Ron Nasty and Dirk McQuickly. During one noise jam, they gave the distinguished British musician a Rat distortion pedal to use and watched as his eyes slowly lit up, the one-time singer of classics like "Ouch!" joining modern drone-psychedelicist Sonic Boom in the timeless noise-sphere. The crew from Lambchop met them in Amsterdam and stayed on the tour for a few days. Miraculously, Kurt Wagner's gang had caught on in Europe thanks to Christof Ellinghaus and City Slang.

"We'd get offered a show at Royal Albert Hall, and then I'd come home and sand floors," Wagner remembered. "And I thought that was beautiful. I was convinced that you could make records and have a normal life."

Advance copies of *And then nothing turned itself inside-out* had drawn attention, including a four-star lead review in *Rolling Stone*, and nearly all of it focused on the album's quiet and the degree of personal exposure in the lyrics. Rob Sheffield concluded, "if the connection between rock and roll and romance still means anything to you, if guitars play a key role in your bodily chemistry, if you don't gag at the idea of record geeks having sex, and if you don't turn the page as soon as you read the words 'influenced by the Velvet Underground,' *And then nothing turned itself inside-out* will open you up to intense new pleasures." Three weeks before the album's release, *The New York Times* published a Q&A with Ira and Georgia, and nudged Georgia a little too sharply.

"Do you ever think about performing less, maybe having

your own kids? And would that mean the end of your careers?" the *Times*'s Kerry Lauerman asked them.

"That's none of your business," Georgia replied. "My mother doesn't even know the answer to that question."

But to the extent that Ira and Georgia had taken nothing and turned it into something, the fact that they were married was a point of interest in their band, making love songs more real and sad songs even sadder. "The way I feel when you laugh is like laughing," Ira had sung in "The Crying of Lot G," "The way that I feel when you cry is so bad," and the sentiment seemed to scale outward through the band's music, the kind of fan-internalized love songs now occasionally played at weddings. Whether lyrics depicted literal facts about their relationship was immaterial. It was as far as they were willing to go in explaining themselves.

"When people reacted so strongly to the words on *And Then Nothing*, I was really taken by surprise," Ira said. "I wrote most of them and I remember when I would show them to Georgia and James and Roger, there was always that 'Do you think this is OK?' moment. Once they had read them, I thought, 'All right, that's the end of that!' Even though I can think back and remember Robert Christgau writing about the lyrics to 'Autumn Sweater.'"

But while the lyrics may have piqued the interest of some listeners, life in Hoboken continued on. They'd quit going to the softball game when it had hopped to Manhattan, Georgia first, then Ira. They had lives outside Yo La Tengo, with large families spread across New York and New Jersey. If Ira and Georgia managed to find a formula to balance a relationship and a joint career, it wasn't one that could or would be shared beyond whatever was bared on record.

Just past forty, they'd paid back the various no-interest loans to their parents, from Will Rigby's disastrous *Sidekick Phenomenon* to finishing *Painful*, and built a public career on the notion of a priori love—an engine hidden from view, its only evidence every record they ever released. "Once I got used to it, I enjoyed the fact that people think it's autobiographical," Ira remarked not long after *And Then Nothing* came out.

It was around this time too that Ira made a small theatrical appearance, as a monologist at the Upright Citizens Brigade's A.S.S.S.S.C.A.T. theater. Phil Morrison had gotten involved with the New York–based improv-comedy group, directing several videos for them and placing their cast members in commercials when he could.

In the improv comedy format known as the Harold, developed by Del Close in the mid-'60s, a monologist will often speak on a theme suggested by the audience before the troupe improvises a series of scenes. Ira did fine. "He was shy, but ready to talk," noted Morrison. But Ira, ordinarily possessed of a practically infallible memory, was so terrified of being onstage without band, guitar, or shield that he would be able to recall almost none of the experience later, let alone the audience's suggestion.

At no point in Yo La Tengo's history did the band ever need a justification to learn a new Kinks cover. They'd played some twenty or more over the years. Actually presented with a reason—namely the imminent and seemingly improbable appearance of Ray Davies in their practice space ready to play—they figured out another half dozen.

One of rock's original contrarians, the fifty-six-year-old ex-Kink had decided to record live demos for his first solo album. Introduced to Yo La Tengo and their music by a mutual friend, Davies had become a fan and tapped them as one of three bands to rotate through three performances at the Jane Street Theater in the West Village. Ira's longtime hero traveled to Jersey City for a few dreamlike rehearsals.

"He was very loose in the practice room," Georgia recalled. "We brought up 'Ring the Bells,' and he said, 'You sing it.' So I sang it and he played organ. It all sounded amazing when he was playing it."

"We ended up toying with each other in rehearsals, because we were all Kinks fanatics, so we would suggest some fairly obscure songs to do," James remembered. "Ray would hem and haw, saying, 'The Kinks never really played that one live' or something else to put us off, and he would counter with some equally obscure song, genuinely thinking he would throw us off the trail because there's no way we could know it. Of course, we knew everything he suggested, because we were Kinks geeks, and Ray would be silently kicking himself, coerced into playing these long-forgotten gems."

"One was 'You Shouldn't Be Sad,' a fake Mersey song," Ira remembered. "It was understandable why he wouldn't want to do it. It was the only one he wouldn't even try. At some point during a lull, we started playing it anyway. The showman in him couldn't resist and he did a sort of very campy sing-along."

The shows at the 280-capacity theater were good fun and, the following year, Davies summoned the band to his Konk Studios in London to track several tunes. "There was one new song, kind of unformed, that was really cool," Georgia remembered. "It reminded me of the Clean." But they never completed the tracks, and never got copies.

And then nothing turned itself inside-out made it into the *Billboard* Top 200, peaking at #138, and in the end sold just under 300,000 copies, slightly less than *I Can Hear the Heart Beating as One* but still well above all that came before, and—in general—ecstatically received. What happened afterward was mildly perplexing to Yo La Tengo, but more so to the rest of the professional music world.

Measured in inflation-adjusted dollars of how much the average American citizen spent annually on recorded music, sales had risen constantly since the post-disco dip in the late 1970s, around the time Ira had established himself at *New York Rocker*. By 1992, the year after *Nevermind* and the first great indie explosion, they surpassed disco, sagged momentarily after the grunge gold rush, and soared even higher still by the turn of the century. In many ways, Yo La Tengo's record sales mirrored this chart exactly.

Napster, introduced in June 1999, took the country's colleges by storm. Sales shot downward as Karlheinz Brandenburg's mp3 format caught on. Decent bandwidth spread the grid across the continent as broadband access rose by 50 percent between 2000 and 2001 alone, and doubled again over the next two years until it was in fully one-third of the nation's households. In the message of the Electronic Frontier Foundation, an Internet-based civil liberties union, everything that could be expressed as bits would be expressed as bits: all text, sound, or image.

For indie rock, this amounted to a massive deregulation that shattered or forced the reinvention of nearly every single pillar its system had been based on: college radio, fanzines, record sales, and distribution. It took a few years, but the game was altered rule for rule.

Fanzines transformed. PitchforkMedia.com's audience would grow to 150,000 daily readers over the next few years. "It was like, how many more Yo La Tengo fans could there possibly be?" editor Ryan Schreiber later mused to *Wired*. The traditional act of collecting was leveled too. Obscure songs that had been the province of Byron Coley and Phil Milstein's record scum networks were, within the decade, instantly accessible to anybody who knew how to search for mp3s online.

Stranger was the ubiquity of the formerly arcane in the mass media. At the end of 2000, Volkswagen launched an advertising campaign that featured the song "Pink Moon" off the album of the same name by British folksinger Nick Drake, who'd committed suicide in 1974 and had remained a cult favorite since. The ad was a hit, and the sales of the album increased some 500 percent and stayed there. The spot's directors were Jonathan Dayton and Valerie Faris, who had gotten their starts in the mid-'80s on the MTV show *The Cutting Edge*. They'd been turned on to Nick Drake by premier indie record dork Peter Buck, of R.E.M.

Drake was not the exception. Built atop old indie networks, a crate-digging cottage industry bloomed in New York that championed underground sounds, old and new, to television and film. Tim Barnes, a Hoboken-based free-jazz drummer, worked as a music director and placed recordings by fellow free-jazz drummer Milford Graves, home-recording power poppers the Apples in Stereo, and the Chicago-based the Sea and Cake, whose first show was opening for Yo La Tengo at Lounge Ax in 1993. The Brooklyn-based Agoraphone Music Direction licensed "Monk Time," theme song of the '60s GI quintet the Monks, to Powerade. Music directors grew as commonplace as booking agents or DJs.

The leader of the licensing revolution was Richard Hall, whose Octopad Yo La Tengo had encountered at Lollapalooza in 1995, though they never met. Recording as Moby, Hall licensed every song on his 1997 album *Play* to commercials for Nordstrom department stores, American Express, and dozens of others. He argued that his music stood a better chance of being promoted, heard, and sold when placed in advertisements than if he relied on more traditional means. He got paid well too. "Independent" was beginning to take on new connotations, and it described nearly everybody. While income and exposure from record-company advances, sales, college radio airplay, and MTV rotation shriveled, potential new audiences emerged everywhere.

The Flaming Lips had appeared on *Beverly Hills, 90210* and, around that time, Matador circulated a press release that claimed Pavement had failed an audition for the show after a fistfight with one of the show's heartthrob stars. But it took that show's spin-off, *Melrose Place*, to sell a soundtrack featuring Dinosaur Jr. and Paul Westerberg, and the teen-oriented shows of the WB Network, launched in 1996, to turn licensing into an industry of its own that soon bordered on subgenre.

When the station created a new show called *Gilmore Girls* in 2000, they requested permission to use Yo La Tengo's version of "My Little Corner of the World" in the show's pilot episode. The band declined. The producers commissioned a soundalike cover.

CHAPTER 15

A Plastic Menorah

Paradise was not lost. Improbably, it was not only within grasp, but open to all. You just had to get yourself across the Hudson in the early winter, likely via a PATH train from the city, followed by a long walk down Washington Street or a $4 taxi ride from the cab stand above the station. The cab would follow the River Walk that the Knickerbockers once took from the ferry, first renamed River Road and, lately, Frank Sinatra Drive.

It would go by the spot where Ira and Georgia met the Dioxin Field gang, a perfectly good ball game–ready empty lot turned multistory parking garage, then ribbon around the base of Castle Point, past the fenced-off entrance to Sybil's Cave, where the Stevens family once sold mineral water. Off to the right, the west side of Manhattan would glitter, spotlights twisting over the World Trade Center site, attacked only a few months earlier.

Finally the cab would arrive at the traffic light at Hudson and Eleventh. To the left, a tiny wedge of hilly park marked the spot as part of the former Elysian Fields, though there was hardly room to have a game of catch, let alone play ball. To the right, the menacing, shuttered hulk of the Maxwell House plant, its vacant parking lot and the ghost of the Savannah

Oval. It had been closed for almost ten years, but nobody had quite figured out what to do with it yet.

The buzzed band that season across the river in Gotham was the Strokes, whose muscular songs evoked '70s New York. Their singer, Julian Casablancas, was the son of the former Miss Denmark and an international modeling agency owner, whose clients soon stocked the band's shows at the Mercury Lounge, the flagship venue of Manhattan's now comically gentrified Lower East Side. A few blocks from where the Fugs once roamed, American Apparel would soon set up shop. When CBGB closed, it was replaced by a John Varvatos boutique that sold used LPs at prices that would enrage anyone who'd ever set foot inside an actual record store. The hipster had gone global and mutated into a caricature of the ugly American en route. If the Strokes seemed destined to veritably flame out after one great album, it's because they did. That Hanukkah, in 2001, what was going on in Hoboken and downtown Manhattan remained as different as it had always been.

When the traffic light at Hudson and Eleventh blinked green, a half block later, Maxwell's. Depending on arrival time, Yo La Tengo would be up front, eating dinner with the crew and whoever else was on the evening's bill. Todd Abramson would be keeping an eye on the table service, occasionally bringing out food if needed, as the audience slowly trickled in from the cold and hooked around past the jukebox to the filling coat rack and toward the back room.

"For a couple of years, the notion of having some kind of holiday party where we would maybe just play free for our friends seemed like a good idea," Ira said. "We just wanted to do some kind of commemorative something-or-other. And then it would come around and we'd be like, 'Yeah, this is exactly what the world needs, another Christmas party,'" he laughed. "So, the idea would just go by the wayside."

Ira joked to Todd about playing the eight nights of Hanukkah, a riff on the Feelies' holiday shows. Entranced by the ridiculousness of the idea, they committed: eight shows, different opening acts for each, all benefits for various causes, plus stand-up comedy and appropriately audacious guest stars. Or, at least, the band would invite appropriately audacious guest stars. That the band had total access to a home base like Maxwell's was more anachronistic than ever, a hip rock club in a sleepy burg. "That was always a pretty comfortable place," Ira said. "Relatively comfortable," he amended. "As comfortable as we got." Ira and Todd made calls and the first Hanukkah shows were scheduled for December 2001.

If one arrived after the openers started, it was a good bet that the band was down the short hall that connected the dining room to the stage area. At the bar's rear was a reliable rotation of onetime *New York Rocker* writers, Hobokenites, Kaplans, Hubleys, Dioxin Field softballers, WFMU DJs, members of Hypnolovewheel and Antietam, current Matador staffers, and former Dutch East employees. Phil Morrison reprised his role as a roadie for the first time since the '80s. The band purchased an electric menorah, placed it on an amp next to Georgia as they set up the gear on the first night, and screwed the first bulb until the light popped on.

The reunited Yung Wu opened the December 9 show, a Feelies spin-off led by percussionist Dave Weckerman that Ira had presented at Folk City within weeks of taking over Wednesdays there. The Feelies had broken up in 1991, but Weckerman, Stan Demeski, and Glenn Mercer still played every week in Mercer's basement in varying configurations. They performed one new song and most of their 1987 Coyote EP, *Shore Leave*. Terry Adams of NRBQ joined YLT on keyboards, and they debuted a post-9/11 cover of Sun Ra's "Nuclear War." The next night, Tara Key added guitar for large parts of the set.

With each show, Yo La Tengo's circles overlapped at Maxwell's—dozens of narratives potentially set to entwine. The band moved a full complement of gear from their practice space to the small stage, left it set up, and spent most afternoons hanging out and rehearsing with guests.

The year before, comedian Todd Barry had opened for the band at Maxwell's and made jokes about Belle and Sebastian.

The crowd loved it, and something about palate-cleansing laughter before the very different experience of a two-hour Yo La Tengo show made sense. In the winter, having a stand-up—performing between the opening band and Yo La Tengo themselves—also made for a fairly literal warm-up. For Hanukkah, the band booked Barry, the Upright Citizens Brigade, H. Jon Benjamin and Jon Glaser, and others.

Earlier that fall, just before Hanukkah, *Mr. Show* co-creator David Cross had taken the first steps toward actually staging a comedy tour in rock venues. "It makes nothing but sense when you take comedy out of a comedy club," he said later. The traditional venue for his medium had "a much different energy and vibe and restrictions to it. It's usually in a strip mall somewhere or it's expensive and there's a cover. You can't do all-ages, there's a two-drink minimum. It just felt better and more natural." Still on tour, Cross signed with Sub Pop, the Seattle-based label that had issued Nirvana's first album. Maxwell's saw comedy of its own that year too, including a bill that paired Sub Pop poster-children the Shins with comedians Tim Heidecker and Eric Wareheim of HBO's *Tim and Eric Awesome Show, Great Job!*

Yo La Tengo's eight nights of Hanukkah, which would become a semiregular tradition over the coming decade, amounted to an eight-night mini festival of stand-ups hosted by a band. It only further solidified the relationship between the music and comedy scenes, and very specifically between Yo La Tengo and a slowly spreading network of comedians who became collaborators with the band in dozens of ways in the years to come.

All these factors, helped especially by the routine of the eight nights, combined to give the shows a gravity of their own, each somehow more than a rock show, but an opening into a world more real than what the ticket-driven concert industry had transformed concerts into. Memories piled up quickly: guests who met onstage and soon married, interludes with visiting underground luminaries, a few superstars and band heroes, soul legends, food critics, matinee indie idols, comedians playing music, musicians doing stand-up, nieces, nephews, and Ira's mother.

Across the eight nights of Hanukkah's first installment in 2001, Yo La Tengo played some 123 different songs, including first-time covers of the Beatles' "Eight Days a Week" (soon a Hanukkah theme), and—with Jon Spencer—Pussy Galore's "You Look Like a Jew." New songs included "seasonal numbers" by great Jewish songwriters like Joey Ramone (né Jeffry Ross Hyman) and Richard Hell (né Richard Lester Meyers), a lineage that encompassed George Gershwin and the Angry Samoans.

One song with at least partially Jewish authorship that got a pair of airings, and one to begin the second night, was "So Sedimentary," written by John and Faith Hubley (née Elliot) with Quincy Jones and recorded by James for Dump's 1993 album, *Superpowerless*. It was arguably the hardest cover the band performed during the week of what were, in actuality, some of the hardest shows the band had ever played.

Twenty-six years and twenty-five films after being diagnosed with cancer, Faith Hubley died in New Haven at the age of seventy-seven, two days before Hanukkah's start. She'd just finished *Northern Ice, Golden Sun* and had gotten sick very suddenly. She insisted that Emily attend its December 10 premiere at UCLA. None of the Yo La Tengo shows would be canceled, either. In between, Emily made it to Hoboken as many nights as she could.

In 2002, James made his father a birthday mix of '60s and '70s funk and soul songs, adding Sun Ra's "Nuclear War" to the end for good measure. Written in 1984 during the reignited Cold War, it highlighted the stardust-loving jazzman's stone cold assessment of the situation: "Nuclear war: it's a motherfucker."

"Oh, my dad would like that," James recalled thinking. "He likes the word 'motherfucker.' Who doesn't?" The next time the two talked, the elder McNew informed his son, "I love that song! Who is that? That guy's crazy!"

"Well, Dad, if you liked that, we actually played that song in Prospect Park over the summer! I got to finish the show by saying 'motherfucker' over and over again, over a huge PA system in front of twelve thousand people! Beat that!" For James, it was a major rock-star moment.

Yo La Tengo's free summer show had brought fans from across gentrified Brooklyn, swollen with artists and commerce in a way that Hoboken—and even Manhattan—never had been. It seemed like everybody James knew was at the show. They'd been riding high. In the spring, *The Onion* had made them a point of reference: "37 Record-Store Clerks Feared Dead in Yo La Tengo Concert Disaster." Ira, Georgia, and James were nothing but honored.

At Prospect Park, the band played hits, including the slow version of "Big Day Coming," "Moby Octopad," and "Speeding Motorcycle," alongside a few new songs in the running for their yet-to-be-recorded next album, and closed the set with eleven minutes of hushed drift under the stars, from *The Sounds of Science*—a nearly two-hour set of dreamy instrumental music they'd come up with the year before to accompany a program of French filmmaker Jean Painlevé's underwater documentaries at the San Francisco Film Festival. At Prospect Park, it segued into the slinky groove of "Nuclear War," James on second snare.

"I have nothing but the most beautiful memories associated with that show," James said. "It easily propelled us through the rest of the summer as far as writing songs and playing together."

It was the band's first real year off the road. They played at WFMU in the spring, did three East Coast *Sounds of Science* shows, including Lincoln Center in New York, and made two one-gig trips to London and Barcelona, respectively. But besides Hanukkah, that was it. It was a natural time to take a break, but Faith's passing had been hard on Georgia. Though the band's productivity continued—exactly as Faith would have loudly demanded—the mood was frequently melancholy.

One year post-9/11 and several months away from war in Iraq, "Nuclear War" became the band's first topical single, not to mention a semicomedic showcase for James. In addition to a fifteen-and-a-half-minute version with Other Dimensions in Music, there was a Mike Ladd remix; a YLT trio take; and one with a children's chorus that featured Will and Emily's kids, Max and Leila Rosenthal; Ray Hubley's kids, Hilary and Isaac; Michael Hill's kids, Claire and Stephen; Dave Rick's daughter, Sophie; and others, all gleefully told it was OK to say "motherfucker" for the afternoon.

On December 9, three days after the end of their second Hanukkah run, which had seen Ray Davies, David Byrne, and Ronnie Spector come to Maxwell's, "Nuclear War" inexplicably cracked *Billboard*'s Top 100 Hot Singles chart, rocketing all the way to #10. With the volume of new singles released and the now-pernicious industry-wide sales plague, it had taken fewer than ten thousand copies to make it, yet there they were, nine spots from Madonna and sandwiched between a wholesome girl-group named TG4 and Robin Thicke, the soon-to-be-wildly-successful pop-star son of sitcom dad Alan Thicke.

To celebrate, James forged a two-column ad from *Billboard*, complete with creases, and posted it to their website. "The whole world was watching, so we kept it real. We bought matching PATH trains and had Maxwell's gold-plated. We hired Donald Trump to roadie for us. We bought Hanukkah. We were bigger than Jesus, The Beatles, and Tupac combined." They slipped in a reference to a "Sir Christopher Gerard of Matador Records" and signed off, making sure to highlight— by way of a pull quote from a fictional CNN interview—"Put out a record where you say 'motherfucker' over and over again, Larry."

Given the down vibe, they'd thought to ironically call the new album *Beach Blanket Bingo*, but discovered they couldn't name an album after a movie. "*Summer Sun* was a particularly stressful record to make, because it may have felt like doing something different," Ira reflected later.

They'd done a lot of work, as usual, since *And Then Nothing*. They'd played with the Other Dimensions horns, released the *Danelectro* EP (three instrumentals they'd made up one afternoon when James brought in a sweet-sounding new bass, plus remixes), written and played live film scores, and collaborated with Mac and David and Sonic Boom and Neil Innes and Ray Davies and tons of others.

"It was the record right after my mom died," Georgia said of the songwriting. "Which I think worked in some way that was hard to place." Emily had taken the family movie screen and Faith's 16-millimeter projector to her family's home in Maplewood, New Jersey. The Hubley piano went into Yo La Tengo's practice space in Jersey City, where it became the centerpiece of the new songs the band assembled, a maturation both musical and symbolic.

Eventually, the songs seemed to be in the correct state of unfinished, and they went to Nashville for five weeks. Like *And Then Nothing*, the new material tended toward the sparse, though now held together with the pop sensibilities first breached in the drum-machine bossa nova of "Center of Gravity."

One song, eventually known as "Nothing But You and Me," would feature a lo-fi electronic hi-hat in conversation with a gentle live cymbal part while impressionistic piano chords made forward motion. Elsewhere, the band tried moody soul-jazz grooves, some of which naturally acquired layers of vibraphone, distant feedback, and unexpected chord changes. Some, like "Tiny Birds," sung by James, came out like classic pop, with stacks of acoustic guitars, reverb, brushed drums, organ, and piano: the tools of a studio band. All seemed to emerge from the same place. "On a beach overseas icy water slaps at our knees, and the buoy was signaling as if it knew we were far from home," Georgia sang on "Winter a Go-Go." It was somewhere near there.

"I'd say this record is about coping," Ira would tell former *Jersey Beat* contributor Jim DeRogatis, by then an editor at the *Chicago Sun-Times*. "I don't think it's a particularly despairing record, but I'm not sure how upbeat it is."

"If it's not tense, there's something wrong," Roger Moutenot once observed about working with Yo La Tengo.

"Almost every single time we were convinced, at some point, 'We have to start from scratch, it's a disaster,'" Ira attested. "I don't relax that easily. I tell a sort of jokey story of going to a spa with Georgia. She was sort of worried about me. My joke was 'Maybe this is what it feels like to relax,' and then fainting, like, seconds later. You feel like, 'All this angst and tension went into the making of it, maybe that's required.' I don't really believe that, but it's hard to behave in any other way sometimes."

"We get a lot of real work done that way," James said.

One tension the band felt during the fall 2002 sessions in Nashville arose from something most bands would want, and something most bands of Yo La Tengo's stature had presumably gotten over long ago: people were paying attention.

Writers and listeners had read into Ira's lyrics before, and Ira had been able to ignore it, but *And Then Nothing* had changed that. "Writing the words I wrote on *Summer Sun*, it did not feel possible. I felt the spotlight in a way I don't think I had felt before that. It stands to reason that maybe we all felt that way recording, in a way that sort of upped certain pressures that were always there. We spend a lot of time trying to pretend no one else is listening, just playing to the three of us, or four of us if Roger is there, who is the only other opinion that matters. Probably, after *Summer Sun*, we had to redouble our efforts in that department. Our ability to do that had maybe slipped away on that record."

"I'm not averse to pillow talk, but I prefer a private joke," he sang on "How to Make a Baby Elephant Float," an index of punch lines without setups. On "Moonrock Mambo," he reeled off abstruse couplets about Tara Key, Mr. Met, *Simpsons* character Professor Frink, and New Orleans pianist Eddie Bo.

Everywhere, the music was infused with melancholy. "Could it be that it's the season of the shark?" Ira posed on "Season of the Shark," mixing universal pop tropes ("Do you need someone to hide behind?") with reticence and emotion steeped in obscurity, but also welcoming harmony arrangements and warm keyboards. There were virtually no rock songs on the album at all, save "Little Eyes," which became *Summer Sun*'s first single by default.

After the basic recording was finished, Other Dimensions in Music had joined YLT for a whole set on the second night of Hanukkah. The next week James and Ira met Roy Campbell Jr., William Parker, and Sabir Mateen at Shelter Island Studios in New York, where the band was mixing.

"It was hard not to give them every track," James said as the musicians improvised over the songs. The horns, Parker's bass, and Mateen's flute transformed everything they touched. On "Beach Party Tonight," which became the album's opening cut, they drifted subtly in and out, textured bits of light and cloud that gently and completely obscured the song's vocal melody.

The cover was a double exposure taken of the band by Phil Morrison in a swampy New Jersey parking lot on a not-particularly-warm-looking day. Despite the title, beach ball logo, and the Matador press photos of the band posed with surf boards, it was hardly music for summertime fun. Whereas *And Then Nothing* had first-dance-ready love songs like "Our Way to Fall," *Summer Sun* presented a unified front of winter gray.

Beyond the long lines and security theater that engulfed the nation's wartime airports in the spring of 2003, the friendly skies got even friendlier with new singles by Yo La Tengo, Stephen Malkmus, Cat Power, and others appearing on a new Rock United in-flight playlist.

Not that indie rock on airplanes was any major surprise, but it was a sign of the times, representative of a new series of global relationships forged by "Sir Christopher Gerard," who had suddenly sold 50 percent of Matador in a deal that was less a sellout than a merger. The Rock United segment, in fact, was credited to "Beggars Group and Matador Records present . . ."—a branding that represented a subtly new, but significant, configuration of global gears that had begun to turn on behalf of Yo La Tengo.

In many ways, Martin Mills's conglomerate the Beggars Group was Matador's Anglo equivalent. Like their closest competitor in Rough Trade, Beggars had begun in a London record store and grew over the years as they founded an additional pair of renowned imprints, XL and 4AD, and eventually absorbed Rough Trade itself.

Chris and Gerard had never stopped looking for new inroads into the market. The Alternative Distribution Alliance, a company Warner Bros. had established to rent their distribution channels at a slight profit, was one path. It was a method for independent labels to have access to the new, weird America. Walmart had long been the nation's biggest music retailer, but the landscape beyond was a tangle of chain stores like Best Buy and Target, much like the Korvette's where Ira had first picked out the "Ruby Tuesday" single.

The merger with the Beggars Group was plenty symbolic, too: the joining of strains of American and British indie rock that had mutually rejected each other twenty years ago. Chris Lombardi and Gerard Cosloy retained full control over Matador, Beggars moved into the offices, and Matador employees took on new titles. They'd released the debut full-length by Interpol, *Turn on the Bright Lights*, in August 2002, and the first American album by the New Pornographers, *Electric Version*, in May 2003. Both bands would take Matador into the top 20 in a matter of years.

Summer Sun's wintry moods seemed a peculiar candidate for pop success, but stranger hits had happened. The band had just come off a critically acclaimed album that saw them sustaining a long-building popularity. The label hired outside publicists and plotted a full media strategy, replete with a trip to South by Southwest routed around a hurried return flight that saw the band go directly from the airport to their WFMU Marathon obligation.

As *Summer Sun* publicity rolled out, Ira's former *Village*

Voice music editor Robert Christgau embodied the continued attention most literally, declaring that he had to see Ira and Georgia's digs to truly understand the album. It was one of the only times they'd allowed an on-duty writer over for a visit.

"It's a modest third-floor condo in Hoboken, theirs for 10 years now," the dean of rock critics reported. "Big L-shaped living-dining-cooking area, big bedroom with big TV and the bed made for my visit, and smaller, well, junk room. If these lifers haven't solved the storage problem, there's no hope for the rest of us, but facts are facts. What should have been the dining-room table was covered with piles of CDs that Georgia says were even higher before the couple got back from a European trip. For Georgia's birthday, Ira had arranged to have new hardwood flooring installed while they were gone. All their stuff had to be removed and put back, and though some of the vinyl is now out of order, sparing Georgia (and himself) that domestic ordeal was genius."

Not everybody was convinced. In a cruel review that dismissed the album as "pleasant," *Pitchfork* writer Eric Carr described "Let's Be Still," a ten-minute pastoral with the Other Dimensions guys blowing breezily across the top as "indie-muzak." Due, perhaps, to negative reviews, but as much to the sales plague around the industry, *Summer Sun* sold some 132,000 copies, the worst returns since *May I Sing with Me*.

It was arguably the first external jolt in the twenty years since Yo La Tengo picked up instruments. But this gentle intrusion of real life was also a perfectly Yo La Tengo–like development, something to navigate and think through carefully.

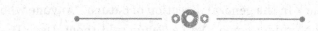

CHAPTER 16

Prisoners of Love

The first leg of the tour closed at the Beacon Theatre in New York. Perhaps knowing to play the hits, they began with members of the Sun Ra Arkestra in full sparkling costume on stage and did "Nuclear War." They closed with the same, the YLT children's auxiliary belting "motherfucker" in a crowded theater. Though not too crowded. The former movie palace with its 2,900-seat capacity was a tad above Yo La Tengo's popularity level and empty seats abounded in the balconies. Also, the Flaming Lips were playing across town.

The Arkestra were new friends. Yo La Tengo had contacted them when they'd played the previous weekend in Philadelphia, where many of the musicians still lived in the same house they once shared with their bandleader, who had died in 1993—or, in the parlance of Sun Ra himself, perhaps merely ascended back in the general direction of Saturn. "Anyone who wants to should just come," Yo La Tengo told them. Dave Davis, Tyrone Hill, and Danny Ray Thompson did and, like the Other Dimensions in Music guys, fit right in, improvising on-the-spot horn arrangements.

"We thought it was just for the night, but it was such a blast," Ira said. "We were back to traveling in two cars; we ended up just driving down to D.C., and just took 'em to D.C.

From there, after the show, they took the train back to Philly. It was pretty amazing watching them do that."

Another tour mate that spring was Merge Records' Mac Mc-Caughan, on the bill with his new band Portastatic and often playing with Yo La Tengo. In Montreal, McCaughan reconnected and crashed with an old Superchunk fan and friend, Howard Bilerman, who had become a recording engineer on various projects that surrounded the Godspeed You! Black Emperor collective. A few weeks after Mac passed through on the Yo La Tengo tour, Bilerman recorded demos with a new local act called the Arcade Fire that he would soon pass back to Mac and Merge.

More low-key than the loudmouths at Matador, Merge had found a rhythm of its own. McCaughan and Laura Ballance's label remained an unconditionally loving home to favorites like the Clean and Lambchop, as well as a host of new stars, like Spoon (who hadn't panned out on Matador) and songwriter Matt Ward, who preferred to go by "M.," as he would remind Ira several times upon being introduced otherwise when he sat in with Yo La Tengo during shows that spring. Within a few years, both would find major success.

Yo La Tengo's career had come to an unforeseen and mostly silent turning point. The completion of *Summer Sun* and its touring cycle was a logical epilogue to the creative, critical, and popular successes of the previous two albums. And when it was over, they were in another new place that looked less like Kansas than ever.

In their ten years of full-time band-dom, they'd always walked a thin but comfortable line of profitability that was based, in some part, on the percentage of people in the United States who, like them, spent money on recorded music. It was a natural resource relied on by their segment of the American marketplace, and—for them—there was a massive, Dust Bowl–like drought. People stopped buying music. But it was also this period more than any other that all of Yo La Tengo's rules and designs and reluctances anticipated. It was a vision of patience, inherited as much from Ira's Depression-reared parents as Faith and John's fervent independence.

The result was Yo La Tengo, as their most comfortable and creative possible selves, individually and collectively, locally and globally, in maturity. They had Matador, Maxwell's, WFMU. They had commercial work. They had a career, momentum, and an internal band clock that continued to tick slowly and (mostly) smoothly years after its very intense windup. They had an active repertoire of music that existed as something of value apart from the 99¢ per song Apple was now charging in the new iTunes Store.

They were always touring, it seemed, and for the very good reason that it was steady, well-paying work. They'd gone back to the two-van method mainly after the *And Then Nothing* bus, but got a bigger ride if the occasion called for it. In the late spring of 2004, they hit a swath of cities they visited infrequently, including their first ever show in Little Rock, Arkansas, and brought Antietam along for a good chunk of the ride, which was capped by a three-night Memorial Day engagement at the Fillmore in San Francisco.

Another reason for the tour was a lucrative gig at the third installment of Bonnaroo, the massive festival spawned by the jam-band scene in 2002. Like indie rock, the separate-but-equal post–Grateful Dead world had found itself absorbed into the cultural mainstream, no more so than at (and by) Bonnaroo. Established by New Orleans promoters Superfly, the festival drew some 90,000 attendees in its third year, when Yo La Tengo rolled up in their tour bus.

The band's set started as Bob Dylan ended, and concluded opposite the start of a headline slot by James's Charlottesville nemesis, Dave Matthews. The band's contrarian move du jour was to take questions from the crowd.

"What does Yo La Tengo mean?" somebody asked.

"It's Spanish for 'China Cat Sunflower,'" Ira replied.

In early 2004, crews arrived to tear down the Maxwell House factory. Pinnacle Ltd. and Toll Brothers, companies that specialized in suburban homes, presented a plan for $500 million of condos, storefronts, and office space. There would be a beach on the river, to pay tribute to the site of John Cox Stevens's yacht club, and a baseball field, on what was said to be the spot of the Knickerbockers' first. Neither was ever built.

When the condos went up, a sign appeared outside—THE FOLLOWING ITEMS OR ACTIVITIES ARE NOT PERMITTED ON OR AROUND THE LAWN—and specified eighteen potential infractions, the second of which read: "Use of aluminum, wooden, or other bats for hitting any softball or baseball or other object that endangers the safety of the public." So it went.

Down the block, Steve Fallon sold 1039 Washington for $1.275 million and moved to Delaware to open a vintage toy and gift shop with his boyfriend in the coastal community of Rehoboth Beach. At Onieals, over near Georgia and Ira's old place, one could catch Skanatra, a ska tribute to Frank Sinatra.

The comedians H. Jon Benjamin and Jon Glaser—Conan O'Brien, Comedy Central, and UCB improv vets—hit with seemingly new one-joke characters every night, pathologically committing to whatever might arise. At the Cat's Cradle in North Carolina, they were Soundtrackapella, a gag they'd done once on Tom Scharpling's *Best Show*, doing vocal versions of movie themes. They came on midway through Yo La Tengo's set, which—for seventeen nights in the early autumn of 2004—swelled into something like a variety show during the Swing State Tour to raise money for the John Kerry presidential campaign.

Benjamin and Glaser riffed on homeschooling, matching tattoos, an anecdote about asking Ray Parker Jr. if he was afraid of ghosts, and bun shops before—nearly fifteen minutes in—singing their one and only a cappella rendition of a movie theme. As Yo La Tengo had made sure to advertise and enforce, guests and comedians on Yo La Tengo's Swing State Tour would not appear as opening acts, but onstage in the midst of an extended set by the headliners. Other nights Glaser and Benjamin became Hans Weber and Gustav Schnabel and, at one point, Superman and C-3PO. They baited the audience constantly. Musical guests appeared as part of the band, who would back them for a few spotlight songs each night. The tour made it as far as Kansas City before turning south, like a rolling Hanukkah revue.

The first leg featured comedian/drummer Fred Armisen, then into his second season at *Saturday Night Live*. Sue Garner, their old friend from a half dozen hometown bands, came along too. And then the Arkestra, in Ira's words, "just showed up" somewhere in Pennsylvania and planted themselves onstage. "We did Sue's song 'Asphalt Road' with no rehearsal," Ira remembered happily. "They just instantly heard something and started playing. I could see Sue's face light up. You could hear them form these parts as if they knew it." Just as a member of the Bonzo Dog Band had jammed with a member of Spacemen 3 under Yo La Tengo's watch, now representatives of Sun Ra's Arkestra would find themselves onstage with the new wave of comedy.

Damon and Naomi, James's pals since *And Suddenly . . .*, did four shows. They picked up David Kilgour for the second half of the tour, some of Eleventh Dream Day, and in Nashville (naturally) Lambchop and friends. Mac McCaughan appeared in Chapel Hill, as did Chris Stamey of the dB's, playing cello, no less. Billed as the Chris Stamey Experience, Yo La Tengo had just backed him on a quick mini album recorded at the relocated Water Music in Hoboken, *A Question of Temperature*, which included garage takes on Television and a public-service announcement about voting.

A new Georgia/Ira duet in the setlist that fall was a bit of *Fakebook*-like his/hers folk pop: Spooner Oldham and Dan Penn's "I'm Your Puppet." "I'm yours to have and to hold," Georgia sang to Ira's "Darling, you have full control," another excellent song called out, another way to sing about love. And most nights, they invented reasons to—slightly later in the set—let Jon Benjamin and Jon Glaser sing "PT Cruiser." Set to the same changes as Spooner and Penn's "Puppet," the audience would usually gasp upon recognition of what Glaser and

Benjamin were about to do to the song Ira and Georgia had just used as an expression of vulnerability.

"I consider making a joke—or at least attempting to make a joke—so much more of a risk than, you know, bearing your feelings in a rock song," James observed to *The Believer* in 2005. "Because everybody does that now. I mean everybody."

The 1962 expansion of Major League Baseball that included the creation of the New York Mets triggered several decades of growth for the sport. By the turn of the twenty-first century, the number of professional baseball clubs had almost doubled, and the need for professional ballplayers along with it.

The so-called New York Rules adopted and endlessly adapted at Elysian Fields had first hopped to the Brooklyn neighborhoods of Greenpoint and Williamsburg, where the game was first hyped (preemptively) as "the national pastime" in 1856. In an ecstatic collision of play and business, the rules spread throughout the country, to Latin America, and eventually around the world. Leagues developed, and—awhile later—so did a system of baseball academies operated by North American clubs, especially in the Dominican Republic. With the influx of Spanish-speaking players in professional baseball over the 1980s and 1990s, a call of *"Yo la tengo"* in the outfield of a Major League Baseball team was no longer a probable cause of collision—though the Mets still figured out ways to lose important ball games.

In the same way, "indie" integrated into the American landscape and became a fundamental condition of the modern world. Sales dropped so precipitously and acts rocked from nowhere and back so quickly that everybody was in the same boat. True independence had always been existential, but it was more so now than ever. No label from Matador to the biggest platers, and no media outlet from *Rolling Stone* to the indie superpower website *Pitchfork* could ensure any band's success.

The underground was dumb with music. The number of professional artists, writers, and musicians in the United States had nearly doubled between Ira's thirteenth birthday in 1970 and the time he settled in New York a decade later. It almost doubled again by the turn of the century, rising from .57 percent of the national population to nearly .9 percent. In the eleven years after Yo La Tengo's first South by Southwest appearance in 1995, the number of bands that performed at the convention doubled to an estimated 1,400. But it wasn't only in Austin where people had music constantly shot at them, as James had once observed about South by Southwest.

It came from iPods programmed by music-loving clerks in restaurants and bookstores and coffee shops. Other public places featured piped-in sounds from the 133 commercial-free music channels offered by Sirius and XM, the two satellite mega-giants who had launched in 2001 and had more than three million combined listeners by late 2004.

Though their companies' executives often paid lip service to their FM forebears, the satellite services' programming was an almost complete rebuke to the freeform radio of the '60s. While the services enthusiastically advertised hundreds of genres of music and talk, nearly all were segregated into their own channels, each calculated to its particular demographic. On-air personalities block-recorded mike breaks of preselected playlists in faceless Manhattan office towers, music-for-all programming utopia rendered as blandly as possible. Despite the huge slowdown in people paying for music, the listening audience did nothing but grow as music became more public and ephemeral than anytime since before its mechanical reproduction and mass distribution.

Wired editor Chris Anderson coined the theory of the Long Tail to describe the phenomenon of artists being rediscovered or finding long-term followings in an age where the costs associated with the reproduction and distribution of media were approaching zero. The A-Bones, the New York garage band who once shared bassist Mike Lewis with Yo La Tengo and whose guitarist, Bruce Bennett, played with YLT each year during the WFMU pledge drive, had been broken up for more than a decade when, seemingly from nowhere, they were offered an obscene amount of money for a one-off reunion show in Las Vegas.

But Long Tail–style rediscovery was something the A-Bones had specialized in well before anyone had coined a term for it. For the band's founders, Billy Miller and Miriam Linna, punk had merely been a supercharged continuation of a long tradition of obscure garage and R&B that stretched deep and wide. From a loft in downtown Brooklyn, they had maintained an obsessive fanzine called *Kicks*. They had a jukebox and massive parties on weekends, founding Norton Records in 1986 as a tribute to "Wild Rock" with 7-inches by surf guitarist Link Wray and crazed rockabilly singer Hasil Adkins. The two lovingly oversaw an all-vinyl empire through the rise and fall of the CD, as they specialized in impossible-to-find reissues, never-before-heard deep finds, and the occasional contemporary band deemed worthy to carry the flame.

After their one-off in Las Vegas, Yo La Tengo invited the A-Bones to play Hanukkah, and the band stayed together. In New York, they hit the bar circuit with a surprising enthusiasm, where Ira and Georgia became fixtures at the gigs.

On the Lower East Side, a few blocks from the Williamsburg Bridge, a former winery called Tonic had become a reliable home for experimental music of all stripes, the members of Yo La Tengo (and countless other acts) often to be found in the audience. Within six years of its 1998 opening, the rent had doubled, and the venue faced eviction. If such a fate had befallen Maxwell's, Yo La Tengo might not have happened.

Economists had begun to consider gentrified (or gentrifying) zones such as Hoboken and Brooklyn as centers for "creatives," or some other variation of what former secretary of labor Robert Reich called the "symbolic analytic" industries. In Brooklyn, especially, the number of bands multiplied in the first decade of the twenty-first century at a rate that made Hoboken in the early 1980s seem quaint.

A month of benefit concerts for Tonic followed their rent hike, and Yo La Tengo played two. The sets featured onetime Pere Ubu member Garo Yellin on cello, and Ira on Tonic's baby grand piano for much of the night. The former Heatwave keyboardist led jazzy instrumental versions of the Lyres' "Don't Give It Up Now" and the Move's "I Can Hear the Grass Grow." Ira was becoming an increasingly confident and enthusiastic piano player.

The Tonic benefits raised some $80,000 for the club via shows by Yoko Ono and others, but there was little that anybody could do in the long run. The idea that a band could relax and spend a while getting its act together while living on the cheap was more or less banished from Manhattan, whose own culture industries had zoomed upscale at an alarming rate.

A few months after the benefits, developers announced the construction of Bernard Tschumi's BLUE Residential Tower, which soon hovered over the avant-garde jazz club like an aqua-obsessed Mondrian. A press release trumpeted it as the first residential building with a full-time doorman on the Lower East Side.

Within weeks of BLUE's opening and immediate noise complaints, Tonic announced its closing. The global city's encroachment was rarely more palpable, though odds were that there were BLUE residents who had some Yo La Tengo in their iTunes libraries.

Boho roots or no, Yo La Tengo's music had found its way into the canon of a particular subset of fashionable society. Like comedy, indie rock and parts of the literary world grew to exist increasingly in parallel. A few years earlier, novelist Jonathan Lethem had published a story inspired by Yo La Tengo's version of "Speeding Motorcycle" called "The National Anthem."

"The Mets go on signing haggard veterans and I think there's no hope at all," Lethem concluded, "but you can be certain Giuseppe and I will be out at Shea having our hearts broken this May, as always. In our hearts, it's always spring, or 1969, or something like that. I only wish we had some out-fielders who could catch the ball."

Mostly, the new sensibility formed around *Timothy Mc-Sweeney's Quarterly Concern*, an irregularly formatted fiction journal based out of San Francisco. Established by novelist Dave Eggers in 1998 as an anti-stodgy literary outlet, *McSwee-ney's* initial cultural moment was born from the mid-'90s West Coast tech boom. Traditionally recognizable boho hipness was never far from the ironic, obsessive wordplay; footnote humor; and semiprecious sincerity that *McSweeney's* championed. In March 2003, they launched *The Believer*, a literary magazine that, with equal earnestness, published an annual music issue that focused heavily on indie rock. Its first install-ment was accompanied by a compilation CD featuring Merge's latest breakthrough act, Spoon (a one-time Matador signee) covering *Electr-o-Pura*'s "Decora."

The following year, they published an interview with Yo La Tengo in the company of reports about the Eleventh Annual H. P. Lovecraft Film Festival and professional women's bas-ketball, an advice column by Amy Sedaris, and interviews with Steve Martin and novelist Tobias Wolff.

"We're fond of . . . allowing serious thoughts to come through, hopefully, with some degree of comedy," Ira told writer Matthew Derby. "I think a lot of times it's easier to get through to the core of things through humor. I'm staring at the case for [the British version of] *The Office* on DVD right now . . . This maybe be shallow, but I really feel that *The Office* is as pene-trating about humanity, if not more so, as Harold Pinter. The comedy makes the experience of that show more bearable and also unbearable simultaneously."

The band moved the practice space out of big-box hinterlands beyond Jersey City back to downtown Hoboken, into a loft in the former Neumann Leathers tannery a few blocks from where the train tracks tangled into Erie Lackawanna station.

In the new room, quiet songs sounded fine, and loud songs sounded even better, perhaps because it'd been so long since they'd focused on them. They also began to sign on to do film scores with increasing frequency.

The most entertaining work, arguably, was for John Cameron Mitchell's raunchy *Shortbus*. Emily Hubley had done some animation sequences for Mitchell's breakthrough glam musical, *Hedwig and the Angry Inch*, and Mitchell had even shown up one Hanukkah to do some of the numbers.

"The scenes we scored we saw again and again, thousands of times," James said of the *Shortbus* assignment, "which was fun 'cause there was a lot of—Mom, I'm sorry—there was a lot of *fuckin'* in that movie. We went there and it was like, 'Oh, OK, well, the guitar comes in when you see that testicle, and it just sort of builds.' It was kind of a fun way to work, I've got to say."

Since scoring the *Sounds of Science* a few years earlier, they'd gotten used to playing with screens and working to order, sometimes deconstructing their own melodies per producers' requests. The assignments had started coming down the pike quickly. *Game 6* featured a screenplay by novelist Don DeLillo and starred Michael Keaton and Robert Downey Jr. as opposing playwright and critic, and was set on the evening of October 25, 1986, the night of the Mets' penultimate World Series game against the Boston Red Sox, for which Ira had a bet going with Phil Milstein. Clearly the right band for the job, Yo La Tengo spent months at work on *Game 6* nearly simultaneous to a job that struck even closer to home than that: the feature debut by their friend Phil Morrison. Titled *Junebug*, the band used "Green Arrow" as a starting point and built upward.

Still another film assignment the band took on that year was *Old Joy*, which starred singer-songwriter Will Oldham. The sophomore feature by director Kelly Reichardt, a Boston-reared filmmaker whom Yo La Tengo had met initially through Christmas (or maybe Big Dipper), the spacious short-story adaptation was a vehicle for Reichardt's quiet, slow rhythm—an on-screen patience Yo La Tengo found highly compatible. The soundtrack was an excuse to collaborate, as well, with another Hoboken neighbor in guitarist Smokey Hormel, heir to the Hormel meat fortune and exquisite session and touring guitarist for Beck, Johnny Cash, and Neil Diamond, among many others.

Reichardt's mournful realism was born from an innately intimate style. Her most recent film, *Ode*, was a forty-eight-minute reimagining of Bobbie Gentry's #1 hit, "Ode to Billy Joe," that Reichardt had shot on saturated Super-8. The film featured Superchunk's Jon Wurster in a rare dramatic turn, as well as YLT's version of Sun Ra's "Dreaming." Soon, Reichardt wouldn't need to resort to lower fidelity to be able to work directly with her actors.

In recent years, technological advances had allowed the indie film world to build further bridges toward its rock-and-roll brethren. In 2004, JVC introduced the GR-HD1, the first affordable handheld high-definition camcorder. The cost of film processing removed, underfunded filmmakers could shoot footage that was of high enough quality to project theatrically. Combined with the ubiquity of laptops and cheap (or downloaded) editing software, it gave independent filmmakers a personal freedom in production and distribution that musicians had known since at least the mid-'70s.

It allowed Yo La Tengo to score films in the comfort of their practice space, and granted filmmakers like Reichardt the freedom to personalize their filmmaking even further. On her next picture, the acclaimed *Wendy and Lucy*, Reichardt would travel to rural Oregon with star Michelle Williams to shoot sequences one-on-one. It was a kind of independent filmmaking as removed from the frenzy of the Sundance Film Festival as Yo La Tengo's music was from South by Southwest.

But even Sundance came calling once. The band had plenty of business there when they visited in early 2005, when both *Game 6* and *Junebug* premiered. They also backed Daniel Johnston, subject of a debuting new documentary by filmmaker Jeff Feuerzig, a show that earned the descriptor, rare in the Yo La Tengo world, "drunken." For the occasion, and being in Utah, they learned the Osmonds' "One Bad Apple."

Still frothing with an endless stream of conversational invective, Gerard Cosloy took to the Internet's ever-changing new technologies with aplomb. In 2003, he launched *Can't Stop the Bleeding*, a sports-blog sequel to *Conflict*. "It's sort of a profane version of the Associated Press," he said later, and declared "there are occasionally moments where the blog is a lot funnier than *Conflict* ever was."

For all of his ongoing obsessions with music, Gerard was a likewise manic sports fan, with an enthusiasm level that had him covering semipro and indie sports leagues alongside his (occasionally) beloved Mets. It was also a chance for a fresh start free from the baggage of nearly a quarter century of running vitriol, observations, and theories about music that began with the first issue of *Conflict* in 1979. He found all new enemies.

As Matador had integrated with Beggars Group, the label had grown more global. Through New York often enough, Gerard moved to London for a few years, before the merger, where he'd established the small label 12XU to import American records in the United Kingdom, and settled in Austin in 2004. Later, Chris moved to California with his girlfriend and had a child.

While both Cosloy and Lombardi remained utterly integral to Matador, many of the label's day-to-day managerial operations fell to Patrick Amory, a medieval historian with a PhD from Cambridge and part of the crew since the Dutch East days on Long Island. Eventually, Gerard and Chris made Patrick president of the label and an equal partner in Matador.

Despite his day job, Gerard took *Can't Stop the Bleeding* seriously. "I see no reason why the current formula of tits = hits, pseudonymous commentary and heavy petting of [*Deadspin* editor] Will Leitch's baloney pony can't continue for another few years at least," he wrote. "Whether or not I'm providing any sort of alternative is for others to judge."

Shortly after his relocation to Austin, Gerard launched

Matablog as well, and became the company's official public voice if, in fact, he ever wasn't. The blog picked up almost exactly where *Conflict* had left off fifteen years previous, as Gerard called out lesser fans and passionately defended Yo La Tengo.

Pitchfork had held its first music festival during the summer of 2006, drawing 35,000 people to Chicago's Union Park for a bill that featured a reunited Mission of Burma, Yo La Tengo, and others. In a post titled "Yo La Tengo vs. Sea of Humanity," Gerard came out guns ablaze, and managed to promote songs from Yo La Tengo's yet-to-be-released album in the bargain.

"Even by the usual zero-attention span standards, the claim by one local jackass that Yo La Tengo were 'so quiet 'til the last song I did not know they were playing' is kinda off the charts," he wrote in the early *Matablog* post. "Never again is the word 'quiet' likely to be employed when describing songs like 'Pass The Hatchet' or 'Watch Out For Me Ronnie,' though I can't deny even the loudest of bands come off as somewhat muted for someone whose head is up their ass."

CHAPTER 17

Popular Songs

The horn arranging, at first, didn't go much better than the first time they'd tried it. Working with "one keyboard that had one crappy saxophone sound and one keyboard that had a crappy trumpet sound" the band tried to sketch parts for two new songs, only to be politely told by the arranger that they should try again. Which they did.

The two songs would also wind up as the first two featured tracks from the new album they were working on at Roger Moutenot's brand-new Hap Town studio in south Nashville—not far from Kurt Wagner's place—although only one would be released as a proper 7-inch. Both "Beanbag Chair" and "Mr. Tough" found the band back on new ground: bouncing soul-pop as influenced by NRBQ and Sun Ra as by obscure soul singles.

"Mr. Tough," especially, attacked a classic Yo La Tengo theme. "Pretend everything will be all right," they sang, James's high sweetness on top. In that way, it was a keynote for the album, whose unspoken mission seemed to be to discover new ways for Yo La Tengo to be unmistakably themselves. The song also shouted it out to Todd-O-Phonic, Maxwell's co-owner Todd Abramson mile-a-minute WFMU persona.

Songwriting had taken place glacially through the daily practicing that started not long after the Tonic benefits in

2005, interrupted by trips to Japan and Europe, some more *Sounds of Science* shows at museums and other uptown (and uptownish) venues, and another Hanukkah with its statistical, almanac-style memory markers.

When they made it to Nashville in early 2006, the batch of songs they brought with them was more eclectic than any they'd yet hatched, and far more polished than any they'd entered the studio with in a decade. "I Should Have Known Better" was garage rock with a carefully dropped Farfisa break. James's "Black Flowers" had a gentle bed of brass under strummed acoustic guitar and high harmonies. "The Room Got Heavy" chased their previous album's jazz leanings into a swinging groove with a cool-as-a-cucumber Georgia vocal.

"I think there are songs on [it] that are very similar to other songs of ours," Ira had said when *Summer Sun* came out. "We just decided that it doesn't matter. If something is particularly similar to something we've done before, it might make it harder for us to like it. But if we do like it, even though it's similar, then that's good enough."

Ira and Georgia had seen country/folk session legend (and onetime Bob Dylan sideman) David Mansfield play with Michael Hurley a few years earlier, adding unrehearsed mandolin and violin parts. "David just made everything special," Ira remembered. Georgia suggested inviting him for Hanukkah, and Mansfield sat in for nearly a whole night of quiet songs. Based out of Nashville, the band visited him at his home studio, where he added layers of strings to the Georgia ballad "I Feel Like Going Home" and "Black Flowers."

For each open-feeling instrumental like "Song for Mahila," there was sculpted, textured pop like "The Race Is on Again," where Ira picked out a sparkling melody on an electric twelve-string. The set was book-ended by noisy jams that crossed the ten-minute mark. At the head of the first LP was "Pass the Hatchet, I Think I'm Goodkind," a Kraut rock–influenced noise wall that cycled around a six-note McNew bass line and old-fashioned mixed-low vocals from Ira.

And stretched across the second disc's final side was the

intentionally typoed "The Story of Yo La Tango," which couched feedback-buried autobiography in the band's most dramatic guitar build yet. "With nothing to lose, we lost, and suffered every cost," they sang, with what sounded remarkably like second thoughts.

Former Grant Lee Buffalo leader Grant-Lee Phillips had been a regular on the WB's show *Gilmore Girls*, playing a pseudonymous street performer. The role gave his career a sustained boost. For the show's sixth-season finale, between typical WB melodrama, the writers worked music into the subplot in a most appropriate way.

Discovered performing on a street corner in the show's fictional town of Stars Hollow, Grant is given his big break, and the town is immediately overrun by musicians trying to repeat his success. It was a thoroughly meta way to promote a new album. Sonic Youth's Thurston Moore and Kim Gordon turned up with their teenage daughter, Coco, to play a song from their forthcoming *Rather Ripped*, the last album of the Geffen contract they'd signed in 1989.

As it happened, after *Gilmore Girls'* producers had commissioned a copycat "My Little Corner of the World" for their pilot episode, James had become a fan of the show anyway. He'd started to contribute a column to the Yo La Tengo website, "On the Couch with James." Like Georgia and Ira, James was a pretty committed television fan. "ABC's Family Channel is showing reruns of *Gilmore Girls* a few times a day, which is pretty amazing," he noted. "Along with *Arrested Development* and *Monk*, it's the only non-animated American drama/comedy worth a shit from this decade. It's smart and sweet and hilarious and subtle and subversive and it doesn't treat its audience like morons. So what's it doing on the Flanders channel? I dunno, I'm just happy to see it."

"We were still trying to come up with a sequence in advance of mastering, which involves choosing the mixes and putting them in order," Ira remembered of the band's trip to the *Gilmore Girls* set. "There was a lot of stuff going on at that exact moment, maybe not the best time to pick up and go out to L.A., but I think we were afraid of James never speaking to us again. It turned out to be so much fun. Just in every way."

True to form, Yo La Tengo used the opportunity to play an alternate three-guitar arrangement of "The Story of Yo La Tango," a new song that almost nobody had heard in advance of the episode's May 2006 airdate, and not even scheduled to be one of the album's singles. "We ran headlong in our way," Ira sang during the band's thirty seconds of screen time. "We tried so hard."

"We are currently not answering that question," Ira told writers when queried about why the band chose the title for the new album, but the confident comic directness was hard to miss. *I Am Not Afraid of You and I Will Beat Your Ass* was sourced from comments by Knicks small forward Kurt Thomas. Reviews were positive, *Pitchfork* back on board with an 8.3 and their increasingly important Best New Music rating.

"A Pitchfork 9.1 is more influential to the audience and the retailers than a *Rolling Stone* or *New York Times* review," Gerard wrote in a public roundtable about the state of indie moderated by Sleater-Kinney's Carrie Brownstein and published on her National Public Radio blog, *Monitor Mix*.

"A 4.5 can kill a record," noted Portia Sabin, of Olympia's still-thriving Kill Rock Stars. "Unfortunately."

"Agree on the *Pitchfork* thing," Mac McCaughan chimed in, "though I do think that a 9.1 helps more than an average number hurts."

"If any of us were really great at galvanizing public sentiment/handing out the learning lessons, we'd be less dependent on *Pitchfork*," Gerard said. "And that's our fault, not theirs."

I Am Not Afraid of You also found itself with a satellite radio hit in "Mr. Tough," which hovered in or around Sirius's Left of Center's Top 10 all autumn. The album rebounded admirably from the *Summer Sun* dip, entering the charts at #66 with a bullet, selling 206,000 copies on the back of another eight full months of shows between the album's September 2006 release and Hanukkah 2007. Though a massive comedown from "Nuclear War," it was the band's highest chart placement for an album yet.

It was a relative achievement—by then, the entrance point for the *Billboard* Top 200 had shrunk to 5,000 records sold in a week. Even so, it also showed an indie rock fanbase that made up an increasing percentage of the music-buying public. For Yo La Tengo, it was an unquestionable success, especially as the music industry's infrastructure began to crumble along with the national economy.

Several chains, including Tower Records, went out of business. Along with eighty-nine other vacated locations around the country, they abandoned their block-long storefront at 4th Street and Broadway that had given name to Other Music, the small record store across the street.

Other Music survived, even thrived. They sold advance-surcharge-free tickets to shows at Tonic, Maxwell's, and elsewhere. In classic record-store fashion, two of their employees, Dave Portner and Noah Lennox, even spawned a wildly successful band, Animal Collective. Yo La Tengo came through frequently, and had tricked the place out into a beach party for the 2003 release of *Summer Sun*. Unlike Pier Platters, though, Other Music was happy to sell CDs, and confined vinyl to one large wall.

Not that they'd been able to stock much Yo La Tengo on that side of the store lately. The vinyl pressing plant Matador employed, 33 1/3, filed for Chapter 11 bankruptcy and locked their doors with nearly all of Matador's masters up through May 2006 inside. In an interview, Patrick Amory admitted that it would take considerable effort to recover most of the Yo La Tengo albums. At WFMU's annual record fair, it was often easier to find a member of Yo La Tengo than to find Yo La Tengo records.

When they were done with their *I Am Not Afraid of You* tour duty, they toured some more. The concert ticketing industry had been deeply unfun and complicated for years but grew more so as it, too, got sucked into the Internet's maw. For each show, the band made sure tickets were available without fees from at least one real-world, offline location, usually a record store.

The bike ride from Hoboken to Jersey City was about fifteen minutes. After some training sessions, Ira officially got a key to WFMU and, in June 2007, pulled his first shift as a fill-in DJ. The new world hadn't been wholly destructive to the old one. WFMU had escaped the dead college campus in East Orange and bought a modest building in downtown Jersey City, two blocks from the PATH train to the World Trade Center. No longer would DJs and bands tread through scary bus systems and questionable parking lot security. They'd liberated a few signs from the school buildings to decorate the new place.

Owned by Auricle Communications, a nonprofit corporation, its board of directors, including station manager Ken Freedman and others, kept WFMU operating as a noncommercial radio station. Committed to independent freedom of expression they still refused any kind of funding that would require them to thank sponsors on the air, relying almost entirely on their annual pledge drive, though diligently hunted down matching grants, including a large amount via New York attorney general Eliot Spitzer to found a Free Music Archive.

With the exception of a Monday-through-Friday show of *Jewish Moments in the Morning*—an important pledge base, no doubt—WFMU continued to pipe 1,250 watts of freeform music into the atmosphere. But by 2001, they'd gotten themselves online. As they maintained their transmitting tower in East Orange, they became, in one of their mottos, "the freeform station of the nation." But its reach went even further. Their terrestrial radio ratings sank in accordance with industry numbers, but WFMU's listenership remained steady.

As more and more colleges began to sell off their radio stations to deal with budget deficits, Ken Freedman organized seminars called "How to Save College Radio," which encouraged students to autonomize the way WFMU had and create a third-party organization to help.

Ira dubbed himself "Ira the K," after '60s DJ (and fifth Beatle) Murray the K, and picked up the occasional slot. Still exceedingly nocturnal, only partially by choice, he had no problem handling a few turns in the graveyard hours between two and six a.m., where he piloted the station board alone in the Jersey City studio until sunrise. Ira mixed selections from his own still-sprawling collection with music from the station's New Bin, selected by music director Brian Turner.

No slouch when it came to rock knowledge, Ira admitted the slots were "intimidating. In any category, there's stuff I like, but there's someone at WFMU who knows *everything* more than I do," he said. More fill-ins than not, he'd dedicate songs to Georgia, listening at home. He was on a half dozen times a year, when the band wasn't off somewhere.

A typical night might see him jump from topical songs about outer space from Sun Ra and The Scene Is Now to birthday wishes for Jerry Garcia, new psychedelic jammers Wooden Shjips to Randy Newman demos and novelty records, dropping in old favorites and dropping in droll mike breaks. He took advantage of freeform's non-boundaries. One Thanksgiving, he had his brother Neil—a WFMU regular—phone in a live reading of a shared favorite, Albert Brooks's participatory *Comedy Minus One* LP. In addition to their annual covers performances, Yo La Tengo could frequently be found at station events. A few times, James sat in to play underground hip-hop on Noah Uman's *Coffee Break with Heroes and Villains*.

Tom Scharpling's *Best Show on WFMU* had grown into the station's most popular program. With particular freeform logic, *Best Show* became an expansive and surreal conversation between the charismatic, curmudgeonly Scharpling, Jon Wurster, comedians, musicians, and a cast of bizarre regular callers, to whom the host acted the straight man. Scharpling wound up with writing jobs both for HBO's *Monk*, produced by WFMU DJ (and Hollywood script doctor) Andy Breckman and *Tim and Eric Awesome Show, Great Job!*

For the Marathon drives, during which Scharpling racked up bigger numbers with each passing year, he assembled new CD compilations, including a song-for-song tribute to Paul McCartney's *RAM* titled *TOM*, with tracks from Death Cab for Cutie, Ted Leo, Mac McCaughan's Portastatic, Dump, and others. It was the first activity for James's Dump alter-ego in some time.

With a somewhat accidental self-defeat, the most recent Dump album, *A Grown-Ass Man*, had been released on the same day as *Summer Sun*, but it'd been a productive run up until then. James had befriended Shrimper's founder, Dennis Callaci, and found a way to put out even more fussless records. Dump's 2001 collection of Prince covers—*That Skinny Motherfucker with the High Voice?*—had become an essential bootleg after it had been struck from the Shrimper catalog for copyright infringement but mostly because of James's wonderful reinventions of the Prince canon, transforming party jams like "Erotic City" and "1999" with cool vulnerability, singing the latter over a woozy 7/4 loop. After a half decade of inactivity, James had started to book the occasional Dump gig in a new duo lineup, as well, with bride-to-be Amy Posner on keyboards. The bassist remained active aside from Yo La Tengo, occasionally working with neighborhood friend and Def Jux producer El-P and others. He would soon learn more Japanese, building friendships with Yura Yura Teikoku—an underground Tokyo trio founded in 1989 who shared many similarities with Yo La Tengo—and others.

More than ever, it was obvious that Yo La Tengo was a band. During Hanukkah, James had taken responsibility for the mix CD-Rs they'd started to sell at the merch table every year, a different one each night put together by band members, friends, and associates ranging from novelist Jonathan Lethem to Japanese labelmate Cornelius to underground hip-hop figurehead RJD2. Organized and responsible, James assembled them all in his apartment.

Over the years he came up with perhaps dozens of answers to questions about whether he felt like a third wheel in Yo La

Tengo. "I don't even think about it," he would say, or "I get my own room on the road," or "Someone's got to hold the camera."

While he only lasted a few gigs in Antietam, Ira did become a semipermanent keyboardist for the A-Bones, who gigged once a month or more around the New York area. Georgia moonlighted too, with the Mad Scene, led by Hamish Kilgour of the Clean, mostly playing guitar.

"The thing that blows my mind is that [Ira's] been on a couple of road trips with us, which is utterly thankless," said A-Bones guitarist Bruce Bennett. "It's enough of a novelty for us that we don't mind sleeping on people's floors and stuff like that, but that's not those guys' scene at *all*. Nobody in that band has slept with their head next to a cat box in twenty years now."

Being an A-Bone opened up its own possibilities, especially as the band signed on for gigs backing Texan R&B songwriter Ray Sharpe, Flamin' Groovies leaders Roy Loney and Cyril Jordan, and others. Tied to the Ponderosa Stomp, a New Orleans festival and organization that overlapped happily with Norton Records, Yo La Tengo took a turn as well and played behind Louisiana swamp popper Tommy McLain at a show at Brooklyn's McCarren Pool.

"The only reasons the A-Bones stayed together were Magnetic Field and plane tickets from Spanish promoters," Bruce Bennett noted of the Brooklyn Heights club where the A-Bones played frequently and who, in early 2008, announced their imminent closing. Yo La Tengo joined the A-Bones for Magnetic Field's final night. Billed as the Condo Fucks, Ira, Georgia, and James took on a new song list of covers previously untouched by Yo La Tengo. Some of them were garagelike, like Cleveland forebears the Electric Eels and Richard Hell. Others, like the Kinks' "This Is Where I Belong" and "Shut Down" parts 1 and 2 by the Beach Boys, fit in with the closing theme of the night. Everything had feedback squealing around the edges, threatening to overtake the songs in the middle.

When Matador released James's more-or-less raw recording of the rehearsal, eventually titled *Fuckbook*, the sleeve saw the concept through all the way. The band got new names—Georgia Condo, in reference to the painter and onetime bassist in the Boston art-punk outfit the Girls—and a new history. Greenwich, Connecticut's Condo Fucks did not quite measure up to the level of self-obfuscation of bands like Times New Viking, their new labelmates on Matador whose "thing" sometimes got branded as "shitgaze," but it was arguably better than being lumped in with what the word "indie" had come to mean.

The new satellite radio merger SiriusXM had produced a new channel. "The roots of indie rock started on college campuses across North America," it claimed. "SiriusXM brings the spirit and the passion of those early days of indie rock with Classic College Radio!" Another piece of advertising copy read: "Re-live the days of alternative rock when it truly was an 'alternative,'" metalevels spiraling outward from the scare quotes.

If one critic had dismissed *Fuckbook*'s f-bomb tactics as "old nerds playing dress-up," he'd also misinterpreted the band's reasons for playing music. There was so much new product that, for music magazines, releases a few months old were often considered old news, their buzz depleted. *Fuckbook* might've been a few things—overdriven, a nom de plume—but it couldn't have been any less ambitious or interested in competition or shock or costumery.

New bands went viral with a quick vibration, and suddenly they were national or global. *Pitchfork* editor Ryan Schreiber picked Toronto's Broken Social Scene out of the site's promotional slush pile, gave them a 9.2, and that—plus FACTOR grants from the Canadian government—were all the ignition they needed. If the group that hung out and tried different things at its own pace had become rare in Manhattan, it had become equally rare in what Bill Wasik dubbed the "hipster archipelago," too. *Fuckbook* was an anti-assertion with no dress-up involved. Yo La Tengo had never needed a message, only excuses to play.

On tour, the band pursued another way to stay small, which

they titled the Freewheelin' Yo La Tengo. In their stripped-down setup—Ira on acoustic guitar, Georgia on snare and hi-hat only, James on electric bass—they planned out only a song or two before they asked for questions from the audience and spat back quick-witted answers while letting the subsequent conversational flow dictate the night's setlist. Even Georgia talked sometimes.

Though both concepts may have seemed continuations of their *Beat Your Ass* flaunted confidence, Freewheelin' was at least partly a solution to the theoretical problem of economic touring. They rented a minivan. Simply, it was a way to return to the graceful and mostly crewless years that allowed for diversions on the road. It was also something new to do, and a reason to play in places amenable to very quiet music, which they continued to enjoy. Kurt Wagner of Lambchop came along for a roll through the South.

One mark of the band's place in the firmament came just before Thanksgiving 2007, when the Writers Guild of America declared a strike. The details were arcane but had to do with the way the economic structures of the film and television industries would handle compensation and writing credit for new media, from viral video to reality shows. Some 12,000 unionized writers were suddenly on hiatus.

The cast of *Saturday Night Live* organized a one-off strike performance at the 150-seat Upright Citizens Brigade Theatre in Chelsea. Before a star-studded audience, the ensemble performed too-racy-for-network outtakes. The host was actor and awkward teen sensation Michael Cera. Yo La Tengo were the musical guests. They'd still never appeared on the actual show. Naturally, they pushed their still-current single, "Mr. Tough."

Several strike-challenged comedians from *The Daily Show*, *SNL*, and elsewhere soon found their way to Hoboken for the fifth installment of Hanukkah, back after a year off for *Beat Your Ass* tour duty. Reunions included the dB's, Redd Kross, and Versus. Mega-guests were My Morning Jacket frontman

Jim James (night 3), the New Pornographers (night 7), essayist Sarah Vowell (night 5), and *SNL* star Amy Poehler (night 5). Plus the Clean; new Matador signees and YLT tour buddies Times New Viking; and Dew-Claw, led by Hypnolovewheel's Stephen Hunking and featuring Dave Rick on guitar, who joined YLT onstage for the first time in twenty years.

Most specially, Alex Chilton came up from New Orleans for extended encores over the weekend and joined the band for the kind of happily tossed-off covers they'd learned, in large part, by watching him.

"It's a Saturday mitzvah," piped up one of the band's younger relatives from the front row of the back room.

"With or without a menorah," Ira added. The electric menorah, balanced as usual between Georgia and James, had a handwritten Out of Order sign affixed to it.

"What does that mean?" the Tennessee-born Chilton asked.

"She said, 'It's a Saturday mitzvah,' which is a good thing," Ira explained. "So, with or without a menorah, it's a good thing." He paused. "Just kind of beatnik jive talk."

It earned a laugh, but the joy of that interaction—Yo La Tengo and Alex Chilton together at Maxwell's singing Big Star's "Jesus Christ" over the holidays—*was* kind of beatnik jive talk. Since Ira's days as a barely legal columnist, he'd been near the center of the still-cozy community of first-generation obsessives lumped under the "indie" umbrella for their self-made jobs as music journalists and DJs and label magnates and promoters.

Maxwell's over Hanukkah became a place where the ley lines entangled, where one could step into the eight-days-a-week continuum between the Velvet Underground at Max's Kansas City and the eternal now of live music. For eight utopian nights, it is what a band at a local bar might feel like anywhere— everyday life blown into magical detail.

When Alex Chilton died suddenly of a heart attack a year and change after he appeared at Maxwell's, most who'd caught his extended encores with Yo La Tengo surely thought of the Hanukkah mitzvah. But it is also doubtful that anyone present at Maxwell's didn't know, at that exact moment, exactly how special Chilton's appearance was, and feel the warm, amazed glow that people often try to channel by invoking the far-off innocence of a Christmas morning.

Twenty-five years into Georgia and Ira's musical relationship, Yo La Tengo's shows were a ritualistic celebration of something that wasn't mysterious at all but clearly, unambiguously good, and achieved in an honest, transparent way. They were a band that was *exactly* the sum of its parts, of three talented and driven musicians whose entire personal and professional lives grew from a carefully monitored tumble between chance and uncompromising logic. No one in Yo La Tengo, least of all Ira, had any more of a game plan in the early twenty-first century than they had twenty-five years earlier. They could only move from decision to decision as they always had, with an eye on some light, somewhere, that couldn't be compromised.

In the American marketplace, the signifiers known as "indie" remained fashionable. That same holiday season of *Saturday Night Live* and Alex Chilton, *Juno*—a caffeinated modern comedy about teen pregnancy filled with Sonic Youth T-shirts—was a box-office smash. Its soundtrack joined Zach Braff's *Garden State* as the latest band-breaking phenomenon. In this case, the breakouts were the Moldy Peaches, a costume-wearing anti-folk duo from the East Village who'd actually disbanded a few years earlier.

An oft-repeated story about the film's music direction was that the Moldy Peaches had been chosen by teenage star Ellen Page herself. Director Ivan Reitman and writer Diablo Cody's original concept had featured a soundtrack comprised entirely of Yo La Tengo songs.

In Hoboken, Yo La Tengo had familiar new neighbors, about to record their Matador debut in their own loft across the Neumann Leathers lot. By the time Sonic Youth released *Rather Ripped*, the last album of their eighteen-year, nine-album, major-label experiment, the name "Geffen Records" on the album art was virtually an ancient rune, long since gulped into the Universal Music Group, David Geffen himself a decade into other ventures.

Sonic Youth and Gerard Cosloy had made peace around the same time the band relocated their Echo Canyon studio from lower Manhattan to downtown Hoboken. After the ease of *Fuckbook*, Yo La Tengo, too, began to contemplate the virtues of recording at home, which they'd done for more and more of their soundtracks.

The band had quickly grown to love their Neumann Leathers space, a short bike ride from Georgia and Ira's place. It was a wide room with space for their road cases, Faith's old piano, drum parts, baffling, lots of ephemera, and a permanent place to leave their gear set up in the middle. The cue cards for their off-air *Saturday Night Live* appearance hung over the couch.

When the building's owners threatened to turn the complex into condos, Yo La Tengo was all too ready to headline a benefit at Maxwell's to preserve it. Though they closed with the Flamin' Groovies' "You Tore Me Down," for once the benefit helped, and the band's practice space was saved. Former City Council president Richard Del Boccio argued that Neumann Leathers' tenants represented one of the last sources of exported industry in Hoboken. The zoning board rejected the condo plans unanimously.

It was an excellent home base to have. For most bands Yo La Tengo's age and a quarter century into a career, later years often see a natural thinning of activity, especially between album and tour cycles. For smaller acts, slow periods might be caused by the increasing responsibilities of life, jobs or families or diminishing returns on the road. For larger bands, it might stem from success itself, with no reason to get together five days a week when not touring or recording, band members maybe even living in different cities. As a compact unit—they only had to support two households, after all, and no children—Yo La Tengo had plenty of advantages. They also still loved to play.

As they made plans to record another album, there was high-profile work to attend to, like a gig on *Conan O'Brien* as the backing band for Merge artists She & Him, the indie-folk super-duo of songwriter M. Ward and actress Zooey Deschanel. There was also another visit to South by Southwest that consisted of more gigs than ever, including parties for the Independent Film Channel (with My Morning Jacket) and Other Music (playing the opening song in honor of the show's locale, the French Legation Museum: Jacques Dutronc's "Et Moi, Et Moi, Et Moi"). But there was legitimate family business, too, with the release of Emily Hubley's feature debut, *The Toe Tactic*, which fused live action and animation with a full YLT score.

Roger Moutenot came to Neumann Leathers. Songs pushed, sometimes strained, into new territories, such as the dense, keyboard-driven single "Here to Fall," which featured strings by Richard Evans, a '60s bassist for the Sun Ra Arkestra who'd gone on to become a '70s soul-jazz arranger for the likes of harpist Dorothy Evans and vocalist Marlena Shaw. But there was plenty that sounded like Yo La Tengo, sometimes elegantly, such as the *And Then Nothing*–like Georgia ballad, "By Two's" (typoed intentionally in honor of a high-modernist painting by Barnett Newman). "If It's True" was, after so many years, the band's first his/hers pop original, as lighter-than-air and hummable as it was textured and complex.

Titled *Popular Songs*, the seventy-three minutes once again made for a double-LP. Three long jams lived on the second disc. "I don't think it's coincidental that we haven't done it before," Ira noted of the sequencing. "There was just something about watching it all explode in the end."

"It's easy to overlook the sound that's on display through the bulk of *Popular Songs* as more of the same," Rob Mitchum wrote in *Pitchfork*, "but it's also uniquely Yo La Tengo in a way that has taken 25 years to reach vintage status."

As part of Matador's "Buy Early, Get Now" campaign, one of the label's many active attempts to keep listeners purchasing their wares, fans were offered mp3s of a pair of album demos. Both were fairly long and sounded almost nothing like the album tracks whose names they bore, "Periodically Double or Triple" and "Nothing to Hide," the album's two singles.

On the former, with piano, an echoed drum-machine beat,

distended loop, and synth-patch string swells, Ira sings what sounds like a pretty complete set of lyrics over a logical movement through different sections of a song that establishes a mood closer to mysterioso string-funk than the bopping confection it became in its final conception. Except for the faintest glimmer, it is a wholly different song. "Nothing to Hide," as well, barely resembles what it would become, a long guitar jam with a few particular changes that—each time they come to them—sound just about right. In each case, one hears why the band needed to keep going, able to make something intriguing to themselves, still, after all this time.

For the September record release in New York, the band filled the cavernous Roseland Ballroom, a 3,200-capacity swing-era hall with a sweeping balcony that was their biggest headlining show to date. *Daily Show* correspondent John Oliver, who'd charmed everyone with his British pronunciation of "Hoboken" at Hanukkah, hosted. The Black Lips opened, and Susquehanna Tool & Die Co. played in the lobby. Behind the band was a giant screen, where the Joshua Light Show—along with *Beat Your Ass* cover painter Gary Panter—provided visuals.

Yo La Tengo had first played with the Joshua Light Show a few years before, at Anthology Film Archives, the venerable theater founded by avant-garde filmmaker and critic Jonas Mekas just down Second Avenue from the site of the old Fillmore East. The band had improvised three sets behind a screen while the Joshua Light crew fragmented James Brown concert footage off a disco ball, among other psychedelic tricks.

Popular Songs entered the Top 200 at #58, but despite generally positive reviews, "Nothing to Hide" failed to ignite at XMU, the new indie-leaning station on satellite radio following XM and Sirius's summer 2008 merger. The album sold poorly—less than 100,000 copies in its first six months—and effectively boggled the band, who'd been generally good at ignoring album sales reports. Shows continued to sell out, but even bigger questions loomed in view for Yo La Tengo and independent bands of their ilk, posed in no better form than the name of *Popular Songs*.

"There are a lot of reasons that the title appealed to us," Ira remembered. "I'm not sure we've even thought about the reasons it seems to resonate." One way that it did was to call into relief the ways that fandom, the very conceit on which Georgia, Ira, and the band had come together, had evolved into something harder and harder to recognize.

The nationwide vinyl resurgence was illustrative of what popularity truly meant. There had been perhaps a half dozen "vinyl is back" moments since the cassette surpassed the format in the mid-'70s, but there were the numbers to prove it this time. In 2008, Rainbo Records, a seventy-year-old plant in California and one of the country's largest, reported it had switched to twenty-four-hour-a-day operation to meet the new demand. The year before, a coalition of store owners had organized a National Record Store Day where labels could sell exclusive releases and drive customers to shops. The second edition resulted in the highest day for vinyl sales since 1991.

Stores held parties and shows. In Brooklyn, Yo La Tengo DJed. The reunited dB's issued their first new music with Chris Stamey in twenty-five years and played at Atlanta's Criminal Records, owned by Record Store Day cofounder Eric Levin, a longtime fan. But despite the sales, vinyl barely charted in the bigger scheme of the music industry.

As the economy began its freefall during the last years of President George W. Bush's second term, more and more pillars of indie rock's old world seemed to topple daily into ruin. Colleges sold their FM bandwidth to National Public Radio affiliates and other high bidders. Touch and Go, the important Chicago-based label and distributor, downsized almost to nonexistence. Several national ad-driven music magazines reverted to volunteer staffs of writers, who inadvertently evoked the zine era in their pro bono copy filings. Another prominent magazine, *The Fader*, found a business model as the publishing wing of a marketing firm, Cornerstone.

While bohemia and economics had collided during the

first tech boom, the second caused the seemingly irreparable entwining of demographics and fandom. Blogs had seemed like clearly visible conversations, and a natural enough continuation of zine culture. But a wave of new technologies broke through quickly thereafter, from the embeddable video of YouTube to the band-organizing platforms of MySpace. Social networks like Facebook and Twitter combined for nearly one billion worldwide users by the turn of the decade.

The vaster conversation about music increasingly collapsed into smaller and smaller spaces as users became channels unto themselves, broadcasting pithy thoughts and cultural preferences to the networks around them. Communal acts of fandom, once shaped by local customs specific to one's subcultural niche, were flattened into a monochromatic array of statistically quantifiable clicks.

With new numbers to crunch, the corporate sponsorship of rock continued to redefine "independence" in even newer and unimagined ways. Bands that recorded primarily for small indie labels, such as California's Best Coast and Wavves, released music exclusively through sponsors such as Converse, longtime manufacturer of Ira's footwear of choice. The shoe company also announced plans to open Rubber Tracks, a 5,200-square-foot recording studio in Brooklyn.

OK Go, guided by former YLT manager Jamie Kitman, split from their major-label contract and partnered with State Farm Insurance, Samsung mobile phones, Range Rover, and other giant companies to fund their popular YouTube videos. It wasn't selling out, they argued. It was "buying in."

Despite the craziness, or perhaps because of it, indie rock's cycles continued, sometimes at hilariously accelerated speeds, speaking unfathomable new lingo: new waves of fans to fall madly in love with new waves of albums, songs, artists, scenes, labels, microtrends, and tags to describe American underground rock.

Even *Hipster Runoff*, a blog dedicated to a piercingly satirical take on buzz bands, didn't have much with which to needle Yo La Tengo. When they deconstructed Amazon's Top 100 indie albums, which ranked *I Can Hear the Heart Beating as One* at #20, they commented, "Think that they are probably 'good' but seem 'old.' Was probably 'cooler' to like them 8 years ago."

While bands like *Pitchfork* favorites LCD Soundsystem sold out Madison Square Garden, music recognized as indie rock frequently sounded more like disco, an unexpected circle to close. In American music criticism, "rock" became a dirty word, as it had in the United Kingdom in 1981, spawning heated debates between so-called rockists and poptimists. Situated in the former camp, old-fashioned Velvet Underground fans might all but be accused of racism for their elevation of the electric guitar in the pop dialogue. But of the ten guitar-oriented bands among the top fifteen full-lengths on the *Village Voice*'s 2011 Pazz and Jop Critics Poll, Yo La Tengo was only a step removed from a half dozen of them, either via friends, recent co-bills, or record-company affiliation. Arcade Fire, recording for Mac McCaughan and Laura Ballance's Merge, took home a Grammy for Album of the Year.

In Austin, Gerard Cosloy continued to pump out blog posts, tweets, and merciless late-night insults. Though he'd lost a lifetime's worth of arcana in a 2009 house fire, it did nothing to dim his affection for the local scene. In 2010, Matador issued *Casual Victim Pile*, a blistering nineteen-track compilation of new Austin punk bands. The next year, Gerard revived 12XU to do a vinyl-only sequel with another eighteen groups.

Around the borough of Manhattan, Georgia, Ira, and James still got out more nights than not when they were home, seeming to hit every gig by every one of their friends' bands, or check out something new, be it a film or gig or restaurant or a weird Korean spa or a Knicks game or something else entirely. Like their record-company owner, they operated on the faith of total fans that, no matter what, at all times there was something amazing going on somewhere.

In late 2010, "Mr. Tough" appeared on the season finale of *Bored to Death*, an HBO series penned by novelist Jonathan Ames and that starred sensitive indie heartthrob Jason Schwartzman. (Like many actors his age, Schwartzman had his own indie band too, Coconut Records.) The track's inclusion owed much to Ira's former Music for Dozens partner Michael Hill, whose new job had him supervising music for various cable series.

On one hand, Yo La Tengo were more willing to place songs than ever. The alternate "Today Is the Day" had even featured in *MLB2K6*, a baseball video game. But for the most part, the new independence looked a lot like the old independence: a navigation of the music world via collaborators they trusted. And if one of those options wasn't available, they could feel it out otherwise, as when they scored a mainstream summer teen comedy in Greg Mottola's 2009 film, *Adventureland*, their first non-independent film gig.

All too appropriately for a Yo La Tengo jaunt into corporate America, the film was released by Miramax, a division of Disney, a relationship that put a Hubley in the employ of the Mouse for the first time in more than a half century. Director Greg Mottola recalled how hard it had been to convince the band to contribute. "They wanted some assurance that the music wouldn't end up in *Escape to Witch Mountain 2* or something." The film opened at #6 nationwide, Yo La Tengo's soundtrack humming out from almost two thousand screens.

They played the first American installment of All Tomorrow's Parties, the small-scale, sponsor-free British festival, at a decaying Borscht Belt resort with their reunited guitar-noise peers in Dinosaur Jr. and My Bloody Valentine. The festival helped establish a new trend in indie rock: bands playing their classic albums in their entirety. Sonic Youth had done *Daydream Nation*. Dinosaur Jr. did *You're Living All Over Me*. Dozens got into the act. The Feelies, who'd reunited that year, did *Crazy Rhythms*—but they'd never had a problem playing the same songs in the same order anyway.

Yo La Tengo continued to resist the nostalgia. When City Slang requested that they perform *Fakebook* to mark its twentieth anniversary as well as the founding of the German label, they declined, though happily brought Dave Schramm to

Berlin to play an acoustic-oriented set in the spirit of the album.

They also established a connection with the enormously popular band Wilco, a continuation of one of their longest-running relationships. Wilco frontman Jeff Tweedy was married to Sue Miller, once part-owner of Chicago's Lounge Ax and who had booked Yo La Tengo's first Second City appearance in April 1986 at West End (bassist: Mike Lewis) and many subsequent gigs. Though they hadn't stayed in touch, Tweedy had opened for Yo La Tengo (bassist: Stephan) in 1987, during his band Uncle Tupelo's first trip to St. Louis, the nearest big city to their hometown of Belleville, Illinois.

With Wilco, they opened the occasional show in a Minor League Baseball stadium, such as Coney Island's KeySpan Park (now MCU Park), where they used the visitors' clubhouse as a dressing room and came out of the dugout waving. In South Bend, Indiana, they played Stanley Coveleski Regional Stadium, named for the Indians pitcher who first uttered the phrase "a worrying thing." Later, most of Wilco would visit Hoboken over various nights of Hanukkah, where the old barriers between big and small felt imaginary again, at least when Yo La Tengo was around, music at its natural scale.

Wilco, along with other bigger bands that Yo La Tengo began to share bills with, such as My Morning Jacket and the National, had carved a new space in American music in a promised land beyond major labels, jam-band earnestness (and audiences), and indie sensibilities. They toured a lot and began to play guest-filled multinight runs of their own.

Another such veteran act that Yo La Tengo increasingly crossed paths with was the Flaming Lips, who had recently covered "Sugarcube" with the Oklahoma City Philharmonic. Singer Wayne Coyne declared *Popular Songs* one of his favorite albums of all time. Justin Vernon, a twentysomething folk-singer known as Bon Iver, took the same demographic by storm, sometimes performing a cover of *Beat Your Ass*'s "I Feel Like Going Home." A newer New Jersey via Brooklyn act, Real Estate, talked of their love for Yo La Tengo and the Feelies.

YouTube brimmed with other such tributes: A California street performer named Winston K did "Season of the Shark." The glossy L.A. indie-pop outfit Airborne Toxic Event did an oddly note-for-note "Sugarcube," the band's most popular tune by that particular metric. A new buzz band from England called Yuck claimed their influence from '80s American indie pop. "We had a massive Yo La Tengo phase," their guitarist would claim. "I'm not saying that's ended." They named one of their songs "Georgia."

The next year would see Yo La Tengo stage a new tour that featured an audience-spun wheel of chance (borrowed from WFMU) to determine the first set of the night from wedges that represented Painlevé-less *Sounds of Science* perfor-mances, Dump (with Georgia and Ira backing), the Free-wheelin' Yo La Tengo, songs that began with "s" (for which they learned *Electr-o-Pura*'s previously unplayed "(Straight Down to the) Bitter End"), and titles that featured people's names. There was also a wheel wedge labeled "Sitcom Theater," for which they would be booed in Chicago during a table reading of a *Seinfeld* episode, "The Chinese Restaurant"—a whole new kind of Jewish-penned cover and a remarkable achievement for a twenty-six-year-old, to cheerfully provoke their generally mild-mannered fan base to jeers. At another show, they read through the episode of *Judge Judy* where Johnny Rotten's for-mer drummer sued him for breach of contract and assault.

And when occasionally they would play the type of room that was too big, where the audience might be hearing the drums through the PA rather than directly from Georgia's sticks, and the scale of everything started to swerve help-lessly off-course, there was always Hoboken. James would strike up a friendship with the Brooklyn band Oneida, and play bass and drums for the duration of one of their legendary ten-hour gigs.

They would ponder whether to release another album, if it would be a worthwhile way to communicate themselves in the second decade of the twenty-first century, or if there was some better way to do it. It was another choice to make, but first to think, worry, and think some more about.

"We don't ever want to do things just because an alarm clock goes off and it's time to make a record," Ira said. "We want to feel like we're doing something smart at the right time. So a lot of things go into thinking about that. It's hard to know what to make of this world."

In late 2010, Yo La Tengo lingered, as well, on the *New York Times* best-seller list in much the same way they'd dominated MTV in the "Glory Days" video twenty-five years earlier. This time it was a tiny, innocuous cameo-by-reference in Jonathan Franzen's latest novel, *Freedom*.

But for Georgia, Ira, and James, there was just Hanukkah to handle, a new batch of guests (most of Wilco, a reunited Mofungo, Mission of Burma), and a new batch of covers. Since the first Georgia and Those Guys shows, and the WFMU benefit gigs, they'd now tried well over a thousand songs over the years. There was a children's chorus from the Elysian Charter School of Hoboken who would sing heartrending versions of "Sugarcube," "Stockholm Syndrome," and "Mr. Tough." They'd gotten as far as the answering machine of Victor "Moulty" Moulton, the one-armed, hook-handed Barbarians drummer immortalized on the *Nuggets* box, Ira hearing the same distinct voice that delivered the monologue on the 1966 Barbarians single. But Moulty didn't make it.

During the afternoon of the first Hanukkah gig of 2010, employees milled around the club, hung advance schedules for the next few months of shows, and prepared for the eight sold-out nights. Yo La Tengo was in and out of the back room, getting ready for a show that would feature M. Ward, Todd Barry, and Gene DiNapoli, also known as "New York Elvis."

By the door to the kitchen, James stopped, stared at the wall, stared at the wall again, and fired off a tweet from the band's account alongside a photo of the club's posted calendar and uncharacteristic triple punctuation.

"Come on @maxwellsnj, seriously???" it read.

Blocked out for eight nights were the venue's favorite children, "Yo La Tango."

Acknowledgments

Thank you to Paul Blanding, for playing me "Green Arrow" in the desert.

Thank you to my mom and dad, Lois, Mel, Jeanette, and Bea, for making it possible that I could get to the desert in the first place.

Again (and again), Caitlin.

To the Heads: Bill Stites and Ariella Stok.

Thank you to my agent, Paul Bresnick, for making this book into reality, even if he spelled it "Yo La Tenga" for a few months, and my editor, Patrick Mulligan, and associate editor Travers Johnson. Thank you to Jason Gross and Will Hermes for pointing me in the correct direction.

My first stop after confirming that this book was happening was Kenneth Thomas of the Sunsquashed site, who kindly provided me with thousands of hours of Yo La Tengo recordings, plus lots of other goodies. Likewise, much research would not have been possible without the lovely assistance of Dave Rick, who graciously provided his collections of *New York Rocker* and *Conflict* on extended loan.

To every editor who ever let me cover Yo La Tengo or other music I love, especially Pete Gershon (who assigned initial features about Yo La Tengo and WFMU for *Signal to Noise*), Josh Jackson at *Paste*, Josh Baron at *Relix*, Rob Harvilla and Maura Johnston at the *Village Voice*, and Grayson Currin at *Indy Week*.

To Ken Freedman, Brian Turner, Liz Berg, and all WFMU DJs past or present, especially overnighters. To Andy Schwartz, Laura Levine, and everybody listed on every masthead of *New York Rocker*. To Nils Bernstein and the staff at Matador Records, Todd Abramson and Maxwell's.

To people who got things done (specifically facilitated the arrival of very useful information in my hands or on my computer screen): Meghan Eckman, Howard Wuelfling, Bertis Downs, Mary Mancini, Jeff Roth at *The New York Times*, Fales Library at NYU, Hoboken City Clerk's office, Hudson County Register of Deeds, Hoboken Historical Society, Hoboken Public Library, Sanborn Maps, archive.org, Brooklyn Public Library, Jim Testa, Byron Coley, John Thorn, Emily Hubley, and Scott Williams.

To various pals and YLT brahs who helped with reading, moral support, scanning, fact-checking, leads, recordings, and general righteousness, both short-term and long: Ted Barron, Chris Pascerella, Jack Chester, Michael Slaboch, Michael Barthel, Anthony Weiss, Dom DeVito, Neil DeMause, Dan Lynch, Jeff Lazar, Liz Clayton, Holly George-Warren, Richard Gehr, Matt Van Brink, Tim Holmes, Gabrielle Kerson, Karen Griswold, Aaron Mullan, Rob Mitchum, Grayson Currin, Chris Weingarten, Jon Sumber, Brian Robbins, Jürgen Fauth, Charles Morogiello, Barry Smolin, Russell Kahn, Akron/Family, Megafaun, Oneida, Mike Rosenthal, Shannon Forney, Vlada Fengenev, Studio 77, and 315 Seigel Street.

Double-thanks to everybody on the interviews list.

To the copy editors at Gotham Books for surviving a manuscript with both Janet Waegal and Janet Wygal.

And, like, totally: Georgia, Ira, and James.

Notes

In addition to the interviews, books, and articles listed below, several other resources were used. For "The Elysian Fields" prologue, I consulted property records at the Hoboken City Clerk's office, Hudson County Register of Deeds in Jersey City, as well as Sanborn fire insurance maps, the Hoboken Historical Society, the Hoboken Public Library, and the New York Public Library. A lot of other information came from a hard drive containing several hundred Yo La Tengo live recordings from 1985 to the present, as well as scanned YLT ephemera, archives of the Yo La Tengo e-mail digest, and other material. Also worthy of additional shout-outs are Megan Eckman, who generously provided transcripts of interviews conducted for her *Parking Lot Movie*, as well as the blessed website that is archive.org, which saved me on a daily basis from the dreaded 404s.

Bassists

Dave Schramm (*Georgia and Those Guys*, 1983)
Terry Karydes (*A Worrying Thing*, 1982–1983)
Dave Rick (1984–1985)
Mike Lewis (1985–1986)
Clint Conley (1986)
Steve Michener (1986)
Stephan Wichnewski (1986–1989)
Chris Stamey (1986)

Wolf Knapp (1988)
Tony Maimone (1988)
Robert Vickers (1989)
Al Greller (1990)
Gene Holder (1990)
Wilbo Wright (1990–1991)
Janet Wygal (1990)
Tim Harris (1991)
James McNew (1991–present)

Interviewees

Todd Abramson, Maxwell's
John Beers, Happy Flowers
Bruce Bennett, the A-Bones
Rob Berends, Paperclip Agency
Nils Bernstein, Matador Records
Fred Brockman, the Kinetics
Rick Brown, Information, Fish and Roses
Irwin Chusid, WFMU
Byron Coley, writer
Clint Conley, Mission of Burma
Gerard Cosloy, *Conflict*, Homestead Records, Matador
  Records
Michael Cudahy, Christmas
Steve Daly, Coyote Records
Guy Ewald, Maxwell's
Jim DeRogatis, *Jersey Beat*
Jad Fair, Half Japanese
Steve Fallon, Maxwell's
Gaylord Fields, WFMU
Ken Freedman, WFMU
Bobbie Gale, Atlantic Records
Sue Garner, Fish and Roses
Karen Glauber, A&M Records
Danny Goldberg, Atlantic Records
Richard Grabel, *New York Rocker*

Mark Greenberg, The Coctails
Tim Harris, Antietam
Michael Hill, *New York Rocker*
Nicholas Hill, WFMU
Gene Holder, the dB's
Peter Holsapple, the dB's
Emily Hubley, filmmaker, sister
Georgia Hubley, Yo La Tengo
Stephen Hunking, Hypnolovewheel
Lyle Hysen, Das Damen
Adam Kaplan, brother
Ira Kaplan, Yo La Tengo
Neil Kaplan, brother
Terry Karydes, A Worrying Thing
Tara Key, Antietam
David Kilgour, the Clean
Hamish Kilgour, the Clean
Jamie Kitman, manager
Wolf Knapp, Antietam
Bob Lawton, booking agent
Laura Levine, *New York Rocker*
Michael Lewis, Lyres
Chris Lombardi, Matador Records
Craig Marks, Homestead Records
Sabir Mateen, Other Dimensions in Music
Mac McCaughan, Superchunk
Mike McGonigal, *Chemical Imbalance*
James McNew, Yo La Tengo
Glenn Mercer, the Feelies
Bill Million, the Feelies
Phil Milstein, What Goes On
Phil Morrison, filmmaker
Glenn Morrow, *New York Rocker*
Jim Napolitano, Maxwell House
Chris Nelson, *New York Rocker*
Peter Occhiogrosso, *SoHo Weekly News*
Dave Rick, Yo La Tengo

Will Rigby, the dB's

Rick Rizzo, Eleventh Dream Day

Kevin Salem, Yo La Tengo

Tom Scharpling, WFMU

Dave Schramm, Yo La Tengo

Andy Schwartz, *New York Rocker*

Steve Sheldon, Rainbo Records

Robert Sietsema, Mofungo

Maynard Sipe, the Maynards

Richard M. Smith, landlord

Chris Stamey, the dB's

Paul Stark, Twin/Tone Records

Jim Testa, *Jersey Beat*

Roy Trakin, *SoHo Weekly News*

Brian Turner, WFMU

Michael Vickers, Go-Betweens

Janet Waegal, *New York Rocker*

Kurt Wagner, Lambchop

Ken Weinstein, Atlantic Records

Janet Wygal, the Individuals

Sources

Introduction: The Story of Yo La Tango

1 *"Wo La Tengo"*: Maxwell's ad, *Village Voice*, January 30, 1985.
1 *"Not exac. clear"*: Gerard Cosloy, "Yo La Tengo, CBGB's 2/22/86," *Conflict*, February 1986.
1 *There was a show:* "Top Billing" via http://yolatengo .com/fun.html.
2 *"yo la tengo!"*: Roger Angell, *Five Seasons*, p. 73.
2 *"Doesn't matter what you did"*: Lawrence Ritter, *The Glory of Their Times*, p. 123.
4 *"Some of those bands"*: "The Bashful Basher," *DRUM!* magazine, February 2001.
5 *"Exceptionally well-connected"*: Robert Christgau, "Consumer Guide," *Village Voice*, September 5, 1989.
6 *There's always been*: Neil Kaplan, "Making It Work: The Story of My Stabbing," *The New York Times*, January 21, 1996.
8 *"It was another way"*: "It Takes Three To Tengo," *New York* magazine, May 12, 1997.

Prologue: The Elysian Fields

10 *"I found a Scotch saddler"*: John Thorn, *Baseball in the Garden of Eden*, p. 33.

10 *"We used to have dinner"*: Monica Nucciarone,
      Alexander Cartwright, p. 147.

12 *"the largest using"*: "News and Notes of the Advertising
      Field," *The New York Times*, May 3, 1939.

Chapter 1: The Hudson Line

18 *"A Community of Your Kind"*: As reproduced in Jane
      Northshield, *History of Croton-on-Hudson*, p. 156.

20 *"I remember vividly"*: On recording of Yo La Tengo,
      January 10, 2008, Carrboro, NC.

20 *"a set for a"*: Linda Greenhouse, "Feminist Effort Grows
      in Croton," *The New York Times*, April 5, 1970.

23 *"Dots have taught"*: "Dots Obsession—Love
      Transformed Into Dots," Haus der Kunst, February
      2007, gallery notes.

24 *"It seemed kinda natural"*: "It's kinda like nothing
      matters as much as music," *Florida Times-Union*,
      September 12, 2003.

24 *"I don't think that I ever"*: Ibid.

25 *"It was completely"*: *chickfactor*, spring 1995.

26 *"And then, ladies and gentlemen"*: "Kinks Mania (Would
      You Believe?) In Central Park," *Melody Maker*,
      September 1972.

30 *"the father of"*: Ira Kaplan, "My Dozen," *eMusic.com*,
      May 2006.

31 *"Lou Reed is back"*: Danny Fields in Schinder, *Alt-
      Rock-A-Rama*, p. 24.

31 *"Although the Geeks"*: Kaplan, "The Epistemological
      Ontology (on a Non-Verbal Level) of the Geeks," *SoHo
      Weekly News*, November 3, 1977.

32 *"Once people pass"*: Kaplan, "Swinging Singles," *SoHo
      Weekly News*, February 2, 1978.

32 *"I love NRBQ"*: Kaplan, "Songs to Sing in the Shower,"
      SoHo Weekly News, March 16, 1978.

33 *"It's rock and roll reality"*: Kaplan, "Beserkley Non-
      Chartbusters," *SotHo Weekly News*, April 6, 1978.

33 *"Even if they never"*: Kaplan, "Heartbreakers/Cutthroats
        at Max's Kansas City," *New York Rocker*, June 1979.

Chapter 2: New York Rockers

36 *"I managed to catch"*: Kaplan, "Rocks Off," *SoHo Weekly
        News*, November 9, 1978.
36 *"I had a friend"*: *chickfactor*, Spring 1995.
37 *"The stage show's"*: Ira Kaplan, "The KISS Are Alright,"
        SoHo Weekly News, August 30, 1979.
37 *"American Punk Rock"*: "Collector of Rock Scene Faces
        Crisis," *The New York Times*, December 17, 1972.
39 *"I took over this paper"*: Andy Schwartz, "To Our
        Readers," *New York Rocker*, February 1978.
40 *"rock warlord"*: Fred Goodman, *The Mansion on the Hill*,
        photo inset.
50 *"Apart from a few"*: "Byron Coley," *Vice Rettsounds*
        blog, June 3, 2011.

Chapter 3: At Home with the Maypos

53 *"Our parents' stuff"*: "Emily and Georgia Hubley of the
        Royal Family of Animation," chickfactor.com, 2002.
53 *"a great relaxation"*: "A Family That Profits from
        Fantasy," *The New York Times*, January 24, 1967.
53 *"I remember feeling happy"*: "Emily and Georgia Hubley of
        the Royal Family of Animation," chickfactor.com, 2002.
53 *"I couldn't really explain"*: Ibid.
54 *"had wonderful teachers"*: "Faith Hubley: An
        Interview," *Film Quarterly*, Winter 1988–1989.
55 *"I think my parents"*: Ibid.
55 *"Darling, we didn't"*: Ibid.
56 *"I owed the world"*: Ibid.
57 *"Kind of like"*: "A Cel of One's Own," *New York* magazine,
        April 12, 1993.
57 *"Who the hell"*: Richard Schickel, *The Disney Version*,
        p. 153.

57 *"It was very modern"*: Michael Denning, *The Cultural Front*, p. 417.

57 *"We have but one"*: Schickel, *The Disney Version*, p. 153.

58 *"very far into"*: Amid Amidi, *Cartoon Modern*, p. 140.

58 *"I am an artist"*: Scott Bruce and Bill Crawford, *Cerealizing America*.

59 *"he had started"*: "Faith Hubley: An Interview," *Film Quarterly*, Winter 1988–1989.

59 *"anthropomorphic wash"*: Amidi, *Cartoon Modern*, p. 95.

59 *"He wasn't sure"*: "Faith Hubley: An Interview," *Film Quarterly*, Winter 1988–1989.

60 *"It was like being kids"*: Ibid.

60 *"one-minute documentary"*: Ibid.

61 *"We heard the boys"*: Susan Saccoccia, "Legendary Animator Carries on Tradition," *Christian Science Monitor*, November 24, 1995.

61 *"The last commercial"*: Joshua Klein, "Faith Hubley," *The A. V. Club*, March 22, 2000.

62 *"They started to punish"*: Ibid.

63 *"I thought this was"*: "Faith Hubley: An Interview," *Film Quarterly*, Winter 1988–1989.

66 *"No, no, no, no"*: "It Takes Three to Tengo," *New York* magazine, May 12, 1997.

Chapter 4: Music for Dozens

68 *"I keep up"*: "I Read New Rocker" by the dB's, from *Ride the Wild Tom Tom*, Rhino, 1993.

70 *"the Bongos are proud"*: Kaplan, "SoHo A-Go-Go," *SoHo Weekly News*, October 8, 1980.

72 *"We don't go"*: Greg McLean, "Up & Down with the Feelies," *New York Rocker*, June 1980.

73 *"We're seasonal thinkers"*: "Update: The Feelies," *New York Rocker*, February 1982.

73 *"Songs that are"*: McLean, "Up & Down with the Feelies," *New York Rocker*, June 1980.

73 *"I don't think music"*: Ibid.

75 *"I'm sure I was"*: Richard Barone, *Frontman*, p. 73.

75 *"The only thing"*: Kaplan, "In A Sense Abroad," *SoHo Weekly News*, March 4, 1981.

76 *"We thought it"*: Gina Arnold, *Route 666*, p. 86.

76 *"You can bet"*: Kaplan, "In A Sense Abroad," *SoHo Weekly News*, March 4, 1981.

76 *"When he finally"*: Barone, *Frontman*, p. 74.

76 *"The English simply"*: Arnold, *Route 666*, p. 86.

76 *"I didn't bother"*: Ira Kaplan, "In A Sense Abroad," *SoHo Weekly News*, March 4, 1981.

77 *"We hated England"*: Arnold, *Route 666*, p. 86.

78 *"pioneering efforts have led"*: "Demons of DOR," *New York Rocker*, July 1981.

78 *"The space is tentatively"*: Michael Hill, "Maxwell's Last Dance," *New York Rocker*, September 1981.

79 *"It remains, without"*: Kaplan, "SoHo A-Go-Go," *SoHo Weekly News*, September 22, 1981.

79 *"They're level-headed"*: Vic Varney, "Athens, GA," *New York Rocker*, March 1981.

80 *"I go just"*: Kaplan, *Bad Brains*, ROIR, 1981, liner notes.

82 *"The current local"*: Cosloy, "Anti Pasti/Gang Green/Ice Age," *New York Rocker*, March 1982.

84 *Photo editor Laura Levine*: "Birthday Bomb," *New York Rocker*, July 1982.

Chapter 5: Georgia and Those Guys

88 *"The new residents"*: William Geist, "Quiched Hoboken," *The New York Times*, March 23, 1982.

88 *"You could sense"*: Barone, *Frontman*, p. 53.

88 *"We seem to"*: Robert Palmer, "How Hoboken Became Mecca for Rock Bands," *The New York Times*, March 31, 1982.

88 *"We were drawn"*: Kerry Lauerman, "Questions For Yo La Tengo: Band Mates," *The New York Times*, February 6, 2000.

89 *"No one was"*: Arnold, *Route 666*, p. 91.

92 *"The new fad"*: Jim Testa, "The Beat," *Jersey Beat*,
March 1983.

99 *"If anything, it"*: "Don Knotts, Henry Winkler, and
Drums . . . Oh My!," DrummerGirl.com, November
1997.

101 *"white soul"*: Jim Testa, "The Band That Plays Together,"
Jersey Beat, March 1984.

101 *"To solve this"*: Byron Coley, "Yo La Tengo: The Long &
Short of It," *Loaded*, #1 (undated).

101 *"Guitarist & bassist wanted"*: Reproduced in Yo La
Tengo, *Ride The Tiger*, Matador, 1996.

101 *"got the impression"*: Cosloy, "Greetings," *Conflict*,
March 1984.

102 *"He was fascinated"*: Michael Azerrad, *Our Band Could
Be Your Life*, p. 350.

103 *"'Bands' means bands"*: Al Flipside, "Bands That Could
Be God," *Flipside*, August 1984.

103 *"Incredible as it"*: Cosloy, *Conflict*, August 1984.

103 *"Most of these"*: Cosloy, "lieslieslies," *Conflict*, August
1984.

105 *"Most fall blissfully"*: Kaplan, Yo La Tengo, *Ride The
Tiger*, Matador, 1996.

106 *"They took our"*: Ibid.

108 *"Unfortunately, though we"*: Ibid.

110 *"We played Maxwell's"*: Andrew Earles, *Hüsker Dü*, p. 146.

Chapter 6: Yo La Tengo

112 *"Yolo Tango"*: CBGB ad, *Village Voice*, March 27, 1985.

112 *"Looks may be"*: Dave Sprague, "Hoboken's Next
Generation," *Matter*, August 1985.

113 *"It was like paying"*: Charles Aaron, "Hanging Curve,"
Village Voice, August 14, 1990.

115 *"an almost tangible"*: John Leland, "Sideswipes," *Spin*,
February 1986.

116 *"You guys have"*: Azerrad, *Our Band Could Be Your Life*,
p. 354.

118 *"At its worst"*: "The Hoboken Sound," WNYW, aired
        October 18, 1985.

121 *"Cognoscenti could challenge"*: Ira Kaplan in Schinder,
        Alt-Rock-A-Rama, p. 320.

122 *"A mixed-bag"*: Cosloy, "Luxury Condos Coming To Your
        Neighborhood Soon," *Conflict*, late February 1986.

123 *"My favorite retarded"*: Steve Albini, "Homestead
        Records: Frontier Days," *Magnet*, August 25, 2006.

123 *"I guess I was trying"*: Arnold, *Route 666*, p. 90.

124 *"The things that"*: Bob O'Brien, "The Hoboken Sound,"
        WNYW, aired October 18, 1985.

125 *"without really anyone's"*: C. Du Bois, "A Free Form In
        New Jersey," *Upsala Gazette*, March 18, 1969.

125 *"Find some outrageous"*: Jesse Walker, *Rebels on the Air*,
        p. 97.

126 *"Freeform essentially means"*: Du Bois, "A Free Form In
        New Jersey," *Upsala Gazette*, March 18, 1969.

126 *"experimenting with tape loops"*: Lou D'Antonio, Amy
        Foerster, and Liz Berg, "Born Again," *Great Moments
        in WFMU History* trading cards, March 2006.

127 *"It behooves me"*: Irwin Chusid, internal memo, WFMU,
        June 1978.

128 *"The trick is"*: "Rx For College Radio Cutbacks: 'Sell' Your
        Stations, Labels Urge," *Billboard*, November 29, 1980.

130 *"We find Yo La Tengo"*: Cosloy, "Yo La Tengo, CBGB's 2/
        22/86," *Conflict*, late February 1986.

131 *"The type of rock"*: Sheffield, "President Yo La Tengo,"
        Spin, July 1989.

132 *"We had to set"*: Ira Kaplan in Schinder, *Alt-Rock-
        A-Rama*, p. 320.

134 *"There was nothing"*: On recording of Yo La Tengo,
        December 10, 2010, Hoboken, NJ.

135 *"It was like being thrown"*: John Stancavage, "The
        Accidental Guitar Hero," *Tulsa World*, January 27,
        2010.

136 *"Sorry, we can't"*: On recording of Yo La Tengo, March 3,
        1987, Albany, NY.

Chapter 7: Road Food, Good Food

139   *"We returned [at] threeish"*: "Reviews of Bands That Have Stayed At Your House," *Escandalo*, #5 (undated).

141   *"We pulled up"*: "BBQ & A," *Time Out New York*, May 29, 1996.

142   "Route 128 Revisited": Kaplan, "Tenderly," *Village Voice*, October 27, 1987.

143–144   *"Always August shows up"*: Ira Kaplan in Schinder, *Alt-Rock-A-Rama*, p. 321.

147   *"The house soundwoman"*: Kaplan in Schinder, *Alt-Rock-A-Rama*, p. 321.

149   *"house soundman decides"*: Ibid.

153   *"As you know better"*: On recording of Yo La Tengo, November 12, 1988, Chicago, IL.

155   *"wedges of pure meat"*: Coley, "Yo La Tengo: The Long & Short of It," *Loaded*, #1 (undated).

155   *"Wait! You can get free food"*: "June 1, 2007," YoLaTengo.com, June 1, 2007.

Chapter 8: Fakebook

161   *"It wasn't like we were trying"*: "Homestead Records: Frontier Days," *Magnet*, August 25, 2006.

162   *"Yo La Tengo have quietly"*: Cosloy, "The Asparagus Song," *Conflict*, Spring 1987.

164   *"Sleepily correcting some softcore"*: Kaplan, "Yo La Tengo: Annotated Discography," MatadorRecords.com, 1997.

167   *"He had many boosters"*: Nick Hill, "Daniel Johnston and Yo La Tengo Collaborate on the Music Faucet, February 4, 1990," WFMU.org, April 5, 2006.

168   *"I heard you got"*: On recording of Daniel Johnston with Yo La Tengo, WFMU, February 4, 1990.

169 *"Genuine songs buried"*: Cosloy, "Slay Tracks: 1933–1969," *Conflict*, Fall 1989.

171 *"Wholly wonderful"*: Jim Greer, "Heavy Rotation," *Spin*, October 1990.

171 *"I don't think there's ever"*: Jim DeRogatis, "They Got It," *Jersey Beat*, 1990.

173 *"That was really the first time"*: "Timeline," *Exclaim!*, March 2000.

Chapter 10: Big Day Coming

190 *"There are times"*: David Browne, "The Independents See Vultures Circling Overhead," *The New York Times*, October 27, 1991.

192 *"Are all your guests"*: On recording of Yo La Tengo, WFMU, August 25, 1991.

192 *"Christmas bassist/And Suddenly editor"*: Cosloy, "lieslieslies," *Conflict*, Fall 1991.

193 *"Every good gig"*: "The Oral History of Matador Records," *MySpace Music*, September 28, 2010.

194 *"We thought we could"*: Ibid.

197 *"I think this album"*: Georgia Hubley, "Yo La Tengo: Annotated Discography," MatadorRecords.com, 1997.

198 *"I like Greg Ginn"*: Azerrad, *Our Band Could Be Your Life*, p. 374.

199 *"We saw an incredible number"*: Charles Cross, *Heavier Than Heaven*, p. 217.

199 *"Regular studios"*: Earles, *Hüsker Dü*, p. 197.

204 *"Not to wax transcendental"*: Jim Greer, "Slanted and Enchanted," *Spin*, January 1992.

204 *"laughing nervously"*: "What's Your Worst Matador Experience?," *Escandalo*, #6 (undated).

205 *"we were gonna have"*: "The Oral History of Matador Records," *MySpace Music*, September 28, 2010.

205–206   *"For the first time in 150 years"*: C. Carr, "The Bohemian Diaspora," *Village Voice*, February 4, 1992.

206   *"The independent labels"*: John Broven, *Record Makers and Breakers*, p. 60.

207   *"negotiating ties"*: "No Buy, But Matador Talking," *Billboard*, November 28, 1992.

208   *"I walked out"*: Larry Crane, *Tape Op*, p. 124.

210   *"The social scene"*: Arnold, *Route 666*, pp. 86–87.

211   *"persevere"*: Yo La Tengo, *Big Day Coming* 7-inch, Matador, 1993.

Chapter 11: Hot Chicken

213   *"opportunist labels"*: John Cook, Mac McCaughan, and Laura Ballance, *Our Noise*, p. 70.

213   *"We are of the opinion"*: *Billboard*, April 10, 1993.

213   *"I was in an airport men's room"*: *The Boston Globe*, October 27, 1993.

213   *"Are you ready"*: "The Oral History of Matador Records," *MySpace Music*, September 28, 2010.

217   *"I saw a lot of value"*: "Wake Ooloo/Feelies interview," *Perfect Sound Forever*, September 1996.

218   *"blip on the radar"*: Interview with Derek Weiler, May 6, 1994.

219   *"executive civil war"*: Eric Boehlert, "Matador is a hip but unprofitable label best known for launching Liz Phair," *Rolling Stone*, June 27, 1996.

221   *"white-knuckle experience"*: Georgia Hubley, "Georgia Hubley's Top 10," Criterion.com, 2010.

222   *"Hot chicken is"*: Georgia Hubley, "Yo La Tengo: Annotated Discography," MatadorRecords.com, 1997.

223   *"The greatest thing"*: Crane, *Tape Op*, p. 123.

Chapter 12: Electr-o-Pura

226 *"the current crop"*: John Greenwald, "Will Teens Buy
      It?", *Time*, May 30, 1994.

228 *"Like on the vinyl"*: Interview with Fred Mills, *Magnet*,
      August 1995.

228 *"Three of independent filmmaking's"*: Matador Records
      press release, 1995.

228 *"Someone told me"*: On recording of Yo La Tengo, *7-Up
      Listen-Up!* radio hour, May 1995.

230 *"I kept imagining"*: Bryan Charles, *Wowee Zowee*,
      p. 40.

230 *"I was smoking"*: Rob Jovanovic, *Perfect Sound Forever*,
      p. 152.

231 *"The revenge of"*: Neil Strauss, "They're Normal? And
      They're Pop Stars," *The New York Times*, June 22,
      1995.

234 *"Maxwell's has always operated"*: "A Crisis For A
      Hoboken Institution," *The New York Times*, May 3,
      1991.

235 *"We didn't play loud"*: "They've got it," *Newark Star-
      Ledger*, August 30, 1997.

239 *"ghost ship between formats"*: Neil Strauss, "The Sorry
      State of New York Radio," *The New York Times*,
      February 4, 1996.

239 *"most major label records"*: Cosloy, "PAVEMENT/
      ATLANTIC/MATADOR," *alt.music.alternative*, April
      18, 1994.

241 *"shouting the praises"*: Cosloy, "What We Talk About
      When We Talk About (Courtney) Love," *Matablog*,
      November 24, 2010.

241 *"That is complete"*: Eric Boehlert, "Matador is a hip but
      unprofitable label best known for launching Liz
      Phair," *Rolling Stone*, June 27, 1996.

241 *"Cosloy is a rare"*: Ibid.

243 *"We spent an afternoon"*: Ira Kaplan, "Yo La Tengo Sell
      Out," YoLaTengo.com, 2003.

Chapter 13: Rocket #9

248 *"I see a beach"*: Uncredited poem, *I Can Hear the Heart Beating As One*, Matador, 1997.

249 *"It's too good"*: On recording of Yo La Tengo, Charlottesville, VA, January 9, 2008.

250 *"This couple comes up"*: "Forever Tengo," *Time Out New York*, February 17, 2000.

252 *"Is he in Yo La Tengo?"*: *Rock, Rot & Rule*, Stereolaffs, 1999.

253 *"Do the math"*: Ibid.

256 *"I've spent more time"*: Kaplan, "My Dozen," eMusic.com, May 2006.

257 *"let us go through"*: "A Chat With Ira Kaplan," *Polyethylene Radio*, December 1998.

257 *"Today, it's microbrewed"*: Jim Testa, "Remembrance of Things Pasta," Jersey Beat, c. Spring 1997.

258 "The Simpsons *is*": "Yo La Tengo Do 'The Simpsons,'" MTV News, October 26, 1998.

Chapter 14: Our Way to Fall

261 *"I think it was '97"*: "The MP3: A History of Innovation and Betrayal," *The Record* blog, NPR.org, March 23, 2011.

262 *"I think I was"*: "Roundtable Discussion: The Role of the Record Label," *Monitor Mix* blog, NPR.org, November 16, 2009.

266 *"We went through a weird"*: "The Oral History of Matador Records," *MySpace Music*, September 28, 2010.

267 *"With Capitol there"*: Ibid.

270 *"We'd get offered"*: Cook, McCaughan, and Ballance, *Our Noise*, p. 215.

270 *"if the connection"*: Sheffield, "Married, with amplifiers," *Rolling Stone*, March 2, 2000.

270–271 *"Do you ever think"*: Lauerman, "Questions For Yo La Tengo: Band Mates," *The New York Times*, February 6, 2000.

271–272 *"Once I got used"*: "State-of-the-heart rockers managing to keep it real," *The Atlanta Journal-Constitution*, September 17, 2000.

274 *"It was like"*: Dave Itzkoff, "The Pitchfork Effect," *Wired*, September 2006.

Chapter 15: A Plastic Menorah

279 *"It makes nothing"*: John Wenzel, *Mock Stars*, p. 99.

282 *"The whole world"*: James McNew, "Billboard magazine," YoLaTengo.com, December 2002.

283 *"I'd say this record"*: DeRogatis, "Yo La Tengo still growing with 'Summer Sun,'" *Chicago Sun-Times*, June 6, 2003.

284 *"If it's not tense"*: Crane, *Tape Op*, p. 123.

287 *"It's a modest"*: Christgau, "Beating As One," *Village Voice*, April 15, 2003.

287 *"pleasant"*: Eric Carr, "Summer Sun," *Pitchfork*, April 9, 2003.

Chapter 16: Prisoners of Love

293 *"I consider making"*: "Rock Band," *The Believer*, May 2005.

293 *"national pastime"*: John Thorn, *Baseball in the Garden of Eden*, p. 109.

294 *The number of professional artists*: Richard Lloyd, *Neo-Bohemia*, p. 66.

295 *"symbolic analytic"*: Ibid., p. 115.

296 *"The Mets go on"*: Jonathan Lethem, *Men and Cartoons*, p. 160.

297 *"We're fond of"*: "Rock Band," *The Believer*, May 2005.

298 *"The scenes we scored"*: On recording of Yo La Tengo,
       Charlotte, NC, January 8, 2008.

300 *"I see no reason"*: "Featured Blog: Can't Stop the
       Bleeding," *Sports Tech Now*, January 2008.

301 *"Even by the usual"*: Gerard Cosloy, "Yo La Tengo vs. Sea
       of Humanity," *Matablog*, July 31, 2006.

Chapter 17: Popular Songs

304 *"ABC's Family Channel"*: James McNew, "On the Couch
       With James," YoLaTengo.com, August 2005.

305 *"A Pitchfork 9.1"*: "Roundtable Discussion: The Role of
       the Record Label," *Monitor Mix* blog, NPR.org,
       November 16, 2009.

311 *"The roots of indie rock"*: "Channel 319: Classic College
       Radio," SiriusXM.com, 2011.

311 *"old nerds playing dress-up"*: Christopher Weingarten,
       @1000TimesYes, April 4, 2009.

311 *"hipster archipelago"*: Bill Wasik, "Hype Machine,"
       Oxford American, November 2007.

316 *"It's easy to overlook"*: Rob Mitchum, "Popular Songs,"
       Pitchfork, September 1, 2009.

318 *"There are a lot"*: "Catching Up with Yo La Tengo,"
       PasteMagazine.com, September 2009.

320 *"Think that they are probably"*: Carles, "Amazon.com
       made a list of the 100 greatest indie albums of all
       time," *Hipster Runoff*, April 8, 2009.

321 *"They wanted some"*: "Hoboken's Finest," *New York*
       magazine, September 13, 2009.

323 *"We had a massive"*: "Yuck Reflect on 'Massive Yo La
       Tengo Phase,'" *Spinner*, March 7, 2011.

324 *"Come on @maxwellsnj"*: Yo La Tengo, @TheRealYLT,
       December 1, 2010.

Bibliography

Books

Amidi, Amid. *Cartoon Modern: Style and Design in Fifties Animation*. San Francisco: Chronicle, 2006.

Angell, Roger. *Five Seasons: A Baseball Companion*. New York: Simon and Schuster, 1977.

Arnold, Gina. *Route 666: On the Road to Nirvana*. New York: St. Martin's, 1993.

Attfield, Nicholas William James. *You're Living All Over Me*. New York: Continuum, 2011.

Azerrad, Michael. *Our Band Could Be Your Life: Scenes from the American Indie Underground 1981–1991*. Boston: Little, Brown, 2002.

Barone, Richard. *Frontman: Surviving the Rock Star Myth*. New York: Backbeat, 2007.

Blush, Steven, and George Petros. *American Hardcore: A Tribal History*. Los Angeles, CA: Feral House, 2001.

Bonomo, Joe. *Sweat: The Story of the Fleshtones, America's Garage Band*. New York: Continuum, 2007.

Broven, John. *Record Makers and Breakers: Voices of the Independent Rock 'n' Roll Pioneers*. Urbana: University of Illinois, 2009.

Bruce, Scott, and Bill Crawford. *Cerealizing America: The Unsweetened Story of American Breakfast Cereal*. Boston: Faber and Faber, 1995.

Charles, Bryan. *Wowee Zowee*. New York: Continuum, 2010.

Coley, Byron. *C'est La Guerre: Early Writings, 1978–1983*. Montreal: L'Oie de Cravan, 2011.

Colrick, Patricia F. *Hoboken*. Charleston, SC: Arcadia, 1999.

Cook, John, Mac McCaughan, and Laura Ballance. *Our Noise: The Story of Merge Records, the Indie Label That Got Big and Stayed Small*. Chapel Hill, NC: Algonquin of Chapel Hill, 2009.

Crane, Larry. *Tape Op: The Book About Creative Music Recording*. Venice, CA: Feral House, 2001.

Cross, Charles R. *Heavier than Heaven: A Biography of Kurt Cobain*. New York: Hyperion, 2001.

Dannen, Fredric. *Hit Men: Power Brokers and Fast Money Inside the Music Business*. New York: Vintage, 1991.

Denning, Michael. *The Cultural Front: The Laboring of American Culture in the Twentieth Century*. London: Verso, 1998.

DeRogatis, Jim. *Let It Blurt: The Life and times of Lester Bangs, America's Greatest Rock Critic*. New York: Broadway, 2000.

DiClerico, James M., and Barry J. Pavelec. *The Jersey Game: The History of Modern Baseball from Its Birth to the Big Leagues in the Garden State*. New Brunswick, NJ: Rutgers University Press, 1991.

Duncombe, Stephen. *Notes from Underground: Zines and the Politics of Alternative Culture*. London: Verso, 1997.

Earles, Andrew. *Hüsker Dü: The Story of the Noise-pop Pioneers Who Launched Modern Rock*. Minneapolis: Voyageur, 2010.

Felt, Ivan, and Harris Conklin. *Believeniks!: 2005, the Year We Wrote a Book About the Mets*. New York: Doubleday, 2006.

Fletcher, Tony. *All Hopped up and Ready to Go: Music from the Streets of New York, 1927–77*. New York: W.W. Norton, 2009.

Fletcher, Tony. *Remarks Remade: The Story of R.E.M.* London: Omnibus, 2002.

Foster, Edward Halsey, and Geoffrey W. Clark. *Hoboken: A Collection of Essays*. New York: Irvington, 1976.

Foster, Robert. *From Another Time: Hoboken in the 1970s*. Hoboken: Hoboken Historical Museum, 2007.

Frank, Thomas, and Matt Weiland. *Commodify Your Dissent: Salvos from The Baffler*. New York: Norton, 1997.

Frank, Thomas. *The Conquest of Cool: Business Culture, Counterculture, and the Rise of Hip Consumerism*. Chicago: University of Chicago, 1997.

Gimarc, George. *Punk Diary: The Ultimate Trainspotter's Guide to Underground Rock, 1970–1982*. San Francisco: Backbeat, 2005.

Goodman, Fred. *The Mansion on the Hill: Dylan, Young, Geffen, Springsteen, and the Head-on Collision of Rock and Commerce*. New York: Times, 1997.

Greif, Mark, Kathleen Ross, and Dayna Tortorici. *What Was the Hipster?: A Sociological Investigation*. New York: N+1, 2010.

Gunderloy, Mike. *How to Publish a Fanzine*. Port Townsend, WA: Loompanics Unlimited, 1988.

Hans, Jim. *100 Hoboken Firsts*. Hoboken, NJ: Hoboken Historical Museum, 2005.

Hermes, Will. *Love Goes to Buildings on Fire: Five Years in New York That Changed Music Forever*. New York: Faber and Faber, 2011.

Heylin, Clinton. *From the Velvets to the Voidoids: A Pre-punk History for a Post-punk World*. New York: Penguin, 1993.

Jovanovic, Rob. *Perfect Sound Forever: The Story of Pavement*. Boston: Justin, Charles, 2004.

Kasher, Steven, and Lou Reed. *Max's Kansas City: Art, Glamour, Rock and Roll*. New York: Abrams Image, 2010.

Lethem, Jonathan. *Men and Cartoons: Stories*. New York: Doubleday, 2004.

Lloyd, Richard D. *Neo-bohemia: Art and Commerce in the Postindustrial City*. New York: Routledge, 2006.

Marten, Neville, and Jeffrey Hudson. *The Kinks: Well Respected Men*. Chessington, Surrey: Castle Communications, 1996.

McInerney, Jay. *Bright Lights, Big City: A Novel*. New York: Vintage Contemporaries, 1984.

McNeil, Legs, and Gillian McCain. *Please Kill Me: The Uncensored Oral History of Punk*. New York: Grove, 1996.

Moore, Thurston, and Byron Coley. *No Wave: Post-punk, Underground, New York, 1976–1980*. New York: Abrams Image, 2008.

Northshield, Jane. *History of Croton-on-Hudson, New York*. Croton-on-Hudson, NY: Croton-on-Hudson Historical Society, 1976.

Nucciarone, Monica. *Alexander Cartwright: The Life Behind the Baseball Legend*. Lincoln: University of Nebraska, 2009.

Oakes, Kaya. *Slanted and Enchanted: The Evolution of Indie Culture*. New York: Henry Holt and Company, 2009.

Peterson, Harold. *The Man Who Invented Baseball*. New York: Scribner, 1973.

Petrusich, Amanda. *Pink Moon*. New York: Continuum, 2007.

Reynolds, Simon. *Rip It up and Start Again: Postpunk 1978–1984*. New York: Penguin, 2006.

Ritter, Lawrence S. *The Glory of Their Times; the Story of the Early Days of Baseball Told by the Men Who Played It*. New York: Macmillan, 1966.

Sanders, Ed. *America: A History in Verse the 20th Century*. Woodstock, NY: Blake Route, 2008.

Schickel, Richard. *The Disney Version: The Life, Times, Art and Commerce of Walt Disney*. London: Pavilion/Michael Joseph, 1986.

Schinder, Scott. *Rolling Stone's Alt-Rock-A-Rama: An Outrageous Compendium of Facts, Fiction, Trivia, and Critiques*. New York: Delta, 1996.

Shargel, Baila Round, and Harold L. Drimmer. *The Jews of Westchester: A Social History*. Fleischmanns, NY: Purple Mountain, 1994.

Shaw, Philip. *Horses*. New York: Continuum, 2008.

Thorn, John. *Baseball in the Garden of Eden: The Secret History of the Early Game*. New York: Simon & Schuster, 2011.

Turnbull, Archibald Douglas. *John Stevens, an American Record*. New York: Century, 1928.

Wald, Elijah. *How the Beatles Destroyed Rock 'n' Roll: An Alternative History of American Popular Music*. Oxford: Oxford University Press, 2009.

Walker, Jesse. *Rebels on the Air: An Alternative History of Radio in America*. New York: New York UP, 2001.

Walsh, Jim. *The Replacements: All Over but the Shouting*. St. Paul, MN: MBI, 2007.

Wenzel, John. *Mock Stars: Indie Comedy and the Dangerously Funny*. Golden, CO: Speck, 2008.

Selected Articles

Archibald, Lewis. "John Hubley: Animation comes of age," *Film Library Quarterly*, Spring 1970.

Betrock, Alan, editor. *New York Rocker*, January 1976 through March 1978.

Bodayla, Stephen D. "Hoboken and the Affluent New Yorker's Search for Recreation, 1820–1860," *New Jersey History*, Fall 1977.

Christgau, Robert. "Beating As One," *Village Voice*, April 15, 2003.

Coley, Byron. "Yo La Tengo: The Long & Short of It," *Loaded* #1 (1989).

Cosloy, Gerard, editor. *Conflict*, March 1994 through Fall 1991.

Derby, Matthew. "Rock Band," *The Believer*, May 2005.

Fritch, Matthew. "Homestead Records: Frontier Days," *Magnet*, August 25, 2006.

Geist, William. "Quiched Hoboken," *The New York Times*, March 23, 1982.

Gross, Jason. "Feelies Interview," *Perfect Sound Forever*, September 1996.

Hayden, Philip A. "Historic Background and Development of the Maxwell House Site," Richard Grubb & Associates, March 30, 2005.

Hirschberg, Lynn. "Gerard Cosloy Is Hipper Than You," *New York Magazine*, May 8, 1995.

Ickeringill, Nan. "A Family That Profits From Fantasy," *The New York Times*, January 21, 1967.

Itzkoff, Dave. "The Pitchfork Effect: How a tiny web outfit became the most influential tastemaker on the music scene," *Wired*, September 2006.

Kaplan, Ira. Articles & columns in *SoHo Weekly News*, November 3, 1977 through November 10, 1981.

Kaplan, Ira. "Peter Stampfel: Foe of the Bad, Pal of the Good," *Loaded #2* (1989).

Kaplan, Ira. "Interview: Neil Young," *Spin*, March 1993.

Kaplan, Ira. "Live! Velvet Underground," *Spin*, September 1993.

Leland, John. "For Rock Bands, Selling Out Isn't What It Used to Be," *The New York Times*, March 11, 2001.

McGilligan, Pat. "Faith Hubley: An Interview," *Film Quarterly*, Winter 1988–1989.

McNew, James, editor. *And Suddenly . . .* , #3 (1988).

The Onion, "37 Record-Store Clerks Feared Dead in Yo La Tengo Concert Disaster," *The Onion*, April 10, 2002.

Palmer, Robert. "How Hoboken Became Mecca for Rock Bands," *The New York Times*, March 31, 1982.

Schwartz, Andy, editor. *New York Rocker*, March 1978 through November 1982.

Stax, Mike. "Norton Records: The First Quarter Century," *Ugly Things*, Spring 2011.

Uncredited, "The Elysian Fields of To-Day," *Harper's Weekly*, October 25, 1890.

Wasik, Bill. "Hype Machine," *Oxford American*, November 2007.

Wilson, John S. "Collector of Rock Scene Faces Crisis," *The New York Times*, December 17, 1972.

Wood, Mikael. "The Oral History of Matador Records," *MySpace Music*, September 28, 2010.

Yo La Tengo, "Annotated Discography," MatadorRecords.com, 1997.

Discography

Please consult Yo La Tengo's Annotated Discography at Matador.com.

Selected Non–Yo La Tengo Discography

It is worthwhile to explore the complete catalogs (and related tendrils) of nearly every artist listed here, but these albums represent a core of the music in *Big Day Coming*.

13th Floor Elevators. *The Psychedelic Sounds of the 13th Floor Elevators*. International Artists, 1966.

A-Bones, the. *Daddy Wants a Beer and Other Million Sellers*. Norton, 2004.

Antietam. *Antietam*. Homestead, 1985.

Antietam. *Burgoo*. Triple X, 1989.

Big Star. *#1 Record*. Ardent/Stax, 1972.

Big Star. *Radio City*. Ardent Stax, 1974.

Big Star. *Third/Sister Lovers*. PVC, 1978.

Black Flag. *The First Four Years*. SST, 1983.

Bongos, the. *Drums Along the Hudson*. PVC, 1982.

Bongwater. *Double Bummer*. Shimmy Disc, 1989.

Bonzo Dog Band. *The Doughnut in Granny's Greenhouse*. Liberty, 1968.

Brian Eno. *Here Come The Warm Jets*. Island, 1974.

John Cale. *Paris 1919*. Columbia, 1973.

Alex Chilton. *Like Flies on Sherbert*. Peabody, 1979.

Christmas. "(The Ballad of the) Invisible Girl" 7-inch. Iridescence, 1984.

Christmas. *In Excelsior Dayglo*. Big Time, 1986.

Clean, the. *Anthology*. Flying Nun, 2002.

the dB's. *Stands for Decibels*. Albion, 1981.

the dB's. *Repercussion*. Albion, 1982.

the dB's. *Ride the Wild Tom Tom*. Rhino, 1993.

Deep Wound. *Discography*. Damaged Goods, 2006.

Devo. *Hardcore Devo, vol. 1 & 2*. Rykodisc, 1990–1991.

Dinosaur. *Dinosaur*. Homestead, 1985.

Dream Syndicate. *Days of Wine and Roses*. Ruby/Slash, 1982.

Dump. *Superpowerless*. Brinkman, 1993.

Dump. *I Can Hear Music*. Brinkman, 1995.

Dump. *A Plea for Tenderness*. Brinkman, 1997.

Dump. *That Skinny Motherfucker with the High Voice?* Brinkman, 1998.

Eleventh Dream Day. *Prairie School Freakout*. Amoeba, 1988.

Fall, the. *The Complete Peel Sessions*. Castle Music, 2005.

Feelies, the. *Crazy Rhythms*. Stiff, 1980.

Feelies, the. *The Good Earth*. Coyote, 1986.

Fish and Roses. *Fish and Roses*. Twin/Tone, 1987.

Flamin' Groovies. *Teenage Head*. Kama Sutra, 1971.

Flamin' Groovies. *Shake Some Action*. Sire, 1977.

Fleshtones, the. *Roman Gods*. IRS, 1982.

Half Japanese. *Half Gentleman/Not Beasts*. Armageddon, 1980.

Happy Flowers. *My Skin Covers My Body*. Homestead, 1987.

Richard Hell & the Voidoids. *Blank Generation*. Sire, 1977.

Holy Modal Rounders. *The Holy Modal Rounders*. Prestige, 1964.

Michael Hurley, the Unholy Modal Rounders, Jeffrey Frederic, & the Clamtones. *Have Moicy*. Rounder, 1976.

Hüsker Dü. *Zen Arcade*. SST, 1984.

Hypnolovewheel. *Space Mountain*. Alias, 1991.

Individuals, the. *Fields*. Plexus, 1981.

Daniel Johnston. *The Early Recordings of Daniel Johnston*. Dualtone, 2003.

Kinks, the. *Something Else by the Kinks.* Pye, 1967.

Kinks, the. *The Kinks Are the Village Green Preservation Society.* Pye, 1968.

Lambchop. *How I Quit Smoking.* Merge, 1994.

Lambchop. *Thriller.* Merge, 1997.

Peter Laughner & Friends. *Take the Guitar Player for a Ride.* Tim Kerr, 1994.

Pep Lester and His Pals. *The Mathematical Genius of Pep Lester.* Forced Exposure, 1988.

Love. *Forever Changes.* Elektra, 1967.

Lydia Lunch. *Queen of Siam.* Ze, 1980.

Barbara Manning. *Lately I Keep Scissors.* Heyday, 1989.

Minutemen, the. *Double Nickels on the Dime.* SST, 1984.

Mission of Burma. *Signals, Calls, and Marches.* Ace of Hearts, 1981.

Modern Lovers, the. *The Modern Lovers.* Beserkley, 1976.

Nico. *Chelsea Girl.* Verve, 1967.

NRBQ. *All Hopped Up.* Red Rooster, 1977.

Pavement. *Slanted and Enchanted.* Matador, 1992.

Pere Ubu. *The Modern Dance.* Blank, 1978.

Phantom Tollbooth. *Power Toy.* Homestead, 1988.

Ramones. the, *Ramones.* Sire, 1976.

Raunch Hands, the. *Stomp It!* Egon, 1984.

R.E.M. *Chronic Town.* IRS, 1982.

Replacements, the. *Hootenanny.* Twin/Tone, 1983.

Will Rigby. *Sidekick Phenmenon.* Egon, 1985.

Rutles, the. *The Rutles.* Warner Bros., 1978.

Scene Is Now, the. *The Oily Years.* Bar/None, 1995.

Patti Smith. *Horses.* Arista, 1975.

Soft Boys, the. *Underwater Moonlight.* Armageddon, 1980.

Sonic Youth. *Bad Moon Rising.* Homestead, 1985.

Sneakers. *Nonsequitur of Silence.* Collector's Choice, 2006.

Sun Ra. *Singles.* Evidence, 1996.

Superchunk. *Superchunk.* Merge, 1990.

Talking Heads. *'77.* Sire, 1977.

Tall Dwarfs. *Fork Songs.* Flying Nun, 1991.

Television. *Marquee Moon.* Elektra, 1977.

Times New Viking. *Rip It Off.* Matador, 2008.

Trypes, the. *Explorer's Hold.* Coyote, 1984.

Urinals, the. *Negative Capability.* Warning Label, 1997.

Richie Van. *My Little Corner of the World.* Art, undated, private press, circa early 1970s.

Various artists. *Bands That Could Be God.* Radio Beat, 1984.

Various artists. *Casual Victim Pile.* Matador, 2010.

Various artists. *Human Music.* Homestead, 1988.

Various artists. *Luxury Condos Coming to Your Neighborhood Soon.* Coyote, 1985.

Various artists. *No New York.* Antilles, 1978.

Various artists. *Nuggets: Original Artyfacts from the First Psychedelic Era, 1965–1968.* Elektra, 1972.

Various artists. *Start Swimming.* Stiff America, 1981.

Various artists. *Tape #1.* Private press, 1980.

Various artists. *WFMU Archival Oddities,* vol. 1 & 2. WFMU, 2002–2003.

Velvet Underground and Nico, the. *Velvet Underground and Nico.* Verve, 1967.

Velvet Underground, the. *White Light/White Heat.* Verve, 1968.

Velvet Underground, the. *Velvet Underground.* Verve, 1969.

Velvet Underground, the. *Loaded.* Atlantic, 1970.

Velvet Underground, the. *1969: The Velvet Underground Live.* Mercury, 1974.

Yung Wu. *Shore Leave.* Coyote, 1987.

Index